Dialogue and Disputation in the Zurich Reformation

Dialogue and Disputation in the Zurich Reformation

Utz Eckstein's *Concilium* and *Rychsztag*

EDITION, TRANSLATION AND STUDY

Nigel Harris and Joel Love

PETER LANG
Oxford • Bern • Berlin • Bruxelles • Frankfurt am Main • New York • Wien

Bibliographic information published by Die Deutsche Nationalbibliothek
Die Deutsche Nationalbibliothek lists this publication in the Deutsche Nationalbibliografie; detailed bibliographic data is available on the Internet at http://dnb.d-nb.de.

A catalogue record for this book is available from the British Library.

Library of Congress Control Number: 2013930486

Cover design by Lucy Buchan.

ISBN 978-3-0343-0960-8

Peter Lang AG, International Academic Publishers, Bern 2013
Hochfeldstrasse 32, CH-3012 Bern, Switzerland
info@peterlang.com, www.peterlang.com, www.peterlang.net

Printed in Germany

Contents

Preliminary remarks

The idea for the present book arose out of doctoral research into Utz Eckstein funded by the Arts and Humanities Research Council, carried out by Joel Love, and supervised by Nigel Harris. While significant parts of the introduction, and several of the elucidatory notes, draw on the resulting 2008 thesis, our editions and translations of Eckstein's texts represent an entirely new and fully collaborative project. Moreover a considerable amount of additional research, particularly into Eckstein's life, the textual history of the *Concilium* and *Rychsztag*, and various aspects of their theological and cultural environment, has been undertaken by Nigel Harris in the context of a period of study leave awarded by the University of Birmingham.

We would like to thank our academic colleagues, particularly Graeme Murdock, who helped to supervise an earlier piece of research; David Hill and Ulrike Zitzlsperger, who examined the PhD thesis and gave crucial advice about the 'next stage'; the late Ben Benedikz for philological support; Ron Speirs and Robert Swanson for practical help; and Sania Reddig, Alan Suter, Antje Pieper, Robert Evans, Elystan Griffiths, and Joanne Sayner for many timely morale-boosts.

Joel Love thanks Adrian Newman, Mike Murkin, Jacki Graham, and the staff of St Martin in the Bull Ring, Birmingham (where he worked throughout his PhD), as well as Janet Bonner and the Information Services team at Birmingham University Library. Our thanks also go to the Rare Books and other specialist librarians of the British Library, Zentralbibliothek Zürich, Bayerische Staatsbibliothek, and Diözesanarchiv Chur. Other libraries that have served us are the Bodleian and Taylorian in Oxford, the Cambridge University Library, the John Rylands Library in Manchester, the Koninklijke Bibliotheek/ Bibliothèque Royale in Brussels, the Universitätsbibliothek Bern, the University of Cumbria's Harold Bridges Library in Lancaster, and Birmingham Central Library.

Our thanks also to those who have read and commented on the work represented here, including Adele Rees and Victoria Bø. Ed Porteous, Katie Day, James Walters, Jane Packman, Ben Pacey, and Aurelio Ramos Caballero have also contributed immeasurably – as, in the crucial final stages, have Alun Ford, Karin Voth Harman, Justin Gau, Catriona Laing, and Melanie Marshall. As well as the Birmingham German Department, Chris Newlands, Jill Novell, and the people of Lancaster Priory have supported us as we brought the work to (its current level of) completion. James and Patricia Love and Claudette Garnier, as well as the long-suffering Harris family, have frequently sacrificed their dining-room tables to the work of translation. Finally, we would of course not have been able to carry out any of this without the prevenient work of many earlier scholars.

Hall Green and Lancaster
November 2012

Introduction

The sixteenth century was a time of rapid socio-political change, far-reaching religious conflict, and an explosion of new media. The intermingling of these and other factors resulted in a substantial increase in the quantity of literature produced in the major European vernaculars, in the number of people who came into contact with it, and hence in the importance of texts for the shaping and nurturing of public opinion. This is why the vernacular literature of the time is of interest not just to students of literature, but also to those concerned with social, religious, or intellectual history. Much of this literature, however, remains in practice impenetrable, not least to readers of English, because of a lack of reliable editions and translations, and indeed of approachable analytical studies. A case in point is provided by the works of the Swiss Reformation author Utz Eckstein (c. 1490–1558), whose dialogues,[1] all datable to the mid-1520s, have much to tell us about the priorities and perspectives specifically of the Zurich (Zwinglian) Reformation, as well as representing a unique moment in the development of the dialogue as a literary and polemical form – but which have, nevertheless, hitherto been largely neglected by scholars.

With the exception of Johann Scheible's uncritical and unreliable reprints in his self-published compendium *Das Kloster*,[2] Eckstein's works have not been edited since the sixteenth century. Moreover the only really substantial study of him remains the book-length article of

1 We use this term throughout for convenience only. *Dialogus* is one of the many names applied to such texts by contemporaries, though clearly what they understood by it differs from our own assumptions, deriving as these do from later theatrical and cinematic conventions.

2 Johann Scheible, *Das Kloster: weltlich und geistlich; meist aus den älteren deutschen Volks-, Kinder-, Curiositäten- und vorzugsweise komischen Literatur*, 12 vols (Stuttgart: the author, 1845–9). The Eckstein texts are in vol. 8 (1847), pp. 705–826 (*Concilium*) and 827–92 (*Rychsztag*).

Salomon Vögelin, published as long ago as 1882.[3] Vögelin's work remains invaluable, particularly as an introductory guide to Eckstein's life and writings (the contents of which are summarized with abundant quotation from the originals); and he also situates Eckstein accurately within the context of contemporary intellectual debates in Switzerland (notably, for example, those involving the Alsatian Humanist and polemicist Thomas Murner). His account of Eckstein's biography needs updating, however; and, when considering Eckstein's literary achievement, he is apt to fall prey to the prejudices of his age. Almost at the outset, for example (p. 93), Vögelin refers to Eckstein's works as 'Reimereien' ('doggerel'), and he several times characterizes them as markedly inferior to the dramas of the Zurich author's Berne-based contemporary Niklaus Manuel.[4] Eckstein was, one fears, always destined to frustrate the attempts of such nineteenth-century scholars as Vögelin and Jakob Baechtold to celebrate the Swiss dramatic tradition, for the simple reason that his dialogues are not plays.[5]

Since Vögelin, substantial progress in Eckstein research has been made only with regard to the author's life. Four articles, all based on newly discovered original documents, have fleshed out our knowledge of Eckstein's biography considerably. First, in 1926, Adrian Corrodi-Sulzer established that, in 1535, Eckstein was appointed to the post of

3 Salomon Vögelin, 'Utz Eckstein', *Jahrbuch für schweizerische Geschichte,* 7 (1882), 91–264.

4 See Vögelin, pp. 93, 179, 225. The works of Manuel have recently benefited from an excellent modern edition, whose appearance is indeed one of the motivating factors behind the production of this volume: Niklaus Manuel, *Werke und Briefe. Vollständige Neuedition*, ed. by Paul Zinsli and Thomas Hengartner (Berne: Stämpfli, 1999).

5 See Baechtold's *Geschichte der deutschen Literatur in der Schweiz* (Frauenfeld: Huber, 1892), pp. 293–7. For him, Eckstein's 'pamphlets' have only the outward form of dramas ('haben vom Drama lediglich die äußere Form'). Rather, they are 'crude conversations', which are 'inappropriately weighed down with theological ballast, repetition of Zwingli's arguments, and quotations from the Church Fathers and secular history' ('derbe Gespräche, mit theologischem Ballaste, Wiederholung Zwinglischer Argumente, Zitaten aus den Kirchenvätern und der Profangeschichte ungebührlich beschwert' – p. 247). Given that nearly all of Eckstein's quotations are in fact from the Bible, these last words already make one question how well Baechtold knew the texts.

Deacon in Niederwenigen.[6] Ten years later, Oskar Vasella published a revealing document, from the *Induzienverzeichnis* of the Diocese of Chur, which gives us information about Eckstein's place of origin (Esslingen am Neckar, in Swabia), his whereabouts in 1522 (Weesen, in the Canton of St. Gallen), his material poverty, and indeed his domestic arrangements.[7] In 1953, Peter Hegg's study of documents in the Staatsarchiv Zürich enabled him to pinpoint the dates of Eckstein's death (7th October 1558) and burial (two days later, in the city's leading church, the *Grossmünster*);[8] and, building on another discovery by Hegg, in 1960 Paul Zinsli published and interpreted the only surviving letter in Eckstein's own hand, dating probably from 1531 or 1532, in which he appeals for help from Zwingli's successor Heinrich Bullinger.[9] Subsequent accounts of Eckstein's life have merely summarized the known material, rather than adding to it.[10]

With regard to the study of Eckstein's works, there is sadly little to report. No twentieth- or twenty first-century scholar has undertaken a substantive reassessment of these, and the brief treatments that have appeared in histories of literature have tended to rehearse, apparently uncritically, the judgements of Vögelin and Baechtold.[11] This is true

6 Adrian Corrodi-Sulzer, 'Zu Ůtz Eckstein', *Zwingliana*, 4 (1926), 337–40.

7 Oskar Vasella, 'Neues über Utz Eckstein, den Zürcher Pamphletisten', *Zeitschrift für schweizerische Kirchengeschichte*, 30 (1936), 37–48.

8 Peter Hegg, 'Ein unbekannter Apiarius-Druck', *Schweizerisches Gutenbergmuseum* [*sic*], 39 (1953), 51–65.

9 Paul Zinsli, 'Notvolles Prädikantendasein', *Reformatio*, 9 (1960), 327–33. Peter Hegg's own story, meanwhile, was a tragic one: he died in 1955 at the age of 27. This represented a major loss to Eckstein studies, not least in that Hegg was planning, in the context of his doctoral thesis, to edit his works.

10 See notably Willy Müller, 'Der Reformationsdichter Utz Eckstein' (unpublished *Lizenziatsarbeit*, University of Zurich, 1970), pp. 3–24; Hans Ulrich Bächtold, 'Eckstein (Acrogoniaeus), Utz (Ulrich)', in *Biographisch-Bibliographisches Kirchenlexikon*, vol. 17 (Herzberg: Bautz, 2000), pp. 296–9 – with excellent bibliography.

11 This is broadly true, for example, of the following: Frida Humbel, *Ulrich Zwingli und seine Reformation im Spiegel der gleichzeitigen, schweizerischen volkstümlichen Literatur*, Quellen und Abhandlungen zur schweizerischen Reformationsgeschichte, 4 (Leipzig: Heinsius, 1912), especially pp. 17–18, 140–6; Josef Nadler, *Literaturgeschichte der deutschen Schweiz* (Leipzig: Grethlein, 1932), pp. 158–9; Emil Ermatinger, *Dichtung und Geistesleben der*

even of relatively recent publications. In his 1984 history of German Reformation drama, for example, Wolfgang F. Michael continues to speak the language of the nineteenth-century *geistesgeschichtlich* tradition in characterizing Eckstein as a direct follower of Manuel, who however failed to understand the latter's 'actual instrument', the stage, producing instead 'pure, sometimes long-winded dialogues' or 'really boring pamphlets' wholly lacking in action or theatricality, but including 'uncouth' attacks on their opponents.[12] Moreover, in what is probably the most recent published comment on Eckstein, Claudia Brinker echoes Jakob Baechtold in referring to his dialogues as 'theologically overloaded' ('theologisch überfrachtet').[13]

Only two post-war Germanists have published substantial work on Eckstein. In a 1961 thesis, Hans Stricker uses his works, and those of other sixteenth-century dramatists, as sources for material about contemporary Swiss life and *mores.*[14] He describes and briefly discusses, for example, Eckstein's perspectives on peasants (pp. 88–92), modish clothing (p. 17), and the Turkish Emperor (pp. 25–7), as well as what he sees as Eckstein's self-presentation as a Swabian (n. 103, p. 157). Some of Stricker's conclusions are highly questionable, however, such as his assertions that Eckstein's works show no influence of the social ethics of Zwingli or that, as a Swabian, he was incapable of

---

deutschen Schweiz (Munich: Beck, 1933), pp. 159–63; and (notably less prejudiced) Hans Rupprich, *Die deutsche Literatur vom späten Mittelalter bis zum Barock: Das Zeitalter der Reformation, 1520–1570. Geschichte der deutschen Literatur von den Anfängen bis zur Gegenwart,* ed. by Helmut de Boor and Richard Newald, IV, 2 (Munich: Beck, 1973), pp. 64–5.

12 'In das unmittelbare Gefolge Manuels gehört Utz Eckstein [...] Aber Eckstein verkannte Manuels eigentliches Instrument: die Bühne. Seine Werke sind reine, z. T. langatmige Dialoge geworden. An eine Aufführung hatte Eckstein offenbar nicht gedacht. Zudem werden seine Angriffe pöbelhaft. Aus dem Mangel an Handlung, dem Fehlen des Bühnengerechten entstanden hier recht langweilige Pamphlete': Wolfgang F. Michael, *Das deutsche Drama der Reformationszeit* (Berne: Lang, 1984), pp. 38–9.

13 Claudia Brinker, 'Von den Anfängen bis 1700', in *Schweizer Literaturgeschichte*, ed. by Peter Rusterholz and Andreas Solbach (Stuttgart: Metzler, 2007), p. 44.

14 Hans Stricker, *Die Selbstdarstellung des Schweizers im Drama des 16. Jahrhunderts*, Sprache und Dichtung, n. s., 7 (Berne: Haupt, 1961).

understanding the 'deep meaning' ('tiefen Sinn') of the Swiss 'national Reformation' (p. 115).

Somewhat more persuasive, finally, is the work of Ninna Jørgensen, whose prime interest is in the typology of peasants, fools, and priests in Reformation literature, but who discusses Eckstein in two sections of her 1988 monograph.[15] In the course of her treatment of fools (pp. 34–41), she sets Eckstein's presentation of himself as Balaam's ass, and of Murner as a false prophet, in the context of other contemporary uses of this biblical motif. Then, in a later discussion of peasants (pp. 117–26), she points especially to the significant discrepancy that obtains in Eckstein's works between the (generally) admirable 'symbolic' peasant disputants and the more negatively conceived 'real life' peasants whose attitudes they talk about. Furthermore she examines the farmers' (in her view, idealized) consultation at the beginning of the *Rychsztag* – an analysis to which our delineation of the three main 'ground rules' that undergird this consultative process is considerably indebted (see below, pp. 33–6).

The foregoing should already have demonstrated that the time for an adequate modern assessment of Eckstein and his achievement is ripe; and it is clear to us that such an assessment can realistically only begin on the basis of an edition and appropriately annotated English translation of his two most extensive and important works, *Concilium* ('The Council', 1525) and *Rychsztag* ('The Diet', 1526). The bulk of this volume is therefore devoted to those tasks. It is supported by an index of people, places, and subjects, and by the present introduction, which will discuss Eckstein and his works, and situate them within the wider religious, social, and cultural context in which they were produced. More specific questions of local, biographical, or literary detail are discussed in the elucidatory notes that accompany the translations.

15 Ninna Jørgensen, *Bauer, Narr und Pfaffe: Prototypische Figuren und ihre Funktion in der Reformationsliteratur,* Acta Theologica Danica, 23 (Leiden: Brill, 1988).

Utz Eckstein (c. 1490–1558)

In spite of the assiduous researches mentioned above, we still know almost nothing of Eckstein's background or education: his works show, for example, that he must have received some kind of university education, but we have no idea where or when. His birthplace is established beyond reasonable doubt, however, in the document from Chur printed by Vasella.[16] This begins with a reference to a 'Dominus Ůdalricus Egkstein de Eßlingen, parcium Sueuorum' – a formulation that seems designed specifically to indicate that this Ulrich Eckstein originated in Esslingen 'of the Swabians', i.e. Esslingen am Neckar (near Stuttgart), rather than the identically named town in the Canton of Zurich. Dated 26th November 1522, the document also indicates that Eckstein was active as a Catholic priest in Switzerland before the beginning of the official Zurich Reformation in 1523: he is described as a chaplain active at the church of St Nicholas in Weesen (a place which, coincidentally or not, held considerable importance also for Zwingli).[17] Eckstein's personal circumstances, however, were clearly far from uncomplicated: the annual payments he is recorded as having to make to the Bishop of Chur include three gulden for the absolution of the sin of 'public fornication' committed with a concubine, with whom he has also sired children ('absolucione publice fornicacionis sue prolis procreationis cum soluta non coniuncta'). Moreover this is a sum that he was clearly ill-equipped to pay: the Bishop is recorded as having allowed him to get away with paying just one gulden, on account of his learning and poverty ('ob doctrinam et paupertatem'), and on condition that he is not subsequently appointed to a more remunerative benefice ('melius beneficium') elsewhere.

Notwithstanding such generous treatment, however, Eckstein must have committed himself to the Evangelical cause relatively soon after 1522: certainly by 1525 he is recorded in Zurich as the author of

16 Vasella, p. 42. A translation into German is given by Müller, p. 3.

17 His uncle Bartholomaeus was parish priest and rural dean there, and it was the site of the small school at which he received his initial education.

the *Concilium*, a polemical work that is absolutely shot through with Zwinglian perspectives.

For whatever reason, Eckstein's literary career seems already to have ceased by 1527 at the latest, but there is abundant evidence to suggest that he remained dedicated to the Evangelical cause. This is implied especially strongly by his often short-term occupancy of a number of benefices: at Thalwil (1527–8), Rorschach (1528–31), Zollikon (1534–5), Niederwenigen (1535), and Uster (1535–58), from which post he retired shortly before his death 'due to old age and illness'.[18] The reason for the rather nomadic nature of Eckstein's career is not altogether clear. Certainly all the places in which he ministered were strategically important locations for the implementation of Zurich's policy of spreading reformed spirituality throughout the surrounding rural areas, and hence it seems possible that Eckstein was regarded as something of a pioneer, or even a 'troubleshooter'. On the other hand, at least some of his moves may have been dictated by poverty, the demands of a numerous (if eventually legitimate) progeny,[19] and by a somewhat restless and difficult temperament. Certainly Vögelin's detailed account of Eckstein's career in Rorschach (pp. 234–46) reveals a pastor who was initially successful in furthering the Zwinglian cause, but who provoked some opposition due to a certain excess of zeal, and who was eventually forced to leave by events beyond his control – namely the reimposition of Catholicism by Diethelm Blaarer, the new Abbot of St. Gallen, in 1531 (also the year of the Second Kappel War, and Zwingli's death).

The nature of Eckstein's personal relationship with Zwingli has given rise to much speculation. The only actual evidence of it that we have is, however, a somewhat ambiguous letter by Zwingli, dated 9th December 1528, to the St. Gallen Humanist and reformer Vadianus (Joachim von Watt): 'We have sent Ulrich Acrogoniaeus ['Eckstein'] to the people of Rorschach', Zwingli writes, 'mainly because he has been tried by many misfortunes and, at the same time, has seen a great deal. His judgement [or 'natural understanding'] is greater than his

18 Quoted by Vögelin, p. 259, from a document in the Staatsarchiv Zürich.

19 In the letter to Bullinger printed by Zinsli (p. 370), Eckstein pleads for assistance on behalf of a pregnant wife and six children.

learning, though this latter is greater than his happiness. He wants us to recommend him to you'.[20] Overall these words come across as something of a backhanded compliment, in which recognition of Eckstein's judgement and experience is mitigated by doubts as to his intellectual abilities and a hint that he is a somewhat demanding, 'high maintenance' colleague. Certainly it is hard to see in them any hint of a warm or close relationship between the two men.

In spite, however, of his later peripatetic career 'in the provinces', his apparent personal distance from Zwingli, and indeed his position as a Swabian 'outsider', there can be no doubt that, at least for the duration of his brief literary career, Eckstein was close to the centre of things in Zurich and wrote primarily for a locally defined Swiss readership. Even though, for example, both the *Concilium* and the *Rychsztag* ostensibly depict supranational fora, their focus remains firmly Swiss. They include frequent allusions to recent events in Zurich, such as Zwingli's brandishing of a 'rabbit cheese' before Johannes Faber at the First Zurich Disputation of 1523 (C 448–50/93), 945–6/123, 1352–4/147),[21] or the abolition of the Mass there in 1525 (C 3239/257); they often mention important theologians and polemicists known throughout the Holy Roman Empire (Murner, Johannes Faber, Andreas Karlstadt, Johannes Bugenhagen, and others), but only in relation to their involvement in specifically Swiss matters, and by nicknames that were presumably transparent to Zurich readers 'in the know';[22] and they make patent allusions not just to the *Karsthans* dialogue and to Murner's *Geuchmat*, but also to less well-known texts that were produced and printed specifically in Zurich.[23] Luther, by

20 Quoted by Müller, p. 14: 'Rorschachensibus Huldrychum Acrogonieum hac potissimum causa misimus, quod multis malis exercitus est, ac simul multa vidit. Iudicio prestantior est quam eruditione, quamquam et illa maior est foelicitate. Hic cupit tibi per nos commendatus esse'.

21 References to the *Concilium* and *Rychsztag* are given throughout in this form: 'C' or 'R' as required, followed by the line number(s) of our German edition and, after the forward slash, the page number(s) of our English translation.

22 Murner, for example, is often called 'Murnarr', Faber is always 'Hans Schmid', and Bugenhagen is 'Pomerantz'.

23 Notably Erhard Hegenwald's *Handlung der verſamlung in der löblichen ſtatt Zürich, vff den xxix tag Ienners / vonn wegen des heyligen Euangelij*; and *Das*

contrast, is conspicuous only by his absence – with the exception of the briefest of accounts of his views on the Eucharist (C 2778–88/229–31) and some critical references at the very end of the *Concilium* (C 4154–87/307–9). Furthermore, Eckstein reaches for local Swiss examples when trying to explain theological concepts, such as the relation of the colours and livery of Basle to the city itself, which he uses as a model for the relation between bread and wine and the body and blood of Christ (C 3137–43/251). This is anyway, of course, a quintessentially Swiss perspective on the Mass, and one of many examples in his dialogues that enable us to discern the strong influence of Zwingli, and indeed of Erasmus as mediated by Zwingli.[24] So strong is this influence, indeed, that Murner took the *Concilium*, apparently seriously, to be the work of Zwingli himself (in his *Responsio* to it of 1525);[25] and it is both the strength and perhaps the weakness of Eckstein's dialogues that they were singularly appropriate for a very specific place and time – Zurich in the early years of its Reformation.

gyren rupffen. halt inn wie Johans Schmid Vicarge ze Coſtentz / mit dem büchle darinn er verheißt ein waren bericht wie es vff den. 29. tag Jenners. M.D.xxiij. ze Zürich gangen ſye (both Zurich: Froschauer, 1523). There has long been a school of thought to the effect that Zwingli himself wrote the *Handlung der verſamlung*; and Keith Dennis Lewis has suggested, with reasonable but inconclusive evidence, that the *Gyrenrupffen* may be the work of Ulrich von Hutten: see his 'Johann Faber and the First Zürich Disputation: 1523. A Pre-Tridentine Catholic Response to Huldrych Zwingli and his Sixty-Seven Articles' (unpublished PhD thesis, Catholic University of America, 1985), pp. 316–47.

24 For a survey of the complex relationship between these two great figures see Gottfried W. Locher, 'Zwingli und Erasmus', *Zwingliana*, 13 (1969–73), 37–61.

25 See the title: *Murneri responsio libello ciuda[m] insigniter & egregie stulto Vlrici Zvuyngel apostate / heresiarche, ostendens Lutheranam doctrinam infamiam irrogare / & verbum dei humanum iudicem pati posse* (Lucerne: the author, 1525).

Eckstein's works

Eckstein seems to have written exclusively in German. Indeed, in the *Rychsztag* he berates his opponent Thomas Murner (at least via the words of the privileged speaker Weybel Reychart, R 2005–10/427) for preferring to use Latin. Plainly he also had a strong preference for verse dialogues (which he sometimes also refers to, revealingly, as 'disputations'). His two most important works, which both fall into this category, are edited and elucidated at length in this volume: the *Concilium* is a fictionalized, indeed highly imaginative representation of a Council of the Church, whereas the *Rychsztag* draws on procedures associated with arbitration or the legal tribunal. Both texts feature peasant characters (especially in the Swiss context, they ought really to be called 'farmers') who dispute with representatives of ecclesiastical and/or secular authority; and they both disclose the framework and rhetorical structures of a formal urban disputation. As such, they use their dialogue structure to reflect particularly tellingly the Swiss predilection for ordered communal consultation – as a means not only of resolving differences, but also of providing both a platform and a forum for the expression of divergent views.

For all their manifest fictionality, though, both *Concilium* and *Rychsztag* are firmly wedded to, and directly inspired by, identifiable contemporary events and processes. It is therefore hardly surprising that the actual subjects discussed in them will hold relatively few surprises for the reader who knows about the early years of the Zurich Reformation. The agenda to be considered at Eckstein's *Concilium* is stated at the work's outset: prayers to the saints, the authority of the Pope, the doctrine of purgatory, the nature of the Mass, tithes and other payments to the Church, and auricular confession. Other issues which subsequently arise as it were unannounced are fasting, pilgrimages, and the validity of canon law. Several of these questions were of course major preoccupations for progressive thinkers throughout the German-speaking lands around 1525, though one is struck by Eckstein's relative lack of interest in indulgences, in justification by faith, and for that matter in the characteristically Swiss issue of images and

icons. The *Rychsztag*, for its part, reflects the extent to which the reformers' agenda was changed, at least temporarily, by the farmers' uprising of later 1525. Accordingly it foregrounds issues of authority and rebellion, and features a lengthy debate between the farmer Pur Eygennutz and his influential opponents about the justifiability of tithes, interest, and taxes.

Within Eckstein's oeuvre the *Concilium* and *Rychsztag* stand out for their length, literary quality, and importance as contributions to the contemporary theological and political debate. They also make a coherent pair, in that they speak into essentially the same set of circumstances and indeed make a number of cross-references to each other. Such considerations, along of course with limitations of time and space, have led us to focus our attention in this volume primarily on these two texts. In what follows, however, we propose briefly to summarize and discuss his other works, with particular reference to points relevant also to the *Concilium* and *Rychsztag*.

Eckstein wrote two other dialogues, generally known as the *Dialogus Christus mit Adam* ('Dialogue of Christ with Adam') and the *Klag des Gloubens* ('Lament of Faith').[26] The relative chronology of these four works is difficult to establish with any confidence. Certainly the *Concilium* and *Rychsztag* must have originated late in 1525 and in 1526 respectively. The former text features, for example, the marginal date 'Anno M. D. XXV' adjacent to a reference to events that occurred 'this year' ('in diſem jar', C 3283–4/259); a statement that, since the First Zurich Disputation (of 29th January 1523) 'the third year has almost turned' ('das jar ſchier drümal vmmhar iſt', C 454/93); and references both to events that were at their zenith in the first half of 1525 (notably the 'Peasants' War'), and to others that happened only in the September or early October of that year – such as Karlstadt's return to Saxony and the publication of Johannes Bugenhagen's *Contra novum errorem de sacramento corporis et sanguinis*

26 The full titles are *Dialogus. Ejn hüpſche diſputation / Die Chriſtus hat mit Adam thon* ([Zurich]: [Froschauer], [1525?]), and *Klag des Gloubens der Hoffnung vnd ouch Liebe, über Geyſtlichen vnd Weltlichen Stand der Chriſtenheit.* (Zurich: Froschauer, [1525?]).

Domini.[27] The *Rychsztag*, meanwhile, is quite explicitly a sequel written almost immediately after the *Concilium* (see Pur Eygennutz's opening remarks, R 104–57/319–23); moreover it repeatedly refers to the 'Peasants' War' as having been raging 'last year' (see R 728/355, 865/363, 2201–2/439), and indeed to Eck and Luther's 1519 encounter in Leipzig as having happened seven years previously (R 2035/429).

Eckstein's other two dialogues, however, are more difficult to date, not least because they contain far fewer references to contemporary socio-political developments. Arguing *ex silentio*, Vögelin suggests that the absence, in the *Dialogus*, of any concerted discussion of the subjects debated at the First Zurich Disputation of late January 1523 indicates that the work's composition must have pre-dated that gathering. Given that we now know that Eckstein was still ministering in Weesen under the authority of the local Catholic bishop almost exactly two months previously, however, this analysis no longer seems tenable. On the other hand, Müller's view that the *Dialogus* must *post*-date the *Concilium* and *Rychsztag* because its 'more conciliatory, milder tones' and avoidance of 'crass contrasts' render it Eckstein's 'most mature work' seems to us to constitute a misreading of all three texts.[28] On the contrary, the *Dialogus*'s almost exclusive concentration on broader theological questions, relative lack of lexical creativity, and absence of any real engagement with other texts or views imply to us that it is, if anything, a *less* mature piece than the works edited here. The same is largely true also of the *Klag des Gloubens*: although it uses a greater number of enlivening dramatic

27 See Doctor Gryff's speech at C 2757–822/229–33; and, especially, Volker Gummelt, 'Die Auseinandersetzung über das Abendmahl zwischen Johannes Bugenhagen und Huldrych Zwingli im Jahre 1525', in *Die Zürcher Reformation: Ausstrahlungen und Rückwirkungen*, ed. by Alfred Schindler and Hans Stickelberger, Zürcher Beiträge zur Reformationsgeschichte, 18 (Berne: Lang, 2001), pp. 189–201. On the many negotiations and machinations concerning Karlstadt's return to Saxony from exile in Rothenburg ob der Tauber see Hermann Barge, *Andreas Bodenstein von Karlstadt*, 2 vols (Leipzig: Brandstetter, 1905), vol. 2, pp. 312–72.

28 Müller, p. 62 ('versöhnlichere, milder gestimmte Töne') and p. 70 ('Wahrscheinlich Ecksteins reifstes Werk [...] Wir finden nicht mehr so krasse Gegensätze').

devices and a broader range of characters than does the *Dialogus*, it too lacks the level of individual characterization evinced by the *Concilium* (in which seven different farmers speak to named Catholic theologians) and, again, allows less scope for the foregrounding of alternative voices and opinions that we see as particularly characteristic of the mature Eckstein. Towards its end the *Klag* does, however, give us at least one revealing clue as to when it might have originated. A representative of the aristocracy makes a clear reference to the 'Peasants' War' and to his class's need to kill and stab those who are rebelling, citing as he does the authority of 'many doctors throughout the German lands' and, in particular, 'one who writes that hell is now empty and that devils have entered into the peasants'.[29] It is hard not to see in this a reference to Luther's notorious treatise *Wider die mördischen und reuberischen Bawren*, written in April 1525.[30]

On the basis of these considerations, then, we are inclined to suggest that the *Dialogus* was composed in 1524 or (more likely) early 1525,[31] the *Klag* and the *Concilium* in the first and second halves of 1525 respectively, and the *Rychsztag* in 1526. This is in line at least with the relative chronology suggested by Vögelin and, much more recently, by Hans Ulrich Bächtold in his 2000 entry in the *Biographisch-Bibliographisches Kirchenlexikon* (pp. 297–8). Moreover it reinforces the view expressed by Bruce Gordon that 1525 was a particularly 'remarkable' (if frenetic) year for Zwingli, in which he was supported by men who 'employed their diverse talents in a vast array of tasks'. He cites as examples Leo Jud, Kaspar Megander, and Hein-

29 'So hoffen ich wir habind gwalt / Das wirs thoetind vnd erſtaechind / wie wir moegind vns an jnn raechind / Denn wir habend deſſe gſtand / von vil Doctorn durch Tütſche land / Eyner ſchrybt er meyne doch / es ſige laer das helliſch loch / Tüfel ſygind in Puren gſchloffen' (Miv^r).

30 See *D. Martin Luthers Werke* (*'Weimarer Ausgabe'*), 120 vols (Weimer: Böhlau, 1883–2009; hereafter *WA*), vol. 18, pp. 357–61.

31 On the slight but possibly significant evidence adduced by Vögelin (p. 101) to the effect that the 'E' initial and other typographical features that appear in Froschauer's edition of the *Dialogus* are not found in the printer's output before 1525. Froschauer's prints are, however, often difficult to date.

rich Uttinger; but one wonders whether, at least in respect of that single year, Eckstein too might justifiably be added to the list.[32]

It is time to turn to individual texts. The *Dialogus Christus mit Adam,* which we take to be Eckstein's first published work, remains true to its title by imagining a discussion between Christ and Adam. The title page sets love, faith, and good works in opposition to prayers, images, and 'what God demands from us'[33] in a confrontational *mise en page* that will reappear in the *Concilium* and *Rychsztag*, thereby preparing the reader for a polemical attack on the traditional piety of the old Church and a call for repentance. The key to this dialogue is straightforward: every word uttered by Christus conveys spiritual wisdom, while Adam's speeches are to be understood as 'fleshly' (*Dialogus*, Aiiii^{v}). The work as a whole, then, is informed by a marked dualism, derived ultimately from the habitual opposition of πνευμα and σαρξ in the New Testament,[34] as interpreted in the light of Greek philosophy. It is a distinction that underpins all of Eckstein's thought[35] and can also be found, for example, in Erasmus's *Enchiridion* and in Zwingli's understanding of the Eucharist.

Inevitably, then, the conversation recorded in the *Dialogus* is very one-sided, Adam's role being to ask questions, while Christus offers comprehensive answers.[36] Moreover this monologic[37] didactic-

32 Bruce Gordon, *The Swiss Reformation* (Manchester: Manchester University Press, 2002), p. 68.

33 'was Gott von vns erfordre' (Ai^{r}).

34 See for example John 3:6 and Galatians 5:16.

35 Fascinatingly, it is even hinted at in his letter to Bullinger: 'jn Summa, Der trüw gott welle fürston, das min fleysch nit thüge / Darzů es lust hätte, wie wol der jnner mensch / vß gottes krafft fast kempfft vnd widerstaat' (Zinsli, p. 370). When it comes to defending and fighting for the Gospel, in other words, the inner man is willing (and indeed active), but the flesh is weak.

36 As such, the text fits Schwitalla's (generic) description of a *Befragung*. See Johannes Schwitalla, *Deutsche Flugschriften 1460–1525: Textsortengeschichtliche Studien*, Reihe Germanistische Linguistik, 45 (Tübingen: Niemeyer, 1983), pp. 97–8.

37 The terms 'monologic' and 'dialogic', which derive ultimately from Mikhail Bakhtin, are important for our conception of Eckstein's approach and achievement. Most 'Reformation dialogues' are, in spite of their form, in Bakhtinian terms 'monologic': that is, they tend to reduce the 'multiple voices and

ism is enhanced by the use of examples,[38] many of which draw direct parallels between the contemporary situation and the biblical narrative (the clergy, for example, are compared to the Pharisees – Avi^{v}).

Adam begins by asking why so many people remain unmoved by the reformers' preaching, and Christus replies that, since human beings are 'fleshly', spiritual truth does not appeal to them. Indeed, many even amongst those who call themselves Christians do not actually follow God's teaching;[39] and those who do preach the truth are rejected by the world, just as Christ himself was. Christus goes on to assure Adam of the reality of future judgement with a reference to Sodom (Aviii^{r});[40] but Adam misguidedly infers from his words that good works will be enough to guarantee entry into heaven (Bi^{v}). Using a formula from the Epistle of St James, rather than St Paul (something a Lutheran would be reluctant to do), Christus argues, in reply, that only faith makes human works pleasing to God: 'If you but believe in me, that is a pure work before my father' (B^{v}),[41] whereupon Adam asks why anyone should bother with good works, if salvation comes by grace and Christ has already paid the penalty for sin (Ci^{r}). The answer Christus gives is simple, and consistent with Luther's principle of justification by faith (if somewhat misogynistically phrased): human religiousness is 'like a cloth soiled by a menstruating woman'

---

consciousnesses within a text to a single version of truth imposed by the author' (Phyllis Margaret Paryas, in *Encyclopaedia of Contemporary Literary Theory. Approaches, Scholars, Terms,* ed. by Irena R. Makaryk (Toronto: University of Toronto Press, 1993), p. 596). Parts of Eckstein's dialogues are clearly like this. We maintain, however, that, for their time, they also include a very high level of 'dialogicity': they are, for example, manifestly in dialogue with the 'truths' of other works and authors, allow these some prominence, ascribe to them some validity, and allow their own truths to be shaped or modified by them.

38 These are usually highlighted in the margins using the word 'Exempel' (see Avii^{r} and Aviii^{r}, for instance).

39 Cf. Matthew 25:31–45. Using a metaphor that will occur repeatedly in the *Concilium*, Christus says that the clergy 'devour widows' houses' (cf. Luke 20:46–47 and Matthew 23:14).

40 This is also an echo of Christ's words in the Gospels (Matthew 10:15 and 11:24; Luke 10:12).

41 'So man an mich gloubt alleyn / das werck ist vor mym vatter reyn'.

(Ci^{v}).[42] By contrast, faith in the grace of God will lead to the sharing of Christ's righteousness with all who are drawn to him (Ciiii^{v}).

Eventually, the dialogue turns to familiar Reformation questions regarding images and cults of the saints. Relatively little is said about the latter, though Christus argues in favour of venerating those saints who feature in the Bible, in preference to more recent ones (Dii^{r}). As to images, Adam initially defends their use with the apparently reasonable remark that people are forgetful and need physical reminders, for example of Christ's sufferings (Cvii^{r}). Nevertheless, Christus is unambiguous in his response: 'seeking help where there is none is the greatest idolatry' (Di^{r}).[43] Ultimately, he says, images are a human invention, designed to maximize the temporal wealth of the Church.

As a whole, then, the *Dialogus* is concerned with *theological*, rather than *political* questions;[44] what is missing is any real practical element, since the dialogue makes no direct reference to specifically Swiss circumstances or events. This is not the case with the *Concilium* and *Rychsztag*, which, as we have seen, not only deal in specifics, but also avoid the one-sidedness of Christ's dialogue with Adam by presenting a greater diversity of opinions and variety of perspectives.

The *Klag des Gloubens,* which we regard as Eckstein's second dialogue, uses personified virtues, chief among them Faith and Hope, to expose the moral and theological failings both of the papal curia and of the secular nobility of the Empire. This takes place in a Council of the Church that also functions as an Imperial Diet – fora which recur, the former in the *Concilium* and the latter in the *Rychsztag* (with the difference that, in place of personifications, named Catholic and Evangelical figures are used). Faith and Hope go to Rome, where they are met by the Pope and his knights in great pomp.[45] On hearing their

42 'Wie ein bſchiſſen tuoch / Das da kumpt von einer zytigen frouwen'. Cf. Isaiah 64:6.

43 'Das man […] ſuocht hilff da keine ſy / das iſt die gröſt abgöttery'.

44 This is also noted by Vögelin, p. 100 (the emphases are his).

45 This scene echoes Manuel's *Vom Papst und Christi Gegensatz* (1522), and possibly even Melanchthon and Cranach's *Passional Christi und Antichristi* (1521), which both contrast the wealth and luxury of the papal curia with the poverty and simplicity of Christ. Not that this was exactly an uncommon trope

complaints, the Pope calls a general Council,[46] at which two more virtues, Truth and Righteousness, debate with a papal official, the 'Fiskal', about the innovations of Evangelical teaching. Among the items discussed is Eucharistic theology, a central aspect of the Zurich Reformation that will also reappear in the *Concilium* (which however, uses biblical proof-texts much more than does the *Klag*).[47]

Next comes a confrontation between Truth (representing the common people) and two representatives of the nobility of the Empire, at 'Rappsburg' in the 'German lands' (Jvi^{v}). Subjects discussed include taxes levied in anticipation of a Turkish invasion, the harsh treatment that the common people receive at the hands of their lords (which is compared to the tyranny of Pharaoh, Saul, and Nero), and the general lasciviousness of the nobility.[48] This section is much more detailed than the corresponding passage in the *Rychsztag*, although in both the actions of the nobility are partly excused with reference to positive royal role models from the Hebrew Bible. It is suggested that according to biblical precedent (King David, for example), lords are entitled to subdue peasant uprisings by any means whatsoever, including the use of violence.[49] However, Truth argues that such actions overstep the God-given limits of feudal authority: God has given the 'sword' of punishment to the nobility, but they may only use it in his name and in the pursuit of justice (thus anticipating the political views we will find expressed in the *Rychsztag*). Truth even

---

at the time – it also undergirds much of Erasmus's *Moriae encomium* (1511), for example.

46 This means of settling theological disputes was in reality widely advocated by reformers and Catholics in the Empire and beyond throughout the 1520s. See for example G. R. Potter, *Zwingli* (Cambridge: Cambridge University Press, 1976), pp. 124–5.

47 Vögelin (p. 105) notes that the speeches of Truth and Righteousness are so scurrilous and polemical that the possibility of mutual understanding is excluded from the beginning. He also argues, however, that this is not the point of the scene; rather, Eckstein is concerned 'to spit out all his poison against the priests of Baal' ('dass der rerformirte Autor sein ganzes Gift gegen das Baalspriesterthum […] ausspeien könne').

48 Vögelin (p. 107) notes the obvious delight with which Eckstein enumerates stories of adultery from the Bible and classical literature at this point (Li^{v}).

49 Miv^{r}: it is at this point that the passage quoted above (in n. 29) appears.

dares to suggest that the ideal form of government would be a republic under a leader like Moses, Samuel, or a Roman Consul (Mv^{r-v}).

Unlike the *Dialogus,* then, the *Klag* does concern itself – at times in a decidedly radical way – with practical matters. Some of these recur in the *Concilium* and *Rychsztag*, although the later texts focus on a different set of even more local circumstances.

In addition to these four dialogues, three satirical songs from 1526/7 have been attributed (albeit for the most part only on the basis of their titles and dates) to Eckstein. They are more overtly polemical in tone, and either thematize the Baden Disputation of 1526 or respond to the intertextual debate that followed it.[50] As such, they have a different function from that of the dialogues, which anticipate and prepare for that disputation. The songs are: (a) *Die Badenfart*; (b) *Ein Anders Lied, von Hansen Faber Vicari*; and (c) *Vff Doctor Thomas Murners Calender, Ein Hübsch Lied.*

Taken together, these songs are an exercise in Evangelical 'spin', claiming as they do that the Baden Disputation of 1526 (at which Eck, in Zwingli's absence, scored an emphatic triumph over Evangelical representatives led by the Basle reformer Johannes Oecolampadius) actually constituted an Evangelical victory. Hence they are in many ways more 'closed' or monologic texts than are Eckstein's dialogues (as well as being arguably inferior in literary terms). If their attribution to Eckstein is genuine, this suggests that, later in 1526 and in 1527, he may have felt the need to turn away from a literary form that proved useful in the Zurich context only during the lead-up to a disputation. We are inclined to wonder, however, whether these songs have only become associated with Eckstein's name because they very obviously censure three figures of whom he had already shown marked disapproval in his dialogues. Faber and Murner are, after all, mentioned in the titles of (b) and (c) respectively; and (a) not only alludes sarcas-

50 For a full account of this disputation see the standard account of Leonhard von Muralt, *Die Badener Disputation 1526*, Quellen und Abhandlungen zur schweizerischen Reformationsgeschichte, 6 (Leipzig: Heinsius, 1926); also, more recently and in English, Irena Backus, *The Disputations of Baden, 1526 and Berne, 1528: Neutralizing the Early Church*, Studies in Theology and History, 1/1 (Princeton: Princeton Theological Seminary, 1993).

tically, in its title, to Murner's *Ein andechtig geistiche Badenfart*, but proceeds to denounce both Murner and Eck. They seem, then, to contain the sort of thing that Eckstein *might* have wanted to say; and so the opportunity to attribute them to Eckstein might simply have seemed too attractively plausible an opportunity to miss.

Eckstein, contemporary Zurich, and beyond

The remainder of our introduction will be concerned primarily with issues that we see as centrally important for the understanding and interpretation of Eckstein's works, and especially of the *Concilium* and *Rychsztag*. We will consider in turn their reception and thematization of the Swiss tradition of communal consultation; their essentially Zwinglian theology; their social and political perspectives; and their literary qualities. In this short preparatory section, however, it is important to delineate, however lightly, certain key aspects of Eckstein's context, both in Zurich and in the German-speaking lands more generally, in the hope of enabling the reader to situate the discussions to come more precisely within a broader picture.

One must remember first of all that, in essence already since the high-profile First Zurich Disputation of late January 1523, Zwingli had been 'very much in control'[51] of religious life in Zurich. His rise, since his appointment as *Leutpriester* ('People's Priest') of the *Grossmünster* in 1518, had been swift and, for the most part, sure-footed. Zwingli built on widespread calls for reform in the Church, not only from Humanists (including Faber, Murner, and Eck),[52] but also from

51 Gordon, p. 61. His chapter 'Zwingli and Zurich' (pp. 46–85) is a good introduction to the early years of the Zurich Reformation.

52 It is easy for us to be misled by the pervading *ad hominem* viciousness of early sixteenth-century polemics into thinking that its various authors had always been strangers and enemies. In fact, Zwingli and Faber were on cordial terms until about 1522, having made common cause over the issue of the irresponsible preaching of indulgences by the Franciscan Bernardino Sansone in 1518–19;

Luther and other radical thinkers; and his preaching came increasingly both to reflect and to influence the religious thinking of his fellow burghers. His calls for changes to the language and style of worship, as well as to the administering and ordering of other areas of life that had until then been within the purview of the Catholic hierarchy, won many supporters also among Zurich's city council. Indeed, above all by means of the Disputation of 1523, which exonerated Zwingli of all charges of theological error, the council could be said to have initiated the implementation of his ideas. From 1523, changes came not without hesitation or resistance, but nevertheless at an impressive pace: in the space of a very few years ornaments were removed from churches, the Mass was abolished, the veneration of saints largely condemned, monasteries dissolved, and many of the day-to-day appurtenances of late-medieval and early sixteenth-century Christianity *de facto* eliminated (pilgrimages, processions, auricular confession, and extreme unction, to name but a few). In many ways, then, Eckstein, as a Zwinglian, was writing from a position of strength, and one which had been made possible not least by the effective use of a process of disputation not altogether dissimilar from the ones portrayed in his own *Concilium* and *Rychsztag.*

One must bear in mind also, however, that this early stage of the Zurich Reformation had multi-layered implications that reached far beyond the city itself. Initially, it gave rise to a protracted and embittered literary controversy, the first stage of which raged between the First Zurich Disputation of 1523 and the Baden Disputation of 1526. The proceedings of the 1523 Disputation were initially publicized in Hegenwald's partisan (if theoretically eyewitness) pro-Zwinglian account,[53] but this prompted an angry reply from Faber, pointedly called *Ain warlich vnderrichtung*, in which he accuses Hegenwald,

---

until then also, Faber had been a personal friend and correspondent of Vadianus; and all three, along with Eck, continued to revere Erasmus, and had at least attempted to befriend him. Meanwhile Eck taught not only Faber, but also such later Protestant luminaries as Urbanus Rhegius and the Anabaptist Balthasar Hubmaier. Murner seems, it is true, to have been something of a waspish outsider; but often the world of Reformation polemics must have seemed, in personal terms, a small and bizarrely close-knit one.

53 The *Handlung der verſamlung* (as n. 23 above).

amongst many other things, of deliberately presenting him as a satan, rather than an angel, and as a denier of Christ ('vß einem engel ein Sathanam machen / vnnd villeycht das ich ouch Chriſtum verleugnet hette', Aiv^{v}).[54] The *warlich vnderrichtung* in turn inspired another polemic composed from a Zwinglian perspective, the *Gyrenrupffen*. Meanwhile a pamphlet war developed between Eck and the Schaffhausen pastor Sebastian Hofmeister; and Murner entered the fray on numerous occasions, in both Latin and German, not least by means of his *Responsio* to Eckstein's *Concilium.*[55] One must not forget, indeed, that the latter was very much part of this literary war: he takes up many of the issues from the original disputation and from the pamphlets that discussed it; and much of the last third of the *Rychsztag* is occupied by what amounts to a reply to Murner's *Responsio.* Certainly Eckstein saw his works as active contributions to an ongoing intertextual debate in the German-speaking lands.

A further layer of tension and conflict arising from the Zurich Reformation was that between the city and its neighbouring cantons, especially in those rural areas which were under joint control (such as nearly all of the parishes to which Eckstein was subsequently sent). It is true that Schaffhausen, Appenzell, and St. Gallen embraced Zwinglianism as early as 1523, but most of the areas surrounding Zurich (such as Zug, Schwyz, Lucerne, Uri, and Unterwalden) remained staunchly Catholic, and became increasingly opposed to the Zurich Reformation after several notorious acts of iconoclasm had been perpetrated there in the closing months of 1523. Moreover the situation was soon complicated still further by the implementation of comparable – though far from identical – reformations in Basle (under Oecolampadius) and Berne (where Manuel played a role analogous to, if maybe more important than, that of Eckstein in Zurich). In short, the Zurich Reformation and its repercussions 'had put before the Swiss Confederation an unfamiliar problem. For all its regional diversity and local identities, the Confederates had been bound by one religion. It was perhaps the one thing that united them, and now one of the most

54 *Ain warlich vnderrichtung wie es zů Zürch auff den Neünundtzweintzigiſten tag des monats Ianuarij nechſtuerſchynen ergangen ſey* ([Freiburg]: [Wörlin], 1523).

55 Backus (pp. 1–17) provides a valuable summary of this sequence of events.

powerful of the Confederates had fallen into heresy'.[56] It is against this troubled backcloth that, in the mid-1520s, calls for a representative disputation to resolve these differences became increasingly urgent. The much anticipated disputation did, of course, eventually take place, at Baden in 1526, though when Eckstein was writing the *Concilium* and *Rychsztag* its exact location had not yet been decided. The contemporary debates surrounding the desirability and efficacy of the traditional Swiss practice of consultative decision-making go a long way, however, towards explaining Eckstein's use of such a model in both of the texts presented in this volume. The ways in which he does this will be explored in greater detail in our next section.

Meanwhile the theological implications of Zwingli's utterances and actions were also occupying many minds, not just in Switzerland, but also in the wider Empire. Theologians were quick to compare Zwingli's views with those that had informed the various Lutheran reformations which were then being established, especially in such imperial free cities as Augsburg and Nuremberg – and they were finding many similarities. Whilst it is true that 'Zwingli probably owed more to Luther than he imagined or was willing to allow',[57] shrewd minds were also able, however, to detect from an early stage some crucial differences between the two – notably in the matter of the Eucharist, and in Zwingli's much greater indebtedness to Humanism in general and to Erasmus in particular. Gordon (p. 68) identifies Eck, 'the best Catholic mind in the German-speaking lands' (not that he is exactly presented as such in the *Concilium*), as someone who readily discerned ways in which a wedge might be put between Luther on the one hand and Zwingli (and Oecolampadius) on the other. Not that these reformers, or indeed Eckstein, were exactly reluctant to distance themselves from Luther. In part, no doubt, such an attitude reflects the fact that the relationship of their cities to the Pope differed greatly from that of Luther and the cities of the Empire, for reasons of Realpolitik involving Rome's reliance on Swiss mercenaries for the protection of the papal states.[58] Hence it was

56 Gordon, p. 69.

57 A. G. Dickens, *Reformation and Society in Sixteenth-Century Europe* (London: Thames and Hudson, 1966), p. 111.

58 See for example Potter, pp. 30–2; Gordon, p. 27.

relatively easy for Swiss reformers to present themselves as offering, as it were, a 'third way' that was distinct both from traditional Catholic and from German Evangelical perspectives. Certainly Eckstein can and does distance the Zurich Reformation from Lutheran ones, while simultaneously lambasting Catholicism and arguing that his views are thoroughly grounded on Scripture. The ways in which he does this will, in turn, be discussed in greater detail below.

Finally we must mention that the Zurich Reformation, along with others particularly in the South and West of the Empire, had profound socio-political implications. These became crystallized in the so-called 'Peasants' War' of 1525 (better thought of as a series of loosely connected farmers' and artisans' uprisings). Whilst, in Switzerland, the physical damage caused by these uprisings was insignificant compared to what happened elsewhere, and there was little if any loss of life, they nevertheless clearly surprised and shocked both the reformers and their territorial rulers – we can see this also in Eckstein, whose *Rychsztag* evinces a rather different perspective on the farmers and their relationship to secular authority from that which informs the earlier *Concilium*. Specifically in Zurich and its hinterland, the farmers' principal grievance concerned their obligation to pay tithes and taxes to the city government and to other interested parties – such as nearby abbeys (see for example R 310–15/331, 624–6/349). Rather as with Luther in Saxony, the arguments used by the Swiss farmers placed Zwingli in a difficult position: he did not support the abolition of tithes, but was conscious that those who did often used aspects of his theology, or at least of his language, in support of their claims.[59] In particular, numerous pamphleteers argued that the spiritual freedom enjoyed by an Evangelical Christian ought also to release him or her from the obligation to make onerous financial payments. Rightly or wrongly, the response of Zwingli and his supporters was generally to pin the blame for such theological confusion on the radical Anabaptists who were beginning, in the mid-1520s, to influence

59 Zwingli's most authoritative statement about tithes and interest payments is a section in his *Wer Ursache gebe zur Aufruhr*. See *Huldrych Zwinglis sämtliche Werke*, ed. by Emil Egli and others, 14 vols, Corpus Reformatorum, 88–101, III (Leipzig: Heinsius, 1914), pp. 355–469 (especially pp. 388–404).

public opinion in and around Zurich. Eckstein does this in the *Concilium* and *Rychsztag*, as well as presenting substantial debates about authority, rebellion, tithes, taxes, and interest payments. These and other aspects of his political and social ideology are therefore discussed in greater detail in our third section below.

Eckstein and the Swiss communal consultation

As we have stated, both the structure and the content of Eckstein's *Concilium* and *Rychsztag* are informed by specifically Swiss forms of decision-making. Many members of the Swiss Confederation (*Eidgenossenschaft*), both urban and rural, had long since – and in marked contrast to the many feudal territories of the Empire – developed models of government that relied on the active participation of a large number of their (male) citizens. Not only were the voices of individuals taken into consideration at the village level, but the same principle was also applied to the dealings of the constituent parts of the Confederation with one another. We can see this tradition reflected in various ways in both the *Concilium* and the *Rychsztag*. Moreover Eckstein casts his *Concilium* also as a supranational organ of corporate decision-making, namely a Council of the Church – a forum that, especially in the fifteenth century, had been put forward by many canon lawyers as embodying a higher authority even than that of the Pope; and the *Rychsztag* draws on procedures associated with arbitration or the legal tribunal, in which various parties state their rival claims and await judgement from a magistrate. Finally, in addition to these long-established models for airing disagreements and arriving at a decision, Eckstein draws on the newer conventions of the urban disputation (such as the presence in the *Concilium* of two officers whose role is to facilitate the debate, the 'Herold' and 'Weybel').[60]

60 'Herold' is close in meaning to English 'herald'; but 'Weybel' is not really translatable. It could be used to designate persons fulfilling an enormous range

Given both the importance and the diversity of these various channels of influence, it is perhaps hardly surprising that Eckstein begins his *Concilium* by articulating a number of 'ground rules'. The first of these is the acknowledgement by all parties of the authority of the Council as a competent judge in the questions to be discussed. Eckstein thus presents it, at least at first, as precisely the sort of authoritative tribunal demanded by Faber at the First Zurich Disputation. This ground rule initially takes the reader by surprise: for one thing, Eckstein seems, through it, to be breaking with one of the central principles of Zwingli and almost all the other Evangelical reformers, namely that they will not submit to any arbitrator but the Word of God – a position which Zwingli did indeed articulate at the First Zurich Disputation. Moreover the spiritual authority of the Council is itself almost immediately called into question by the Weybel (normally a voice whom Eckstein privileges), when he states: 'Often in a Council, someone asks another person to put him right. The Holy Spirit doesn't do this: he does not regret tomorrow what he does today. His power endures for ever. Christ has told us what to do; and if we now do what he has commanded, we need no human rules (C 879–86/119)'. Here, in other words, he seems to be undermining the foundations of the very form of conciliarism which has just been established, by showing that its authority is merely human and its decisions are not definitive.

We are, then, presented early on with rather a confusing state of affairs: the overriding principle of *sola scriptura* is mitigated to a degree by the need to defer to a human decision-making body, which, however, is itself intrinsically flawed. And this paradox, or tension, is not really resolved as the text progresses – any more than it was, one suspects, in the 'real life' politics of 1520s Zurich. Eckstein will certainly have accepted Zwingli's view that biblical interpretation is not contingent and does not depend upon any human authority; on the

---

of administrative, legal and/or economic functions, on behalf of a lord or a community. See *Schweizerisches Idiotikon*, 17 vols (Frauenfeld: Huber, 1881–[2022]), XV, 109–22 (hereafter *SI)*. In Eckstein's works, the Weybel's main roles are to introduce participants and to summarize their arguments, but in practice he frequently does more than this, to the extent of seeming to act at times as the mouthpiece of the author.

other hand, he will have been well aware that, in practice, 'religious truth was determined by Protestant ministers in dialogue with their magistrates: the ministers interpreted Scripture, and the magistrates sat in judgement on their interpretations' – so that 'in actual fact, it was magisterial sanction of Protestant interpretations of Scripture that institutionalized the Reformation'.[61] Ultimately, then, through his first, deceptively simple ground rule, Eckstein is both problematizing and acknowledging the process by which Zwingli's interpretation of Scripture actually came to be established as the norm for Zurich in the 1520s.

Certainly Eckstein seems to see no intrinsic conflict between his first ground rule and his second, namely that Scripture alone is to constitute the admissible evidence. He presents this principle, perhaps bizarrely, as a local Swiss custom: 'take up God's Word – that's what we use in our valley' (C 507–8/97).[62] While such an approach to authority in 1520s Zurich can only have been a recent development (unless it be understood as aspirational or anachronistic), the statement we have quoted undeniably presents the community as consciously and deliberately choosing the terms of the debate. And in what follows, in fact, the *Concilium* contains a remarkably high level of biblical argumentation and interpretation from both sides of the argument, Evangelical and Catholic. This alone is enough to set it apart from other dialogue texts of the German-speaking reformations, most of which show no such willingness to 'hear otherness'. For example, in the discussion of the Mass in the *Concilium*, both the Catholic doctor and the Evangelical farmer urge one another to restrict themselves to the text of Scripture, which to a large extent they do – something that suggests furthermore that Eckstein possessed an almost 'modern' awareness of the ambiguity of much Scripture.

The third ground rule governing the *Concilium* is the underlying assumption that the debate it contains will be conclusive, resolving the

61 Steven E. Ozment, *The Reformation in the Cities. The Appeal of Protestantism in Sixteenth-Century Germany and Switzerland* (New Haven, CT: Yale University Press, 1975), p. 146.

62 The reference to 'our valley' is naturally suggestive of Swiss topography and identity.

issues concerned once and for all. In this respect Eckstein is for certain reflecting the utopian hopes of many struggling with the uncertainties and complexities of 1520s Switzerland, rather than depicting anything that was likely actually to happen. Even though, as Jørgensen points out (p. 122), the specific ground rules of the *Concilium* correspond to those identified by Moeller as typical of the urban disputation,[63] in practice, after the First Zurich Disputation, no Catholic spokesperson would ever agree to such conditions. In the *Concilium*, Eck (as the initial speaker for the Catholic cause) is, quite simply, doomed to defeat from the moment he agrees to them (C 515/97).

In addition to these ground rules, further local decision-making principles and processes appear as the disputations progress. A notable example of the latter is the village consultation, or 'vmbfraagen' (cf. R 397/337). This procedure is hinted at in the *Concilium*, as, one by one, the farmers are encouraged to offer their advice 'according to the custom of our land' (C 770/113); but it is played out above all in the early part of the *Rychsztag*. The 'vmbfraagen' is in essence an open oral conversation, in which the village Weybel actively seeks to elicit different or (in his words) 'better' opinions (R 398–9/337); and it is informed by the understanding that every villager is a stakeholder with the right to contribute. The farmers who speak argue from experience as well as principle, and occasionally make *ad hominem* attacks on one another. When no unanimous decision emerges, the Weybel suggests a simple show of hands (R 802–3/359). Unsurprisingly, the majority favours Eygennutz's proposal, namely that he should represent their interests before the Diet at Richtal[64] – this is, after all, the outcome demanded by the logic and the drama of the text (and by Eckstein as the author). Nevertheless the decision is shown to be reached only through a discussion that includes opportunities for hearing other points of view; and the absence of the (normally ubiquitous)

63 Bernd Moeller, 'Zwinglis Disputationen: Studien zu den Anfängen der Kirchenbildung und des Synodalwesens im Protestantismus', *Zeitschrift der Savigny-Stiftung für Rechtsgeschichte,* Kanonistische Abteilung, 56 (1970), 275–334; 60 (1974), 213–364.

64 Notwithstanding the inherent irony involved in sending a character called 'Eygennutz' to represent the interests of the whole community.

Bible references in this part of the text implies that many of the views expressed may be at odds with Eckstein's position as expressed in the prologue. It would seem, then, that Eckstein found it important to depict the workings of this village consultative process, even though doing so might militate against a straightforward communication of his own (monologic) views.

A further stipulation of the debate in the *Concilium* is that a matter must be established by the testimony of two witnesses (see C 803–6/115). This is both a biblical principle[65] and a recognition of the consultative nature of the urban disputation. Consensus is sought, in order that a binding decision may be reached. This principle is, however, carefully balanced against the demands of fairness. As Amma Krůg observes: 'it's not our way to have two against one, I've never seen that before' (C 1427–8/151). Eckstein, indeed, makes some show of not being one-sided both in the *Concilium* and in the *Rychsztag*, where Iohann Schydman, the town clerk ('Stattschryber'), emphasises the fairness of the Imperial Diet in finding guilt on both sides (see the speech beginning R 1674/409).

Finally, there is the principle of appropriate behaviour. In the *Concilium*, the Herald criticizes Luther and Karlstadt for their unchristian disunity, apparently distinguishing between proper ways of dealing with disagreement (such as a disputation) and improper ones, characterized as 'bickering like a pair of washerwomen' (C 4156/307).[66] Similarly, in the *Rychsztag*, Murner is roundly rebuked by Weybel Rychart for 'raging' and 'shouting', rather than seeking sound, rational arguments from God's Word (R 2021–3/429).

All, or nearly all of these various principles reflect contemporary reality, and, if followed, would create the conditions necessary for a genuinely consensual model of decision-making. To that extent they reflect both Swiss habits and Swiss aspirations, and do so in ways that

65 In Deuteronomy 19:15: 'A single witness shall not suffice to convict a person of any crime or wrongdoing in connection with any offence that may be committed. Only on the evidence of two or three witnesses shall a charge be sustained'. In Matthew 18:16: 'Take one or two others along with you, so that every matter may be confirmed by the evidence of two or three witnesses'.

66 This is one of several examples of Eckstein phrasing his polemic in gendered terms.

will doubtless have heightened the appeal of Eckstein's texts to a Swiss audience. In spite of all this, however, we must never forget that Eckstein ultimately wishes to use the apparently 'open' dialogic format of both the *Concilium* and *Rychsztag* as monologic platforms for his own views. This tension is never resolved; and one suspects that the texts would be weaker if it were.

Eckstein's Zwinglian theology

The principal theological positions reflected in the *Concilium* and *Rychsztag* are, in our opinion, a pervasive if not unproblematic biblicism, an integrated approach to soteriology centring on Christ and the cross, a distinctively Zwinglian approach to the Eucharist, and a broad-based challenge to the authority of the Pope and his clergy. These will now be addressed briefly in turn, along with some matters of less central significance, which however also contribute to our understanding of Eckstein's, and Zwingli's, theological project.

As we have seen, Eckstein follows Zwingli in making Scripture the explicit starting point for his theology. This was a fundamental tenet of all Evangelical reformations, including the Lutheran reformations of the imperial free cities and those at Berne and Basle. In English, the principle tends to be referred to as 'biblicism', and in German as *das Schriftprinzip*. Certainly both *Concilium* and *Rychsztag* are characterized by a thoroughgoing biblicism, which is reflected not only in the many references to biblical passages (more accurately, chapters) printed in their margins, but also in frequent appeals to 'God's Word' within the texts themselves. Having said that, Eckstein can appear inconsistent in his application of the principle. For example, the prologue to the *Concilium* imagines God rebuking his people for having served him in vain with the words: 'I did not tell you: "Pay for lots of Masses"' (C 223/79); but later in the same work we find the Herald (with whom it is reasonable to assume Eckstein normally agrees) declaring that 'what is not at odds with his

commands, all Christians should adhere to rigidly' (C 3992–4/299). The first passage suggests, in other words, that one should only do what is positively commanded by God, whereas the second implicitly deems anything that is not prohibited by Scripture to be permissible. In Zwinglian terms, this discrepancy is reasonable and defensible, in the light of the reformer's clear differentiation between religious matters (such as the former) and political, social, or economic ones (such as the latter); it differs markedly, however, from Luther's approach, which is to treat both theological and other questions on the basis of an 'inclusive' *Schriftprinzip* (i.e. whatever the Bible does not forbid can be admitted).

To an unusual degree, and perhaps especially in the *Concilium*, a conscientiously biblicist approach is pursued both by Evangelical farmers and by their Catholic opponents. Indeed they compete to see who can adduce the fullest and most explicit range of Scriptures to support their positions – not that the verses chosen are by any means always apt or persuasive. The Catholic Doctor Fritz is proud, for example, to offer seven sayings ('sprüch') from Scripture as evidence for purgatory (C 1934–6/181). Moreover, following Zwingli,[67] characters from both sides state repeatedly that the words of Scripture are 'clear' (usually 'klar' or 'heiter'). This is asserted more frequently by the Evangelical speakers, however; and it is noticeable that Catholic representatives are apt to stress the clarity of Scripture when they are arguing in favour of something to which Eckstein (and presumably most of his readers) will have been unequivocally opposed: Doctor Gryff does this when promoting transubstantiation, for example, Fridle Landfarer when advocating purgatory, and Faber when claiming that Job prayed to a saint.[68] Such misuse of the *Schriftprinzip* is far from pervasive amongst the Catholics (Doctor Stroubutz, for example, argues very ably, also from Scripture); but there are certainly occasions where the reader is persuaded to reflect that a biblicist approach can be dangerous when adopted by the 'wrong' people, and to acknowledge again Eckstein's subtle use of irony. At times, in other

67 Especially his treatise *Von Klarheit und Gewißheit des Wortes Gottes*, edited in *Sämtliche Werke*, I, 328–84.

68 See, respectively, C 2810–15/231; 1847–51/175; 1198–1203/137.

words, he is able simultaneously to pursue both an open, dialogic agenda and a closed, monologic one.

There is no reason to suspect authorial irony, however, in the occasional statements made by the farmers about their own exegetical practice and/or the extent of their literacy (and hence ability to access God's Word). One thinks, for example, of Joß Hechelzan's exemplary awareness that passages need to be interpreted in context: 'the verse provides its own interpretation, if you look at what comes before it in the same chapter' (C 1994–6/183–5). And Hans Ofenrůß's pride in being able to tell Doctor Lentz that he too 'can find all the scriptures you've mentioned' (C 2321–2/203) will similarly strike most readers as justifiable, rather than in any way arrogant or ignorant.

With regard to the parts of the Bible that Eckstein's characters use, one can perceive a particular emphasis on the Hebrew Scriptures: the marginal references tell their own story in this respect, as do several individual speeches, such as that of Růdolff Fürsichtig in the *Rychsztag* (R 1265–1350/385–91). This is, of course, a markedly different 'canon within a canon' from that of Luther, with his special fondness for the Pauline epistles. Like Luther and Zwingli, however, Eckstein appears to have held a low view of the Apocrypha: no one gainsays Joß Hechelzan's dismissive comment on the Maccabees, 'which isn't part of the canon: even a farmer like me knows that [...] that book has no authority at all with the Jews' (C 1947–51/181). Nevertheless the *Rychsztag* modifies this impression somewhat, with its occasional use of the apocryphal parts of Daniel and, especially, its series of quotations from the Wisdom of Solomon (R 1419–43/395).

When considering Eckstein's soteriology, the reader especially of the *Concilium,* and indeed of the *Dialogus mit Adam,* readily notices that he adopts a more integrated approach than is commonly found in other contemporary Evangelical texts. That is to say, he combines an emphasis on the importance of justification by faith with a theology of the Eucharist, and of good works, that also reflects his soteriology. Much of what he says for example in his (monologic) prologue to the *Concilium* is, admittedly, fully in line with Luther: he presents salvation as a free gift that cannot be bought, sold, or earned (for example, by 'good works'); and nor can God's grace be confined to any particular place (cf. C 2985/241, 3046–7/245), a perspective which of

course has distinct implications for the Eucharist and for pilgrimages. Equally reminiscent of Luther is a hermeneutic that draws a distinction between 'law' and 'grace', based on the fulfilment of the law in the death of Christ.[69] On the other hand, the *Concilium* prologue also contains an impassioned call to repentance in stark language taken from the Hebrew prophets; and Eckstein is apt to imply elsewhere also that salvation is in some way conditional both upon repentance and upon certain forms of Christian behaviour. A good example would be the Weybel's disquisition about penance (C 2630–67/221–3), which draws heavily on the law, the prophets, and the more legalistic parts of Matthew's Gospel. In line with this, perhaps, Eckstein emphasises only the eternal aspects of salvation: in this life it seems to entail only duties, and there is little sense that the gospel transforms, excites, or liberates.

His soteriology does unequivocally resemble Luther's, however, insofar as it is built on a theology of the cross, in which the death of Christ is taken as a unique and sufficient sacrifice not to be repeated in the Mass (see C 1611–18/163). In a polemical *coup de grâce*, Eckstein even has the Catholic Murner agree to something very much like this (C 1539–44/157–9), when he cites Isaiah 53:4 to the effect that Christ has borne our sins. His opponent Cleywi Fenchmul, here for certain speaking on Eckstein's behalf, is quick to follow this logic through to its conclusion, by emphasizing the sacrificial implications of such a statement, and asserting that, in consequence, the only 'sacrifices' God requires of us are those of praise and of ourselves (C 1657–9/165). The centrality of Christ for salvation, and the role of the individual in responding to it are moreover contrasted with many areas of Catholic practice which Eckstein regards as clerical inventions used to exploit the people. When discussing purgatory, for example, Joß Hechelzan says that no such place can exist, although the judgement to which it points is real enough (C 1939–44/181); rather, salvation is

69 This allows Eckstein to sidestep some of the commands of the Hebrew Scripures, although he retains others. See for example Hans Ofenrůß's statement: 'Circumcision need no longer concern you, and nor need sacrificing the blood of cattle to God; the blood of Christ has done away with all other sacrifices' (C 2581–3/217–19).

a free gift that cannot be earned, either by saints or by the suffering of souls in purgatory. The Weybel therefore suspects that purgatory is the brainchild of the Antichrist (a rare reference in Eckstein's works to this ultimate polemical figure), or at least thought up by the greed of the priests (C 2141–50/193).

Vögelin argues, reasonably enough, that the principal focus of Eckstein's 'theological exposition' is the Mass.[70] This is hardly surprising, given that the Eucharist presented a particular problem to the Zwinglian reformers of the 1520s: their theology of it was, after all, their most obvious departure from the faith and practice both of their Catholic neighbours and of their Lutheran fellow reformers. Whilst Luther detects the real presence of Christ in or around the consecrated elements ('consubstantiation'), and the Catholics understand them to be transformed literally into his body and blood ('transubstantiation'), Zwingli thinks that the bread and wine are merely symbols of Christ's death (a 'memorialist' view of the Eucharist).[71] A true farmers' Mass, in the words of the *Concilium*, therefore involves always thinking of Christ's sufferings, rather than engaging in any sacrifice (C 1697–8/167). Or, in the rather more sophisticated language of Lee Palmer Wandel, 'Zwingli's position, labelled 'symbolist' or 'spiritualist' by his opponents, held that a cognitive and somatic connection existed between the bread of the ritual and Christ's body, but not a physical connection autonomous of human perception'.[72]

It is indeed in the *Concilium*'s debates about the Eucharist that the sharpness of Eckstein's dualistic distinction between the flesh and the spirit is at its clearest. A good example is the exchange between the Catholic Doctor Gryff and the farmer Claus Rebstock about the

70 Vögelin, p. 133: 'Die Messe ist das Hauptinteresse der theologischen Exposition […] für den Verfasser'.

71 See also Cyril Charles Richardson, *Zwingli and Cranmer on the Eucharist* (Evanston: Seabury-Western Theological Seminary, 1949).

72 See her book *The Eucharist in the Reformation: Incarnation and Liturgy* (Cambridge: Cambridge University Press, 2006), pp. 72–3. Also Diarmaid MacCulloch, *Reformation: Europe's House Divided* (London: Allen Lane, 2003), pp. 147–8; and Walther Köhler, *Zwingli und Luther: Ihr Streit über das Abendmahl nach seinen politischen und religiösen Beziehungen*, 2 vols (Leipzig: Eger & Sievers, 1924).

interpretation of 1 Corinthians 11 (C 2940–85/239–41). The former insists on a literal, physical interpretation of Scriptures such as Mark 14:22 and Luke 22:19, and argues that St Paul supports such a reading through his specific references to the *body* of Christ in 1 Corinthians 11: 24, 27, and 29.[73] Claus Rebstock, however, claims that this text also supports *his* view of the Eucharist, since St Paul's instructions to 'proclaim' (v. 26) and 'remember' (vv. 24–5) can be interpreted as evidence for Zwingli's Eucharistic theology; and he proceeds to tell Gryff: 'you really are a foolish man to see bread as flesh [...] You have to eat him only in the spirit' (C 2998–3003/243). Ultimately, indeed, Eckstein seems to regard the Catholics' arguments about the Eucharist as simply the best example of their pervasive tendency to confuse flesh with spirit. He, by contrast, habitually resolves both biblical and practical paradoxes by distinguishing the physical from the spiritual sense, often radically. For example his spokesman Rebstock anticipates a possible counter-argument from Matthew 28:20 ('remember, I am with you always, to the end of the age') by saying that Christ is 'with us' spiritually, even though he also said that he would *not* always be with us in physical terms (C 3020–43/245).

For all his concern for 'correct' Evangelical doctrine, however, Eckstein's objections to many Catholic practices frequently come across as not so much theological, as pastoral. A certain pastoral urgency already informs his calls for repentance at the beginning of the *Concilium*; and he objects to the Catholic system of financial payments surrounding the Mass (including tithes, fines, and the endowment of Masses for the dead), not least because they are backed up by the threat of excommunication, and hence weigh heavily on the people in a variety of ways. These points are made strongly, and at this stage credibly, by Eygennutz in the *Rychsztag* (R 833–48/361, 936–41/367); and, in the *Concilium*, the privileged speaker Amma Krůg complains (in a tirade whose rhetoric is reminiscent of Manuel and of another contemporary Swiss dramatist, Pamphilius Gengenbach) that the clergy have not just deceived farmers, but also robbed them of their

73 Far from post-dating the gospel accounts, as Eckstein and his contemporaries believed, St Paul is actually our earliest source on first-century Eucharistic practices.

houses and fields (C 1702–51/167–71). Worst of all, the Mass stands as a symptom of a Catholic soteriology that locates grace in a physical place and seeks to control it corruptly by means of money and outward works, thereby distracting people dangerously from the spiritual work of faith and repentance. Eckstein's intermittent use, here and elsewhere, of the first person plural shows the extent to which he identifies with the plight of the common people.

Such criticisms of Catholic theology and practice as these inevitably also involve criticisms of the papacy as an institution. We have seen above in our discussion of the *Klag des Gloubens* that Eckstein, like many of his contemporaries, enjoyed highlighting the discrepancies between the humility of Christ and the simplicity of his apostles on the one hand, and the pomp and power of the papacy on the other. He does this also in the *Concilium*, as well as challenging the fundamental legitimacy of the papal office. The stakes are high here, because, if the Catholic theology of the papacy is correct, then Zwingli is proved to be a heretic on his own terms (as was pointed out at the First Zurich Disputation and reiterated in the *Rychsztag*). In the *Concilium,* Eck attempts a demonstration from Scripture of the validity of the Pope's claims, but is immediately condemned by his own mouth when, in the space of six lines, he reveals his almost complete reliance on the Fathers and refers to the Pope by a (Freudian) slip of the tongue (or rather, of Eckstein's pen) as his 'god' (C 515–20/97). Meanwhile Thoman Klotz refutes Eck's use of the classic pro-papal proof-text, Matthew 16:18–19, by playfully appropriating the words of Christ: 'I will break down the gates of your church using your own words' (C 672–3/107).

Furthermore there are hints in this section, and indeed throughout the *Concilium,* that the farmers (who after all frequently refer to themselves in the first person plural) are developing their own nascent sense of ecclesial identity, defined by adherence to the authority of Scripture (as opposed to the Pope, the Fathers or canon law, which define the Catholic position). Paule Kachelmůs describes what amounts to an alternative church which, in stark contrast to the confusions of the Catholics, might be able to bridge the gap between the visible and the invisible, the temporal and the eternal. And this Church needs no earthly head, which is why Paule is able to ridicule the very idea of a

truly authoritative papacy, by asking which of the historical Popes will be the head of the Church when God finally reveals it in heaven (C 824–30/115).

Some less central theological issues (at least in the Swiss context) are also discussed from time to time. These include the veneration of relics at pilgrimage shrines, of which Eckstein essentially disapproves. Pilgrims only end up with tired legs and empty purses, the Weybel argues, while the real beneficiaries are the priests who dreamed up the relevant saint or miracle in the first place (C 2680–7/225). Moreover the plenary indulgences that could be obtained on some pilgrimages are rejected on theological grounds. Following the pattern in which Catholic abuses are criticized and an Evangelical corrective is suggested, the Herald reminds us that, instead, 'God does not sell indulgences, and forgives sin and guilt free of charge' (C 427–9/91).[74] Further, cults of saints in general are rejected, on the basis of Eckstein's christocentric soteriology, but also because they too result from a confusion between the physical and the spiritual realms (St Antony's burdensome cosmic responsibility for all pigs, discussed by Knüchel Fritz in C 1114–23/133, furnishes a good example of how ridiculous the implications of early modern Catholic practices could become).

Two important Catholic practices are not so easy to ridicule, however. Confession and fasting are both taught in Scripture, and hence cannot be rejected; but they too need to be reinterpreted. In an attempt to do this, Hans Ofenrůß insists that no biblical evidence can be found for the practice of auricular confession, and that there is certainly no warrant for charging a fee to hear someone's confession. Hans's Evangelical alternative is in line with both Scripture and Eckstein's communalism: one farmer should confess his sins to another, or to God (C 2331–72/203–5). True penitence, meanwhile, is a matter of the heart (C 4095–7/303–5); and, of course, God's forgiveness is free.

Fasting, for its part, was a delicate issue in the Zurich context, not least because the Swiss Reformation could be said to have begun when several supporters of Zwingli ostentatiously broke the Lenten

74 See also n. 358 on the *Concilium* (p. 227 below).

fast of 1522 by eating sausages at the house of the printer Christoph Froschauer.[75] In his speech on fasting to the *Concilium* (C 1352–421/ 147–51), the Weybel shows that he is not opposed to fasting *per se*, quoting Zwingli (at the First Zurich Disputation) as asserting that we are not told not to fast. Such a double negative is of course far from a wholehearted endorsement, but the Weybel's (and Eckstein's) biblicism constrains him to say that Christ did indeed teach his disciples how to fast (cf. Matthew 6:16–18). The important thing is that Jesus says fasting should be done secretly, in marked contrast to the public practices and controls surrounding late-medieval fasting. Again, the purpose of the rules (and fines) that surrounded fasting is identified as clerical greed; and, through the Weybel, Eckstein also points to the corrupt paradox that regulations about fasting are enforced more rigorously than those regarding more serious moral infringements, such as adultery.

It is important to point out, however, that, for all of his anticlericalism, Eckstein is plainly aware of the existence of well-intentioned Catholic clergy. This can be seen not least towards the end of the *Rychsztag,* where the Herald offers advice on how to spot such priests, and how to treat them appropriately (R 2332–52/445–7). After all, there were learned and well-intentioned Humanists on both sides of the confessional divide, and both Zwingli and Eckstein had been Catholic priests before the Zurich Reformation. Eckstein is no doubt concerned to uphold the integrity of the better of his former colleagues, whilst also keeping the channels of communication with enlightened Catholics open – at least in principle, and until after the proposed Swiss disputation had taken place. There is no doubt that in this as in so many other respects Eckstein will have identified himself with Zwingli's position. Certainly, whilst nuances differ and priorities are not identical, it is entirely reasonable to describe his theology as essentially Zwinglian in nature.

75 Zwingli claimed to have been present on the occasion, but not to have eaten any sausage – though 'he also raised no objection' (Potter, p. 75). The best source for the reformer's views on fasting in general is his *Von Erkiesen und Freiheit der Speisen*, in *Sämtliche Werke*, I (Berlin: Schwetschke, 1905), 74–136.

Eckstein on politics and society

Eckstein's views on socio-political matters also reflect positions current in Zurich in the mid-1520s. These issues come to the fore towards the end of the *Concilium*, and are taken up again in the opening two sections of the *Rychsztag*. The main subjects discussed are the financial obligations placed on the common people, the legitimacy and nature of temporal authority, the immoral and socially damaging behaviour of both the clergy and the farmers, and an assortment of wider social ills.

The terms used by Eckstein to denote obligatory financial payments made by farmers to lords appear in various combinations, and are frequently impossible to translate (or differentiate from each other) with confidence. The two most commonly employed, however, are 'zins', which tends to refer to interest payments, but can also imply taxes or other duties owed to the Church; and 'zähend', whose basic meaning is 'tithe'. The principal locus for the discussion of problems associated with these is the final section of the *Concilium*, in which the farmer Pur Eygennutz (whose name means, significantly, 'selfishness' or 'self-interest')[76] encounters Doctor Stroubutz. Their discussion differs from the preceding sections from a structural point of view, not only because of its greater length, but also because Eygennutz is the only farmer character to speak first, before his educated opponent. In every other section, it is the Catholic doctor (the representative of the incorrect opinion) who begins, and the second, Evangelical speaker who then offers superior arguments from Scripture and undermines his interlocutor through polemical attacks. From the very outset of this section, then, there are clear indications that Eckstein may wish to distance his own views from those of Eygennutz.

The latter begins by expressing his inability to understand why the farmers must continue to pay tithes that were previously levied by

76 This was an important term for Zwingli, which he used as a kind of shorthand to describe egotistical and/or stubborn opposition to the cause of reform. See especially *Eine treue und ernstliche Vermahnung an die Eidgenossen,* in *Sämtliche Werke*, III, 97–113, especially 107–11.

the old Church. He perceives the current situation to be different in three respects: firstly, there has been a huge religious upheaval (he now considers himself to be 'Evangelisch'); secondly, he feels that 'God's Word' has freed him from all previous obligations; and thirdly, he has formed the expectation that 'all things would be held in common' (C 3226–40/255–7). It is important for Eckstein to address arguments such as these because of their topicality in the context of the 'Peasants' War', and also because they represented a certain danger to the cause of the Zurich Reformation: they suggest, after all, a need to go beyond the reforms instituted by Zwingli and the Zurich council, and as such represent 'radical' or 'Anabaptist' views of a kind that were increasingly threatening the newly established orthodoxy in Zurich.[77] Doctor Stroubutz counters them here by arguing that Eygennutz has mistaken the freedom proclaimed in Scripture for a holiday from his debts, because he has failed to interpret the Bible spiritually, and is motivated purely by temporal considerations (C 3269–84/ 257–9); the charge is reminiscent of similar statements made by Christus in the *Dialogus*. In reply, Eygennutz alludes to the law of Moses, which stipulates that all debts should be cleared after seven years, and to St Luke's injunction (6:35) to 'lend, expecting nothing in return' (C 3361–8/263). It is of course clear that he understands this passage from the perspective of a debtor, rather than that of a lender. In any event Stroubutz denies the validity of such biblical statements for the Christian life, insisting that Eygennutz's very status as a borrower points to God's judgement upon him: he quotes Deuteronomy's statement (15:6) to the effect that the faithful will lend to many nations, but will not borrow (C 3370–87/263–5).[78] Instead of worrying about temporal matters, Stroubutz argues, a Christian should trust God and continue paying tithes and taxes, since these will not affect his or her eternal life (C 3339–52/261–3). Finally, in a passage that amounts to an apology for usury, Stroubutz points out that society could not

77 Pur Eygennutz, indeed, readily admits his indebtedness to the Anabaptists, in C 3259–64/257 and C 3625–30/277.

78 In appropriating this promise, Stroubutz personalizes it by making the relevant pronoun singular rather than plural (the biblical text refers to a whole nation).

function if people did not repay their debts (C 3660–74/279–81).[79] Throughout, then, the Catholic apologist Stroubutz[80] evinces a certain economic conservatism – with which, however, perhaps surprisingly for the modern reader, Eckstein and for that matter Zwingli are likely to have been broadly in agreement.[81]

With regard to temporal authorities also it is easy to see Stroubutz as Eckstein's mouthpiece. He notes that authorities are not explicitly forbidden by Scripture, and are indeed mandated to protect widows and orphans (a favourite trope throughout the *Rychsztag* as well), and to keep the peace (C 3309–16/261). On this basis, he characterizes the uprisings of the common people as contrary to God's Word and motivated by self-interest ('von Eygnem nutz', C 3316). Instead, he argues, the farmers should submit to God, who will punish whom he will; and he contrasts the self-interest of Eygennutz with the simplicity and pacifism of Christ, in a harangue that draws heavily on the Psalms and the Gospels[82] and, in its rhetoric, is frequently reminiscent of Luther (C 3722–73/283–5). With regard to the rule of law, the paying of taxes and repaying of debts, and submission to temporal authorities – even corrupt ones (C 3632–45/279) – Stroubutz is (like Eckstein and Zwingli, and again like Luther) something of an idealist. For all of them, rich and poor are equal in the face of divine judgement; and this should guarantee a spirit of mutual dependence as well as of individual responsibility before God. In a phrase that echoes Luther's *Von der Freiheit eines Christenmenschen*, for example, Stroubutz urges Eygennutz to 'be subject to all human creatures' (C

79 Cf. Lewis Hyde, *The Gift: How the Creative Spirit Transforms the World* (Edinburgh: Canongate, 2006 [1983]), pp. 111–42.

80 There is no justification for regarding Stroubutz as an Evangelical (*pace* Müller, p. 26), though Jørgensen is right to point out (p. 124) that his views are doubtless similar to those formed by the Zurich Council when faced by unrest in their own rural hinterland.

81 See for example Dieter Demandt, 'Die Wirtschaftsethik Huldrych Zwinglis', in *Beiträge zur Wirtschafts- und Sozialgeschichte des Mittelalters. Festschrift für Herbert Helbig zum 65. Geburtstag*, ed. by Knut Schulz (Cologne: Böhlau, 1976), pp. 306–21.

82 Gospel idealism such as this may also be a sign of Erasmus's influence (cf. the *Enchiridion*).

3652/279). Christian love is the key to this attitude of submission, as well as to the successful functioning of society as a whole. On the other hand, Eckstein seems to allow no other mechanism than civic authority for seeking redress in cases of abuse. His idealism is therefore coupled with a powerful trust in the support of the local civic authorities for the Evangelical cause. Like many others, after all, the Zurich reformers had a strong interest in maintaining the sociopolitical *status quo*.

If Stroubutz's (and Eckstein's) gospel idealism seems impractical, it is worth noting that Eckstein himself seems actually to have lived largely in accordance with it, faithfully and in no little poverty. Certainly he seems to feel able to occupy a certain moral high ground when discussing the corrupt and exploitative behaviour of many of his fellow clerics. Through privileged voices such as those of the Herald in the *Concilium* and Mayor Salomon and Bernhart Erenuest in the *Rychsztag*, he regularly accuses them of self-interest and of leading the people astray with human inventions not commanded by God. Both *Concilium* and *Rychsztag* give examples of clerical corruption, usually involving extortion, drunkenness, and sexual immorality. Perhaps the most poignant example, given its deliberate echo of the Gospels, tells how the rich local abbot systematically fails to offer drink to a hungry and thirsty farmer, and will only give him food that his dogs will not eat (R 310–48/331–3, cf. Matthew 25:42). The situation is made all the more disgusting, we are told, not only because of the monastery's wealth, but also because the monks themselves are lazy. They live by the sweat of the farmers' brows, and contribute nothing,[83] because even their worship is pointless. All of this is particularly deleterious because clerical corruption has a trickle-down effect on the whole of society. According to the Herald at the end of the *Rychsztag*, clergy, nobility, and farmers are guilty of seeking their own interests rather than the mutual benefit of all, even to the point of robbing others of what is rightfully theirs (R 2201–32/439–41).

That said, the dignity of the farmers, on whom all other parts of society rely, is reiterated several times in the *Rychsztag,* often indeed

83 This is one of the clearest indications that Eckstein's concept of masculinity is bound up with the notion of working the land (as Adam did).

using the concept of 'sweat'. Yet they are oppressed, neglected, and insulted by everyone, including by certain speakers in the *Concilium* – notably by the supercilious Murner, who opines that common people are good only for chopping wood and ploughing (C 1526–8/157 – a view that Amma Krůg later turns on its head with the statement: 'A farmer pulling his plough can understand that Christ has suffered enough, has died once and can't die any more', C 1702–4/167). Such statements as this confirm that Eckstein uses his peasant characters to help him show how easily theological truths can be grasped by 'ordinary' people. Nevertheless, as the *Rychsztag* especially shows, he is by no means blind to the farmers' faults. And, notwithstanding the abuses of the clergy, religious, and territorial lords, he insists that they too should 'turn to God, rather than destroying castles and monasteries' (R 144–5/321).

Here as elsewhere, Eckstein reveals that, for all his sympathy for the plight of the farmers, he is writing from an urban perspective and in support of specifically urban forms of government: 'we still need some kind of authority over us, whether it's located in castles or in a city, for that is what God himself has ordained' is the chastened Eygennutz's summary, in the *Rychsztag*, of some of Stroubutz's arguments from the *Concilium* (R 147–9/323); and he himself goes on to suggest, somewhat optimistically, that the villagers 'might still find somewhere in the imperial free cities some godly and honourable men who would take our suffering to heart' (R 160–3/323).[84]

Finally it must be pointed out that, whilst he is primarily concerned with the behaviour of and relationships between the farmers and their temporal and ecclesiastical lords, Eckstein also permits himself some sideswipes against wider social ills, including pride, drunkenness, swearing and blasphemy, and the wearing of fine clothes, especially in the French style. Farmers dressing above their station, and women showing off their breasts are singled out for special criticism, rather as they are in Brant's *Narrenschiff,* Murner's *Geuchmat* and *Narrenbeschwörung*, and other examples of satirical

84 Jørgensen (p. 125) is correct to point out, however, that in sixteenth-century society the notion of the state as a potentially disinterested source of authority must be seen as a utopian aspiration, rather than a practicable reality.

Humanist literature.[85] Interestingly, Stroubutz answers his own question as to 'why things are so bad at this time' by blaming those at the very top: 'God has given us children for princes, and we are all leading a sinful life. Kings are the same as the common people [...] one king is always after another one's kingdom' (C 3613–18/277). The reference to excessive youthfulness may well reflect the fact that Emperor Charles V was but twenty-five when these words were written; and ignoble, acquisitive empire building was of course a defining characteristic of the Italian Wars that rent Europe asunder, at least intermittently, for much of the first half of the sixteenth century. But the implication is clear: for Eckstein, it was still possible to hope for good government, but the most promising places to look for it were cities like Zurich.

The *Concilium* and *Rychsztag* as literature

The two texts edited and translated here differ from much vernacular dialogue literature of the period, including dramas such as the carnival plays of Niklaus Manuel, in a variety of instructive ways. Perhaps the most obvious way is that, within the limitations imposed by the use of rhyming couplets, they make a seemingly genuine attempt to mimic elements of real spoken communication. For one thing, the characters' speeches tend to be fairly short and naturalistic – though there are lapses in this regard, most obviously when, in the *Concilium*, the Catholic Doctor Laurentz is harangued for over 600 lines by a series of three Evangelical characters without being given the opportunity to reply (his opponents' occasional injunctions to him to listen constitute less a persuasive concession to dialogue form than an opportunity to alert the reader to points that Eckstein wishes to stress). Nevertheless, at various points not least in the *Rychsztag,* for example, we really do

85 For a lively new description of sixteenth-century fashions, see Ian Mortimer, *The Time Traveller's Guide to Elizabethan England* (London: Bodley Head, 2012), pp. 156–90.

get a sense of the cut and thrust of genuine debate. This is true certainly of the peasant 'vmbfraagen' discussed above, but also of the discussions at Richtal between Eygennutz, Ludeman Pfeffersack and Mayor Salomon (R 932–1189/367–81), and indeed, for all its manifest stylization, of the entertaining showdown between Murner and Balaam's ass (R 1834–986/417–27) – a section which also contains some good examples of Eckstein's gift for what might euphemistically be termed earthy, unsophisticated plain-speaking.

At the same time, and only superficially paradoxically, Eckstein is manifestly keen that his characters should not only take up one another's exact words, but should also respond to them rationally and in some detail – as distinct from being content with the kind of sloganizing invective that one not infrequently meets in dialogue texts from this era. Here again we see not just a desire to encourage a sense of realistic communication, but also a concern on Eckstein's part to present his texts as basically 'fair' hearings. For all their clear Evangelical orientation, the dialogues are unusual, indeed remarkable, for the extent to which they allow valid alternative points of view to be expressed and heard. As we have seen, already in the *Concilium*, and perhaps especially in its sections on the Mass, the Catholic speakers express sophisticated and well formulated theological views; and the debate between Eygennutz and Stroubutz about tithes and taxes is, as we have seen, not so much even-handed as positively slanted in favour of the latter. The *Rychsztag* then takes this process a stage further by presenting Eygennutz as being comprehensively out-thought and out-argued by the 'establishment' figures who oppose him: to the extent indeed that he eventually experiences a form of conversion, vowing never again to rebel or to withhold his tithes (R 2469–86/455).

This (for its time) unusual willingness to engage in a genuinely dialogic process must not, of course be exaggerated. Both of our dialogues do, after all, seek at times to discredit their opponents (such as Murner and Johannes Faber) by means of emphatically monologic polemical attacks. Monologic sections open and close the *Concilium*, occupying nine sides at the beginning (one sixteenth of the whole text) and at the end comprising the lengthy speeches of Stroubutz and the Herald, both of which reiterate and reinforce views expressed in the

prologue. Indeed, the only 'new' element in the Herald's speech is his vituperative criticism of Luther and Karlstadt (C 4154–87/307–9), which gives a twist to the usual practice of 'Reformation dialogues' to end with an assessment (almost invariably positive) of Luther.[86] Eckstein's monologic voice is also discernible in the words of the Weybel, whose role is ostensibly to introduce each pair of disputants and to summarize their arguments, but who becomes increasingly vocal about his own sympathies for the Evangelical position as the text progresses. Moreover, especially in the *Concilium*, Eckstein regularly privileges Evangelical interpretations through such devices as repetition, the relative length of speeches, the use of rhetorical questions, and marginalia.

Overall, then, Eckstein's works combine monologic and dialogic, didactic and polemical elements in a way that is quite unusual for so-called 'Reformation dialogues' – but is a familiar feature in Erasmus.[87] Nor is this the only aspect of Eckstein's works that seems to reveal the influence of Humanist folly literature of the kind we associate most readily with the Rotterdam master. For one thing, Eckstein has a wide range of targets, including monks and theologians as well as foolish commoners and greedy lords, rather as Erasmus, Brant, and indeed Murner do in the *Moriae encomium*, the *Narrenschiff*, and the *Narrenbeschwörung* respectively. And one could hardly have a more quintessentially Erasmian motif than that of the 'wise fool', into which Eckstein transforms himself, in the guise of Balaam's ass, when attacked by Murner in the *Rychsztag*.

When one adds to these features the Swiss and 'Reformed' elements of Eckstein's theology (his integrated soteriology, Humanist influences, christocentrism, gospel idealism, and emphasis on the dualism of body and spirit), as well as his communal political views, one begins to see that the *Concilium* and *Rychsztag* are in many ways intrinsically different from most other so-called 'Reformation dia-

86 See Joel Love, 'Peasants in Dialogue with Authority: Three Literary Dialogues of the German Reformation' (unpublished MPhil thesis, University of Birmingham, 2004), pp. 109–10.

87 See the changes in tone that occur in the various sections of the *Moriae encomium*, for example.

logues'. So much so, indeed, that they could even be said to problematize that whole generic construct – to which they are conventionally, and rather lazily, assigned. The notion of the 'Reformation dialogue', as adumbrated by Johannes Schwitalla and others, is after all founded on the identification of a number of characteristic genre markers, most of which, quite simply, are not present in Eckstein.[88] Rather, the two dialogues offered here could perhaps be more accurately designated 'textualized disputations', standing as they do in printed form between two oral disputations (Zurich in 1523, Baden in 1526), and attempting as they do to recreate the dialogic patterns of such oral exchanges for Eckstein's own monologic ends. Moreover a foregrounding of the term 'disputation' points neatly to the essential Swiss-ness of these texts: they are, after all, imaginative representations of a fundamentally Helvetian, and urban, approach to public debate and decision-making; and their flavour is consistently and very specifically Zwinglian.

Textual history of the *Concilium* and *Rychsztag*

Between them, the two texts edited here are found in six sixteenth-century prints, which in the following are designated 'A' to 'F' in strict chronological order. Not all of these are dated, and none is explicitly acknowledged to be the work of a particular printer; but, in each case, the relevant metadata can be (and have been) established reliably

88 Schwitalla, *passim*. See also Elspeth Ann Davidson, 'An Examination of German Reformation Dialogues, 1520–1525' (unpublished PhD thesis, University of Stirling, 1982); Fiona M. K. Campbell, 'The Dialogue as a Genre of German Reformation Literature' (unpublished PhD thesis, St Andrews University, 2000). Problematic genre markers in Eckstein's context include the convention of the dialogue taking place in a casual and spontaneous context, an essential one-sidedness in the arguments (coupled with a reluctance to 'hear otherness'), and an expectation that dialogues involving many speakers will be particularly confrontational in tone.

enough by specialist librarians, working on the basis of a detailed knowledge of the printers involved. The prints are:

A: *Concilium. / HIe in dem bůch wirt diſputiert / Das puren lang zyt hett verfürt / Heilgen fürbit / ouch des baſsts gwalt / vom Fägfhür / ouch was dMäſs innhalt,* [Zurich]: [Christoph Froschauer], [1525]. Copies used: London, British Library, C.107.aa.18; Zürich, Zentralbibliothek, AW 6083.

B: *Rychſztag. Der Edlen vnd Pauren bricht vnd klag / z fridberg ghandelt auff dem Rychßtag,* [Zurich]: [Christoph Froschauer], [1526]. Copy used: Zürich, Zentralbibliothek, Gal Ch 292/2.

C: *Concilium. / HIe in dem bůch wirt disputiert / Das puren lang zyt hat verfürt / Heylgen Fürbit / Ouch des Bapsts Gwallt / vom Fägfhür / ouch was dMäſs innhalt,* [Zurich]: [Christoph Froschauer], [1526]. Copy used: Zürich, Zentralbibliothek, Gal Ch 292.

D: *Der Bawren Reichßtag vnd Concilium. Weß ſicher die ſieben Bauren auß ſieben Landtſchafften vereynigt / vnd zů antwurt geben dem Cardinal Campeio vnd ſeinen mitgeſandten auff das verkündt Bäpſtiſch Concilium / wa bei ſie bleiben wöllen / in ſieben artickel geſtelt / alles verantwurt mit red vnd gegenred auß heyliger Geſchrifft / luſtig vnnd kurtzweilig zůleſen,* [Strasbourg]: [Jakob Cammerlander], 1539. Copy used: London, British Library, C.107.b.20.

E: *Concilium. / HIe in dem bůch wirt diſputiert / Das Puren lang zyt hett verfürt / Heilgenfürbit / ouch des bapſsts gwalt / vom Fägfhür / ouch was dMäſſs innhalt,* [Berne]: [Matthias Apiarius], [c. 1550]. Copy used: Bern, Universitätsbibliothek, ZB Rar 256.

F: *Reichstag: / oder / Verſammlung der Bawren / gehalten zu Fridberg im Rychthal / darinnen / die gemeine Klag der jetzigen Welt gehört vnd erörteret wirdt. / Concilium: / Darinnen die Bawren mit den Doctoribus der heiligen Geſchrifft von geiſtlichen Sachen diſputieren vnd entſcheiden. / Klag / des Glaubens / der Hoffnung / vnd auch der Liebe / vber alle Stend der Chriſtenheit / der Geyſtlichen vnd Weltlichen. Alles vor 65. Jaren von dem Wolgelehrten und frommen Mann / Utz Eckſtein beschriben / vnd jetz allen frommen Chriſten zu gutem / vnd / in vilen ſchwären fürfallenden Sachen zum bericht widerumb / an tag gebracht,* [Basle]: [Sebastian Henricpetri], 1592. Copy used: London, British Library, C.107.aa.22.

In sum, this means that we have five sixteenth-century prints of the *Concilium* (A, C, D, E, and F), and two of the *Rychsztag* (B and F: in spite of its statement implying the contrary, D only has the *Concilium*). The *Concilium* has in many ways the more complicated textual history, not least in that these five editions can be divided into two distinct versions, the first represented by A and E, and the second (which

seems to have been the only one known to Scheible and Vögelin) by C, D, and F. The differences between these versions are marked, and, at least in the cases of A, C, and E, start to become apparent already on the books' title pages. After the initial list of seven theological 'hot potatoes' and naming of the participants, A (as always, copied almost 'slavishly' by E)[89] proceeds as follows: 'Reader, do not neglect to buy me. See the one up against the other: for this book brings you both seriousness and humour. Turn your heart towards God's Word alone. With Danhuser's privilege' (C 17–21/67). Print C shares the initial sentence of self-promotion,[90] but then says something quite different: 'I'm bringing you many strong words which tell you about the sacrament, that Christ's body wasn't sent into the bread. If you want to hear the lament of all the world, read about it in the *Peasants' Rychsztag*'.[91] C, then, removes the statement preparing the reader for 'both seriousness and humour' and the curious phrase 'cum priuilegio Danhusers'[92] – changes which, taken together, arguably denude the title page of a certain sense of playfulness. More significantly, though, it takes the opportunity to underline the importance that discussion of the Eucharist will have in the work that follows, and to advertise the *Rychsztag* – as indeed, at the other end of the text, does a 68-line closing speech by Pur Eygennutz, who reflects back on his experiences at the *Concilium*

89 'Sklavisch' is the word that Hegg quite correctly uses (p. 60) to describe the carefulness with which E generally copies even A's errors.

90 Whilst direct address is not uncommon in the dialogue literature of the Reformation, it is unusual to find the book itself engaging in this kind of sales pitch. Arguably the statement prepares the reader for Eckstein's subsequent use (not least in the prologue that follows immediately afterwards) of monologic forms.

91 For the German text see p. 66 below.

92 It is not possible plausibly to relate these words to an actual person (such as the distinguished Nuremberg Humanist Peter Dannhauser; Hegg (p. 63) mentions also the Salzburg nobleman Franz von Tannhausen and the Strasbourg printer Conrad Danhuser). Rather, a tradition had developed, especially since the first printing of the folk ballad of Tannhäuser in 1515, of seeing that fictionalized poet as a principled opponent of an unforgiving Pope – and hence as a kind of proto-Protestant. See Dietz-Rüdiger Moser, *Die Tannhäuser-Legende* (Berlin: de Gruyter, 1977), especially p. 11. The formulation is of course also a play on the wording of the imperial privilege ('Cum privilegio Caesaris maiestatis').

and then expresses his determination to 'go and make an appeal at the Reichstag'.

Quite apart from anything else, of course, all this means that C's text of the *Concilium* must post-date the *Rychsztag* – and hence cannot have been printed before 1526. Moreover the sense conveyed of C being perhaps a more theologically serious version of the work with a particular emphasis on the Mass is borne out by a number of other changes and additions in the text that follows. Such a shift of emphasis might for example explain the perceived need for the 107-line addition about priestly (and especially papal) arrogance and worldliness that follows A's line 869, or the patent attempt to 'clean up' the scatalogy of A 305–8; it almost certainly is the reason behind the 28 extra lines after A 382 that stress that God wants no sacrifice other than that of the heart; and it must surely have prompted the very extensive, 285-line addition (after A 2822) to the discussion of the Eucharist between Claus Rebstock and Doctor Gryff. That this section is intended to serve a primarily didactic, monologic purpose is evident immediately from the fact that only two of these lines are assigned to the Catholic spokesman, Gryff. Moreover Rebstock's words clearly reflect the extent to which the divisions not only between Zwingli and Catholic apologists, but also between him and the Lutheran Bugenhagen had become more clearly focused since the composition of the first edition of the *Concilium*. Rebstock homes in unerringly on the two questions which, especially since the publication of his *Responsio ad epistolam Ioannis Bugenhagii* (on 23rd October 1525), Zwingli seems to have recognized as the most important and divisive issues: the words of institution (specifically, does 'is' mean 'actually is', or can it mean 'signifies'?), and the question of whether Christ can be really present (in consequence *either* of 'transubstantiation' *or* of 'consubstantiation') in the human body.[93] Hence the first of Rebstock's two long supplementary speeches reminds us that, for example, when Christ describes the disciples as 'salt', he is not commenting literally on their physical composition, any more than Pharisees could be said *actually* to devour widows' houses, or God to brandish a winnowing fork. Then, in his second speech, he proceeds to draw so strong a

93 See Gummelt, *passim.*

contrast between the spiritual and physical elements of human and divine nature as to make the very notion of Christ's 'real presence' entering a human stomach appear positively absurd.

The longer version of the *Concilium* that appears in our prints C, D, and F, then, quite clearly does not represent the work in its original form. The earlier version, transmitted in A and E, is almost certainly closer to that; and this, along with its paucity of significant errors and the fact that Scheible's nineteenth-century edition is a 'straight' transcription of C which there seems little need to duplicate, is the reason why we have chosen to use it as the base text for our new edition – whilst also offering the extra material of C, D, and F in an appendix. That said, there are at least some grounds for thinking that there may once have been a still earlier, first version of the *Concilium* which is now lost. Hegg reminds us (p. 62) that Murner, in his *Responsio,* berates the author of the *Concilium* for having published his scurrilous work anonymously; yet our earliest print, A, clearly names Eckstein as its author, albeit at the very end of the text (C 4198/309). One might of course surmise that Murner did not feel inclined to read his copy of A the whole way through, in the context of what was doubtless a highly irate perusal of it; and it is perhaps worth noting that something seems to have motivated Eckstein, when composing the *Rychsztag*, to give his name at the very beginning of that dialogue, rather than the very end. Nevertheless it remains possible, though far from certain, that Murner is genuinely alluding to an anonymous version of the text which is no longer extant. At least some of C's extra material might, after all, have been cut by A from a pre-existent version (by no means all of it would appear out of place); and one can identify at least one error in A (which E subsequently corrects) that might well have resulted from overhasty 'cutting and pasting': in 2823, A fails to notice that there has been a change of speaker, and hence omits the necessary reference to Claus Rebstock.

Before leaving the textual history of *Concilium*, we must point out that both D and F, whilst clearly representing the same branch of the tradition as does C, are largely independent, indeed decidedly eccentric texts. This is true particularly of D, the product of a Lutheran publishing house, that of Jakob Cammerlander in Strasbourg, in 1539. In many ways it seems that Cammerlander's version of the *Concilium*

is a typical product of his workshop, which, according to Josef Benzing, specialized not least in often free adaptations of already known works, most of them made by his associate Jakob Vielfeld.[94] It is nonetheless perplexing to witness Eckstein's dialogue being recycled in what one would have thought was a decidedly alien context – not least because, for all of the *Concilium*'s multivocality and its author's capacity for 'hearing otherness', this cannot be accomplished without considerable violence being done to the integrity of the text. Hence D omits over 800 lines entirely, including most notably the whole of the prologue and of the Herald's closing speech – though this latter is replaced by one of comparable length, in which readers are requested to submit to the authority of the Church (rather than, specifically, that of the Pope) and to pursue unity and peace by means of a General Council. The example of St Peter and St Paul in Antioch (as recorded in Acts 11) is cited with particular approval. Moreover almost all of the local Swiss references are excised (one thinks, for example, of the numerous mentions of Zwingli's 'rabbit cheese' and the substantial passages detailing the evils of Murner or Faber); and – albeit surprisingly rarely – certain theological statements (notably, of course, those concerning the Mass) are omitted or 'finessed'. The characters also have to be renamed: so Eck becomes the Cardinal Protector of the Empire (and opponent of Councils) Lorenzo Campeggio, Dr Laurentz becomes Hieronymus Emser, Dr Stroubutz Doctor Wolthat, Pur Eygennutz Pur Geier; and, in a particularly extraordinary development, Zwingli becomes Luther. All the peasants are also renamed, a process which, along with those just mentioned, frequently necessitates changes of wording in order to accommodate new rhyme words. Other than entertainment (which will have been promoted also by the inclusion of a woodcut at the beginning and end),[95] the precise purpose of this print is unclear. Clearly, however, it was conceived as some kind of contribution (and, by Protestant standards, a notably

94 See Benzing's article for the *Neue deutsche Biographie* (24 vols, Berlin: Duncker & Humblot, 1953–present), III (1957), 108–9.

95 The same one appears both times. It is a not terribly well executed, generic picture of an enthroned senior cleric (Campeggio?) in discussion with four other, not readily identifiable robed figures.

positive one) to the debate about the value of Church councils, which had been vigorously promoted since 1534 by Pope Paul III, and which, in Germany, was revivified, early in 1539, by the appearance of Luther's most comprehensive treatment of the topic, *Von den Konzilen und der Kirche.*[96] One suspects, indeed, that D also is likely to have been produced earlier in the year 1539, rather than later: it would surely have lost some of its relevance following the final prorogation of the moribund Council of Vicenza on 21st May, and in any event Campeggio died on 19th July.

Print F, meanwhile, which is dated 1592, contains three of Eckstein's dialogues, albeit in a curious order (first *Rychsztag*, then *Concilium*, then *Klag des Gloubens*). It offers far less radical adaptations of these texts than does D, but nevertheless makes many minor changes to lexis, rhymes and, in particular, metre. The result is a text that seems less specifically Swiss, less earthily naturalistic and, above all, far more polished in conventional literary terms. Overall, its combination of 1520s content with a much later sixteenth-century approach to poetic style makes for a somewhat disconcerting read. The extensive introductory material placed by the book's printer, Sebastian Henricpetri, on its title page does imply that the texts might have some relevance to readers seeking to solve difficult problems in the modern age; and certainly the works' theology will have supported the formation of a 'reformed' identity at the end of the sixteenth century. Nevertheless the printer's interest in Eckstein's works seems to have been primarily historical. Hence his statement that the works were written 'by a learned and devout man' sixty-five years previously – a figure which we take (with Hegg, p. 61) as constituting a forgivable miscalculation (or indeed rounding down) on Henricpetri's part, rather than evidence to the effect that the three works in question were written in 1527.

In contrast to the *Concilium*, the textual history of the *Rychsztag* is blessedly straightforward. Given what we have just said about F (the remarks apply equally to all three of its dialogues, including the

96 *WA* 50, 606–50. An excellent account of all of Luther's later writings about Councils is given by Mark Urban Edwards, jr, *Luther's Last Battles: Politics and Polemics 1531–46* (Ithaca, NY: Cornell University Press, 1983), pp. 68–97.

Klag des Gloubens), B is, realistically, the only source that an editor could plausibly use as the basis of an edition; and, fortunately, it offers a good, reliable text.

Approach to editing and translating

As stated above, our edition of the *Concilium* is based on print A, and that of the *Rychsztag* on print B. We seek to reproduce the source texts as accurately as possible, having regard to orthography, punctuation, capitalization, and marginalia (most of which simply give Bible references, thereby underlining Eckstein's desire to present his writings as based on a thoroughgoing biblicism). Words or phrases which appear in larger type in the original texts are printed in bold; italicized marginal references remain in italics. Editorial interventions are made only in cases of manifest linguistic or typographical error, and even then only when a more persuasive reading can be taken from one or more of the other surviving sixteenth-century prints. Subjective conjectures of our own, in other words, are avoided as a matter of principle. Changes we have made to the text are indicated in italics, and recorded in the critical apparatus at the foot of the relevant page. To the basic texts we have added only line numbers, references (in square brackets) to the pagination of the original prints, and the critical apparatus. In the case of both texts, this is a slender one. In respect of the *Concilium* we offer – alongside A's errors – only significant group variants (i. e. readings that *either* A and E *or* C, F, and – where applicable – D have in common). In the case of the *Rychsztag*, for which we have only two sixteenth-century witnesses, we have made the pragmatic decision to provide selected variants from F. Chosen for inclusion are those readings which we regard as potential improvements on or, in some cases, particularly interesting alternatives to the text of B. We feel it would be a pity to lose these from the edition entirely, whilst seeing no point in mechanically recording all of F's myriad tiny emendations.

The translations into English prose seek to take account of the differing requirements of two groups of potential readers: native or advanced readers of German, who will want to consult the English occasionally in order to clarify difficulties in or stimulate reflection upon Eckstein's original wording (hence the need for a parallel edition); and readers more comfortable in English than in German, who will use the translations as their sole or primary means of accessing the texts. The translations therefore aim at an unpretentious clarity, as distinct from having any literary ambitions of their own; and they seek throughout to combine accuracy with readability. That such a goal is a counsel of perfection that must inevitably lead to many uneasy compromises is of course self-evident to us.

Not least for practical reasons (a verse text occupies much more space than a prose one) we have taken care to keep annotations to a minimum on the pages that reproduce Eckstein's original dialogues. The pages containing our English translations, however, generally afford sufficient free space to enable us to offer rather more in the way of supporting material. We discuss difficulties of translation and unusual (or just Swiss-specific) vocabulary; where possible we elucidate references to people, places, literary works, and historical developments that might otherwise remain obscure; and, importantly in our opinion, we give the full text of Bible verses cited or otherwise appealed to by Eckstein (using what we consider to be the most reliable English translation, the New Revised Standard Version).[97] Little detailed research has been done as yet on the way specifically Swiss Reformation writers – with their at times problematic relationship with Luther's methods and their general indebtedness to Humanism – used or abused the Bible; and nothing at all has been done on the precise nature of Eckstein's biblicism. We therefore consider it worthwhile to provide material which should greatly facilitate such future work – at the same time, we hope, as providing a potential extra layer of interest for other readers.

97 *The Holy Bible. Containing the Old and New Testaments with the Apocryphal/ Deuterocanonical Books. New Revised Standard Version. Anglicized Edition* (Oxford: Oxford University Press, 1989).

Edition and translation of the *Concilium*

Concilium

[Ai^{r}] **Concilium.**
HIe in dem bůch wirt diſputiert
Das puren lang zyt hat verfürt
Heilgen fürbit / ouch des ba*p*ſts gwalt
vom Fägfhür / ouch was dMäſs innhalt.
Deßglychen von dem Sacrament.
von Zins / Zähenden / gült vnd rent.
Von Bicht / was die vor Gott nützt /
darumb hie Pur gen Doctor ſitzt.

{**Doctor Eck.**	{**Thoman Klotz.**
{Doctor Faber.	{Knüchel Fritz.
{Doctor Murner.	{Cleywi Fenchmul.
{Doc. Fritz Lindou.	{Ios Hechelzan.
{Doctor Laurentz.	{Hans Ofenrůß.

4 baſts *A*

The Council

Here in this book things will be debated which have long led farmers astray: prayers to the saints, the power of the Pope, purgatory, and what the Mass involves. Also the sacrament,[1] interest payments, tithes, taxes and tributes,[2] and confession and its value before God. To debate these things farmers are seated here opposite learned doctors:

Dr Eck	Thoman Klotz[3]
Dr Faber	Fritz Knüchel[4]
Dr Murner	Cleywi Fenchmul[5]
Dr Fritz Lindou[6]	Joß Hechelzan[7]
Dr Laurentz[8]	Hans Ofenrůß

1 The title page seems to have been intended primarily to catch the eye of the prospective reader, rather than to set out the order in which the topics will be discussed. Nevertheless what amounts to a double mention of the Eucharist does underline its importance in what follows – as well as enabling Eckstein's list to contain seven items, in line with seven's status as a holy number and with late-medieval mnemonics like the seven deadly sins and seven sacraments.

2 See the comment on these terms in the introduction, pp. 46–7.

3 As with all the peasant figures, this is a descriptive name: 'Klotz' means a clod of earth, and was also used of stupid or obtuse people (see *SI* III, 708).

4 As English 'knuckle'; also used of coarse people (and sows on heat – *SI* III, 1447).

5 'Fenchel' is the cognate of English 'fennel', though can also mean 'millet' (*SI* II, 834). 'Mul' (modern German 'Maul') is a colloquial, pejorative term for 'mouth'. The first name, 'Cleywi', can be a form of 'Klee', 'clover'.

6 Fritz Lindou, parish priest of Bremgarten, had claimed after the First Zurich Disputation that he proposed to silence Zwingli with three words. He was in consequence invited by the Zwinglians to appear at the Disputation of Baden, but did not do so. See Vögelin, pp. 123–4.

7 'Card-' or 'Comb-Tooth'. The implied context is flax-gathering.

8 Laurentius Merus (Laurenz Mär), originally from Feldkirch, who, in the course of a peripatetic career, was parish priest in Chur (1522), Zwingli's successor as 'Leutpriester' in Zurich (1522–3), and parish priest in Baden an der Limmat (1523–7) – in which capacity he re-converted to Catholicism. He subscribed his

{Doctor Gryff. {Claus Rebstock.
{Doctor Stroubutz. {Pur eigennutz.

Läſer nit laß / du kouffiſt mich /
Eins gegen dem andren wol bſich
Denn hie wirt brucht ernſt vnd ſchertz
Zů Gotswort allein richt din hertz

Cum Priuilegio Danhuſers.

*[Ai*v*]* **Uorred.**
Du armer Chriſt mit dem namen
wie lang wilt dich Gotzwort bſchamen? *Luce. 9.*
Bſchämen wirt er ſich ouch dinen
dich hilfft denn nit wirſt ſchon grynen
Du bkenſt hie Gott nun mit dem mund
vnd haſt mit jm ein andren pund
Dem gaaſtu doch ſo fulklich nach
ach menſch entſitzſtu nit die rach?
Hör zů was Eſaias ſag
wie ſich din Herr Gott ab dir klag
Das Rind doch ſinen Herren bkent *Eſaie. 1.*

Dr Gryff[9]	Claus Rebstock[10]
Dr Stroubutz[11]	Pur Eygennutz[12]

Reader, do not neglect to buy me. See the one up against the other: for this book brings you both seriousness and humour. Turn your heart towards God's Word alone.[13]

With Danhuser's privilege.

Prologue

You poor Christian in name only, how long will you be ashamed of God's Word? He also will be ashamed of you,[14] and then nothing will be able to help you: you'll certainly whine then! Here on earth you confess God only with your lips, but you are also bound to another, whom you follow so obediently! O man, do you not fear God's vengeance? Listen to what Isaiah says of the Lord God's complaints about you: 'The ox knows its lord

---

name to Eck's closing speech at the Disputation of Baden, and is later recorded as a priest in Überlingen (1527–32) and Feldkirch (1532–45). See Emil Egli, 'Wer war Laurentius Fabula?', *Zwingliana* 2 (1907), 147–51. In the *Concilium* he is treated as a renegade: self-seeking, greedy, and unreliable, he typifies Eckstein's depiction of the Catholic priesthood. See also below, n. 101, 290–1.

9 A name used also by Brant (in the *Narrenschiff*) and Murner (in the *Narrenbeschwörung*), to refer to a corrupt or immoral cleric. 'Grif' could mean 'profit', and the adjectives 'grifgierig' or 'griffig' 'avaricious' (see *Frühneuhochdeutsches Wörterbuch*, 13 vols (Berlin: de Gruyter, 1977–[2015]), VII, 413, 416–17, hereafter referred to as *FWB*).

10 'Rebstock' simply means a vine.

11 'Scarecrow'. The *SI*, however (IV, 2009), has an example from 1535 of the doctors of the Church being called collectively 'stroubutzen'. See Müller, p. 27.

12 'Pur Eygennutz' is the only one of the 'common' characters whose surname is not a play on his peasant status, though 'Pur' (or 'Bauer') does of course mean 'peasant' or 'farmer'. 'Eygennutz', by contrast, means selfishness or self-interest – a characteristic which Eygennutz subsequently personifies.

13 For comments on this paragraph and the next, and for a translation of C, D, and F's alternative wording, see the introduction, pp. 56–7.

14 Luke 9:26: 'Those who are ashamed of me and of my words, of them the Son of Man will be ashamed when he comes in his glory'.

der Eſel zů der kripffen rendt
Das iſt ein vnuernünfftig vich
vnd Iſrael erkennt nit mich
Hör wie in Hieremia ſtand
ſy hand all gnon die lügin zhand
Vnd hand nit wöllen wider keren
keiner der ſich bkenn Gott dem heren
Das er doch ſag / was hab ich thon
ſy rennend wie ein hengſt dauon *Hiere. 8.*
Im lufft weyßt doch ſin zyt der wy
die tub / der ſtorch / die ſchwalm daby *Hiere. 8.*
Bhaltend das zyt jrer zůkunfft
allein min volck iſt on vernunfft
O menſch vngloub hat din hertz bſeſſen
wiltu alſo dins Gots vergeſſen? *Eſaie. 17.*
Sin vatter eret doch ein kind *Malach. 1.*
warumb biſtu o menſch ſo blind
[Aii^{r}*]* Er iſt din vatter vnd ouch herr
du fürchſt jnn nit / gibſt jm kein eer
Verlaaſtu gott du wirſt verlon
wenn er dir wirt engegen gon
Wie ein Löwin vff dem wäg *Prou. 15.*
dich hilfft denn nit kein ſchwärdt noch däg
Denn er wirt gwüß gegen dir kon
als ein Bär dem die jungen ſind gnon *Oſee. 13.*
War wilt denn flühen arme gſchöpfft?
ſo dich die zůkunfft gots erklöpft
Vnd dich vmmgibt groß angſt im hertzen
Gott laßt denn nit mit jm ſchertzen
Du haſt hie zil vnd tag gnůg ghan
es gadt dir wie dem rychen man *Luce. 16*
Der läbt on gotzforcht täglich wol
hatt ouch hie kiſt vnd käller vol
Barmhertzigkeit facht jnn nit an
vnd kam darzů das jm zerran

44 Hiere. 8] *om. ECF*

and the ass runs to its own crib; they are brute beasts, but Israel does not acknowledge me'.[15] Hear what is written in Jeremiah: 'They have all straightaway taken hold of lies, and have not wanted to return to me; there is none who confesses to the Lord God, saying: "What have I done?". They run away like stallions.[16] In the sky the hawk knows its time, and the dove, the stork, and the swallow keep the appointed time of their coming, but my people alone are without understanding'. O man, unbelief has seized your heart – will you then forget your God? A child honours his father;[17] why, O man, are you so blind?[18] He is your Father and also your Lord, but you neither fear him nor give him honour. If you abandon God, you yourself will be abandoned, for he will come upon you like a lioness on the road,[19] and neither sword nor dagger can help you then. He certainly will come upon you, like a bear whose young have been taken from him.[20] Where will you fly to then, poor creature, when God's coming startles you and great dread surrounds your heart? Then God will not let himself be mocked: you will have had life and days enough on earth. The same thing will happen to you as to the rich man who lived well every day without the fear of God, and here on earth filled all his chests and storehouses. Mercy did not move him, and it came to pass that his time ran out.

15 Isaiah 1:3: 'The ox knows its master, and the donkey its master's crib; but Israel does not know, my people do not understand'.

16 Jeremiah 8:5–7: 'They have held fast to deceit, they have refused to return. I have given heed and listened, but they do not speak honestly; no one repents of wickedness, saying, "What have I done!". All of them turn to their own course, like a horse plunging headlong into battle. Even the stork in the heavens knows its times; and the turtle-dove, swallow, and crane observe the time of their coming; but my people do not know the ordinance of the Lord'.

17 Isaiah 17:10: 'For you have forgotten the God of your salvation, and have not remembered the Rock of your refuge'.

18 Malachi 1:6: 'A son honours his father, and servants their master. If then I am a father, where is the honour due to me? And if I am a master, where is the respect due to me?'

19 Probably a rough conflation of several verses: Proverbs 19:12 and 20:2 refer to the king's anger as the growling of a lion, and Proverbs 26:13 speaks of the lazy person saying: 'There is a lion in the road! There is a lion in the streets!'.

20 Hosea 13:8: 'I will fall upon them like a bear robbed of her cubs, and will tear open the covering of their heart'.

Hett in der hell gern waſſer truncken
kein finger mocht er daryn duncken
Gott ſeyt vns vor drumb diſe gſchicht
das ſich ein yeder darnach richt
Kumpt einer in das helliſch fhür
wyn vnd waſſer wirt jm thür
Zween wäg hat er vns für gſchriben *Hiere. 21.*
eine*n* eng / de*n* ander*n* triben *Matth. 7.*
Welcher wil den engen gon
den wyten můs er gar verlon
Sůch gottes wäg / biß nit ſo zag
hör was gott in der gſchrifft dir ſag
[Aii[v]] Du wirſt fürwar kein läben han *Deut. 8.*
nimſtu das gotswort hie nit an. *1. Ioann. 5.*
Denn es iſt grecht / nun zwyfel nit *Pſalm. 23.*
gſundheyt der ſeel fürwar es git. *Pſal. 106.*
Dem Gotswort du nit widerſprich *Eccleſ. 4.*
es iſt kon vſſz dem himmelrich. *1. Pet. 1.*
Wir ſind durch Gotswort wider gborn *Iacob. 1.*
on Gotzwort werdend wir verlorn.
Es iſt nit von den menſchen kon
von himmel hats braacht Gottes ſon
Vom vatter der barmhertzigkeyt *2. Cor. 1.*
die krafft Gots wirt damit vßgſpreyt. *Rom. 1.*
Iſt er gegen vns ſo gütig
warumb biſtu denn ſo wütig?
Wider Gotzwort als ein hund
es kumpt doch nun vſſz Gottes mund. *Eſaie. 55.*
Wie darffſt ſagen ich bin ein Chriſt
ſo du wider das Gotzwort biſt?
Gotzwort vnd Gott ſind vnzerteylt
es hat all vnſer kranckheit gheylt. *Eſaie. 53.*

76 einer, der ander *AE*

In hell, he would gladly have drunk water, but he could not dip his finger into it.[21] God tells us this story so that all might live by it: if anyone comes into the fire of hell, he will have neither wine nor water. God has described two paths to us, one narrow and the other well worn.[22] Anyone who wishes to go down the narrow path must entirely abandon the wide one. Search for God's path; do not be so cowardly. Hear what God says to you in Scripture: 'Indeed you will not have life if you do not accept God's Word here on earth'.[23] For it is just, do not doubt it,[24] and it indeed gives health to the soul. Do not contradict God's Word, for it has come from heaven.[25] We have been born again through the Word of God,[26] and without his Word we are lost.[27] It has not come from man, but God's Son has brought it from heaven, from the father of mercy, and God's power is spread by it.[28] If, then, he is so good towards us, why do you rage like a mad dog against God's Word? For it comes from God's mouth.[29] How can you say 'I am a Christian' when you are against God's Word? God's Word and God himself are inseparable, and his Word has healed all our ills.[30]

21 An outline of the story of Dives and Lazarus, from Luke 16:19–31.

22 Most likely Jeremiah 21:8: 'See, I am setting before you the way of life and the way of death' – with an added reminiscence, of course, of Matthew 7:13–14.

23 Deuteronomy 8:20: 'Like the nations that the Lord is destroying before you, so shall you perish, because you would not obey the voice of the Lord your God'. Also 1 John 5:3: 'For the love of God is this, that we obey his commandments'.

24 Psalm 25:8?: 'Good and upright is the Lord; therefore he instructs sinners in the way'. The discrepancies between Eckstein's texts and these notes in respect of Psalm numbers (especially those between 10 and 113, or 117 and 146) result from the fact that Eckstein uses the Vulgate numeration, whereas our source Bible (like nearly all modern ones) uses the Masoretic one.

25 Cf. Psalm 107:20: 'He sent out his word and healed them, and delivered them from destruction'.

26 1 Peter 1:23: 'You have been born anew, not of perishable but of imperishable seed, through the living and enduring word of God'.

27 Cf. James 1:18: 'In fulfilment of his own purpose he gave us birth by the word of truth, so that we would become a kind of first fruits of his creatures'.

28 Not very close to anything in 1 Corinthians or Romans, though Romans 1:16 does say: 'For I am not ashamed of the gospel; it is the power of God for salvation to everyone who has faith, to the Jew first and also to the Greek'.

29 Isaiah 55:11: '[...] so shall my word be that goes out from my mouth'.

30 Isaiah 53:4: 'Surely he has borne our infirmities and carried our diseases'.

Schry noch zů Gott du wirſt erhört *1. Mach. 4.*
er hat ſin blůt für dich verrert
Das er dir wil barmhertzig ſin *Exodi. 22.*
ſchry du / ſo ſpricht er: Hie ich bin. *Eſaie. 58.*
Keer dich zů Gott / denn er iſt milt *Iohel. 2.*
ſo er dich wil / vnd du nit wilt.
Verfarſtu denn gib jm nit dſchuld
wee dem der nit hat Gottes huld.
Wirſtu nit vſſz dem Gotzwort gborn *Iacob. 1.*
der wäg wirt dir verzünt mit dorn. *Oſee. 2.*
[Aiii^{r}] Ach wandel nit den ruhen wäg *Eccleſ. 32.*
da ſtein vnd dörn wirt ſin din ſtäg
Richt dich vff den wäg des Herren *Matth. 3.*
zeyg jm din wäg er wirt dich neren. *Pſalm. 36*
Denn wiltu in das rych Gots gon
du můſt fürwar dich ſelbs verlon *Luce. 9.*
Darzů lieb han die grechtigkeyt *Matth. 5.*
die warheyt werd dem nächſten gſeyt. *Pſalm. 14.*
Kein lug der nächſt nit von dir wüſſz
gen jm enthalt dich alles bſchiſſz.
Denn Gottes gſicht lůgt vff die armen *Pſal. 10.*
das er ſich jren erbarme
Desglychen ſicht er vff die böſen *Pſal. 33.*
jr dächtnuß wil er hie ablöſen.
Denn ein tag by Gott Ieſu Chriſt *Pſalm. 83.*

122 erbarme] mög erbarmen *CF*

Cry out yet to God, and you will be heard:[31] he has shed his blood for you, so that he might have mercy on you.[32] If you cry out, he will say: 'Here I am'.[33] Turn to God, for he is gracious when he wants you and you do not want him. If you go astray, do not blame him. Woe to him who does not have God's favour! Unless you are born of the Word of God, your way will be hedged up with thorns.[34] O do not walk down the rough path, where you will step on stones and thorns,[35] but turn on to the way of the Lord.[36] Commit your way to him, and he will save you.[37] For if you wish to enter God's kingdom, then you certainly must deny yourself,[38] and also love justice[39] and tell the truth to your neighbour.[40] May your neighbour never know that a lie has come from your mouth; refrain from ever deceiving him. For God's face looks upon the poor,[41] that he might have mercy on them. Likewise he looks upon evildoers – he will blot out the memory of them from the earth.[42] For one day with the Lord God Jesus Christ

31 1 Maccabees 4:10: 'And now, let us cry to Heaven, to see whether he will favour us and remember his covenant with our ancestors and crush this army before us today'.

32 There is no obvious correspondence in or around Exodus 22, the chapter cited.

33 Isaiah 58:9: 'Then you shall call, and the Lord will answer; you shall cry for help, and he will say, "Here I am"'.

34 Hosea 2:6: 'Therefore I will hedge her way with thorns; and I will build a wall against her'. The James citation is incorrect.

35 Cf. Ecclesiasticus (in the NRSV 'Sirach') 32:21–2: 'Do not be overconfident on a smooth road, and give good heed to your paths'.

36 Presumably the instruction in Matthew 3:8 to 'bear fruit worthy of repentance'.

37 Cf. Psalm 37:4: 'Take delight in the Lord, and he will give you the desires of your heart'.

38 Luke 9:23: 'If any want to become my followers, let them deny themselves and take up their cross daily and follow me'.

39 Matthew 5:6: 'Blessed are those who hunger and thirst for righteousness, for they will be filled'.

40 Psalm 15:2–3: 'Those who walk blamelessly, and do what is right, and speak the truth from their heart; who do not slander with their tongue, and do no evil to their friends'.

41 Psalm 11:7: 'For the Lord is righteous; he loves righteous deeds; the upright shall behold his face'.

42 Psalm 34:16: 'The face of the Lord is against evildoers, to cut off the remembrance of them from the earth'.

vil beſſer denn hie tuſend iſt.
Darumb danck Gott zů aller zyt *Pſalm. 33.*
des armen bätt ſich nit verlyt. *Iacobe. 5.*
Es wirt vf gen himmel tragen
lond vns Gott alle not klagen.
Gotzwort tröſt vns in trurigkeyt *1. Theſ. 5.*
all vnſer ſünd an tag gſchrifft leyt
Wär den wäg zů Gott wil finden
der můß die gſchrifft vor durch gründen *Ioannis. 5.*
Gotzwort das lüchtet biß ins rych *Pſalm. 118.*
wär gſchrifft nit hat / verirret glych.
Die gſchrifft von Gott ynblaaſen iſt *2. Petr. 2.*
vnd offnet vns den Ieſum Chriſt. *2. Tim. 3.*
Er iſt ſälig der jr naach gründt
on gſchrifft der menſch nit rům findt.
[Aiii[v]] Gotzwort vnd gſchrifft iſt ein ding
gond in einander wie zween ring
Da weder end noch anfang iſt
darnach richt ſich ein yetlich Chriſt
Wär hie den worten Gots nit gloubt
der wirt dört lyb vnd ſeel beroubt
Dich hilfft nit das du dich druß züchſt
vnd wo man predget das du flüchſt
Du můſt noch hören Gottes wort
wenns dir nit gfalt an yhenem ort
So er ſpricht: Kommend har zů mir *Math. 25.*
den böſen ouch: Gond hin jr
Denn wirſt du kummen oder gon
heſt du den willen Gotz gthon
Das hilfft dich denn / nun zwyffel nit.
kein heilg im himmel dich vertritt
Das ſyg dir gſeyt du armer pur
gotswort blybt veſt ſton wie ein mur
Wär Gotswort gloubt / vermag all ding *Marci. 9.*
O menſch wie wigſt du Gott ſo ring
So du den ſun Gots nit wirſt han

is much better than a thousand here on earth.[43] Therefore thank God at all times:[44] the prayer of the poor is not lost, but is borne up to heaven. Let us tell God of all our sufferings. God's Word comforts us in sadness; Scripture brings to light all our sins.[45] Anyone who wants to find the way to God must first sound the depths of the Scriptures. God's Word illuminates our path right into the heavenly kingdom,[46] and anyone who does not have the Scriptures is straightaway lost.[47] The Scriptures are inspired by God[48] and reveal Jesus Christ to us.[49] Anyone who fathoms the Scriptures is blessed, and without the Scriptures no one can find rest. God's Word and the Scriptures are a single thing: they are interlinked like two rings, where there is neither beginning nor end. All Christians should live their lives by them. Anyone who does not believe God's words in this life will have both body and soul taken from him in the next. It is no use shrinking from God's Word, or fleeing from places where it is preached. Like it or not, you must still hear God's Word, in that place where he says: 'Come hither to me'. He also says to the evildoers: 'Go hence'. Then you will either come or go. If you have done God's will, that will help you, have no doubt. No saint will speak for you in heaven. Let me tell you, poor farmer: God's Word stands fast like a wall, and anyone who believes God's Word can do all things.[50] O man, why do you hold God of such little account that you will not accept the Son of God?

43 Psalm 84:10: 'For a day in your courts is better than a thousand elsewhere'.

44 Psalm 34:1: 'I will bless the Lord at all times; his praise shall continually be in my mouth'.

45 Close to 1 Thessalonians 5:4–11, though with no precise verbal equivalences.

46 John 5:39: 'You search the scriptures because you think that in them you have eternal life'.

47 Close to Psalm 119:5–6: 'O that my ways may be steadfast in keeping your statutes! Then I shall not be put to shame, having my eyes fixed on all your commandments'.

48 2 Peter 1:20–21: 'No prophecy of scripture is a matter of one's own interpretation, because no prophecy ever came by human will, but men and women moved by the Holy Spirit spoke from God'.

49 2 Timothy 3:15 refers to 'the sacred writings that are able to instruct you for salvation through faith in Christ Jesus'.

50 Mark 9:23: 'All things can be done for the one who believes'.

dich werdend alle gſchöpfft verlan
Wie magſt du nun ſo Gotlos ſin
denckſt nit er ſyg gen für dich hin? *Roma. 4.*
Hett dir dient in dinen ſünden *Eſai. 43.*
on in magſt du kein gnad finden *1. Ioan. 5.*
In jm iſt all vollkommenheyt *Colloſs. 2.*
din ſünd er vff jm ſelbs hat treyt *Eſaie. 53.*
Wie lang ſol er durch dfinger ſehen? *Sapie. 11.*
wie magſt du ſin wort verſchmähen?
[Aiv^{r}] Zeyg an was heſt das dich recht mach *Eſaie. 43.*
wär meinſt der red zů diner ſach
Wenn Gott der ſun ſich dinen bſchempt *Luce. 9.*
din grechtigkeit wirt bald dempt
Sin güte zů der bůß dich zücht *Roma. 2.*
die locket dir / din ſchalckheyt flücht
Dſtund loufft vs ee du dich vmmſichſt
denck wär er ſyg / wider den du fichſt
Keer widerumb du irrends ſchaaff *Ezech. 34*
ſtand vf erwach nun von dem ſchlaaff
Es iſt nun zyt / du ſolt vffſton
die werck der finſternus verlon *Roma. 13.*
Wie lang wilt du an wenden taapen? *Eſaie. 59.*
züch ab den Adam / leg an Gots waapen *Epheſi. 6.*
Du biſt doch nun ein erdklotz
nimm an dich den harneſch Gotz
Du gaaſt weerloß / vnd ſolteſt ſtryten
nims ſchwärt in dhand / wie lang wilt beiten?
Din ſchwärt ſol ſin das heilig gotzwort *Hebre. 4.*
mit dem kumpſt du durch dhelliſch port.

All of creation will abandon you. How can you be so godless – do you not think he has given himself up for you[51] and served you in your sinfulness?[52] Apart from him you cannot find grace.[53] In him is all perfection.[54] He has taken your sins upon himself.[55] How long must he turn a blind eye?[56] How can you despise his Word? Show what you have that might justify you.[57] Who do you think will speak on your behalf when God the Son is ashamed of you?[58] Your righteousness will soon be damned; it is his goodness that draws and calls you to repentance.[59] Flee from your wickedness; before you look around you, there will be no time left. Think who he is and whom you are fighting against; turn around, you lost sheep,[60] arise, awake now from slumber. It is now time; you must arise and leave behind the works of darkness.[61] How long will you tap at walls?[62] Put off Adam, and take up the weapons of God.[63] You are a mere clod of earth; put on the armour of God. You are unarmed, but must fight. So take a sword in your hand; what are you waiting for? Your sword should be the holy Word of God;[64] with that you will get through the gates of hell.

51 Romans 4:24–5: 'Jesus our Lord [...], who was handed over to death for our trespass and was raised for our justification'.

52 Probably a generalized reference to the 'suffering servant' of Isaiah 53 (*sic*).

53 Cf. I John 5:12: 'Whoever has the Son has life; whoever does not have the Son of God does not have life'.

54 Colossians 2:9: 'For in him the whole fullness of deity dwells bodily'.

55 Isaiah 53:6: 'The Lord has laid on him the iniquity of us all'.

56 Wisdom 11:23: 'You overlook people's sins, so that they may repent'.

57 Isaiah 43:26: 'Set forth your case, so that you may be proved right'.

58 Luke 9:26 (see n. 14 above).

59 Romans 2:4: 'Do you not realize that God's kindness is meant to lead you to repentance?'

60 Based on the association of Israel with God's sheep that pervades Ezekiel 34.

61 Romans 13:12: 'Let us then lay aside the works of darkness and put on the armour of light'.

62 Isaiah 59:10: 'We grope like the blind along a wall, groping like those who have no eyes'.

63 See the famous list in Ephesians 6:10–17. The notion of 'putting off the old Adam' (cf. 1 Corinthians 15:22) is a consistent preoccupation in Eckstein's dialogues from *Christus mit Adam* to the *Rychsztag*.

64 Hebrews 4:12: 'The word of God is living and active, sharper than any two-edged sword'.

Nimm den glouben für ein ſchilt
on den vor gott nüts gilt
Was nit iſt vſs glouben gſchehen *Rom. 14.*
das ſelb wirt gott nit anſehen
Was aber Gott wil von vns han
Findt man clar in Mattheo ſton *Math. 25.*
Ouch was gott gfall / man klarlich ſicht
wenn er am jüngſten tag richt
Alſo gott denn zmal zů vns ſeyt
jch nacket was / jr hand mich bkleyt
[Aiv^v] Vnd hend mir gen in hunger ſpyß
jn durſt mich trenckt glycherwyß
In kranckheit thettend ir mir pflag
kamend do ich im kercker lag
Nemmend das rych das üch iſt bereyt
zů den böſen er ouch denn ſeyt
Gond hin von mir in ewigs fhür
fürwar dir wirt denn lachen thür
Sprichſt du ich hab ein Mäſs geſtifft
was äben der armen lüt gifft
Von Mäſshan iſt nun wůcher kon
du heſt dem armen das ſyn abgnon
Mit wůcher vnd ſunſt übernutz
dich hilfft nit des Bapſts abſolutz
Hettiſts du den armen glon
das wär dir yetz vil baß kon
Du heſt nit damit dienet mir
der dichs hab gheiſſen lone dir
Ich hieß dich die armen ſpyſen
ſo laſt du dich den Bapſt wyſen
Thetteſt denn das er dich hieß
darumb yetz in der Hell büß
Ich ſeyt dir nit: Stifft vil Mäſsen
hettiſt du min nit vergeſsen
Ich hieß dich gen / ſo heſt du gnon
nüt gůts iſt von dym ſtifften kon

As your shield take up faith, without which nothing is any use before God;[65] he will not look upon anything that does not proceed from faith. But what God wants from us can be found clearly written in Matthew: you can see plainly what will please him when he sits in judgement on the last day.[66] Then God will say to us: ‘I was naked and you clothed me, and you gave me food when I was hungry; likewise when I was thirsty you gave me drink. When I was ill you looked after me; when I was in prison you came to me. Take the kingdom which is prepared for you’. At that time he also says to the evildoers: ‘Depart from me into the everlasting fire, where you will find little to laugh about’. If you say, ‘But I have paid for a Mass to be said’, well, this was as poison to the poor.[67] Paying for Masses has led only to usury, and you have taken from the poor what was rightfully theirs with usury and suchlike extortions.[68] The Pope’s absolution cannot help you. If you had let the poor keep what was theirs, things would now be much better for you. You have not served me in this. May he who told you to do it reward you! I told you to feed the poor, but you have let the Pope guide you, and done what he told you to do. Now, therefore, you must atone for it in hell. I did not tell you: ‘Pay for lots of Masses’. If only you hadn’t forgotten me! I told you to give, but instead you have taken. No good has come of your Masses:

65 An unreferenced allusion to Ephesians 6:16.

66 Matthew 25:31–46, the story of the separation of the sheep and the goats.

67 Doubtless intended as a pun on ‘gifft’, which at the time could convey both the modern German (‘Gift’ = ‘poison’) and the modern English meanings.

68 This statement about usury, and the affective rhetoric in which it is couched, prepares the reader for the later arguments of Pur Eygennutz (from p. 255 onwards).

Nun münch vnn pfaff hend gfült den buch
das ſy ſtunckend wie ein wynſchluch
Hend gfürt darnach ein vnkünſch läben
darzů heſt du din gůt geben
[Av^{r}] Die rychen heſt nun rycher gmacht
yetz fürt der geiſtlich huf den pracht
Vnd vndertruckt den armen man
du heſts mit der Mäſs gfangen an
Drumb gadts wie der grasmucken
den puren yetz in vil ſtucken
Wenn ein grasmuck eyer leyt
denn iſt der gugger ouch bereyt
Supfft vs die eyer der grasmucken
ſin eyer kan er dar ſchmucken
Darus wirt denn ein Guggouch
der frißd zeletſt die graßmuck ouch
Alſo es yetzt den puren gadt
ſy hend lang geätzt den vnflat
Den gucker / das iſt münch vnd pfaffen
hend lang gucket mit vil klaffen
Doch allermeyſt zů Summers zyt
wenn man inen bycht gelt git
Alſo habend ir den gucker gſpiſd
der Moyſes dich ein anders wysd *Deute. 14.*
Das heisd gwüſs gucker eſſen
wo man vfricht eewig Mäſſen.
Sprichſt ich hab hüpſch taflen bereyt
mit gold die bilder daryn bkleyt
Mäſsgwand ggeben / ſtol vnd alben
die Kilchen bgaabet allenthalben
Denn ſpricht der Herr was gadts mich an
von dir wil ich nit der glychen han
Du heſt nun leym vnd holtz bekleyt
jch hatt dir von den armen gſeyt
[Av^{v}] Die ſelben haſt erfryeren lon

227 nun] *om. CF*

all that has happened is that monks and priests have filled their stomachs so full that they have stunk like wineskins, and have then led lives of lechery. That is what you have given your wealth to: you have made the rich richer. Now the pack of priests lives in splendour and oppresses the poor man; and you began it with your Masses. So now many farmers live like the warbler: when the warbler lays its eggs, the cuckoo is also ready, and slurps up the warbler's eggs and puts its own in the nest. So from this one a cuckoo is hatched, who in the end eats up the warbler too. So it is with the farmers nowadays. They have long fed the filthy cuckoo, that is the monks and priests. These have long been lying in wait with their many harangues, especially in summertime, when they are given their confessional fees. In this way you have fed the cuckoo; but Moses shows you a different way.[69] Always endowing Masses is certainly like feeding cuckoos. If you say, 'I have made beautiful altars and adorned their pictures with gold, given chasubles, stoles, and albs, and been generous to churches all over the place', the Lord will say: 'What is that to me? I don't want that kind of thing from you. You have adorned wood and clay, but I had spoken to you of the poor. You have let them freeze to death,

69 Presumably Eckstein identifies one of the 'unclean' birds listed in Deuteronomy 14:11–20 as the cuckoo.

lang laſſen vor der türen ſton
Laſſen hülen wie ein hund
Was nit mocht gon in dinen mund
wurffeſt du zum fenſter vs
kein bättler dorfft dir in din hus
Die armen ſolteſt bkleydet han
die nit hend füchße ſchuben an
Du heſt nun bkleyt die vor bkleyt waren /
mit mäſsgwand der pfaffen ſcharen
Wol ziert mit mengerley gfüllen
das was gantz wider min willen
Sprichſt denn: Ich bin zun heilgen grennt
hab inen öl vnd ancken brennt /
Iung hanen bracht / ouch gelt vnd wachs
eyer / kernen / werch / vnd flachs
Ich hats verbotten ſpricht der Herr
dich nit an valſch propheten keer *Matt. 24.*
Seyt man dir ſchon: Hie Chriſtus iſt *Marci. 13.*
gloubs nit / es iſt der endchriſt *Lucæ. 21.*
Hat man dir ſchon von gott ſelb gſeyt
du ſolteſt nüts han dar treyt
Du ſolteſt nit ſin vsgangen
das rych gotz wirt ins hertz empfangen *Lucæ. 17.*
Heſt du verbrennt vil öl vnd ancken
drumm hend dir müß vnd ratzen zdancken
Die hend nachts deſter baß gſehen
wär beſſer es wär nit gſchehen
Hettiſt öl vnd ancken ggeben
den armen / das wär mir eben
[Avi^{r}] So hettinds damit gſchmeltzt jr ſuppen /
ſunſt ſchmirbt der ſigriſt mit ſin juppen
Vnd zündt den götzen durch die nacht
denn einr den anderen an lacht
Das fröwt biſſicher dheilgen wol
die gſehend nit / ſind hinden hol
Da iſt gnädig Sant Baſtians bog
all götzen vsghült wie ein ſchwyntrog

standing outside your door for ages, and have let them howl like dogs and thrown them food out of the window that you didn't want to eat yourself.[70] No beggar was allowed in your house. You should have clothed the poor, but they're not exactly wearing foxskin jackets.[71] And you have clothed those who were already well supplied – you have clothed the gang of priests with chasubles, beautifully decorated with many linings. That was completely against my will'. If you then say, 'I have run to the saints and have burnt oil and butter for them,[72] have brought them young chickens, and also money, wax, eggs, corn, tow, and flax', the Lord will say: 'But I have forbidden it. Do not turn to false prophets'.[73] If anyone says to you already 'Christ is here',[74] do not believe it; it is the Antichrist.[75] You have been told by God himself that you should not have taken anything to them. You should not have gone outside; the kingdom of God is received in the heart.[76] If you have burnt a lot of oil and butter, mice and rats will have been grateful to you – they will have seen better at night. But it would have been better if it hadn't happened. If you had given oil and butter to the poor, that would have suited me. They would have larded their soup with it. But, instead, the sexton in his robe prepares the grease and lights a flame to idols during the night, because idols like to see each other and exchange smiles. They can't walk and have hollow backs, and St Sebastian's bow[77] comes in handy here, for hollowing out all the idols like pigs' troughs.

70 Similar treatment (meted out to Velti Kybig) is described in the *Rychsztag* (R 310–48/331–3) – with the added piquancy that the scene is set in a monastery.

71 The Swiss German term 'schube' can be applied to various garments, both male and female. See *SI* VIII, 93–7.

72 Presumably Eckstein is envisaging votive oil and butter lamps.

73 Matthew 24:4: 'Beware that no one leads you astray. For many will come in my name'.

74 Mark 13:21–2: 'If anyone says to you at that time: "Look! Here is the Messiah!", do not believe it. False messiahs and false prophets will appear'.

75 The Antichrist is not mentioned in any of the Gospels, though many signs of the Last Times are discussed in Luke 21 (and also Matthew 24 and Mark 13).

76 Cf. Luke 17:20: 'The kingdom of God is not coming with things that can be observed'.

77 St Sebastian was the patron saint of archers, having himself been killed by many arrows (in Rome, c. 300).

Heſt du jung hanen zůtragen
die fraß der pfaff in ſin kragen
Darzü halff jm ſin Källerin
vnd warend beyde vollen wyn
Alſo der pfaff fraß die hanen
ließ dich in eim habermůß zanen
Das wachs brucht er zum ſchyßhus
wenn er wolt zünden eim dräck vs
Das er nit on ein liecht verſchied
da ſaß er vff biß er ward müd.
Die köchin flachs vnd werck nam
zum gällt ſy vnderwylen kam
Das nams / vnn ſagt: Dems gfalt dem gfeltz /
herr Schabion / ich dorfft eins beltz
Die haller wil ich vf kluben
jch dörfft ouch wol einer ſchuben
Alſo heſt du din gůt angleyt
dir wirt ſin lützel danck gſeyt
Hettiſts ggeben Edlen lüten
die vff krucken zk*il*chen ryten
Das käm dir bas am letſten zyt
was hilffts das mans den pfaffen gib?
[Avi[v]] Thů den armen gůts vff erden
das wirt von dir gfordret werden. *Matth. 25.*
Sprichſtu min pfaff hat michs glert
das ich hab zů den heiligen kert
Wenn mir nun was eim kind we
verhieß ichs zů ſant Mikome.
Wenn mir der halß gſchwollen was
ſo kam der pfaff vnd lert mich das
Bring Sant Bläſi ein ſilbre gaab
der hilfft dir der gſchwulſt ab
Vnd henck ein kertzen an den hals
die gſchwulſt vergadt dir eins mals:

305–8 Din blůtigen ſchweyß trůgest jm zů / gwunnen mit groſſer vnrůw / Mit müſſig gon verzart er das / brachtest nun vil ye liebers [lieber *F*] jm was *CF*   318 zklichen *A*

If you have brought young chickens, the priest will have stuffed his face with them, with the help of his housekeeper; and both will have filled themselves to the brim with wine. While the priest was eating the chickens, he no doubt let you bite into some gruel. He also took the wax to the shithouse, because he wanted to light up a turd with it – so that there would be no danger of him dying without a light, and he could sit out there until he got tired.[78] Meanwhile the cook would take the flax and tow, and would sometimes make money out of it. She would take the money and say: 'Like it or not, Herr Schabion,[79] I need a coat, and I'll put together my hellers to buy one. I could also do with a slip'. So, then, you have invested your money wisely, and get little thanks for it. If you had given it to aristocrats walking to church on crutches, that would do you more good at the last day. What's the point of giving it to priests? Do good to the poor on earth, that is what will be required of you. If you say, 'My priest told me to turn to the saints. When my child was in pain, I commended him to St Mikomus.[80] When my neck was swollen the priest came and told me: "Bring a gift of silver for St Blaise.[81] He will cure your swelling. And if you hang a candle round your neck, the swelling will go at once".

78 Whether on grounds of comprehensibility, taste, or a mixture of the two, C replaces this sentence with 'You brought to him blood you had sweated in great labour; but he ate it in his sloth, so you brought him much of whatever he wanted' (for the German see opposite).

79 A descriptive name, presumably for a tailor, given its overtones of 'schappe' (a fabric made of waste silk and gum) and 'schabe', a moth (cf. English 'moth-eaten', or indeed 'shabby').

80 This curious name is conceivably a reference to the tenth-century preacher saint Nikon the Metanoeite – or even, given the context, a garbled reference to St Nicholas of Myra, patron saint of children?

81 Bishop of Sebastea (d. 316), renowned as a healing saint (originally of a boy who was choking to death from a fishbone in his throat). The reference to a candle presumably reflects the ancient ceremony held on St Blaise's Day (3rd February) of blessing candles held next to congregants' throats.

So kam ich denn mit gelt gloffen
das hat der pfaff als verſoffen
Oder verſpilt in dem Brätt
was man zůhin tragen hätt.
Wolt man in dem wirtzhuß karten
hett man dörffen des pfaffen warten
Der gab vns denn haller vmb batzen
die můßtend wir ſur erkratzen.
Die kamend jnn liederlich an
es was als vmb den gmeynen man
Du ſyeſt gwarnet frummer Chriſt
die ax an boum gſetzt iſt *Matt. 3.*
Wirſtu nit würcken rechte bůß
die man durchs Gotzwort lernen můß
Vnd dich allein zů Gott keeren
jnn über alle gſchöpfft eeren.
So wirſtu vor Gott nit beſton
dich hilfft nit zů den heiligen gon.
[Avii^{r}] Denn Gott hats nit gheyſſen dich
darumb gar eben vf ſich
Thů allein das dich Gott heyß
vff erden ich beſſers nit weyß
Wenn so du thůſt das Gott wol gfalt
vff pfaffen gſchwätz du gar nüt halt.
Sprichſtu / ach Gott ich weyß nit wol
welchem ich doch glouben ſol.
Los mir zů ich kan dichs leeren
an was pfaffen du dich ſolt keeren.
Was der pfaff vmb gelt hat feyl
ſůcht er ſin nutz / nit diner ſeel heyl
Da flüch du als ſyg es gifft
es iſt gwüß nit von Gott gſtifft
Wo man dich denn vff Chriſtum wyßt
des namen für all heylgen bryßt
Vnd er dir ſeyt / den rüff nun an

354 nit beſſers *CF*

So I ran to the priest with money. He drank it all, or lost it all at the gaming table which they had brought. If you wanted to play cards in the inn, you had to wait for the priest, and he would give us hellers in exchange for batzen[82] – and it was hard work scratching even them out of him. Of course he came by them easily – they all came from the common man'. Be warned, O faithful Christian: the axe is laid at the tree.[83] If you do not truly repent (which you must learn about through God's Word), turn to God alone and honour him above all creation, you will not be able to stand before God. Praying to the saints won't help you, for God has not told you to do it. Therefore look directly up to him and do only what God commands. I know nothing better on earth than for you to do what pleases God: pay no heed to the chatterings of priests. If you say, 'O God, I don't know whom to believe' – listen to me, I can teach you which priests to turn to. If a priest has things for sale, he is seeking his own advantage, not your salvation. Flee this kind of thing like poison, for it certainly isn't God's work. But you can happily rely on a place where you are directed towards Christ, his name is praised before those of all the saints, and you are told to call on him.

82 Two denominations of coin, the heller originally associated with Schwäbisch Hall and the batzen with Berne ('batz' = 'bear'), and the former worth considerably less than the latter.

83 Matthew 3:10: 'Even now the axe is lying at the root of the trees; every tree therefore that does not bear good fruit is cut down and thrown into the fire'.

dem gloub / vnd laß dich frölich dran
Gott der hilfft vns ſelb vſſz nöten
das ſagend nun all propheten
Wenn ich den Eſaiam bſich *Eſa. 43.*
ſpricht Gott / es iſt kein helffer on mich
Hör was der Iop ſag *Iob. 13.*
gott wirt mir helffen am jüngſten tag
Darzů ſpricht der Hieremias *Iere. 14.*
gott iſt in trübſal vnſer quies
Gottes zwarten ſind all bereyt *Oſee. 13*
wie vns der Oſeas ſeyt *Mat. 18.*
Gott ſelb iſt helffer aller welt *Luc. 9.*
ſo man all gſchrifft für zellt
[Avii^{v}] Seyt anders dir ein bſchorner lur
gloub jms nit du frummer Pur
vertruw du gott on all Cur

Herold.
Nun hörend zů einr nüwen gſchicht
iſt es nun wie man mich hat bricht
So iſt vorhanden doctor Eck
das er die nüwen leer erſteck
Hat bracht von Rom har allen gwalt
das er hie ein Concili halt
Iſt jm vergundt nun überal
von der gantzen gmeind im Wäntal
Er kumpt gen Zürch in dſtatt nit gern
er zug vil lieber gen Lucern
Oder gen Baden diſputiern
da meint er wett ers nit verliern
Des wil jm Zuingle nit geſton
meint vaſt er ſöll gen Zürich kon
Hab er denn glert das Kätzriſch ſy
das ſöll er jnn da bzügen fry
Vor aller welt die jnn hab ghört

383 *om. CDF*. 382 is followed by a 28-line addition in *CDF* (see below, pp. 458–60).

All the prophets say that God himself helps us out of trouble. When I look at Isaiah, God says: ‘There is no helper but me’.[84] Hear what Job says:[85] ‘God will help me at the last day’. Jeremiah also says:[86] ‘God is our rest in trouble’. God’s swords are all prepared, as Hosea says.[87] God himself is the helper of all the world, as all of Scripture relates. If any corrupt scoundrel tells you otherwise, don’t believe him, O Christian farmer. Trust God, and don’t go to any priest’s house.

Herald

Now listen to a new story. If what’s been reported to me is true, Dr Eck has come here to throttle the new doctrines. He has brought with him from Rome all the power to set up a Council, and the whole community of the Wäntal[88] are happy for him to do so. He doesn’t want to come to the city of Zurich, though; he’d rather go and dispute in Lucerne or Baden. He doesn’t think he would lose the disputation there. But Zwingli[89] isn’t prepared to let him do this: Zwingli definitely thinks Eck should come to Zurich.[90] And if (Zwingli says) he has taught anything heretical, then Eck should tell him so freely, before everyone who has heard such teachings.

84 Isaiah 43:11: ‘I, I am the Lord, and besides me there is no saviour’.

85 Cf. Job 13:18: ‘I have indeed prepared my case; I know that I shall be vindicated’.

86 Jeremiah 14:8: ‘O hope of Israel, its saviour in time of trouble’.

87 In Hosea 13:7–16 God makes various threats to destroy Israel, and in verse 16 he predicts that Samaria will ‘fall by the sword’.

88 Presumably the Wehntal, a valley in Canton Zurich. This is arguably an example of Eckstein’s ‘Naturalismus’, as described by Jakob Baechtold (p. 293); but, if so, his naturalism is short-lived. Apart from these few details in the Herald’s opening speech, there are no descriptions of the physical space in which the *Concilium* takes place or of the appearance of its characters.

89 The Swabian diminutive ‘-le’ on Zwingli’s name here is one of the (very few) linguistic features that could be said to betray Eckstein’s Swabian origins. For other examples see Müller, pp. 5–6.

90 Especially between Eck’s attack on Zwingli’s 67 Theses before the Swiss Diet at Baden in August 1524 and the opening of the Disputation of Baden in May 1526, there was indeed continual debate as to where a meeting to resolve the conflict should take place – in contrast to the general consensus that one was necessary. See for example Potter, pp. 154–5, 228–34.

das thůt Eck nit / drumb blypts erwert
Wenn Eck gen Zürch in dſtatt nit gadt
Zuinglin man nit gen Baden ladt
Darumb wirt hie nun bſetzt ein gricht
der zwytracht nach dem gotzwort gſchlicht
Das ouch die ſach deſt minder fäl
bringt Eck mit jm vil Cardinäl
[Aviii^{r}] Vff Eßlen von Rom har gritten
wol bkleyt nach Cardinälſchem ſitten
Breyt hüt vnd ouch rot Caputzen
ſind all har gſandt vom hanff butzen
Der z Rom richt über ſeel / lyb / gůt
gſtücht in eim hohen rätzenhůt
Hat yetz nit ſelb har mögen kon
er bſorgt jm werd ſin ſpitzhůt gnon
So widrig iſt jm alle welt
er müßt nun wider gän das gelt
Von Puren gnon ein groſſe ſumm
mit ablaß bſchiſſen vmb vnd vmm
Drumb hat er botten hie har gſant
der namen werdend nahär gnant
Enbietend ſich dar zthůn mit gſchrifft
das Bapſtum ſyg vff Petrum gſtifft
Dauon der Bapſt hab allen gwalt
das er mög thůn nun was jm gfalt
Darwider iſt der ander teyl
vnd ſpricht / gott hab nit ablaß feyl
On gelt vergeb er ſünd vnd ſchuld
hab einer ſchon nit bäpſtlich huld
Das iſt dem ſtůl zRom vil zenach
der heylikeyt ein groſſe ſchmach
Vnd meint der Bapſt er ſyg ein Herr
drumb ſöll man halten was er leer
So ſeyt das nein der ander teyl
gott ſyg allein der ſünder heyl
Darzů ein houpt der Chriſtenheyt
vnd der Bapſt nit wie Eck ſeyt

Eck won't do this, though, and so it won't happen. But, since Eck won't go to Zurich and Zwingli isn't invited to Baden, a court is now being set up here to resolve the dispute on the basis of God's Word.[91] To strengthen his case still further, Eck is bringing with him many cardinals, who have ridden here from Rome on donkeys and are as well dressed as one would expect cardinals to be, in wide-brimmed hats and red hoods. They've all been sent here by the old Scarecrow[92] himself, who sits in Rome lording it over people's souls, bodies, and pockets in his great rat's hat.[93] He didn't want to come himself: he's afraid someone will steal his pointy hat. Everyone is so against him that he'd have to give back the money he's taken from farmers, a great sum extorted from them everywhere by indulgences.[94] So he has sent messengers here, whose names I will give later. They will seek to show, on the basis of writings, that the papacy was founded on Peter, with the result that the Pope is all-powerful and can do whatever he wants. Against them, the other party says that God does not sell indulgences, and forgives sin and guilt free of charge. At Rome, though, it's regarded as a great blasphemy if the Pope himself hasn't granted the forgiveness. He believes he is a lord, and that people should obey what he teaches. But the other party denies this, saying that God alone saves people and is the head of Christendom – and not the Pope, as Eck says.

91 For comment on the way in which this speech of the Herald establishes the *Concilium* as the kind of tribunal often actually demanded in the 1520s, see the introduction (pp. 32–5).

92 Literally, 'scarecrow in a hemp field'.

93 Presumably the papal tiara.

94 This is one of very few references Eckstein makes to indulgences, which were never sold in Zurich and hence less of an issue there than elsewhere.

[Aviii^v] Nun ſind vorhanden beyd Parthy
lond ſehen welche meiſter ſy
Hie werdend puren Doctor bſton
wie ſy hie ſitzend vff dem plan
Der erſt pur heißd nun Thomma Klotz
bſtadt Ecken an ſtatt des Römſchen gotz
Darnach Schmid Hans Heyeheyen
hett ouch für ſich gnon ein leyen
Der heißd mit namen Knüchel Fritz
Hans Schmid hett noch im hals ein bitz
Vom häſin käß den er Zürich gwan
den Zuinglin vfthett vor yederman
Er wußd dozmal vom Concilj
meint gwüſs / redt er vor der fili
Es wurde eins in jares friſt
das jar ſchier drümal vmmhar iſt
Da ligt nit an / es iſt noch frü
es ſind ouch ander puren hie
Ioß Hechelzan von Hanffdarren
Murner vff Helias karren
Kumpt gfaren vſſz dem Paradyß
jn grauwer kutten vollen lüß
Hett mit jm bracht in grauwen röcken
vil Nolhart mit bättel ſecken
Landfarer Fritz ein glerter man
der treit ſin orden nit mee an
Aber ſins ordens brüder vil
jeder am hals ein pfannen ſtil
Bkleyt wyß vnn ſchwartz nach ordens ſitten
nit wie greuwling dſchůch zerſchnitten
[Bi^r] Von pfaffen ouch ein groſſe rott

462 Nolhart behenckt mit *CDF*

Now both parties are present: let's see who wins. Farmers are going to dispute with learned doctors, as they are seated here in the arena. The first farmer is called Thoman Klotz, and he is opposing Eck (representing the Roman idol). Then Hans Heyeheyen the Blacksmith[95] also has a layman opposite him, who is called Fritz Knüchel. Hans Schmid has still got in his mouth a bite of the rabbit cheese he was given at Zurich, and which Zwingli cut open for everyone there.[96] He knew about the Council then, and certainly said before all the crowd that there'd be one in a year's time. Since then, the third year has practically turned, but no matter: it's still early days. Other farmers are here too, such as Joß Hechelzan of Hanffdarren.[97] And Murner has come to us hotfoot from paradise in Elijah's chariot, wearing his louse-riddled grey habit.[98] He's brought with him plenty of lay brothers in grey clothes and bearing beggars' sacks. Also Fritz Landfarer,[99] a learned man who no longer wears the mark of his order, and many more of his brother monks, each with a panhandle around his neck and dressed in white and black according to his order's custom, but without damaged shoes like the grey ones.[100] There's also a huge pack of priests

95 Eckstein's nickname for Johannes Faber. His family name was Heigerlin, and 'heie-heier' means a clown or buffoon (see *SI* III, 853). 'Blacksmith', meanwhile, translates Faber's Latinized name, derived from his father's profession.

96 In the first Zurich Disputation Zwingli offered Faber a rabbit cheese ('Hasenkäs') if the latter could prove his teachings to be false on the basis of the Bible. See *Das Gyrenrupffen* (Zurich 1523, Hiv^r): 'Du weiſt wol wann man von vnmöglichen dingen redt / das man spricht: Bſchicht das / ſo wil ich dir einen häſinen käs geben' ('you know very well that when people speak of things that are impossible, they say: "If that happens, I'll give you a rabbit cheese"').

97 This fictitious toponym means 'hemp yarn'. Given that 'daren' can also mean 'to damage', a reference back to the Pope as 'hanff butzen' is also implied.

98 See 2 Kings 2. The fact that Elijah did not die on earth, but went directly to heaven, was held to be a sign of his special spiritual status – something claimed here, implicitly and of course ironically, on behalf of Murner. The 'grey habit' reminds us that Murner was a Franciscan.

99 Presumably Fritz Lindou (see n. 6). The surname means 'tramp' or 'vagrant' (see *SI* I, 900).

100 The white and black robes establish these as Dominicans, and the state of their shoes confirms that they are not itinerant mendicants.

wend all by ſton dem Römſchen Gott
Darumb wirt gon nun yetz der gul
an Murner wil Cleywe Fenchmul
Ouch iſt hie der Lentz von Baden
Luther bringt jm groſſen ſchaden
Er mag nit wol mee keller ſin
jm gadt yetz wenig opffers yn
Das trybt jnn / das er har můß
gen jm ſo ſitzt Hans Offenrůß
Doctor Gryff von Straßburg
jſt yetz am Wallenſee Biſchoff zMurg
Da ligt lybhafft Sant Grixen rock
gegem Gryffen ſitzt Claus Rebſtock
Noch iſt ein Doctor heißd Stroubutz
gegem jm ſitzt pur eigennutz
Gem Fridle ſitzt Ioß Hechelzan
drumm weybel Schwynbeltz fach nun an
Vnd frag Hans Ecken ob er well
ſich halten / wie man dſach ſtell
Das er nit naher Appellier
die puren wend ouch all ſchier
Ir ſach an gricht vnd radt hie lon
frag Ecken ob ers ouch well bſton
Darby verkünd jmm vnſre recht
das er allein mit Gotzwort fecht.

Weybel.
Hoch glerter Doctor Io hang netz
wilt du das ich dir ein gricht ſetz
[Bi^{v}] So wirſtu hie mir thůn ein eyd
das zhalten was dir werd für bſcheyd
Oder mir gän die trüwe din
das du nit wölliſt zornig ſin
Wenn man dir wirt nach Pürſcher art
die warheyt ryben in den bart

497 bſetz *CDF*

who want to support their Roman god. So now it's time to start. Cleywi Fenchmul is going to oppose Murner. Lentz of Baden is also here. Luther is causing him a lot of trouble: he can't be a cellarer any more, because not many people are giving him money. That's what drives him to be here.[101] Opposite him sits Hans Ofenrůß.[102] Doctor Gryff of Strasbourg is now Bishop of Murg on the Walensee,[103] where St Grix's tunic lies in all its glory.[104] Claus Rebstock is sitting opposite him. And there's one more doctor, called Stroubutz, and opposite him there is Pur Eygennutz. Opposite Fritz sits Joß Hechelzan. So then, Weybel Schwynbeltz,[105] let's get started, and ask Hans Eck if he's willing to abide by what's been set up and not appeal against anything any more. The farmers are willing to set their case straightaway before court and council. Ask Eck if he's willing to argue against them, and tell him about our rule that he must fight using only God's Word.

Weybel
Most learned Doctor Io hang netz,[106] if you want me to set up a court for you, you will swear me an oath here to do what you are told, or give me your word not to get angry if people rub the truth into your beard in a peasanty kind of way.

101 'Lentz of Baden' is of course Laurentius Merus (see n. 8). The precise circumstances being alluded to are unclear, but are doubtless related in some way to his switches of allegiance between the Catholic and Evangelical parties.

102 Literally, 'oven soot'. 'Ruoß' (or 'Russ') was also used of coarse or wild people (see *SI* III, 1446), in consequence of the perceived savagery of Russians.

103 The Walensee is a large Alpine lake straddling the Cantons of St. Gallen and Glarus, on which the ancient (though never episcopal) town of Murg does indeed lie.

104 'Grix' is a popular variant of 'Gregor', and hence could refer to a number of saints. Given Eckstein's frequent references to the Fourteen Holy Helpers, it is however also conceivable that he has in mind another of their number, St Cyriacus, who helps in resisting temptation on one's deathbed.

105 The surname means 'pigskin'. For a discussion of the term 'Weybel' see the introduction, n. 60 (pp. 32–3).

106 A play on Eck's name, presumably invoking the hanging of nets, and maybe the noun 'handnezi', meaning towel.

Wir ſind ſchlächt puren überal
vnd könnend nüt im Decretal
Wir ſind vff hoher ſchůl nit gſtanden
darumb ſo nimm das gotzwort zhanden
Das bruchend wir in vnſrem tal
vnd bring vns ſuſt nüt überal
Magſt das Bapſtum damit bſchützen
das wirt dich hie vnd zRom nützen
Wiltu das thůn / gib har din trüw
verheyß nit hütt das dich morn rüw

Eck Doctor.

Trüw gib ich dir by minem Gott
von dem ich har gſant bin ein bott
Der iſt ouch aller Chriſten houpt
das hand all vnſer vordren gloupt
Ouch wil ichs mit der gſchrifft zügen
all vätter heyſſend mich nit lügen

Weybel.

Hettiſts langeſt zügt bym Luter
ſo wäriſt du vnd Vyt Suter
Vil müeg vnd arbeyt über xin
do er ward gſchickt gen Baden hin
[Bii^{r}*]* Mit diner Miſſiff für die Eydgnoſſen
haſt ſtarck angrent / doch nüt abgſtoſſen
darzů kätzret ouch den Zuingle
vnd zügſt es nit mit eim dingle

514 Doctor Eck *CF*   522 Hettiſts dann langeſt *CDF*

All of us are simple farmers and know nothing of the Decretal;[107] we haven't been to university. So take up God's Word – that's what we use in our valley – and don't try coming at us with anything else.[108] If you can defend the papacy using God's Word, then that'll do you a lot of good here and in Rome. Will you do that? Give us your word, and don't promise anything today that you'll regret tomorrow.

Doctor Eck

I give you my word in the name of my god, from whom I've been sent here as a messenger. He is also the head of all Christians; all our ancestors have believed this, and I will prove it by the Scriptures. All of the Fathers command me not to lie.

Weybel

If you had said that a long time ago, when you were with Luther, you would have spared yourself and Vyt Suter[109] a lot of trouble and grief – when he was sent to Baden with your missive to the Swiss. You certainly attacked us (but didn't repel us), and you made Zwingli out to be a heretic, without proving it with a single scrap of evidence.[110]

107 Used throughout as shorthand for canon law in general. The text being alluded to is for certain the *Decretals of Gregory IX*, Raymond of Peñaforte's thirteenth-century codification of canon law.

108 This oft-repeated challenge serves not only as a reminder of the classic Evangelical *Schriftprinzip*, but also of the specific words spoken by Zwingli to Faber at the First Zurich Disputation (as recorded by Hegenwald, Dii^{v}).

109 Vyt Suter was an agent employed by the Duke of Austria to negotiate with the Swiss. See Anton Laziadèr, 'Zur Geschichte des zweiten Kappelerkrieges', *Zwingliana*, 6 (1937), 460–2; also Walter Weber, 'Die Datierung von Zwinglis Schrift *Was Zürich und Bern not ze betrachten sye in dem fünförtischen Handel*. Versuch einer Lösung', *Zwingliana*, 12 (1965), 228–31.

110 A reference to Eck's *Missive und embieten* to the Swiss, dated 13th August 1524, and published in Zwingli, *Sämtliche Werke*, III, 304–5. What Eckstein says here is true: Eck's letter accuses Zwingli of having introduced many errors of doctrine ('manig faltig irrung'), of having sullied the faith ('den glouben befleckt'), and of 'doing heretical violence to the Holy Scriptures' ('die heiligen geschrifft kätzerisch verwaltiget') – without, in this context, offering any proof.

Du haſts vor thon ouch me wenn eineſt
mich wundret was damit meineſt
Du reyßteſt vor zyten gen Wien
du biſt nit yetz wie do zmal kien
Ouch zugeſt wol durch fünff Biſtum
vnnd magſt nit eineſt durch Chriſtum
Gen Zürch in dſtatt die ligt in Schwytz
ich gloub dich trybe nun der gytz
Nach gůt vnd eer iſt dir ſo gach
das du dich nempſt eim Helden nach
Du wirſt ye Doctor Eck genant
wär nun dins vatters hof verbrant
Daruff du denn biſt geboren
ſo wurd dim namen nach gſchoren
Alſo haſt vom hof den namen
jr ſoltend üch vor Gott ſchamen
Alſo thůt ouch din xell Hans Schmid
heyßt Heyer von ſinr vordren glid
Doch Eck vor zyten was ein Riß
als ich im Berner Dietrich liß
Der iſt frylich din äni gſin
geborn von Cöln das ligt am Ryn
Vnd du vſſz ſchwaaben land
din heymat iſt mir vaſt wol bkant
Doch heyſſiſt Hans Gick oder Geck
du biſt vormal me gwalt im dreck
[Bii^{v}] Das möcht dir aber zhanden gan
denn wiltu hie ein Puren bſtan
So ſchlach von hand all ſophiſtry

You've also done this more than once before;[111] I wonder what you mean by it. Once you travelled to Vienna;[112] you're not as keen to get about now as you were then. And you went through five dioceses and didn't once visit the city of Zurich (that's in Switzerland, by the way) on Christ's behalf. I think it's greed that's bringing you here now: you're so set on gaining honour and possessions that you're named after a hero.[113] You're called Doctor Eck. If your father's farm, which you were born on, had burnt down, you'd have been deprived of a name. But you have the name from the farm – and you should be ashamed of yourself for it.[114] Your friend Hans Schmid does the same thing: he's called Heyer from his front member.[115] But in earlier times Eck was a giant, as I read in the stories about Dietrich of Berne. I admit he was your ancestor. He was born in Cologne (which is on the Rhine, by the way), and you come from Swabia – I know your homeland very well.[116] But you're really called Hans Gick or Geck;[117] you once used to wallow in the mud more than you do now. This needs to come flooding back to you now, because if you want to beat a farmer in argument, you'll have to get rid of all your sophistries,

111 Eck had indeed been taking an active interest in Swiss affairs, not least via short publications on Zwingli's theology of the Mass, at least since early 1523.

112 Eck's reputation was founded not least on his impressive performance at a public disputation in Vienna in 1516.

113 The giant Ecke, an important literary figure especially in the *Eckenlied*, an epic from the Dietrich von Bern cycle. The strength of Johann Eck's ambition and his liking for material rewards were notorious by 1525.

114 Eck's surname was actually 'Maier'. Eckstein is berating him for having adopted the name of the village in which he was born and in which his father was a bailiff, now known as Egg an der Günz (in the Lower Allgäu).

115 'Heien' can also mean to castrate or rape an animal (*SI* II, 855–6; *FWB* VII, 1454).

116 This is perhaps the most significant piece of evidence presented by Stricker (n. 103, p. 157) to suggest that Eckstein's Swabian origins are detectable also from references within his texts.

117 'Geck' ('fool') is a particularly common nickname for Eck. A 'Gick', meanwhile, is a small incision with a knife.

vnd nit wie allwäg als lut ſchry
Des ſitzt hie gen dir Thoman klotz
den bericht hie mit dem wort Gotz
Das der Bapſt ſyg der kilchen houpt
vnd ob jms Chriſtus hab erloupt
Hat er denn von Gott har den gwalt
das er zů Rom ein gwardi halt
Zügſtu jm das ons Decretal
ſo wirſt zů einem Cardinal

Hans Eck.
Nun loß mir du nun Thoman klotz
der Bapſt ſitzt an der ſtatt Gotz
Von Petro har kumpt diſer gwalt
da jnn Chriſtus zů Bapſt erwalt
An ſinr ſtatt zſin nach jm vff erden *Math. 16.*
was er vflößt dort ſolt loß werden
Was er denn bund ſolt bunden ſyn
alſo ſatzt er jm dſchlüſſel yn
Do Chriſtus diunger all da fragt
Petrus ſich für ander wagt
Do er ſo dapffer Chriſtum bkant
darumb ward er ein felſer gnant
Do zmal ward dkilch vff Petrum gründt
wie man jm bloſſen text findt
Sy iſt nit buwt vff ſand vnd kadt
der Bapſt zů jr die ſchlüſſel hat
[Biii[r]] Sölt er jr houpt nit billich ſin
kron kumpt vom Keyſer Conſtantin?

566 Bzügſt du *CDF*

and not shout as loudly as you usually do.[118] For this purpose Thoman Klotz is sitting here opposite you. Tell him here, from God's Word, that the Pope is the head of the Church, that Christ has allowed him to be so, and that he has the power from God to keep a papal guard.[119] If you can prove all that without referring to the Decretal, they'll make you a cardinal.

Hans Eck

Now you listen to me, Thoman Klotz: the Pope sits in God's stead. This power comes from Peter, when Christ chose him to be Pope on earth after him and instead of him. Whatever he looses on earth shall be loosed in heaven, and whatever he binds on earth shall be bound in heaven.[120] In this way Christ gave Peter the keys: when Christ asked all the disciples, Peter dared, before the others, to confess him boldly. For this reason he was called a rock, and the Church was founded on Peter, as one can find written simply in the text. The Church is not built on sand and mud, and the Pope holds the key to her. Is it not right that he should be her head? The crown comes from Emperor Constantine.[121]

118 Eck was, throughout his career, an enthusiastic preacher and teacher, and was seemingly not prey to modesty or shyness ('Bescheidenheit oder Zurückhaltung') – see Erwin Iserloh, *Johannes Eck (1486–1543). Scholastiker, Humanist, Kontroverstheologe*, Katholisches Leben und Kirchenreform im Zeitalter der Glausbensspaltung, 41 (Münster: Aschendorff, 1981), here p. 12.

119 In Eckstein's time the Pope's Swiss Guard was still a relative novelty, having been set up by Julius II in 1506.

120 Matthew 16:19: 'I will give you the keys of the kingdom of heaven, and whatever you bind on earth will be bound in heaven, and whatever you loose on earth will be loosed in heaven'.

121 This is of course a reference to the Donation of Constantine, a document by which that Emperor supposedly transferred authority over Rome and its Western Empire to the Pope, but which was definitively demonstrated by Lorenzo Vallo to be a forgery (in his *De falso credita et ementita Constantini donatione declamatio*, 1460). The various references in the margin of the German text seem not to refer to any particular source; rather, they serve to indicate the extent to which Eck uses canon law as other speakers use holy writ. Murner does the same in *Karsthans*. See *Karsthans. Thomas Murners 'Hans Karst' und seine Wirkung in sechs Texten der Reformationszeit*, ed. and trans. by Thomas Neukirchen, Beihefte zum *Euphorion*, 68 (Heidelberg: Winter, 2011), p. 16.

Die ſchenck nit widerrüfft mag werden *12. qu. 11.*
von keim keyſer hie vff erden *de rebus.*
Vnd all Keyſer müſſend ſchweeren *Di. 63. Ti*
ſich zhalten nach des Bapſts leeren *Ego Lud.*
Vnd wie die Sonn zů aller friſt
vil häller denn der Mon iſt
Alſo hat es ein vnderſcheyd
zwüſchem Keyſer vnd Bäpſtlichkeyt *Extra. de*
darumb der Bapſt an Got*s* ſtatt ſitzt *ma.et ob.*
was hettind ſuſt die ſchlüſſel gnützt? *cap. Soli.*
Von Petro geerbt nach ſim abgang *ca. Noui.*
der gwalt hat gwärt zů Rom yetz lang *extra de*
Vnd wär ja ſchon kein geiſtlich recht *reb. Iudi.*
hör ob ich nit mit gotzwort fecht
Da Chriſtus ſprach: Du heyſt Cephas
das heyßt ein houpt / verſtaaſtu das?
Drumb wie das houpt das obreſt glid
ein gantzen lyb regiert in frid
Alſo der bapſt der obreſt iſt
wär das nit gloubt iſt kein Chriſt
Wir ſind all durch einandren glider
Der bapſt das houpt / biß nit darwider
Vnd kündeſt du nun decliniern
Matheus wirt dirs bas probieren *Math. 16.*
Vff den Petram es da ſtadt
nun hör was mer naher gadt
Wird ich min kilchen buwen
es hat doch Gott noch nit gruwen
[Biii[v]] Die ſchlüſſel gab er jm darzů
lůg ob ich nit gnůg darthů
Die kilch iſt lang in růw gſtanden
vnd noch / allein in tütſch landen
Wil man nüt daruf mee han
ſy ſähind nit Bapſt noch ban an

595 Gott *AE*

His donation cannot be revoked by any emperor on earth, and all emperors must swear to hold to the Pope's teachings. And just as the sun is at all times much brighter than the moon, so there is a difference between the Emperor and the papacy – in that the Pope sits in God's stead. What use would the keys have been otherwise? The power of the Pope was inherited by Rome after Peter's death, and that power has been held there for a long time now. Without it there would be no canon law. Hear whether I am using God's Word to fight with: when Christ says 'You are called Cephas, that is, a head'. Do you understand that? Just as the head, as the highest member, governs the whole body peaceably, so the Pope is the head of the Church. Anyone who does not believe that is not a Christian. We are all members together, and the Pope is the head. Don't oppose this; and if you decline to believe it, Matthew will put you right. 'On this rock', he says (now hear more about it), 'I will build my Church'.[122] God did not leave it at that: he gave him the keys as well. See if I haven't said enough. The Church has long been at peace, but now, only in the German lands, people are fed up with this: they respect neither the Pope nor his ban,

122 Matthew 16:18: 'And I tell you, you are Peter, and on this rock I will build my church'.

Noch wirt ſy gſton in eewigkeyt
dauon ſyg yetz zmal gnůg gſeyt

Thoman Klotz.
Benefon ertis Iohan nes
wenn der Bapſt an gots ſtatt ſäß
Vnd wär ein houpt der Chriſtenheyt
wie du yetz zmal gnůg heſt gſeyt
So käm der Türck ins himmelrych
wenn er läbt grad dem ſelben glych
Der Türck ſtellt nun vff Chriſten blůt
treyt wie der Bapſt ein rätzenhůt.
Kein herr iſt yetz vff aller erd
der ee dem Bapſt verglycht wärd
Als eben der Türckiſch Keyſer
der Bapſt hat wie der Türck reyſer
Die hat er nit vmb gots willen
ſunder das er möge ſtillen
Die jm nit wöllend ghorſam ſin
frag man den Hertzog von Vrbin
Dem hatt er ouch yngnon ſin land
ſo stadt ſyn rych vff kadt vnd ſand
Der gwalt kumpt nit von ſant Peter
der hat ouch nit wie er trummeter
[Biv^{r}] On andren wolluſt / ſicht man wol
all ſin läben iſt ſünden vol
Er wil nun herr ſin über dwält
es wäre lidig wärs vmb gält
Die gwüßne wil er ouch regieren
die ſeelen vſs dem Fägfhür füren
Hett jm nun gott gen diſen gwalt
(daruon ich warlich lützel halt)
Das er ſöll ſeelen meyſter ſin
ynfüren vnd vſs ſölcher pyn
So iſt er doch ein groſſer wicht
das er nit tür vnd thor zerbricht
Vnd all vergäben vstrybt

and so they will not stand in eternity. Enough has now been said about this.

Thoman Klotz

John[123] of Peñaforte says that, if the Pope did sit in God's stead, and if he really were the head of Christendom, as you have now sufficiently stated, then the Turk would go to heaven. Because his way of life is very much like the Pope's. The Turk seeks to shed Christian blood and wears a rat's hat, just like the Pope.[124] There is now no lord on earth who can better be compared to the Pope than can the Turkish Emperor. Like the Turk, the Pope has soldiers, whom he uses not for God's sake, but to put down those who won't obey him. Just ask the Duke of Urbino: he has taken his land from him.[125] So the Pope's land is indeed built on mud and sand. His power doesn't come from St Peter – Peter didn't have trumpeters of war, as the Pope does. Quite apart from his other lusts, you can see that the Pope's life is full of sin. He wants now to be lord over all the earth. It wouldn't be so bad if it was just about money, but he also wants to rule over our consciences. He wants to lead souls out of purgatory. If God has given him this power (which, truly, I don't think much of), to be the master of souls and to lead people into and out of this suffering, then he really isn't up to much if he doesn't break down purgatory's doors and gates and let out all those who have been forgiven,

123 Either he means Raymond (see n. 107 above), or, more likely, he is setting up a plausible sounding opposing authority (in the best late-medieval/early modern tradition).

124 This cannot refer to Suleiman the Magnificent's renowned four-tier tiara (as famously drawn by Agostino Veneziano), since he was not given this until 1532. Doubtless, however, a comparably magnificent tiara or turban is envisaged.

125 Papal troops (under Leo X) took Urbino from its Duke (Francesco della Rovere) in 1516.

das keine ſo lang drinnen blybt
Denn ſo ers mag vmb gält löſen
ſo ſolt man jnn billich kröſen
Nun das ich kumm vff min probatz
vnd antwurte dinr allegatz
Das der Bapſt ſyg der kilchen houpt
ſag ich Gott habs jm nit erloubt
Keim andren wil er ſin gwalt geben *Eſai. 42.*
min nachpur Hans loß mir eben /
Du ſprichſt ſant Peter hab ſich gwagt
do er von Chriſto ward gefragt
Das er jnn gottes ſun erkannt
darumb ſyg er ein Felſer gnannt
Vnd ſyg vff Petrum gründt die Kilch
jch bſtand dich vmb ein napff mit milch
Ich wöll mit dinen worten
vmb werffen diner kilchen porten
[Biv^{v}] Iſt nun dkilch buwt vff Petrum
ſo machſt du vſſz dem am ein vmm
Du ſeyſt ye Super petram hanc
min gſell Hans Geck hab immer danck
Ich kan baß denn du declinatz
du dörfftiſt aber einr purgatz
Wie ſtadt din tütſch vnd latin zſamen
jch hör wol Petrus het zwen namen
Peter in tütſch / Petra latin
ſo iſt er Peternella gſin
Vnd hat zween namen vff erden
nun welcher můß der recht werden?
Zwar Petrus iſt der recht nam ſin
ſo valt denn dKilch vff Petram hin
Das ſelb vff tütſch ein vels heißd
das plůt vnd fleiſch Petri nit weißd
Das Chriſtus der ſun Gottes ſy
wärs vatters offnung nit dar by
Von oben ab kon in ſin můt
er trůg dozmal kein ſpitzhůt

so that none of them has to stay there any longer. But since he only wants to open it in exchange for money, we really should do away with him. Now let me come to my argument and answer your allegation[126] that the Pope is the head of the Church. I say God doesn't permit it. He doesn't want to give his power to anyone else[127] – listen to me well, neighbour Hans. You say St Peter dared, when he was asked by Christ, to acknowledge him as God's Son, and that for this reason he was called a Rock. And you say that the Church was founded on Peter. I bet you a bowl of milk that I can break down the gates of your church using your own words. Because, if the Church is built on Peter, then you are making an 'am' into an 'um'. You always say 'Super Petram hanc'. I'm eternally grateful to you, friend Hans Geck, but I can decline Latin better than you. You should take a purgative: you're getting your German mixed up with your Latin. I hear that Peter has two names, Peter in German and Petra in Latin. If that's the case, then he must have been Peternella, and must have two names on earth.[128] Now, which is the right one? For sure Petrus is his right name, but the Church has hit upon Petra, which in German means a rock. Peter's flesh and blood wouldn't know that Christ was the Son of God if it wasn't for the Father's revelation of it. His courage came to him from above; and at that time he didn't wear a pointy hat.

126 The Latinizing rhyme pairs 'probatz' and 'allegatz' (660–1) and 'declinatz' and – especially – 'purgatz' (678–9) are doubtless intended to mock the language of canon lawyers such as Eck.

127 Isaiah 42:8: 'I am the Lord, that is my name; my glory I give to no other'.

128 No doubt an allusion to the virgin martyr St Petronilla, who was traditionally identified (one suspects only by dint of her name) as St Peter's daughter.

Kein kron mit gold vnd bärlin bſchlagen
man dorfft do nit ſant Peter tragen
Er hatt kein gwardi / gold / noch hab
weiſt wie er dem lamen antwurt gab? *Act. 3.*
Silber vnd gold hab ich nit
hörzů was ward jm für ſin bitt
Gſundtheyt im namen Ieſu Chriſt
empfieng der lam zur ſelben friſt
Vnd hoppet vor jm in tempel
das iſt vns ein gwüſs exempel
[Bv^{r}] Vnd zügt vns das er arm iſt xin
ouch ſeyſt vom Keyſer Conſtantin
Der heige rychlich bgaabt den ſtůl
das kumpt Ekillen wol dim bůl
Gäb man dir nit ſo vil ducaten
du wurdiſt bald helffen radten
Nach zfragen der ſelben Dotation
jch gloub ſy wurd gmach fürhar kon
Sunſt ſprichſt ſy ſyg langſt veraltet
das iſt einr luge glych gſtaltet
Vnd ſind doch dwort noch vorhanden
wie ſy im alten brieff ſind gſtanden
Darzů hend Conſtantini kinder
nahin regiert nüt deſt minder
Hett der vatter dkron hin ggeben
ſo wärind dkind / merck mich eben /
Enteerbt / darzů nit Keyſer xin
das hat nit gthon der Conſtantin
Sin rädt die hettitz nit zůglon
das Keyſerthůmb ſölte abgon
Du vnd all din Romaniſten
mögend den ſtůl zRom nit friſten
Er wirt mit Gotswort zſchiter gon
es iſt ſchon brennt ein bein daruon *Ierem. 2.*
Der fhürin haf im Ieremias

722 hettinds *CDF*

St Peter didn't wear a crown studded with gold and pearls. He had no guards, gold or possessions. Do you know what answer he gave to the lame man?: 'Silver and gold have I none'.[129] Listen to what the lame man received in return for his request: immediately he received his health in the name of Christ, and went hopping into the temple. That is a sure example to us, and witnesses to the fact that Peter was poor. You also say about Emperor Constantine that he gave generously to Peter's throne; well, little Master Eck, that suits your squeeze very well. If people didn't give you so many ducats, you'd soon try and help investigate that Dotation.[130] I reckon it makes for a comfortable life. Otherwise, you'd be claiming that it had long ago expired. But it's all a lie and, anyway, we now have the words of the original document. What's more, Constantine's children continued to rule after him anyway. If their father had given away the crown, the children – hear me well in this – would have been disinherited, and wouldn't have become emperors. But Constantine didn't do this; and his council wouldn't have allowed the Empire to be taken away. You and all your Romanist friends can't save the Roman throne. God's Word will destroy it. One of its legs has already been burnt away: Jeremiah's seething pot[131]

129 Acts 3:6: 'But Peter said: "I have no silver or gold, but what I have I give you"'.

130 All editions have 'dotation' instead of 'donation' here, presumably deliberately.

131 Jeremiah 1:13 (*sic*): 'The word of the Lord came to me a second time, saying, "What do you see?" and I said: "I see a boiling pot, tilted away from the north"'.

hat verbrennt den ablas quies
Das iſt das gröſt ans Bapſts hof gſyn
das minder vallt ouch bald dahin
Darumb gſell Hans nun bſinn dich baß
vnd lern was da heyſſe Cephas
[Bv^{v}] Das heißd ein Fels vnd nit ein kopff
nun biſt du ye ein armer tropff
Biſt nun ſo lang ein Dräckhuß gſin
vnd weiſt noch nit das wörtlin
Heſt noch Eraſmum nit gleſen
du biſt ob dem Decret gwäſen
Cephas iſt Siriſch nit latin
din Bapſt der möcht wol Cayphas ſin
Der reyß ſin gwand / vnd thett nit not
darumb das Chriſtus ſich nampt Gott
Das was er ouch / vnd wirdts blyben
du můſt nit wider Gott kyben
Alſo der Bapſt nun all die haßd
die mit dem gotswort ſind verfaßd
All ſin leer iſt wider Chriſtum
drumm wirt jm Gott nemmen ſin Biſtum
Vnd wie Cayphas ſin gwand zerreyß
alſo wirt der gantz vmbkreyß
Vom Bapſtthůmb ſton / anhangen Gott
darwider mag kein tüfliſch rott
Sin geyſtlich recht jnn ouch nit bſchützt
din tant darzů jnn nüt nützt
Du wolteſt gern ſin gwallt bſchirmen
man wirt üch bäpſtler anders firmen
Wenn din prob vns noch hie nit ſchlicht
jch wärd denn mit dem Gotswort bricht
Das iſt bißhar von dir nit ghört
jch hoff ich hab mich din erweert
Vnd ſetz nun dſach an biderb lüt
das geiſtlich recht gilt by vns nüt
[Bvi^{r}] Ich bgär gotswort / wems gfalt dem gfeltz

has consumed the indulgence 'Quies'.[132] That was the biggest one at the Pope's court, and the smaller one will soon fall. So then, friend Hans, think better of it, and learn what 'Cephas' means. It means a rock and not a head. You really are a poor fool. Have you been a shit-house[133] as long as you have, and still don't know the word? Haven't you read Erasmus? You've gone beyond the Decretal. 'Cephas' is Syrian, not Latin: your Pope might just as well be Caiaphas, who tore his garments, without needing to, because Christ called himself God. He *was* God anyway, and will remain so. You shouldn't quarrel with God. So the Pope hates all those who are concerned with God's Word. All his teachings are against Christ. And so God will take his bishopric from him, and just as Caiaphas rent his garments, so all those around him will forsake the papacy and turn to God. No devilish mob can prevent that happening. His religious laws won't protect him, and your trumpery won't be any use to him either. You wanted to protect his power, but people will punish you Papists in a different way for this. Because your proofs haven't placated us yet, and won't until such time as you correct me from God's Word – which we haven't heard you do yet. I hope I've defended myself against you, and now place the matter in the hands of some honest people. Canon law is no use to us: whatever anyone else thinks, what I want is God's Word.

132 We do not find this reference easy to interpret. Our best guess is that, rather than 'quies' ('rest', 'ease', hence 'quiet') Eckstein intended the word to be printed as two ('qui es', 'you are/thou art'). This would suggest a link with the Lord's Prayer ('Pater noster, *qui es* in coelis'), and hence, in context, with the Rosary (which opens with the Lord's Prayer). In the early sixteenth century the Rosary was particularly associated with indulgences, and indeed with one of Eckstein's other *bêtes noires,* the rising confraternities. Moreover the Rosary had been particularly promoted (and, in terms of indulgences, rewarded) by a recent Pope, Sixtus IV; and its use had been to all intents and purposes abolished in Zurich by 1525.

133 The combination of Eck's doctoral title and surname lent itself all too readily to puns such as this involving 'dreck'.

frag vmb gfatter weibel Schwynbeltz
Ich wölt wol mee han hie darthon
mir iſt ich wöll by dem bſton

Weybel Schwynbeltz.
Aman krůg vſs der waſſer hütten
radt du nach vnſers lands ſitten
Was dunckt dich gůt nach gſtalt der ſachen
du haſts nun hören beyd machen
Hans Ecken vnd den Thomma klotz
die zween ſchlicht allein das wort Gots
Nach dem vnd ich denn dſach verſton
ſo wil Hans Doctor Eck han
Der Bapſt ſigs houpt der Chriſtenheit
darwider Thomma Klotz ſeyt
Gott geb keim andren ſinen gwalt *Eſaie. 48.*
das ſelb ich warlich ouch halt
Er heige lyb vnd ſeel verfürt
alſo hab Petrus nit regiert
Gott ſyg das houpt der Chriſten kilch
vnd nit der Bapſt vff der Eſel fülch

Amma Krůg.
Ich meins ouch ſammer botz grind
jſts wie ich zun Corinthern find
So mag der bapſt das houpt nit ſin
als wenig ich ſant Peter bin
Hörend wie iſt der ſpruch ſo klar
Ir ſöllend wüſſen all fürwar
[Bvi^{v}] Eins yeden mans houpt Chriſtus iſt *1. Cor. 11.*
wie der vatter ein houpt Ieſu Chriſt
Iſt nun der Bapſt wie ich ein man
ſo gadt jnn diſer ſpruch ouch an
So ſind wir glider miteinander
all bäpſt Gregory / Allexander

797 Gregory vnd Alexander *CDF*

Ask some other people, Weybel Schwynbeltz. Though I'd have liked to say more, I feel I should leave it here.

Weybel Schwynbeltz

Amma Krůg from the water huts,[134] give us your advice according to the custom of our land. What do you think, now that you've heard both Hans Eck and Thoman Klotz discuss the question? God's Word alone must decide the issue between them. As far as I can understand the matter, Dr Hans Eck holds that the Pope is the head of Christendom, whereas Thoman Klotz says that God does not give his power to any other – which is indeed what I also think – and that Dr Eck has misled us in body and soul. So, for him, Peter was not a ruler; rather, God was the head of the Christian Church, and not the Pope riding on the foal of an ass.

Amma Krůg[135]

That's what I think too, by God.[136] If what I find in Corinthians is true, the Pope can't be the head, any more than I'm St Peter. Listen to how clear the words are: 'You should indeed all know that Christ is the head of every man, as the Father is the head of Jesus Christ'.[137] So if the Pope is a man like me, then these words apply to him also, and we are all members together. All Popes, be they called Gregory or Alexander,

134 Or possibly 'water hats'.

135 An 'am' is a wine beaker, or measure of wine (see *SI* I, 211), whereas a 'Krug' (also in modern German) is a jug or pitcher, often used for beer in taverns. On the other hand, 'Amma' can also be a corruption of 'Amtmann', usable to describe various kinds of senior local official. Text D of the *Concilium* obviously imagines Amma's function to have been a legal one: it changes his name to 'Gerichtsman Schauffler'.

136 The expletive literally means – doubtless significantly – 'may God's head help me'.

137 1 Corinthians 11:3: 'But I want you to understand that Christ is the head of every man, and the husband is the head of the wife, and God is the head of Christ'.

Sy ſind wie ich ouch glider xin
dem glöubigen hufen glybet jn
Ia wenn ſy ouch daby hend gloupt
das Chriſtus ſyg der kilchen houpt

Weybel ſchwynbeltz.

Radt ouch drumm Paule Kachelmůß
weyſt etwas gůts nun frölich thüs
Biſt der meinung wie Aman Krůg
ſo hend wir zweyer zügnuß gnůg.

Paule Kachelmůs.

Min ſchwynbeltz was ſol ich ſagen
ich hab in allen minen tagen
Nüt vff dem hanffbutzen ghan
ich ſeytz keim nie ich forcht den ban
Mich důcht allwäg es wär ein trug
von menſchen erdacht nüt denn lug
Ich daacht / ſolt der an gotzſtatt ſin
er gibt nüt vß vnd nimpt nun yn
Das hat doch kein zwölffbott nit thon
man můß jnn tragen als könd er nit gon
Was iſt das für ein geiſtlicheyt
das er alſo ein badhůt treyt?
[Bvii^r] Solt er ſin der glöubigen houpt
botz ſeych ich hab es nie gloupt
Der glöubigen houpt iſt nit hie
kein menſch mit ougen gſachs ouch nye
Dkilchen mag man hie nit kennen
biß Gott wird von einander trennen
Denn wirt der glöubig huf ſchynen
die böſen hülen vnd ouch grynen *Matth. 25.*
Denn ouch all bäpſt da werdend ſtan
welcher wirt denn für das houpt ghan?
Nit einr noch keinr kan ich ſagen

812 btrug *CDF* 813 denn ein lug *CDF*

have been members just like me, incorporated into the assembly of the faithful, if indeed they have believed that Christ is the head of the Church.

Weybel Schwynbeltz

Advise us then, Paule Kachelmůß: if you have anything good to say, then tell it to us with joy. If you agree with Amman Krůg, then we have the two witnesses we need.[138]

Paule Kachelmůß[139]

What should I say, my dear Schwynbeltz? All my days I've had no regard for the old Scarecrow, but I've never said so to anyone for fear of the ban. I've always thought it was a deception made up by men, nothing but a lie. I thought to myself: should he really be in the place of God? He never gives anything, but only takes. None of the apostles did that. People have got to carry him around as if he can't walk.[140] And what sort of religion is it that says he has to wear a bath hat? Is he supposed to be the head of the faithful? I swear to God,[141] I've never believed it. The head of the faithful isn't here, no man ever saw him with his eyes. You won't be able to recognize the Church on earth until God comes to separate the sheep from the goats: then the faithful throng will shine and the evil ones will howl and weep.[142] At that time all the Popes also will stand before God, and who will people think is the head then? Not a single one of those Popes, I can tell you.

138 Undoubtedly an allusion to Deuteronomy 17:6: 'On the evidence of two or three witnesses the death sentence shall be executed; a person must not be put to death on the evidence of only one witness'. One is of course reminded also of the Swiss tradition of collective decision-making.

139 The name is probably best translated as 'stone guts'.

140 A reference to the Pope's ceremonial *sedia gestatoria* – a cause of offence to many of Eckstein's contemporaries and near-contemporaries.

141 Literally, 'God's piss' (see *SI* VII, 138–9).

142 Another summary of Matthew 25:31–46.

denn werdends gan / man wirts nit tragen
Welcher denn iſt ein gůt hirt xin
der fart mit der kilchen gotz hin
Da wirt denn ein hirt vnd ein ſtal / *Ioan. 10.*
die böſen gand ins jamertal
Da wirt ſin hülen vnd zänklaffen
wee denn den bſchornen pfaffen
Die hie vmb ein klein zytlich gůt
hend brot verkoufft für fleyſch vnd blůt
Des eineſt gſtorbnen Ieſu Chriſt
die ſchuld der bäpſten aller iſt
Die hand vns zwungen mit dem ban
das wirs hend für gots lychnam ghan
Alſo hentz vns puren bſchiſſen
da by hentz ouch wellen wüſſen
Was wir denckind vnd heygind thon
es hat als müſſen für ſy kon
Darzů hend all küng vnd heren
ſy müſſen an gotzſtatt eren
[Bvii^{v}*]* Inn darzů küſſen füß vnd hend
hey das ſy botz blater ſalb ſchend
Solt er das houpt der kilchen ſin
ich weyß das ich ſin gwüß bin
Das Chriſtus iſt der kilchen houpt
das hat ouch ſant Paulus gloubt
Hör was er zun Epheſern ſchryb
Chriſtus ſyg das houpt / dkilch ſin lyb *Epheſ. 5.*
Dkilch heyßt hie nit ſtein vnd muren
ſunder all glöubig bäpſt vnd puren
Sy kumpt vffs erdtrich hie nit zamen
biß Gott verſamlet xund vnd lamen
Drumb lond nun den Ecken touben
lond vns ein Chriſten kilch glouben *Ioan. 1.*
Nit fleyſchlich born von mann vnd wyb
die kilch iſt nun ein geyſtlich lyb

847 es] *om. CDF* 850 Inn] Im *CDF* 862 nun] *om. CDF* 863 vnd lond] *CDF*

They'll have to walk then – no one will be carrying them around any more. Anyone who has been a good shepherd of his flock will go up with God's Church to where there is both a shepherd and a stall;[143] but the evil ones will go into the valley of sorrows, where there will be weeping and gnashing of teeth. Woe, then, to the dishonest priests who here on earth have sold bread, for not much money, as if it were the body and blood of Jesus Christ, who died once for all! This is the fault of all the Popes: they have coerced us with their bans so that we might think the bread is actually God in bodily form. In this way they have deceived us farmers. And they have also wanted to know everything that we are thinking and have done. All that had to be brought before them. Also all kings and lords have had to honour them as God's representatives and kiss their hands and feet. A pox on them! Should the Pope be head of the Church? I know and am certain that Christ is the head of the Church. St Paul believed this too. Hear what he wrote to the Ephesians, that Christ is the head and the Church is his body.[144] 'The Church' here doesn't mean something made of stones or walls – it means all of the faithful, both Popes and farmers. It won't come together here on earth, until God gathers together the sound and the lame. So let Eck rage and let us believe in the one Christian Church, which wasn't born in fleshly form from man and woman.[145] The Church is a spiritual body.

143 The image is based, albeit loosely, on John 10:1–18.

144 Ephesians 5:23: 'Christ is the head of the church, the body of which he is the Saviour'.

145 John 1:12–13: 'Children of God, who were born, not of blood or the will of the flesh or the will of man, but of God'.

Sy heyßt darumb ein Chriſten kilch
ſy ißt hie weder můß noch milch
Allein das gotzwort iſt jr ſpyß *Deut. 8.*
vff jrem houpt wachſend nit lüß
Darab bringt mich kein Cardinal
das ſyg nun gnůg gſeyt yetz zmal

Weybel.
Hans Eck du haſt nun wol gehört
die puren ſind dir vil zů glört
Du magſt nun yetz nüt me ſchaffen
man kert ſich nüt an din klaffen
Geyſtlich recht mag hie nüt zügen
eins heyßt ſelb das ander lügen
[Bviii[r]] Man offt in eim Concili ſpricht
das man jm andren wider bricht
Der heylig geyſt thůt ſömlichs nüt
was er hütt macht / jnn morn nit rüwt
Sin gmecht blypt ſton in ewigkeit
was wir ſönd thůn hat Chriſtus gſeyt
Wenn wir nun thůnd das er vns büt
wir dörffend menſchen ſatzung nüt
Er wil ſich nit damit lon eren
was er nit büt als Bapſt*s* leren
Wir eerend Gott damit vergeben *Matth. 13*
lond vns nach ſinem bott ſtreben
Er büt vns nit das wir ſönd han
an ſinr ſtatt ein ſündigen man
Er iſt ſelb der kilchen grund
das wirt vns durch den Paulum kund
Kein andren grund mag man ſetzen *1. Cor. 3.*
er mag vns wol leyds ergetzen

869 *CDF* add 107 lines after this line (see below, pp. 460–7) 871 gloub ich anders ſo ſchieß mich dſtral *CDF* 873 Geck *CD* 875 nun yetz] fürhin *CD* 886 wir dörffend] so dörffend wir *CDF* 887 damit] mit *CDF* 888 Bapſt *AE*

That's why it's called a Christian Church. Here on earth the Church neither eats gruel nor drinks milk: God's Word alone is her food,[146] and no lice grow on her head. No cardinal will persuade me otherwise. But that's enough said for now.

Weybel

Now you've heard it, Hans Eck. The farmers are much too learned for you. There's nothing you can do any more: people won't listen to your chatter. Canon laws are of no use here: one of them gives the lie to the other. Often in a Council, someone asks another person to put him right. The Holy Spirit doesn't do that sort of thing: he does not regret tomorrow what he does today. His power endures for ever. Christ has told us what to do; and if we now do what he has commanded, we need no human rules. It won't honour him if people keep what he didn't command, such as the teachings of the Pope. In keeping them, we honour God in vain.[147] Let us strive to follow his commands (that is, Christ's). He doesn't tell us that we should put a sinful man in his place: he himself is the Church's foundation. Paul makes this known to us: 'No other foundation can be laid'.[148] And he will reward us for our sufferings.

146 Deuteronomy 8:3: 'One does not live by bread alone, but by every word that comes from the mouth of the Lord'.

147 Based on Matthew 15:8–9: 'This people honours me with their lips, but their hearts are far from me; in vain do they worship me, teaching human precepts as doctrines'.

148 1 Corinthians 3 (*sic*): 11: 'For no one can lay any foundation other than the one that has already been laid; that foundation is Jesus Christ'.

Er iſt der grund vnd velß darzů *1. Cor. 9*
man findt allein by jm růw
Er heyßt all dürfftig zů jm kon
keiner nit kumpt on gnad daruon
Er iſt vnſer / vnd wir ſind ſin
drumb iſt er geben für vns hin
ſo wir denn hand das obreſt gůt
wir ſind gheylget durch ſin blůt
Kein läben mag man on jnn han
es ſygind frouwen oder man
Wir ſönd an jm trülich hangen
tag vnd nacht nach jm lon blangen
[Bviii[v]] Bgirig wie ein hirtz des brunnen *Pſalm. 42.*
ſo lang biß wir hend gnad gwunnen
Darumb gſell Hans das ſyg dir gſeyt
wilt gern / nun wider heim reyt
Verkünd dem Bapſt ouch diſe gſchicht
man heig dich mit dem Gotswort bricht
Gott ſyg das houpt / der vels / vnd grund
gnůg züget vſs Sant Paulus mund
Wir hend ouch anders hie ztagen
hörzů ſo kanſts jm ouch ſagen
Es trifft den Römmſchen ſtůl ouch an
jch wil yetz an Schmid Hanſelman

Weybel.
Wol an Schmid Hans Heyerle
nim ouch für dich ein Meyerle
Diſputier ouch hie vor allen
ſol man ouch zun heilgen wallen?
Die Mäſs dörfft ouch einr reformatz
doch Doctor Murner die grauw katz
Wil Mäſs han vnd gouchen bſchweeren
ſag wie ſol man dheilgen Eeren?

897 1.Cor. 8 *AE* 900 keiner nit] gar keiner *CDF* 916 bzugt *CDF* 925 ſol man ouch] ob man söll *CDF*

He is our rock and our foundation, and in him only do we find rest.[149] He commands all who are in need to come to him, and no one comes away without receiving grace. He is ours and we are his: he was given up for our sake so that we might have the greatest good. We are saved by his blood. No one, man or woman, can have life apart from him. We should abide in him faithfully, and should yearn for him day and night, as a hart pants for cooling streams,[150] until we have found grace. So, friend Hans, we're going to tell you to ride home again, if you don't mind, and say this to the Pope: that you have been taught by the Word of God that God is the head, the rock and the foundation of the Church, and that this is fully attested to by St Paul. We've got other things to talk about here today, and if you listen, you can tell the Pope about them too, because they also have to do with him and his throne. It's time for Schmid Hanselman to speak now.

Weybel

Greetings, Schmid Hans Heyerle,[151] you too should take a farmer and discuss with him before us all whether we should go on pilgrimages to saints' shrines. The Mass also needs reforming, but it's that grey cat Doctor Murner who wants to conjure up fools and their Masses.[152] Tell us, though, how should we honour the saints?

149 Cf. the discussion of eternal reward in 1 Corinthians 9:24–7.

150 Psalm 42:1: 'As a deer longs for flowing streams, so my soul longs for you, O God'.

151 This use of the (Swabian) diminutive '-le' in reference to Faber is perhaps particularly significant given the meaning of 'heien' (and its substantive form 'heier') discussed in n. 115.

152 A clever formulation, which enables Eckstein to allude in the same sentence to both of Murner's most celebrated satirical texts, the *Geuchmat* and the *Narrenbeschwörung*. More generally, this signposting of the coming discussion of the Mass is doubtless an encouragement to the reader to persevere, as well as a reminder of the special importance of this subject for the text as a whole. The impression is reinforced by the early mention of Murner, already an unpopular figure in Zurich, whose come-uppance at the hands of a farmer would be eagerly anticipated. Murner was often referred to as a cat in literature of the 1520s: a 'murner' is a tom.

Mag Sant Peter für vns bitten?
oder die sind vff roſſen gritten?
Sant Martin mit Sant Mauritzen?
hie wirt Fritz Knüchel by dir ſitzen

Hans Schmid.

Min gůter Meyer Knüchel Fritz
jch bſorg vnd bruch ich ſchon vil witz
[Ci^r] So gangs mir wie vor zyten Zürich
vnd yetz dem Ecken mit der kirch
Ich wölt vil lieber rüwig sin
ſo ich aber ein Doctor bin
Der heilgen gſchrifft vnd beyder recht
wag ichs mit einem puren knecht
Ich wölte vil lieber klagen
vnd vom gyrenrupffen ſagen
Der häſin käß ligt mir noch inn
bin yetz drum hie das ich jnn gwün
Vnd hett ich Zürich vor diſputiert
ſo hett ich jnn gen Coſtentz gfürt
Da ſeyt man mir / Her Vicari
gott geb nun war ich yetz fari
Bſchäm ich mich vor pfaffen vnd leyen
man ſagt mir yetz Heyenheyen
Das hends im Gyrenbůch gleſen
von Zürchern hab ich das wäſen
Das thůnd allein die handtwercks lüt
ſy habend vff mir nun gar nüt
Ich ſpring wie ein krott im kübel
vſſz dem krantz ſäch ich macht übel

Can St Peter pray for us, or those who rode about on horseback, St Martin and St Maurice?[153] Fritz Knüchel will sit here with you.

Hans Schmid

Fritz Knüchel, my good farmer, I'm worried that I'll need all my wits about me. That was the case with me before at Zurich,[154] and now also with Eck talking about the Church. I'd rather have a quiet life.[155] But since I'm a Doctor of holy Scripture and of both civil and canon law I can venture to dispute with a farmer. I'd much rather talk and lament about the *Gyrenrupffen*: that rabbit cheese is still in me. I've come here now to win it; if I had won it in Zurich previously, I'd have taken it back with me to Constance. There, people said 'My Lord Vicar' to me.[156] But, God save me, wherever I go now I feel shame before both priests and laity, who call me 'Heyenheyen'. They've read that in the *Gyrenrupffen*. That's the name the Zurichers call me – though it's only the artisans who do it.[157] They have no regard for me. I leap about like a toad in a pail;[158] through my laurel wreath I now see evil things

153 These are two soldier-saints: St Maurice († c.287) was a member of the Christian 'Theban Legion', and St Martin of Tours (c. 316–97) began life as a pagan army officer, who refused to fight following his conversion.

154 Almost the whole of this speech is a sustained allusion to the First Zurich Disputation and its literary aftermath.

155 As with Eck's imperiousness and Murner's waspishness, statements like these reflect an attempt on Eckstein's part to characterize his opponents individually and at least to some degree accurately. Faber does seem to have been a warm and irenic personality, who had been very reluctant to take sides in the controversies of the 1520s, in the awareness of how many friends he would alienate: see Herbert Immenkötter, 'Johannes Fabri', in *Katholische Theologen der Reformationszeit*, ed. by Erwin Iserloh, 4 vols, Katholisches Leben und Kirchenreform im Zeitalter der Glaubensspaltung, 44–7 (Münster: Aschendorff, 1984–7), I, 90–7 (pp. 91–2).

156 A reference to Faber's position as Vicar-General of the Diocese of Constance.

157 This is true in respect of the *Gyrenrupffen*, in which Zwingli is notably more polite to Faber than are his less educated supporters.

158 The *SI* mentions this as a proverbial expression (III, 876), but does not otherwise define it. It is also used, similarly obscurely, though again of Faber, in the *Gyrenrupffen* (Ki^{r}).

Wie ein kuo vſſz eim finſtren wald
loß mir noch eins / ich wil bald
hören / vnd ein anders ſagen
jch hette noch vil zklagen
Ouch ſagends ich ſyg Klüpffis ſun
min Knüchel Fritz loß mir nun
Der Klüpffe hab ein ſun ghan
der wär wie ich ein dapffer man
[Ci^{v}] Er ſtäche ein zum fenster yn
der wäre nit daheym gſin
Das hand ſy gſagt / vnd anders mee
es thůt mir in mim hertzen wee
Vnd wurd ich als ein Schneegans alt
die ſchand mir nimmermee empfalt
Die ich zů Zürich hab vff mich gladen
näms waſſer ab / ich für gen Baden

Knüchel Fritz.
Deſſelben halb ſo blyb nun hye
kein Mor der wůſch ſich wyß nye
Du bist ſunſt einr ſchwartzen natur
zürns nit ſagt dirs ſchon ein pur
Dann wöltiſt du dich wäſchen wyß
du müßtiſt bruchen bſundren flyß
Als wenig ein Mor dhut verkeert
als lützel man üch bäpſtleren weert
Das jr keerind üch von ſünden
jch gloub das man kein mög finden
Es iſt vnmüglich daruon lon *Hiere. 13.*
was einr von jugent vf hett thon
Darumb gſell hans nun bſinn dich baß
weyſt wie ich eineſt by dir was
In eim huß das heißd zum rappen
du in diner zipffel kappen
Thetteſt da desglychen mir

like a cow from the dark forest.[159] Let me say one other thing: I'll soon start listening and talking about other things, though I've still got a lot to complain about. They also say that I'm Klüppfi's son.[160] Listen to me now, my good Knüchel Franz: they say Klüppfi had a son (he was a brave man like me)[161] and put him through the window of a house that wasn't his own. They said that, and more things too. It cut me to the quick; and if I live to be as old as a snow goose, the shame which I incurred at Zurich will never leave me. So I ran off the water and went to Baden.[162]

Knüchel Fritz

Stay here now for that very reason: no Moor ever washed himself white. And, anyway, you have such a black nature[163] – don't get angry, one farmer has already said this to you – that, if you wanted to wash yourself white, you'd have to make a special effort. We don't see any of you papists turning from your sin any more than we see a Moor changing his skin.[164] I don't think you'll be able to find an example of that. It's impossible to turn from what you have been doing since your youth. So, friend Hans, think better of it. Do you know that I was with you once before, in a hostelry called the Black Horse, and that you, with your pointy hat, did the same to me?

159 An exact quotation from the *Gyrenrupffen*, Ciii^{r}. The context is that Faber has accused his opponents of claiming victory (i.e. awarding themselves a laurel wreath) prematurely, and is then accused by them of exactly the same thing.

160 'Klüppfen' or 'chlupfen' means to frighten or to take fright (especially suddenly), and the nouns 'Chlupfi' or 'Chlupfi's son' came to be used in various contexts to refer to fearful or cowardly people (see *SI* III, 683–4).

161 Faber is ironically described as 'tapffer' also in the *Gyrenrupffen* (e.g. Aiv^{r}), whereas the Zurich artisans opposing him state 'wir ſind nit klüpffis ſün' (Eiii^{r}).

162 A pun on bathing which is so obvious as to need no further elucidation.

163 One of the epithets used of Faber in the *Gyrenrupffen* is 'rappen', black horse (cf. Aii^{r}). This also may partly explain the otherwise obscure reference to the scene at the hostelry of the same name.

164 Jeremiah 13:23: 'Can Ethiopians change their skin or leopards their spots? Then also can you do good who are accustomed to do evil'.

drumm ligt nit dran gſchichts yetz *o*uch dir
Dir wirt ouch wider gemeſſen
jch hab des ryffen nit vergeſſen
[Cii^{r}] Dich wundret do ab minem grind
drumb fragteſt ob ich hexen künd
Meiſter Iörg Bock was ouch darby
der ſprach / Meinſt das er ein vnhold ſy
Der ſchůlmeister ouch darby ſaß
ſprach zů mir / lönd üch nit kümmren das.
Ich ward dozmal examiniert
du hatteſt ins Göldins huß gſtudiert
Der ſtarb dozmal als ich da was
do ſchnitteſt diner kuo walgraß
Drumb wie es mir zů Coſtenz gieng
alſo man dich ouch Zürich empfieng
Ich meint nit mee zgon für din gſicht
ſo hat vns gott yetz zämen gricht
Wir ſind beyd vſs Schwaben landen
lang zyt in Kalkutten gſtanden
Darumb Schmid Hans fach an ſchmiden
ſag an durch wän hand wir friden
Durch dheilgen oder jr fürbitt?
darby vergiſſz der faſten nit
Sag wie ſol man dheilgen eeren
doch on aller menſchen leeren?

Hans Schmid.
So thůn ichs dar hie offenbar
das all gots heilgen ſigind zwar
Fürbitter gen Gott dem Herren
drumb ſol mans ouch billich eeren
Sant Barblen / vnd ouch ſant Margret
nun ſpricht Dauid der heilig prophet

993 duch *A* 1005 wol graß *CF*

So it doesn't matter that it's now happening to you; you're being paid back. I've not forgotten the frost. At that time you wondered at my skin problem[165] and asked whether I could do witchcraft. Master Jörg Bock[166] was also there, and asked: 'Do you mean whether he's a monster?' Also the schoolmaster was there, and he said to me: 'Don't worry about it'. I was examined there. You were studying at Gulden's house, but he died when I was there; you were cutting sedge for your cow at the time. So what happened to me in Constance is how you're now being received in Zurich. I hadn't reckoned on seeing you again, but God has brought us together.[167] We're both Swabians, and have spent a long time in foreign parts.[168] So then, Hans Schmid, start smithying. Tell me, how do we achieve peace with God: through the saints or their prayers? And don't forget fasting either. Tell us, should we venerate the saints? But don't use any human teachings.

Hans Schmid
I'll show you here very clearly that all of God's saints are indeed intercessors before the Lord God. For that reason you should certainly honour St Barbara and also St Margaret.[169] David the holy prophet

165 *FWB* (VII, 434–6) states that 'grind' can refer to various kinds of skin condition, including leprosy and impetigo.

166 A commonly used nickname for Hieronymus Emser (1478–1527). It is based on his family's coat of arms, which features a mountain goat ('Steinbock'). Zwingli knew Emser while the latter was briefly a student at Basle in 1502. Indeed, he may well have witnessed the incident, involving what we would now call xenophobic abuse of a (sleeping) Swiss fellow-student, which led to Emser's precipitate and inglorious departure from Basle. Zwingli seems never to have forgiven him. See Paul Mosen, *Hieronymus Emser, der Vorkämpfer Roms gegen die Reformation* (Halle: Kaemmerer, 1890), especially pp. 12–13.

167 The specific events alluded to here are, by their nature, impossible to reconstruct. They reflect the fact, though, that, as young men, Zwingli, Faber, and Emser knew each other in Basle. See for example Leo Helbling, *Dr. Johannes Fabri, Generalvikar von Konstanz und Bischof von Wien, 1478–1541. Beiträge zu seiner Lebensgeschichte*, Reformationsgeschichtliche Studien und Texte, 67–8 (Münster: Aschendorff, 1941), especially pp. 45–6.

168 A conjecture based on *FWB*'s interpretation of 'kalekut' (VIII, 494–5).

169 It is not wholly clear why Faber should single out these two saints, save for their general popularity in the Middle Ages and their status as two of the Fourteen Holy Helpers.

[Cii^{v}] In eim bůch das heyßd der Pſalter
wir ſöllind gott vnſeren bhalter *Pſal. 149.*
In ſinen heiligen loben
nun ſind ſy yetz by Gott oben
Vnd bittend Gott on vnderlaß
ſant Martin vnd ſant Niclaß
Sant Veltin mit ſant Wendelin
ſant Anthoni bhütet dſchwyn
Wenn man Gott in heilgen eert
ſo wirt denn allem übel gweert
Das vns von Gott müßd zhanden gon
lůg hab ich nit gnůg dar gthon?

Knüchel Fritz.
Gſell Hans ich wond du wäriſt gleert
jch hab dins glychen nie ghört
Heſt du ſo vil pfründen bſeſſen
vnd heſt den pſalter noch nit fräſſen
Ich wond du kündist Hebreiſch
ſo kanſt du nun Heyenheyiſch
Du heſt mit dem ſpruch nüt probiert
er ist nit recht transferiert
Drumb iſts nit wie du heſt gſeyt
lobend Gott in ſiner herlichheyt
Das bringt Bekodſcho ein hebreiſch wort
lobend gott in ſinem heilgen ort.
Vnd wenn es ſchon (wie du ſagst) hieß
hör ob man ſy anrüffen müß
Sol man Gott in ſin heilgen eeren?
jch wil mich mit dim ſpruch weeren
[Ciii^{r}] Wenn man nun dheilgen eert in Gott
wie helffends denn der armen rott?
So blybt doch Gott allein die eer
all Gots heilgen bgärend nit mer
Vnd all heilgen im pſalter ſchryen
man ſölle Gott all eer verlihen *Pſal. 113.*
Darumm Hans Schmid nun heitz baß yn

says in a book called the psalter that we should praise God, our preserver, in his holy ones.[170] Now St Martin, St Nicholas, St Valentine, and St Wendelin are on high, with God, and are praying to him ceaselessly.[171] And St Antony is looking after the pigs.[172] If you honour God in his saints, you will be protected from all the ills that might come to us from God. See, haven't I already said enough?

Knüchel Fritz

Friend Hans, I thought you were a learned man! I've never heard anyone like you before. Have you got so many benefices without having devoured your psalter? I thought you could speak Hebrew – but in fact you can only speak Heyenheyish.[173] You haven't proved anything by what you've said. The words aren't properly translated. They don't mean, as you say, 'praise God in his holiness'. The Hebrew word 'bekodscho'[174] means 'praise God in his holy place'. And even if it did mean what you said it did, hear me discuss whether we have to pray to the saints. Should we honour God in his saints? I want to argue against those words of yours. For if you honour the saints in God, how do they then help the common people? The honour remains God's alone, and that is all that any of his saints want. And, in the psalter, all the saints cry out that we should give God all the honour.[175] So you'd better heat up your forge a bit better next time, Hans Schmid,

170 Psalm 150:1: 'Praise God in his sanctuary, praise him in his mighty firmament'.

171 Presumably these four saints are mentioned above all because of their popularity in the Middle Ages. St Wendelin (of Trier) may have had a further resonance for an agricultural audience, being the patron saint of shepherds.

172 St Antony of the Desert (251–356), known (for obscure reasons) to be the patron saint of pigs.

173 This and similar comments seem particularly ungenerous when we consider that Faber emerged at the First Zurich Disputation as a learned yet humble Humanist scholar, even in Hegenwald's highly partisan account.

174 A perfectly competent transliteration. One also finds 'b'kadscho', 'beqodhsho', 'b'qädshô', etc.

175 One assumes that Psalm 115:1 is meant: 'Not to us, Lord, not to us, but to your name give glory, for sake of your steadfast love and your faithfulness'.

wenn der ſpruch wil wider dich ſin
vnd bring ein andren / der ist hin

Hans Schmid.
Nun hett es doch ſo lang gewärt
ſolt man ſy han vergeben geert
Das wär doch wol ein groſſe plag
hör wyter zů was Christus ſag
Was jr dem minsten hie hand thon *Matth. 25.*
vſs den minen / das wil ich han
Als obs mir ſelbs wäre bſchehen
alſo wirt Chriſtus ſelbs yehen
Darumb ſol man inen dienen
dann Gott hats verbotten nienen
Sy thůnd doch zeichen das mans ſicht
das weyß ich gwüſs vnd bin ſy bricht
Zů ſant Batten was ein Cappon
wenn eins wolt vmb den altar gon
So hocket er vor jm nider
ließ ſich opfren / floch denn wider
Martin wirt geert fürs kaltwee
Niclaus bhüt dſchifflüt vff dem See
Sant Barbel mag vns erwerben
[Ciii^{v}] das wir nit on gotz lychnam ſterben
Noch ſind vil nothelffer on zal
drumb hat ein yeder pur die wal
Das er anrüff welchen er wil
gſell Fritz der präſten ſind ouch vil
Die vns zůſtond hie vff erden
welcher bald wil ledig werden
Die heilgen mag er rüffen an
ſy helffend mengem biderman
Das ſyg nun gnůg von heylgen gſeyt
ſy nemmend was man zůhin treyt
Wachs / öl / werck / vnd ſüwhammen
vil krucken bringend ouch die lamen
Das hands als von Gott erbätten

because this passage argues against you. Think of another one. We've dealt with that one.

Hans Schmid

It's been going on for so long now – have we been honouring them in vain? That really would be a great pity. Listen to more of what Christ says: 'What you have done on earth for the least of my people I will count as if you had done it for me'.[176] That is what Christ himself will say. It's for this reason that we should serve them; God has certainly not forbidden anyone to do that.[177] But they perform signs and wonders so as to be seen. I know for certain, and have been told, that there was a capon at St Batten,[178] who used to crouch before a priest as he was approaching the altar, offering itself to be sacrificed. Then it flew away again. St Martin is honoured for curing cold-sickness, St Nicholas protects sailors at sea, St Barbara sees to it that we don't die without the body of Christ.[179] And there are countless other helpers in emergency. So any farmer can choose whom he wants to appeal to. Friend Fritz, there are so many illnesses which befall us here on earth that anyone who wants to be free from them can call on the saints. They come to the aid of many an honest man. We've said enough about saints now. They take whatever we give to them, wax, oil, tow, hams, the crutches that lame people bring. They've asked God for all of these things,

176 Matthew 25:40: 'Truly I tell you, just as you did it to the least of these who are members of my family, you did it to me'.

177 This approach is fundamentally and revealingly different from that of Zwingli, who allowed only those practices that were specifically permitted in Scripture.

178 A popular designation for the 'Beatushöhlen' ('caves of St Beatus'), on Lake Thun near Interlaken, a regular destination for medieval pilgrims.

179 St Martin was known for cutting his cloak in half and sharing it with a freezing beggar, and St Nicholas (of Myra) for saving doomed sailors off the coast of Lycia. St Barbara's act of mercy derives from her function as a Holy Helper.

ſy mögend vns ouch wol vertretten
Vnd bitten Gott für unſre ſünd
Mariam mit jrem kind.

Knüchel Fritz.
Schmid Hans nun loß mir ouch yetz zů
du haſt nun gſeyt von vil vnrůw
Die all gotz heilgen müßtind han
weltind ſy helffen yederman
Sinn by dir ſelb wenn ich yetz käm
das mir ein wolff ein ſuw näm
Ein andrer pur käm ouch gloffen
dem wär die ſin ſuſt erſoffen
Dem dritten wär ſin ſuw verfallen
die vierd näm der apt von ſant Gallen
Von eim puren für den fal
[Civr] die fünfft verdurbe eim im ſtal
Die ſechßten hettind bären fräſſen
du magſt hie nun wol ermeſſen
Was vnrůw müßt Antoni han
vnd überlouff von yederman
Was hett er für ewigs läben?
müßt er jnen allen rechnung geben
Solt er im himmel ſchwynhirt ſin?
ich wölt als lieb in dhell hinyn
Wenn ich nun Sant Anthoni wär
ee wölt ich das man dpuren bſchär
Das ich jr ſchwynhirt ſölte ſin
ich hatt das vorig jar ein ſchwyn
Daruon hatt ich ein hammen verheyſſen
das fraſſend dwölff vnd zwo geyſſen
Ich ſinnet da von ſtundan
nun biſtu doch ein thorecht man
Die heilgen hand anders zſchaffen
gibſt hammen vß vnd freſſends pfaffen
Sind wir nit arbeytſälig lüt
dheylgen goumend der ſchwynen nüt

so are well able to represent us before him and ask him, Mary and her child to forgive us our sins.

Knüchel Fritz
Schmid Hans, listen to me now. You've talked about a lot of trouble that all of God's saints would have to go to if they were to help every-one. But think a minute: if it happened to me that a wolf stole one of my sows, another farmer came running up and said that his had been drowned, a third said that his sow had got lost, a fourth that his had been taken by the Abbot of St. Gallen for the sake of its offal, a fifth that his had died in her stall, and a sixth that his had been eaten by bears – think of all the disturbance and overloading that St Antony would then suffer from everyone! What sort of eternal life would he be having? If he had to take account of all of these, would he want to be a swineherd in heaven? If I was St Antony, I'd just as soon go to hell as be given to these farmers as their swineherd. Last year I had a pig, from which I'd promised the priests a ham, eaten by wolves (along with two goats). And I thought to myself then: 'You're a foolish man if you give the priests a ham and they eat it! The saints have got other things to do. Aren't we poor, sad people? The saints won't look after the pigs.

Sy hettind tag vnd nacht zweren
ſöltinds vnſer ſüw erneren
Haſt ſuſt kein andren bhüter ghan?
nun zünd dich Santitöni an
Ich wil fürbaß Gott vertrüwen
mich fiengend erſt an dhammen rüwen
Die ich hatt vßgeben lange zyt
vnd dacht / du hammen jeger bit
Kein hammen ſolt mir me abiagen
[Civ^{v}] ich geb dir dfülle im ſüwmagen
Nun pack dich mit lären henden
der tüfel müß dnollhart ſchenden
Sy hand mir abgnon allerley
hatt ich nit gelt / nun gib ein ey
Wir wend gott für dich bitten
wär bättet für ſy wett der ritten
Nun das ich dir yetz antwurt geb
vnd dinem anzug widerſtreb
Da Chriſtus redt vom letſten zyt
vnd ſpricht: Welcher eim armen gyt
dem minſten etwas in mym namen
Chriſtus meint hie krumm vnd lamen
Das findt ſich an Chriſti worten
er meint dheilgen vor den porten
Die ſöllind wir trencken vnd ſpyſen
das wil ich mit dem text bwyſen *Matth. 25.*
Im himmel dheylgen ouch nit dürſt
ſy eſſend nit me fleyſch vnd würſt
Chriſtus empfilcht vns die armen
der ſöllend wir vns erbarmen
Diewyl wir vff erden läbind
das wir jnen almůſen gebind
Darumb well er vns geben lon
als hettinds wir jm ſelb thon
Din ſpruch wyßt vns vff die armen
der heyligen darfſt dich nit erbarmen
Die in dem himmel oben ſind

They'd have to be on watch day and night if they were going to tend to our sows. Didn't you have any other protector? Get rid of St Antony: from now on I'm going to trust in God'. Then I began to regret giving away the hams that I'd been donating for a long time, and thought: 'Just you hold back, you ham hunter! You're not going to get any more hams off me: I'll give you plenty of pig's stomachs instead. Now go away empty-handed!'. May the devil take all fools! They've taken everything from me: if I didn't have any money, they'd say: 'Give us an egg. We'll pray God for you'. A plague on anyone who prays for them! Let me now answer you and oppose your argument. When Christ speaks of the last times and says: 'He who gives to a poor man, to the lowest of the low, in my name', he means to those who are deformed and lame. These are Christ's words: he means the saints at the gates. They are the people we should give food and drink to, as I will prove from the text. In heaven, the saints aren't thirsty, and they no longer eat meat or sausage; Christ is commending the poor to us. It is they we should have mercy on while we live on earth, by giving them alms. If we do, God will reward us as if we had done it to him. The Scripture directs us towards the poor. You don't need to have mercy on the saints up in heaven:

es iſt das himmelſch hof gſind
Sy eſſend nit me lyplich brot
[Cv[r]] das man jnn geb das thůt nit not
Du haſt ouch hie noch nüt probiert
ein andren ſpruch haſt ouch yngfürt
Den bringſtu nun vſſz dinem grind
vnd ſprichſt das man nyenan find
Das heylgen eer ſyg verbotten
alſo ſagend gottloß rotten
Die vil hand vff der heylgen eer
nit achtend gotz vnd ſiner leer
Iſt es nit gnůg am erſten bott
du ſolt nun haben ein Gott
Söllend wir Gott haben allein
ſo hat kein heylg mit jm gmein
Der tüfel hat den worten gloubt *Matth. 4.*
vnd nit wie du darwider toupt
Sprichſtu nun: Das iſt min allein
ſo hab ich nit mit dir gmeyn
Das wort (allein) ſchlüßt vil vß
da machſtu all heylgen druß
Du můſt hie in dienen lang
ee es obſich in himmel gang
Min meynung haſt nun wol verſtanden
wilt gern ſo nimm ein anders zhanden

Hans Schmid.
Wolan ich hab mich lang gſpart
ich wil noch eineſt vff die fart
Ein veſten ſpruch zeyg ich noch dir
gelt wo du jnn verwerffeſt mir
Der ſpruch zeygt vns heyter an
[Cv[v]] das Iopp der heilig man
Iſt ouch für ein heylgen gwiſen
wie ich in ſinem bůch liſen
Do Iopp in aller kranckheyt was
ſinr fründen einer Eliphas *Iopp. 5.*

they're the heavenly host, who don't eat actual bread any more. There's no need to give them anything, and you haven't proved otherwise. You've brought up another saying, off the top of your head, and told us that it's nowhere forbidden to honour the saints. This is what the godless hordes say who are very keen on honouring the saints but have no regard for God or his teachings. Isn't the First Commandment enough: 'Thou shalt have no other God but me'? Should we indeed only have God? No saint has anything in common with him. The devil believed these words,[180] and didn't rage against them as you do. If you now say: 'That's mine alone, I have nothing in common with you', that word (alone) excludes many things – you exclude the saints, whom you must serve here below, before you and they go up to heaven. Have you properly understood my argument now? If you like, you can take up another one.

Hans Schmid

Very well: I've held myself in for long enough, and will now go back into battle. I'll show you another solid teaching: will you then throw it back in my face? These words show clearly that Job, a holy man, was told about a saint, as I read in his book. When Job was very ill, one of his friends, Eliphaz,

180 Matthew 4:10: 'Worship the Lord your God, and serve only him'.

Hieß jnn zů eim heilgen keren
darumb ſöllend wirs ouch eren
Man mag an dem ſpruch wol ſehen
wenn den alten iſt etwas gſchehen
So hand ſy ſich zun heilgen kert
die lieben heilgen ouch geert
Das zügt vns Iopp der heilig man
laß ſehen mag ich da by bſtan
wils helffen ich hab gnůg thon

Knüchel Fritz.
Diſer ſpruch iſt gůt Ioppiſch
du verſtaaſt jnn gantz Rodoppiſch
Zů welchem ſolt ſich Iopp keren?
man wußt noch nüt von heilgen eren
Dheilgen hattend noch nit glitten
wie kundtend ſy denn für jnn bitten?
Ich mein dheilgen im kalender
lůg wie ſich din ſpruch verender
Sprichſtu / es ſind ſuſt heilgen gſin
iſt waar / ich nit darwider bin
Abraham was vor dem Ioppen lang
der Iopp nit zů dem Abraham trang
Drumb ſind die Iuden witzig gwäſen
hand nit wie wir / dheilgen vßgläſen
[Cvi^{r}] Vnd hand vil heilger vätter ghan
zeig mir ein den ſy hand grüfft an?
Nun ſind ſy wie wir ſünder gſin
gloffen zů Gott ſuſt nienan hin
Der halff jn wie ein vatter ſin kinden
hör wie wir im propheten finden
Du vatter / erlöſer / vnd Herr *Eſa. 63.*
Abraham weyßt von vns nüt mer
Iſrael hat vnſer vergeſſen
da mag nun yederman ermeſſen

1210 ſich] *om. CDF*

advised him to turn to a saint.[181] So we too should honour saints. You can see plainly from these words that, when something happened to the old heroes of the faith, they turned to the saints and honoured them. Job, that saint, also proves this. Tell me, do I have to insist on this? Will it help? I've done enough.

Knüchel Fritz

This passage is very Job-like, though you're actually speaking Rodoppisch![182] What saint was Job supposed to be appealing to? In his day they didn't yet know anything about honouring saints. The saints hadn't yet lived and suffered, so how could they pray for him? I mean the saints in our church calendar. See how different your words would seem to be if you were saying: 'But there were other saints too'. That's true; I don't disagree with that. But Abraham was around long before Job, and Job didn't call on him. The Jews were clever, and didn't single out the saints as we do. They had lots of holy fathers, but show me one they prayed to! No, just like us sinners they ran to God and to no one else. He helped them as a father helps his children. Hear what we find in the prophet:[183] 'You, Father, Saviour and Lord, Abraham doesn't know anything about us, and Israel has forgotten us'. Anyone can deduce from these words that,

181 Job 5:1: 'Call now; is there anyone who will answer you? To which of the holy ones will you turn?'

182 One assumes this term, also used in the *Gyrenrupffen* (Ci^{v}), refers to the language of Rhodes. If so, it is likely to have connoted (misplaced?) learning, riches, and indeed arrogance (the *Gyrenrupffen* reference is to 'dine [Faber's] hochruemende wort in Rhodopo').

183 Isaiah 63:16: 'For you are our father, though Abraham does not know us and Israel does not acknowledge us; you, O Lord, are our father; our Redeemer from of old is your name'.

Wußt Abraham von Iuden nüt
ſo ſind wir Chriſten torecht lüt
Das wir vns wend an dheilgen lon
Chriſtus wil vns doch ſelb byſton
Durch jnn ſo hand wir ewigs leben
er ist vns doch für eygen geben
Die kundtſchafft kumpt von oben ab
der heylig geyſt des zügnuß gab
Das iſt min aller liebſter ſun *Matt. 17.*
der mir wol gfalt / den hörend nun
Dſäligkeit in keim andren iſt *Act. 4.*
denn allein jm namen Ieſu Chriſt *Hebre. 4*
Zů jm ſönd wir in hoffnung gon *Pſalm. 90.*
in trübſal wil er by vns ſton
Zwüſchend gott vnd vns kein mitler iſt *1. Tim. 2.*
denn Gott vnd menſch Ieſus Chriſt *Ioann. 8.*
Er iſt das liecht der gantzen welt *1. Pet. 1.*
vergibt vns dſünd nun on gelt *Rom. 5.*
Frid hand wir allein durch jn
er nimpt all vnſer präſten hin *Eſaie. 53.*
[Cvi^{v}*]* vnd gibt vns ſin gerechtigkeyt *Epheſ. 2.*
hat vns ouch wäg in himmel preyt *Ioann. 14.*
Wir müſſend durch jnn ynhin gon *Ioann. 10.*
on jnn vor Gott wirt niemant bſton *Epheſ. 2.*
Er ſitzt zů des vatters rechten hand

1263 Epheſ. 22. *AE*

if Abraham knew nothing about the Jews, then we Christians are foolish people to want to rely on the saints. Christ himself wants to help us, and through him we have eternal life.[184] He has given himself up into slavery for us; these tidings come down from on high, and the Holy Spirit bears witness to them: 'This is my beloved Son, with whom I am well pleased'.[185] Listen to what he says: 'Blessedness can be found nowhere but in the name of Jesus Christ'.[186] We should go to him in hope.[187] He will help us in trouble.[188] There is no mediator between God and us save the God and man Jesus Christ.[189] He is the light of the whole world,[190] and forgives us our sins without charge.[191] We have peace through him alone.[192] He takes our sins upon himself[193] and gives us his righteousness,[194] and has made us paths leading to heaven.[195] We have to go there through him,[196] and without him no one will be able to stand before God.[197] He is seated at the right hand

184 We would regard the remainder of this speech as Eckstein's clearest and most eloquent statement of his christocentric soteriology.

185 Matthew 17:5: 'This is my Son, the Beloved; with him I am well pleased'.

186 Acts 4:12: 'There is salvation in no one else, for there is no other name under heaven given among mortals by which we must be saved'.

187 Hebrews 4:16: 'Let us therefore approach the throne of grace with boldness, so that we may receive mercy and find grace to help in time of need'.

188 Psalm 91:15: 'When they call on me, I will answer them; I will be with them in trouble'.

189 1 Timothy 2:5: 'For there is one God; there is also one mediator between God and man, Christ Jesus, himself human, who gave himself a ransom for all'.

190 John 8:12: 'I am the light of the world'.

191 1 Peter 1:18–19: 'You know that you were ransomed from the futile ways inherited from your ancestors, not with perishable things like silver or gold, but with the precious blood of Christ'.

192 Romans 5:1–2: 'Therefore, since we are justified by faith, we have peace with God through our Lord Jesus Christ, through whom we have obtained access to this grace in which we stand'.

193 Isaiah 53:4 (see n. 30 above).

194 This reads like an interpretation, rather than a quotation, of the Evangelical *locus classicus* Ephesians 2:8–9.

195 John 14:6: 'I am the way, and the truth, and the life. No one comes to the Father except through me'.

196 John 10:9: 'I am the gate. Whoever enters by me will be saved'.

197 Probably an allusion to Ephesians 2 (*sic*): 12's reference to those who were 'without hope and without God'.

vnser fürbitter vnd heyland *Rom. 8.*
Gegem vatter er vns vertritt
loß zů Hans Schmid wär für vns bitt *Eſaie. 45.*
Sin eer gibt er keim andren nit *Eſaie. 42.*

Weybel
Hans Heyer du haſt nun gnůg ghört
wie Knüchel Fritz ſich gen dir wert
Völlig mit gſchrifft ſo manigfalt
daruf ich me denn vff dins halt
Kuntſchafft iſt nun gnůg dar thon
das wir vns ſöllend an Gott lon
Dheilgen ſind vmb Gotzwillen gſtorben
von wem hand ſy gnad erworben?
Allein von Gott durch Chriſtum Ieſum
vnd hand ſich laſſen drumb kröſen
Enthoupten vnd ouch ſchinden
was mag man gröſſers von inn finden?
durch glouben hands dwelt überwunden *Hebre. 11.*
hab ich zun Hebreern funden
Nun ſinds nach einander gſtorben
vnd keinr von andren gnad erworben
Heylgen eren kumpt nun von gyt
denn es offenlich am tag lyt
Wo man am meiſten zů iſt gloffen
[Cvii^r] hand pfaffen nun deſtme gſoffen
In ſecken hands puren zůtragen
das fullt den pfaffen jren kragen
Wo man am meiſten zů hin bringt
was thůt man denn man plert vnn ſingt?
Das fröuwt bißſicher dheilgen wol
das pfaff vnd köchin ſygind vol
Was möcht nun gůts daruß entſton
denn vnnütz pfarrer vnd Caplon
Deren ſind me denn wyſſer hund
hett es gwäret biß vff die ſtund
So hettinds dwelt gar anſich zogen

of the Father, our intercessor and Saviour. He represents us before the Father.[198] Hear, Hans Schmid, who is really praying for us.[199] He will not give his honour to any other.[200]

Weybel

Hans Heyer, you've heard enough now of how Knüchel Fritz defends himself against you – fully, and with all manner of Scriptures. For that reason I prefer his arguments to yours. He's told us clearly enough that we should trust in God. The saints died for God's sake – so where did they receive grace from? Solely from God, through Christ Jesus. And that is why they let themselves be crushed, beheaded, and skinned. What greater things could be said about them? They overcame the world by faith, as I have read in Hebrews.[201] But they died one after another, without any of them receiving grace from one of the others. The veneration of saints comes only from greed. For it's as clear as day that priests have drunk all the more in places that people go on pilgrimage to. Farmers have brought them sacks full of cash, and they have stuffed their faces on the proceeds. In the places where the most money is brought in, what do they do apart from shout and sing? You can be sure that the saints really appreciate the priests and their cooks filling their stomachs like this. What good can come of it all, apart from useless priests and chaplains? There are more of them about than there are white dogs. If it had all carried on until now, they would have taken in the whole world.

198 Romans 8:26–7: 'Likewise the Spirit helps us in our weakness; for we do not know how to pray as we ought, but that very spirit intercedes with sighs too deep for words'.

199 Various verses in Isaiah 45 support the paragraph's final, rather than penultimate sentence, e.g. 5–6, 14–21.

200 Isaiah 42:8 (see above, n. 127).

201 Hebrews 11:33: '[...] who through faith conquered kingdoms'.

alſo hand die gotz dieb glogen
Pfaff / münch / Nunn / vnd Cartüſer
freſſen der armen witwen hüſer
Vnd thetinds noch hütt by tag gern
weyſt wie gieng es eineſt zBern?
Was hat die ſelben münch verfürt?
ſy hattend ouch vff gyt gſtudiert
Woltend vnſer frowen machen
drumb bſengt mans wie dſchwyn bachen
Das was nun ouch jr rechter ſold
ſy dachtend / man iſt vns nit hold
Wir mögend alſo nit wol bſton
ſönd wir von huß zhuß gon
Wir wend dwelt darzů bringen
das ſy vns lond im Chor ſingen
Vnd treyt vns wyb vnd man zů
denn ſo hand wir gůte růw
Das gſchach nit vmb Märgen willen
[Cvii^{v}] ſy woltend ire büch füllen
Ein groſſes zeichen do zmal gſchach
deßglychen ich nie ſach
Ein ſchnider was Franciſcus worden
das iſt nie ghört im predger orden
Groß zeichen kummend pfaffen wol
es fült inn kiſt vnd kaſten vol
Noch wöllend dpuren nit witzig werden
man findt den meerenteyl vff erden
Die ſprungind noch den alten reyen
wie vil findt man pfaffen vnd leyen
Wol an / gott bkennt die ſinen wol
der tüfel hat ein wytes hol
Daryn findt man ein wyten ſtäg *Hiere. 21.*
jn himmel iſt ein enger wäg *Matth. 7.*
Ein yeder gang welchen er well
gott bhüt vns all vor der hell

1311 vns ſunſt nit *CDF*

This is the way the thieves of God (priests, monks, nuns, and Carthusians) have lied to people. They have devoured the houses of poor widows,[202] and would be perfectly happy still to be doing it today. Do you know what happened once in Berne?[203] What led the monks astray there? They too had studied the art of greed. They wanted to make an image of Our Lady, and so they blanched her like pigs' cheeks. That was what they earned their money with. They thought: 'People don't like us, so we can't keep going very well. But if we went from house to house we would persuade people to give us enough to let us sing in the choir; and men and women would give enough for us to have our ease. So all this didn't happen for Our Lady's sake; they just wanted to fill their stomachs. A real miracle happened then, the like of which I've never seen before: a tailor had become St Francis, something unheard of amongst the Dominicans.[204] Big miracles like this do the priests a lot of good – they fill their chests and coffers. But the farmers don't want to get wise yet; most of them here on earth are still dancing to the old tune. How many people you find doing this, both priests and laity! That's fine, though: God knows his own very well, and the devil has a very wide cave with a broad path leading into it.[205] A narrow path leads to heaven;[206] and everyone can choose to go down whichever one he wants. May God protect us all from hell!

202 An unreferenced allusion to Matthew 23:14.

203 A reference to the notorious Jetzer affair of 1506–7, in which the tailor Johann Jetzer claimed to experience visions of the Blessed Virgin whilst staying in the Dominican house in Berne. This caused a brief but intense sensation, until Jetzer was caught (in costume) trying to stage a Marian apparition, and hence exposed as a fraud. See Gordon, pp. 32–3. One of Jetzer's most outspoken critics was, interestingly, Murner, who published three pamphlets on the scandal.

204 At the height of his fame, in April 1507, Jetzer appeared to receive the stigmata on his hands, feet, and side.

205 Can only be a reference to Jeremiah 22 (*sic*): 13–14: 'Woe to him who builds his house by unrighteousness, and his upper rooms by injustice; who makes his neighbours work for nothing, and does not give them their wages; who says, "I will build myself a spacious house with large upper rooms"'.

206 Matthew 7:14: 'For the gate is narrow and the road is hard that leads to life'.

Hab yetz für gůt min Doctor Schmid
vnd far recht wider heim in frid
Der häſin käß iſt dir noch zſchwär
denn du biſt götlicher gſchrifft lär
Dir wirt yetz zmal von vns kein krantz
gang ſpring mit dem bapſt den Moriſcken tantz
Bſchirmend wol den ablaß kaſten
doch ſag vns vor von der römſchen faſten

Hans Schmid
Ich denck wenn ich ſchon vil ſag
das ich kleins lob von üch trag
Ir wellend nüt vffs bapſts recht han
[Cviii^{r}] ſuſt findt man nit / weißd yederman
Das man ſöll faſten viertzig tag
drumb gilts glych ob ich ſchon nüt ſag

Weybel.
Was haſt du dich denn vsthon
drumb far on häſin käß daruon
Dann häſin käß lond ſich nit eſſen
einer ſyg denn daby gſeſſen
Do Chriſtus hab die faſten botten
es wolt dir Zürich ouch nit hotten
Weiſt noch vff dem Radthuß?
du lieſſeſt wol ein klein vs
Meintiſt vaſt du wöltiſts zügen
nun hieß dich Zuingle nit lügen
Sunder das ſin antwurt was
herr Vicari thůnd jr das
Ein häſin käß wil ich üch ſchenken
jch wil min läbtag dran dencken
So übel gfiel dir doch der käß
jch gloub er wär dir gſaltzen zräß
Das Vicari hütli zugeſt ab

1341 gang] *om. CDF*

Be done with it now, Doctor Schmid, and go back home in peace. That rabbit cheese is still too heavy for you, because you're empty of God's Word. You won't be getting any laurel wreath from us: go and do your Morris dance with the Pope. Guard the indulgence chest well. But tell us something about Romish fasting.

Hans Schmid
I think that, even if I now tell you many things, I'll not get much from you in the way of praise. You're not interested in the Pope's law, and, as everyone knows, you won't find anywhere else the idea that you have to fast for 40 days. But it still applies, whether I say so or not.

Weybel
What have you decided to do, then? Go home without your rabbit cheese, because you can't eat rabbit cheese unless someone else is at table with you. At Zurich too they didn't accept you saying that Christ had commanded fasting. Can you remember still, at the Rathaus? You said something, and wanted to give evidence, when Zwingli told you not to lie. He said: 'My Lord Vicar, if you do that, I will give you a rabbit cheese'. I'll remember that for the rest of my days. You disliked the cheese so much that I reckon it must have been too highly salted for you. As soon as he gave you the present, you took off your vicar's hat.

als bald er dir die ſchencke gab
Er ſagt nit das man nit faſten ſöll
ein yeder faſte wie er wöll
So veer der lyb nun nüchter ſy
ein rein gmüt ſtadt ouch wol daby
On das / faſtend wir vergeben
wie man faſten ſöll / leert Chriſtus eben
in der Bibel allenthalben
[Cviii[v]] heißd er vns die höupter ſalben
Wäſchen das antlitz vnd den bart
vnd redt nach Paleſtiner art
Das iſt wir ſöllind frölich erſchynen
nit vorn menſchen wie glychßner hünen
Das faſten ſol heimlich zů gon *Matth. 7.*
vnd gott allein nun wüſs daruon
Bunden iſts nit an zyt vnd tag
täglich ein menſch wol faſten mag
Gott hets nit für ein bott glon
das wir thügind das er hat thon
Er iſt *.xl.* tag in der wüſte gſeſſen *Matt. 4.*
vnſer keinr blybt ſo lang vngeſſen
Chriſtus hets thon nun eineſt zwar
ſo gbüts der Bapſt vns alle jar
Ma*n* můß jm eyer vnd ancken bzalen
er frißd dhanen / vnd laßt vns dſchalen
Verbüt vns das Gott nit verbüt
alſo betrügt er biderb lüt
äſſe einer fleiſch in der faſten
er müßt gelt gen in Gytkaſten
Die ſünd man jm nit abnäm
wo einer nit mit gelt käm
Den Eebruch den Gott ſelbs verbüt
des ſelben achtet niemandts nüt
Das iſt doch vaſt ein groſſe ſünd

1388 lx. *AE*   1392 Mam *A*

He didn't say that one shouldn't fast, but that everyone should fast as he chooses; and that if our body hasn't eaten, then our spirit too will be pure.[207] Otherwise, we shall fast in vain. Christ also teaches us how we should fast: throughout the Bible he tells us to anoint our heads and wash our faces and beards. He is speaking in a Jewish way: he means that we should appear cheerful before people and not wail as hypocrites do. Fasting should be done in secret, so that only God knows about it.[208] It isn't tied to particular days or times: indeed, you can fast daily. God hasn't given a command to the effect that we should do what he did: he stayed for 40 days in the wilderness,[209] but none of us can go for that long without eating. Christ did this once and for all, but the Pope now tells us we should do it every year.[210] We have to pay him with eggs and butter: he eats the chickens and leaves us with the carcasses. If he forbids us to do something that God doesn't forbid, he deceives decent people. Anyone who eats meat during Lent has to make a contribution to the Greed Box; your sins won't be absolved unless you bring along some money. Nobody bothers about adultery, something that God does forbid. As I see it, that's a very great sin –

207 A phrase that closely echoes Zwingli's views on fasting, and at the same time a good example of Eckstein's own insistence on the duality of body and soul.

208 Matthew 6 (*sic*), 16–18: 'And whenever you fast, do not look dismal, like the hypocrites, for they disfigure their faces so as to show others that they are fasting. Truly I tell you, they have received their reward. But when you fast, put oil on your head and wash your face, so that your fasting may not be seen by others but by your Father who is in secret; and your Father who sees in secret will reward you'.

209 Matthew 4:2: 'He fasted for forty days and forty nights, and afterwards he was famished'.

210 This sentence skilfully implies a parallel with contemporary debates on the Eucharist, with the once-and-for-all death of Christ being set against Catholic notions of his sacrifice being repeated at every Mass. As such it also prepares the reader for the coming debate between Murner and Cleywi Fenchmul (from p. 155 onwards).

wie ich nun allenthalben find
Der achtet weder pfaff noch ley
äß einer in den faſten ein ey
Der můß von ſtund an ſin im ban
[Di^{r}] vnd ſo einr näm eim biderman
Sin wyb / vnd bräch mit jr die Ee
man vergäbe jmm es vil ee
Denn ſo er fleiſch vnd eyer ißd
ob er ſchon nüt drum wüßd
Wenn Fritag oder Sampßtag ſy
nun gib gelt har vnd biß denn fry
Spricht der pfaff / vnd laßt jnn gon
hette er nun vil mee thon
So hett er ouch mee müſſen geben
es iſt den pfaffen gůt läben
Ie gröſſer thaten einer hett thon
ye me er gibt den pfaffen zlon
Dauon gſagt iſt yetzund gnůg
nun wirt reden Amma krůg

Amma Krůg.
Murren Thomma vſs der Gouchmatten
Fritz Landfarer münch in der pfaffen platten
wöllend ir dſach miteinander han
Cleuwe Fenchmul wil mit üch dran
Doch zween an ein iſt nit ſitt hye
jch hab es vormals gſehen nye
Drumb nemm ein yeder ein puren an
hie iſt ouch Ioß Hechelzan
Der wil mit Fritzen diſputieren
vnd gilt ſunſt nüt ynfüren
Denn das die götlich gſchrifft innhalt
des bapſts gſatz gibt nit warm noch kalt
Vnd bringend ſunſt nüt überal
[Di^{v}] wie ſtincktz Decret vnds Decretal
Vch hilfft ouch nit kein Sanction

but no one, priest or layman, bothers about it. If you were to eat an egg during Lent – well, you'd be banned straightaway; but if you took an honest man's wife from him and committed adultery with her, that would of course be much easier to forgive. Because if you eat meat and eggs on Friday and Saturday, even without knowing that you're not supposed to do it, you've got to give money to be let off your sin, or so the priest says. Only then will he remit your sins. And if the person had done more things wrong, he would have had to pay more. Priests have a good life: the more sins you commit, the more money you've got to pay them. But that's enough of that now. It's time for Amma Krůg to speak.

Amma Krůg

Murren Thoma[211] from off the *Geuchmat* and Fritz Landfarer, the monk with his priestly pate, if you want to make common cause, then Cleywi Fenchmul will debate with you. But it's not our way to have two against one, I've never seen that before. So you should each take on one farmer. Joß Hechelzan is here too: he's going to dispute with Fritz; and no one's allowed to bring in anything that's not in the holy Scriptures. The Pope's laws blow neither hot nor cold, and indeed they don't achieve anything at all (things like the stinking decree and decretal, I mean). No sanction will get us anywhere either:

211 Another pun on Murner's name: 'murren' means 'to grumble'.

mit gotzwort můß *es* allein zů gon
Wöllend jr das thůn / ſo ſprechend ja
hie ſitzt nun Cleüwe Fenchmul da

Murner.
Wo iſt nun me des glychen gſchehen
pur heſt du mine gens nit gſehen
Sag warumb bäpſtlichs recht nit gilt
wenn nun ein pur dem anderen ſtilt
mit gotswort mag man jnn nit tödten
warumb heiſt du es lügin löten?
Man mag on bäpſtlich recht nit ſin
als wenig ich on dkutten bin
wo findeſt im Euangeli grad
ein mörder ghöre vff das rad?
Ich mein ouch ander ſtraffen
die man ſtraft mit Henckers waffen
Man möcht doch wol on all Gotswort
recht läben an eim yeden ort

Amma Krůg.
Thomma Thomma du můſt tantzen
bind dkutten zämen / hencks an dlantzen
wie du vor mal me haſt thon
wie wilt mit dim Franciſcus bſton?
Nun hat es ouch ein ſunder bott
vom bapſt nit gheiſſen / noch von Gott
Wenn einer in ein orden kumm
[Dii^{r}*]* das er louff vff den dächeren vmb
Vnd rauwe wie ein grauwe katz
nach müſen gröſſer denn kein ratz
Vnd wens jm gfall das er drus louff
ein ſpieß wie ein kriegsman kouff
Sag an wo ſtadts ins Bapſts Recht
das ein münch im ſpieß fecht?

1438 es] *om. AE*

it has to be God's Word alone. If you want to use that, then go ahead and speak. Cleywi Fenchmul is sitting here ready.

Murner
Where has anything like this happened before? Haven't you seen my geese, you peasant? Tell me why papal law isn't valid. When one peasant steals from another, you can't kill him with God's Word. So why do you call the Pope's law a pack of lies? You can't do without it, any more than I can do without my habit. Where can you find in the Gospel that a murderer should be broken on the wheel? And I'm thinking of other punishments too, punishments you use the hangman's weapons for – you don't need God's Word to experience them everywhere.

Amma Krůg
Thomas, Thomas, you've got to dance – tie the two ends of your habit together and put it on your lance, as you've often done before. How can you go against your very own St Francis? No special representative come from the Pope or from God has ordered that, when you join an order, you should run about on roofs and howl like a grey cat, go mousing for animals bigger than any rat and, if you care to, go and buy a spear as a soldier would. Tell me, where in the Pope's laws does it say that a monk should fight with a spear?

Härus mit dinen argumenten
vergiſs ouch nit der blauwen enten
Du ſprichſt man mög on Gotswort ſyn
jch gloub dir ſchmackte ſunſt der wyn
Wenn man ſchon kein gotswort hab
Hans Schmid ein ſölich antwurt gab
Vnd was der meinung der du biſt
ſtůnd ouch by dem Endchriſt
Din meinung vſs dem tüfel kumpt
wo man das Gotswort dennen rumpt
Das Gotswort engt all Iuriſten
vnd Bäpſtlich recht macht böß chriſten.
Ouch ſagſt von weltlichem gwalt
vnd fragſt wo gotzwort innhallt
Das man dieb vnd mörder ſtraf
jch gloub du rediſt nun jm ſchlaf
Iſt das nit gnůg zan vmb zan /
ſo einer tödt ein andren man?
Vnd vergüßd menſchen plůt
jſts recht das man jm ouch alſo thůt?
Das ich dirs ſag / zürn nit an mich
heſt gůts im ſinn / far nun für dich
vnd ſag vns von der Mäſs ein klein
[Dii[v]] ſo hort es hie die gantz gmeyn
wärs glück denn hat / fürt Brut hein

Murner.
Miſſach iſt ein Hebreiſch wort
ſtadt in der Bibel an mengem ort
Heyßd ouch Miſſa in latin
das mag vff tütſch ein Mäſs ſin
Miſſa ein willig opffer heyßd
ein ſchlächter pur das nit weißd
Die Mäſs hat Gott ſelbs yngſetzt
do er ſich mit den jüngeren letzt
Sprach: Deß ſöllend jr yndenck ſin
das ich wird ggeben für üch hin

Let's be having your arguments, and don't forget the blue duck.[212] You say we can do without God's Word. I think you'd still enjoy your wine if we didn't have God's Word. Hans Schmid gave an answer like that and shared your opinion.[213] He too supported the Antichrist. When you take away God's Word, opinions come from the devil. God's Word hems in all jurists, and papal law makes bad Christians. You also talk about secular authority, and ask where God's Word says that thieves and murderers should be punished. I think you must be talking in your sleep. Isn't 'a tooth for a tooth' good enough? When someone kills another, spilling human blood, is it right that the same thing should happen to him? If you're minded to do good, don't be angry with me for saying that. Now carry on and tell us something about the Mass. If everyone hears it, the lucky one will get to bring home the bride.[214]

Murner

'Missach' is a Hebrew word, which occurs at many points in the Bible. It's 'missa' in Latin, 'Messe' in German. 'Missa' means a sacrifice willingly given – though a simple peasant doesn't know that. God himself instituted the Mass, when he said farewell to his disciples. He said: 'You should remember that I am being given for you'.

212 i.e., a lie. A reference is surely meant to the first chapter proper (following the prologue) of Murner's *Schelmenzunft*, which is entitled 'Von blawen enten predigen' ('On preaching blue ducks'). See *Schelmenzunfft. Antzaigung alles Weltleüffigen můtwillens / ſchalckaiten vnn bübereyen diſer zeit Durch den hochgelerten herren Doctor Thoman Murner von Straßburg* (Augsburg, 1514), Aiv^r.

213 This points to a statement that Faber was at least accused of having made during the First Zurich Disputation. Eckstein has already put forward the opposite view in his prologue (see above, C 85–8/71).

214 i.e., win the contest.

Vnd ſprach darzů: Facietis
das wörtlin by der Mäſs bhept vns
Vnd heißd: Thůnds in miner gdächtnus
was thett er? Er opffret / hörſtus
Er hets vns gheiſſen / vnd ſelb thon
ſolt mans nit für ein opffer han?
Es hat nun lange zyt gewärt
biß yetz ſo iſt die welt verkert
Wil nüt mee han vff Mäſs vnd Gott
das thůt allein die kätzriſch rott
Die wend nüt vff den vättren han
jch wölte ſunſt wol baß dran
Ich hette noch vil Scribenten
ſo habends die für blauw enten
Darumb iſts gnůg yetz zmal
es gilt doch hie kein Decretal
[Diii^{r}] Ich bſorg doch das ſy vmb ſuſt
vnd hab zun puren keinen luſt
Wär wolt ſy leren Meſſz halten?
ein pur der ſolt holtz ſpalten
Vnd ſich neren mit dem pflůg
möcht dmeſſz bſton wär der pfaffen fůg.

Cleüwe Fenchmul.
Herr Thoman du heyſt wol Murnaw
es ist kein wunder biſt ja graw
Dich töupt vilicht der puren witz
was meinſt das vns Meſſzhan nütz
Sag / warumb iſt Chriſtus gſtorben?
hat er vns nit gnůg erworben
Iſt ſin lyden nit völlig gſin
das es der welt ſünd nemme hin?

Murner.
Wär wolt nun darwider ſagen?

1531 ja] schon *CDF*

And he also said: 'Facietis', do this. This word supports us when we say: 'Do this in remembrance of me'. What did he do? He made a sacrifice. Do you hear? He commanded us to do this, and did it himself. So oughtn't we to think that the Mass is a sacrifice? This view has prevailed now for a long time, up until now – when the world is upside down and we no longer have any regard for the Mass or God. It's the mob of heretics that's responsible. They have no regard for the Fathers. I'd like to say more, and have lots more writers to bring in – but you think they're just blue ducks. So that's enough for now: no one accepts any decretal here, I'm afraid they'd all be in vain. And I don't want to talk to peasants. Who would want to teach them to say Mass? Peasants should cut wood and feed themselves by working the plough. It's the priests' job to keep Masses going.

Cleywi Fenchmul

Sir Thomas, you're indeed called Murnaw,[215] and it's not surprising, because you're already grey. Perhaps the wits of us farmers are driving you mad.[216] What do you mean, that Masses help us? Tell me – why did Christ die? Didn't he achieve enough for us? Wasn't his passion enough, when he took away the sins of the world?[217]

Murner

Who would want to deny that?

215 A slightly contrived form of 'miaow', reflecting Murner's presentation as a cat. This is doubtless an intertextual reference to *Karsthans*, the main dialogue part of which begins with Murner's fourfold utterance of 'murnaw'– a noise which Studens immediately identifies as emanating from cats (*sic*) – see *Karsthans*, ed. Neukirchen, p. 12.

216 Literally, 'deafening' or 'numbing you'. The suggestion is that the common people are able, by their wit(s), to inflict on their opponents a form of social silencing.

217 Cleywi Fenchmul's aggressive style of questioning is evidence of Eckstein's considerable skill at individualizing his characters – as for that matter is Murner's contemptuous manner, to which Cleywi is in a sense responding.

er hat vnſer präſten tragen *Eſaie. 53.*
Vnd hat zalt für die gantzen welt
mit ſinem lyb on gůt vnd gelt *1. Petr. 1.*
Wir ſind mit ſinem tod erkoufft *1. Cor. 6.*
dem tüfel vſſz dem rachen groufft

Cleüwi fenchmul.
Höre zů hie jung vnd alt
was Murner für ein meinung halt
Er iſt nit in der gouchmatt gwäſen *Eſaie. 53.*
in Eſaia hat ers gläſen
[Diii^{v}] Hat Gott vnßre präſten tragen? *1. Pet. 2*
wie jr hand ghört den Murner ſagen
So mag die Meſſz kein opffer ſin
ſin tod hat dſünd all gnommen hin
Denn ſo die Meſſz ein opffer iſt
ſo wirt gſchmächt der Ieſus Chriſt
Vnd wär ſin tod nit mechtig gnůg
das wär nit der ſündren fůg
Drumm Meſſzhan iſt nun ſchmähen Gott
nützt niemant denn nun die bſchorne Rott
Noch eins frag ich ee ichs vergeſſz
ſag mir / wär hatt die erſten Meſſz?

Murner.
Sant Peter hat die erſt Meſſz ghan
z Rom findt man noch ein Capell ſton
Darinnen ſtadt noch der alter
Gregori hat ouch Meſſz druff ghalten.

Cleüwi fenchmul.
Das züg mit gſchrifft Doctor Thomma
du haſt das vſſz Lüg gardick gnommen

1540 hat all vnſer *CDF* Eſaie.53.] *om. AE* 1543 1.Cor.6.] *om. ADE* 1548 Eſaie.53.] *om. CDF* 1550 1.Pet.2] *om. CDF* 1566 ghalten zwar *CDF* 1568 bzüg *CDF* 1567–9 *marg.* Lompardica hystoria *CDF*

'He has borne our infirmities', and with his body has redeemed the entire world, without worldly goods or money.[218] We have been redeemed by his death,[219] and snatched from the devil's jaws.[220]

Cleywi Fenchmul

Listen, young and old, to Murner's opinion. He hasn't been in Cuckooville after all: he's read it in Isaiah.[221] But if God has indeed borne our sins,[222] as you've heard Murner say, then the Mass can't be a sacrifice. His death has taken away all our sins. So if the Mass is a sacrifice, then Jesus Christ is reviled. And if his death weren't sufficient, then it wouldn't be any use to sinners. So Masses are an insult to God; they help no one but the tonsured mob. And there's one more thing I want to ask before I forget: tell me, who celebrated the first Mass?

Murner

St Peter did. You can still find the altar he did it on, in a chapel in Rome.[223] Certainly Gregory celebrated Mass on it.

Cleywi Fenchmul

Prove that from the Scriptures, Dr Thomas. You've taken that from Lüggardick,[224]

218 1 Peter 1:18–19 (see n. 191 above).

219 1 Corinthians 6:20: 'For you were bought with a price; therefore glorify Christ in your body'.

220 This is of course a classically Evangelical statement, and hence a polemical own goal with which Murner fatally undermines his argument.

221 Isaiah 53:4 (see n. 30 above).

222 Cf. 2 Peter 2:9: 'The Lord knows how to rescue the godly from trial'.

223 The location is generally reckoned to have been the Basilica of St John Lateran, which houses St Peter's wooden altar inside its high altar.

224 Literally 'Great thick lie'. C, D, and F gloss this as 'Lompardica hystoria', a title sometimes given to the penultimate section of Jacobus a Voragine's *Legenda aurea* – which, however, does not contain an account of St Peter celebrating Mass in Rome.

Oder ſuſt vß eim Römſchen bůch
ſag / hatt er ouch ein alter tůch?

Murner.
Er hat ouch gwüß tůch vnd alb
nun biſtu ye ein grobs kalb
Wie hat er dörffen Meſſz läſen
wär da kein altertůch gwäſen
[Div^{r}] Keiner lißt Meſſz er ſyg denn gwycht
die wyhe der bapſt allein verlycht
Sy iſt ouch von dem Bapſt erdicht

Cleüwe Fenchmul
Ferda ſchwitz Murrenthoman
wo hat Sant Peter dwyhe gnommen?
Er iſt der erſt Bapſt gwäſen
vnd hat Meſſz on gwycht gläſen
Wenn dwyhe was noch nit dozmal
ouch hatt er kein Cardinal
Der jm hett mögen zallter dienen
das er Meſſz hab ghan findt man nienen
Nun loß mir zů du manſt mich dran
hat er zRom ſin erſte Meſſz ghan?
Was thett er ee er gen Rom kem
da er was zů Antiochen?
Da iſt er ein Biſchoff gwäſen
hat er nit ouch da Meſſz gläſen?
Du ſprichſt doch / Gott habs yngeſetzt
do er ſich mit den jüngren letzt
Hat ers denn vnderwägen glon
wie wirt er denn ſo übel bſton
Das ers zů Rom hat erſt angfangen
ſo iſt er vorhin müſſig gangen
Er iſt ein fuler pfaff gſin
wenn er nit thett nach ſatzung hin
Wie kundt er aber Meſſz han
der Canon fieng da noch nit an

or some other Romish book. Tell me, did he also have an altar cloth?

Murner

For sure he had a cloth and an alb. But you're an ignorant pleb, aren't you? How could he have read Mass without an altar cloth? No one celebrates Mass unless he's been ordained, and that ordination comes from the Pope alone. The Pope's the one who made it up.

Cleywi Fenchmul

By heaven,[225] then, grumbly Thoma, where did St Peter get ordained? He was the first Pope, so he must have read Mass without being ordained – because there was no such thing as ordination then. And he didn't have any cardinals either, who might have assisted him at the altar when he celebrated Mass. You can't find any. Listen to me, now you've reminded me of it: did he celebrate his first Mass at Rome? What did he do at Antioch, before he came to Rome? He was a bishop there – didn't he also read Mass? You say God instituted it, when he was saying farewell to his disciples. So did St Peter then go away and forget about it? How can he have behaved so badly as only to get around to doing it when he came to Rome? He must have been very slothful before then: he was a lazy priest if he didn't obey the statutes. But how could he have celebrated Mass, given that the canon hadn't been invented?

225 'Ferda schwitz' literally means 'by St Valentine's sweat' (see *SI* I, 995).

Ouch was nit gſetzt noch keinerley
[Div^{v}] das ghorte zů dem Meſſzgſchrey
Hat denn Sant Peter Meſſz gläſen
vnd iſt noch kein Canon gwäſen
Kein Colect vnd kein Epiſtel
iſts waar? ſo wachßt vf korn / miſtel
Nun ſinn ein yeder frommer Chriſt
das Meßhan wider Gott iſt
Wenn Gott iſt nun eyneſt gſtorben
hat vns allen gunſt erworben
Den wir gem vatter müſſend han *Rom. 5.*
er nimpt kein ander opffer an
Denn das eineſt gopffret iſt
der lyb des Herren Ieſu Chriſt
Das opffer mocht kein menſch geben
denn allein der ſun gotz geb ſin läben
Der iſt ein rechter prieſter gſin
hat durch ſin tod dſünd gnommen hin
Das iſt nun eyneſt vergangen *Rom. 6.*
wirt nimmerme angfangen
Es iſt an eim mal gnůg gwäſen
als wir zů den Hebreern läſen *Hebr. 7. 8.*
Durch die Epiſtel vß vnd vß *& .9. 10.*
hör zů was ſpricht Petrus
Chriſtus eineſt gſtorben iſt *1. Petri. 3.*
hat durch ſin tod vns zůgrüſt
Das er iſt gſtorben nach dem fleyſch
hand wir ererbt ſin eignen geyſt *Roma. 8.*
Wär on den iſt hat kein läben
das zügt Ioannes ouch eben *1. Ioann. 5.*
Ouch kumſtu mit dem Miſſach har
[Dv^{r}] das heyß ein willig opffer zwar
Vnd ſye ein Iüdiſch wort
ſag an / wo ſtadts / an welchem ort?

Murner.
Nun hab ichs all min läbtag ghört

And there was no law or anything else telling you how to caterwaul at Mass either. So did St Peter celebrate Mass when there was no canon, no collect, no epistle? Is that true? That's like mistletoe growing on corn. Now all faithful Christians should consider that Masses are against God, because God has died only once and has earned for all of us the grace we need before the Father.[226] He doesn't accept any sacrifice other than the one that has already been made, namely the body of our Lord Jesus Christ. No man can make that sacrifice, for only the Son of God can offer up his life. He was a true priest, who took away sin through his death. That happened only once, and will never happen again.[227] Once was enough, as we read in Hebrews, right the way through the epistle.[228] Hear what Peter says: 'Christ died once, and has saved us by his death'.[229] By his death according to the flesh we have inherited his own spirit.[230] No one who does not have that spirit has life.[231] John also bears witness to this. But you come to us with your 'Missach' and tell us that it's a Jewish word meaning a willing sacrifice. Tell me, where is that written?

Murner
I've heard all my life,

226 Romans 5:1–2 (see n. 192 above).

227 Romans 6:10: 'The death he died, he died to sin, once for all'.

228 See for example Hebrews 7:27; 9:11–12; 10:12.

229 1 Peter 3:18: 'For Christ also suffered for sins once for all, the righteous for the unrighteous, in order to bring you to God'.

230 Romans 8:3–4: 'For God has done what the law, weakened by the flesh, could not do: by sending his own Son in the likeness of sinful flesh, and to deal with sin, he condemned sin in the flesh, so that the just requirement of the law might be fulfilled in us, who walk not according to the flesh but according to the Spirit'.

231 1 John 5:12: 'Whoever has the Son has life; whoever does not have the Son of God does not have life'.

vnd hab es ouch mine ſchůler glert
Miſſach heyße ein willig gab
wenn einer geb von ſiner hab
Wo es in der Bibel ſtand
Iſt mir yetz zmal nit wol bkand

Cleüwi Fenchmul.
Des Miſſachs bin ich ouch nit pricht
nach dem vnd mich das wort anſicht
So mag es wol Hebreyſch ſin
vnd heyß ein gab wie du fürſt yn *Leuit. 2.*
Was gaben ſind es doch gwäſen? *Deute. 16.*
du *h*aſts gwüß in Moſe gläſen *Exodi. 23.*
Man darff ſich nit nach Moſe richten
Moſes redt von gaben der früchten *Deut. 16.*
Das gadt vns Chriſten nüt me an
wir wend nun fürhin Chriſtum han
Dem gfalt das opffer vnſers lobs *Pſalm. 49*
er fragt nun gar nach keinem ops *1. Petr. 2.*
Wir ſöllend vns ſelb für opffer geben
das ſpricht ſant Peter / merck mich eben
Wir ſygind ein künglich prieſterthůmb
da meint er glöubig vmb vnd vmm
Nit blettlig vnd die gſchirmbt Rott
[Dv^{v}] ſunder all die ſind gwycht von Gott
Drumb ſind wir gwycht durch chriſti blůt *Rom. 3.*
nit von dem Bapſt im badhůt
Das iſt der puren prieſter ampt
vnd heyßts vns Gott allſampt
Das wir ſöllind yndenck ſin
er ſyge geben für vns hin
Vß diſem groſſer danck entſpringt
die gwüßne ouch ein yeden dringt
Das einer by jm ſelber denckt
iſt er für dich ans Crütz ghenckt

1652 baſts *A* 1667f. *marg.* Die recht Mässz *CDF*

and have also taught my pupils, that 'Missach' means a willing gift, which happens when someone gives something from his possessions. But I don't rightly know now where it is in the Bible.

Cleywi Fenchmul

I also don't know about 'Missach', though it seems to me that it might very well be Hebrew and mean a gift, as you say.[232] But what sort of gifts were they?[233] For sure you've read it in Moses.[234] But you shouldn't go by Moses. Moses talks about the oblation of first-fruits, but that no longer has anything to do with us Christians. We believe we have Christ now, and what pleases him is the sacrifice of our praise.[235] He doesn't ask us for any fruit;[236] rather we should offer ourselves as a sacrifice. This is what St Peter says, listen to me well: 'We are a royal priesthood'. By this he means all the faithful, not the pock-marked and painted priestly tribe, but all who have been ordained by God. For we have been ordained by Christ's blood,[237] and not by the Pope in his bath hat. The priestly office of farmers, and what God asks of all of us, is to remember that he gave himself up for us. This is a cause for great thankfulness. Conscience also forces us all to consider in our own minds that he hung on the cross for you

232 The whole of Leviticus 2 is a discussion of grain offerings.

233 Deuteronomy 16 describes the Passover and freewill offerings.

234 Exodus 23:19: 'The choicest of the first fruits of your ground you shall bring into the house of the Lord your God'.

235 Psalm 51:16–17: 'For you have no delight in sacrifice; if I were to give a burnt-offering, you would not be pleased. The sacrifice acceptable to God is a broken spirit; a broken and contrite heart, O God, you will not despise'.

236 1 Peter 2:9: 'But you are a chosen race, a royal priesthood'.

237 Romans 3:24–5: 'They are now justified by his grace as a gift, through the redemption that is in Christ Jesus, whom God put forward as a sacrifice of atonement by his blood, effective through faith'.

Vnd iſt vmb dinetwillen gſtorben
on din verdienſt hat gnad erworben
Vnd biſt jm gfründt in brůderſchafft *Marc. 3.*
das kumpt vſſz der Gottes krafft
Das magſtu Gott nit vergelten
ein grechter ſtirbt für grecht ſelten *Rom. 5.*
Vnd du biſt gſin ein groſſer ſünder
hat für dich glitten nüt deſtminder
Vnd hat dir gſchenckt ſin grechtigkeit
din laſter vff ſim rucken treyt
Herr Gott das ſyg dir lob vnd danck
mer minen glouben ich bin kranck
Das ich die groſſen that verkünd
denn gar nüt gůts ich in mir find
Damit ich vor dir möge bſton
an din gnůgthůn wil ich mich lon
Das iſt ein rechte puren Meſſz
das man ſins lyden nit vergeß
Vnd das wir allweg denckind dran
[Dvi^r] allein das wil er von vns han
Wir ſöllend nit thůn das er hat thon
ſuſt müßtind wir vns krützgen lon
Er hat gſeyt: Thůnds in miner dächtnuß
nun denckend / nit opffrend / hörſt dus?
Dauon ſyg gſeyt yetz nun gnůg
red ouch nun du min Amma krůg.

Amma Krůg.
Ein Pur verſtünde hindrem pflůg
das Chriſtus hette glitten gnůg
Iſt eineſt gſtorben / ſtirbt nit mer *Roma. 6.*
der tüfel ſich an dpfaffen ker
Sy hand dMeſſz für ein opffer ghan
darzů yngnon von yederman
Vnd nüt vßgeben / das heyßt gmeſſen *Matth. 23.*
ouch armer witwen hüſer gfreſſen
Die hands verſchluckt durch lange bätt

and died for your sake; you have won grace through no deserts of your own, and are bound to him in brotherhood.[238] This comes from the power of God, and you can give God nothing for it in return. Very rarely does a just man die for an unjust one,[239] and you have been a great sinner. But he suffered for you all the same. And he has made you the gift of his righteousness, and has carried your sins on his back. Lord God, may you have praise and thanks for that, and increase my faith (for I am weak), so that I might proclaim this great deed. For I can find nothing good in me that might enable me to stand before you; I will rely on your atonement. A true farmer's Mass is this: not to forget Christ's Passion, but always to think of it. That alone is what he wants from us. We don't have to do what he did: that way we'd have to be crucified. He said: 'Do this in remembrance of me'. We only have to remember it, not make a sacrifice – do you hear that? We've now said enough about this. You speak now, Amma Krůg.

Amma Krůg

A farmer pulling his plough can understand that Christ has suffered enough, has died once and can't die any more. May the devil take the priests! They've thought the Mass was a sacrifice. On top of that they've had money from everyone, and not spent any of it – that's to say, they've not given any away. I call that just! They've also devoured poor widows' houses, swallowing them with their long prayers.[240]

238 Mark 3:34–5: 'Here are my mother and my brothers! Whoever does the will of God is my brother and sister and mother'.

239 Romans 5:7–8: 'Indeed, rarely will anyone die for a righteous person – though perhaps for a good person someone might actually dare to die. But God proves his love for us in that while we were still sinners Christ died for us'.

240 Matthew 23:14: 'Woe to you, scribes and Pharisees, hypocrites! For you devour widows' houses and for the sake of appearance you make long prayers; therefore you will receive the greater condemnation'.

der tüfel jnen gholffen het
Sy hand vns puren übermeſſen
das wir ſind vff höfen gſeſſen
Hand buwen korn / vnd darzů wyn
das hat halb müſſen jren ſin
Dritteil / Zehend vnd das vierteyl
wir buwtend / vnd ſy hattends feyl
Das bracht als dmeß weißt menklich wol
ſy maſſend jn ſelber dkeller voll
Daby ſo mochtends herren ſin
vnd warten hüpſcher fröuwlin
Wenn nun ein pur an zügen lag
[Dvi^{v}] ſo kamends mit dem jüngſten tag
Wie Gott ein ſtrenger richter wär
vnd giengend vffz keim huß nit lär
Ein ſchillig galt das Sacrament
ſy ſprachend: Setz ein Teſtament
Kumpt dir vnd din nachkummen dſtatt
ſetz jarzyt vff din huß vnd matt
Alſo ward huß vnd hof verpfendt
dmäſſz hat nüt bracht denn güldt vnn rendt
Das nimmermer wirt abgelößt
biß Gott die gantzen welt abtößt
Das hat das Meſſzhan alles bracht
ſy hand all bſchiſſz vnd liſt erdacht
Biß ſy puren hand betrogen
huß / äcker / matten / an ſich zogen
Der erdbod in der Chriſtenheyt
den gröſſern nutz den pfaffen treyt
Es ſol alles nüt / pfaff / münch / vnn nunnen
der gytz hat überhand gwunnen
Damit ſind puren ouch vergifft
doch hat der Bapſt den anfang gſtifft
Puren ſind nit der anfang gſin
allein die můter Bäpſtin

1714 vnd] *om. CDF*

The devil has helped them; they've walked all over us farmers, so that we've stayed on our farms and grown corn and wine, half of which went to them. A third, a tenth, a quarter: we grew it and they sold it. Like the Mass, this brought in a lot, you know. They've filled their own cellars. And along with that they've wanted to be lords and have entertained pretty young women. When a farmer has been ill, they've come at us with the Last Judgement and said that God is a strict judge; and they've not left any house empty-handed. The sacrament cost a shilling, and they've said: 'Make a provision that will help you and your descendants: set up an annual Mass for your soul[241] to be said in your own house and meadow'. And so you forfeit hearth and home. All these Masses have created are debts, that won't be repaid until God brings the world to an end. Masses have brought all this about. They've thought up all kinds of tricks and twists, so as to deceive farmers and do them out of their houses, fields, and meadows. It's wrong, but the soil of Christendom actually yields up most of its fruits to the priests, monks, and nuns. Greed has got the upper hand. Farmers are poisoned by this as well. But it all began with the Pope: the farmers didn't start it; it was Mother Pope,

241 For this meaning of 'jarzeit' see *FWB* VIII, 323–6.

Die hat ſömliche kind erzogen
die den armen hand den ſchweyß vßgſogen
Wir ſind verfürt durch böß hirten
der tüfel wirt jnen wirten
Da vnden in Nobis huß
ſchlachts helſch fhür zum fenſter vß
Nun loß noch eins Murrenthomma
[Dvii^{r}] weiſt wo har ſygind dmünch kummen?
Es iſt ein ſundere Creatur
vnd ſind nit gſchaffen wie ein pur
Ouch kummends nit von Adams kind
ſchafft das ſy gern allein ſind
In klöſtren vnd wyten garten
jm brättſpyl ires Schöpffers warten
Das laſſends inen nit leyden
der tüfel machts vff wyter heyden
Do Gott hat gſchaffen den Adam
der tüfel es ouch zhanden nam
Vnd macht vff einer wyten matten
ein grauwen münch in groſſer blatten
Der Karſthans ſagt er habs gſehen
vnd ſyg in diner Gouchmatt bſchehen
Doch ſye bſchehen wo es well
zürn nit das ich dirs für zell
Ich hab meng mal an Cantzlen ghört
das dmünchen hand närſchers gleert
Denn das iſt / wie ich yetz hab gſeyt
weyſt wenn man dfladen zſägnen treyt?
Es ſyg ein mal ein pur geſyn
der zug mit fladen zkilchen hin
Vnd als er gieng durch einen wald
ein holen boum fand er bald
Daryn zog er mit den fladen
vnd fraß ſy all / das bracht jm ſchaden
Als er hatt gfüllt den buch vol
do mocht er nit mee vſs dem hol
Vnd wie ſin hußfrouw naher kam

who has brought up plenty of children that have sucked the sweat off farmers' brows. We've been led astray by false shepherds. The devil will look after them. Down below in his house hellish fire blazes through the window. Now listen to another thing, grumbly Murner: do you know where the monks have come from? They're a special kind of creature, not made as farmers are. They're not descended from Adam's children, and so they want to be alone in their cloisters and great gardens, serving their Creator by playing board games.[242] But they're not happy with that: the devil makes them go further afield as well. When God made Adam, the devil also got in on the act and created a grey monk somewhere on a broad meadow. Karsthans says he has seen this, and that it happened in your *Geuchmat*.[243] But wherever it happened, don't be angry that I'm telling you about it. I've many times heard monks preaching things from pulpits that are sillier than what I've just said. Do you know the one about the oatcakes being brought to be blessed? Once, there was apparently a farmer who was bringing oatcakes to church, and as he was going through a forest, he found a hollow tree. He went inside there with his oatcakes and ate them all up. This did him harm, because after he'd filled his belly he couldn't get out of the tree any more; and when his wife came up to him,

242 As can be seen from many manuscript illustrations and later woodcuts, monks seem to have been particularly associated with board games of all kinds, from chess to those involving gambling.

243 A sentence which could hardly place Eckstein's Murner more firmly in the broader context of vernacular Reformation polemics. For the passage in question see *Karsthans* (ed. Neukirchen), p. 20.

[Dvii^v] die ſelb ein ax in dhend nam
Vnd ſprach: Nun wart biß ich dich löß
hüw jm in buch do empfiel ims kröß
Das hab ich von eim Doctor ghört
hats zFriburg im Briſgouw gleert
Ich ſchwür ein Eyd du wäriſts gſyn
ein andren ſpruch fůrteſt ouch yn
Als Chriſtus in dem garten war
hindrem zun hielte die Schwäbiſch ſchar
Vnd hettind dIuden Chriſtum glon
ſo hettind jnn die Schwaben gnon
Ich hab es lang zyt in mir bhan
jch was dozmal ein houptman
Do Chriſtus ward jm garten gfangen
du hatteſt ein ſeckel am hals hangen
Mit der laternen zugeſt vor
jch ſach dich vnderm garten thor
Drumm hab für gůt / min Murren Thommen
das iſt vſs diner predig gnommen
Ich weyß noch mee / das ich nit ſag
du heſt yetz gnůg vff ein tag
Din gſell Fritz můß ouch an dſach
der deckt jm Fägfhür yetz das dach
Das es nit vff die ſeelen ſchny
lůgt ob der Emſer darinnen ſy
Der iſt lang Dachmeyſter gſyn
vnd gfallen durchs dach yn
Drumm weybel Schwynbeltz man jnn dran
das ers anfach mit Ioß Hechelzan

[Dviii^r] **Weybel.**
Doctor Fritz von Gewiler
fach an yetz am Fägfhür filen
Ich denck du ſygiſt drumb har kon
wenn heſt den orden von dir thon?
Du biſt gſin im prediger orden
wie biſt der kutten abworden?

she took an axe in her hand and said: ‘Wait there now for me to free you’. She took the axe to his stomach, with the result that his entrails fell out. I heard this story from a doctor, who preached about it in Freiburg im Breisgau. I’d swear on oath that it was you.[244] You also said that, when Christ was in the garden, a bunch of Swabians were lying in wait behind the fence, and that, if the Jews hadn’t taken Christ, the Swabians would have.[245] I’ve been imagining for a long time that I was a captain when Christ was taken captive in the garden, and that you were there with a sack around your neck, moving forward with a lantern. I saw you under the garden gate. Don’t take it amiss, my moaning friend Thoma. I’ve taken all that from your sermon. There’s a lot more I know, too, that I won’t tell you about – you’ve had enough of it for one day. It’s your mate Fritz’s turn now: he’s going to give purgatory a nice roof, so that the souls there don’t get snowed on.[246] Have a look and see if Emser’s in it. He was a roofer for a long time, and fell down into purgatory from the roof. So, Weybel Schwynbeltz, tell him to start debating with Joß Hechelzan.

Weybel
Doctor Fritz von Gewiler,[247] start getting purgatory ready. I think that’s why you came here. When did you leave your order? You were with the Dominicans, but how did you get rid of your habit?

244 We are not aware that Murner preached any such sermons. Rather, the passage recalls the mockery of contemporary sermonizing that appears in Erasmus’s *Moriae encomium: Desiderii Erasmi Roterodami opera omnia* (20 vols, Amsterdam: New Holland, 1969–2003), IV, 3 (1979), pp. 162–8.

245 Presumably the garden of Gethsemane is meant. This is also perhaps the main passage that dissuades us from supporting Stricker’s argument (n. 103, p. 157) that in the *Concilium*, Eckstein casts Swabia, and by implication himself, in a positive light.

246 The point of this slightly strenuous running joke is, one assumes, that the Catholic party takes purgatory absurdly literally.

247 Yet another alias for Fritz Lindou.

Du hefts mit dir gen Rom tragen
mir kundt din Prior nit ſagen
War du doch hin kon wäriſt
ein pfaffenblatt (ſagt ich) du ſchäriſt
Den gugel hettiſt nit me an
ouch von dir gleyt den Schamprian
Vnd wäriſt zSurſee Doctor worden
ein rote kapp wär yetz din orden
Din Prior ſprach Domernemus
wär er hie / wol käms vns
Wir leytind jm ein kappen an
es zugind hundert roſs dran
Ich ſag nit me / du haſt nun gnůg
der pfarrer horts / der heißd der Krůg
Doch gloubſt mirs nit / züch durch nider
bring mir ein recognitz wider
Vnd thů vns vor hie etwas dar
wo einer nach diſem zyt hin far
Ob ouch gwüſs ein Fägfhür ſy
gotzwort můß ſin allein daby
Vnd denck vns nun keins leerers nit
was Bibel ſagt das fürhar ſchütt

[Dviii[v]] **Fridle Landfarer.**
Es iſt ein Fägfhür gſin von alter
mit Dauid bzüg ichs in dem pſalter
Vnd ander gſchrifft zeig ich noch mee
die gſchriben ſind in der alten Ee
Zum erſten wil ich nemmen für mich
ein vers im Dauid finden ich
Der zeigt vns klar vnd heiter an
wir müſſind durch fhür vnd waſſer gon *Pſalm. 65.*
Vnd darnach wider zrůwen gfürt
das iſt / man wirt im Fägfhür purgiert

Ioß Hechelzan.
Den verß heſt im pſalter gleſen

You took it with you when you went to Rome; but your Prior couldn't tell me where you had gone. I said to him that you had a tonsure but weren't wearing your fool's costume any more, and had given up your cowl; also that you'd become a doctor at Sursee and that your order was now the Red Caps.[248] The Prior said: 'Domernemus'.[249] It'd be good if he was here: we'd put a fool's cap on his head (a hundred horses would have to help us pull it on). I shan't say any more: you've had enough. The priest called Krůg heard it, but don't believe me: get yourself down here and bring me a certificate of indulgence. And tell us something about where we'll end up after this life, and whether there really is such a thing as purgatory. When you talk about it, you can only use God's Word. Don't think about any other teachers: let us just have what the Bible says.

Fridle Landfarer

There has been a purgatory from of old. I can attest it with David from the psalter. And I can also show you more Scriptures from the Old Testament. First of all I will take a verse that I find in David, which shows us very clearly that we have to go through fire and water[250] and thereafter are led to rest – that is, that we are purified in purgatory.

Joß Hechelzan

You've read this verse in the Psalms.

248 From the context, one assumes this means Lindou's doctoral cap, worn perhaps with undue pride.

249 The closest Latin word to this is probably 'dormiamus', 'let us sleep'.

250 Psalm 66:10, 12: 'For you, O God, have tested us; you have tried us as silver is tried [...] we went through fire and water; yet you have brought us out to a spacious place'.

jſt denn Dauid im Fägfhür gweſen?
Wie iſt er wider vßhar kon
das er den verß hett gſchriben nun?
Wir ſind durch fhür vnn waſſer ggangen *Pſalm. 65.*
ſo hett er das läben me empfangen
Vnd hett erſt nahin gmacht den pſalmen
wie ſind jr ſo groß ſchalmen
Das jr vom waſſer nüt hand gſeyt
doch das fhür hat gnůg vßtreyt
Wie hand ir dwort ſo übel ermeſſen
das jr hand des waſſers vergeſſen
Hettind jr ans waſſer gedacht
es hett vns ouch in koſten bracht
Iſt nun waſſer by dem fhür
ſo iſt es mir ein abenthür
Vnd habend dſeelen warm vnd kalt
[Eï] ſo mag man wol (dar für ich halt)
Im fhür ſchwitzen / naher wäſchen
war kumpt der Tüfel mit der äſchen?
Er ſeechtet denn all Münch damit
vnd badetz das der Ritt ſchütt
Darumb gſell Fritz nun heytz baß yn
denn wär Dauid im Fägfhür gſin
Er hett den pſalm nit mögen ſchryben
drumb laß das fhür für trübſal blyben
Dauon Dauid vff erden weyßd
dann fhür ouch hie nüt anders heyßd
Der gantz pſalm ſagt nun von trübſal *Pſal. 150.*
vnd dencktz Fägfhürs nüt überal
Man findt der glychen verß ſunſt ouch
die ſagend von fhür das gibt nit rouch
Spricht Dauid an eim ort ſo ghertz
Herr brenn min nieren vnd das hertz *Pſalm. 25.*
Du haſt mich Herr im fhür probiert *Pſalm. 16.*
kein fhür hat ſin hertz nit brürt
Damit du dſelen brennen wilt
für trübſal fhür by ſant Peter gilt

But had David ever been in purgatory? And how did he get back out of it, so as to be able to write that verse? 'We have gone through fire and water'. This means that he received life, and afterwards wrote the Psalm. And how come you are such fools as to talk a lot about the fire but fail to mention the water? How have you misunderstood the words so badly that you forgot the water? If you'd thought about the water, it would have cost us: if there's water mixed in with the fire, that's news to me. And if the souls have got both warm and cold things in purgatory, then I assume that you'll run a sweat in the fire, and then have to wash. And where does the devil go with the ashes, unless he first puts them over the monks and then bathes them, so that they end up with a fever? So, then, friend Fritz, turn the heat up a bit: because if David had been in purgatory, he wouldn't have been able to write that Psalm. Understand the fire he mentions there as meaning the troubles David knew on earth. Because 'fire' doesn't mean anything else here. The whole Psalm talks about troubles,[251] but it certainly isn't thinking of purgatory all the way through. You can also find other such verses, that speak of fire that doesn't give off smoke. At one point David is brave enough to say: 'Lord, burn my kidneys and my heart.[252] For you, Lord, have tested me in the fire'.[253] No fire actually touched his heart, no fire that you might actually burn souls by. For St Peter, fire means trouble:

251 Psalm 66:12 (as n. 250).

252 Psalm 26:2: 'Prove me, O Lord, and try me; test my heart and mind'.

253 Psalm 17:3: 'If you try my heart, if you visit me by night, if you test me, you will find no wickedness in me'.

Ob wir ſchon hie kummer habend
jn vil trübſal / das nimpt ein end
Vnd wirt der gloub dar durch probiert *1. Pet. 1.*
wie man das gold im fhür purgiert
Das iſt diß ſpruchs der recht verſtand
darumb ſo nimm ein andren zhand

Doctor Fritz.
Nun hör zů was Mattheus ſpricht
[Eiv] mit dim widerſächer vor dich ſchlicht *Matth. 5.*
Ee er dich übergeb dem gwalt
vnd dich der richter innbhalt
Fürwar du wirſt nit mee vsgon
ein örtlin wirt dir nit nachglon
Das iſt das vierteil an eim pfennig
kumpſt du dryn / man ſchenckt dir wenig
Hör me zů was Paulus ſeyt
ein yeder ſin that fürn Richtſtůl treyt *Galat. 6.*
Wie man hett gläbt / darnach es gadt
der Iopp dennzmal für kein ſtadt
Ouch Noe nit / darzů Daniel *Ezec. 18.*
eigne burde treyt ein yetliche ſeel
Darumb ſol man inen gůtzthůn nach
ſo kummends vſs des fhüres raach
Wir all müſſend antwurt geben *2. Cor. 5.*
wie wir hie hand gfürt vnſer läben
Es ſye gůts oder böß
darumb iſt not das man ſy löß
Hie mit bitt vnd andren gaaben
loß wie wir in propheten haben
Ich will inen gen nach irer that *Hiere. 25.*
vnd wie ein yeder gwerchet hat
Darzů ſpricht ouch Solomon
man werde vſs dem kercker gon *Eccleſ. 5.*

1907 ein yeder ſin] Sein yeder *CDF*

'Even if we have many griefs here, and great troubles, this will come to an end. And our faith will be tested by it like gold purified by fire'.[254] That's the correct understanding of your verse: it's time now for you to take another.

Doctor Fritz

Listen now to what St Matthew says: 'Be reconciled with your adversary before he delivers you over to the authorities and the judge takes you.[255] Truly you will never get out until you have paid the uttermost farthing (that is, quarter of a penny)'.[256] Once you go in, you won't be given much. Hear also what Paul says: 'All men should present their works before the judgement seat, and will be treated according to how they have lived'.[257] At that point neither Job nor Noah nor Daniel will be able to stand in anyone else's place; every soul must bear its own burden.[258] So we should do good on their behalf, that they might escape the vengeance of the fire. We must all answer for how we have lived our lives, well or badly.[259] So we need to liberate them here with prayers and other gifts. Listen to what we have in the prophets: 'I will give to them according to their deeds, how each has behaved'.[260] Solomon also speaks about this, saying that we will go out of the prison,

254 1 Peter 1:6–7: 'Now for a little while you have had to suffer various trials, so that the genuineness of your faith – being more precious than gold that, though perishable, is tested by fire – may be found to result in praise and glory and honour when Jesus Christ is revealed'.

255 Matthew 5:25: 'Come to terms quickly with your accuser while you are on the way to court with him, or your accuser may hand you over to the judge, and the judge to the guard, and you will be thrown into prison'.

256 *SI* I, 485–6 confirms that an 'örtlin' was normally worth a quarter of a gulden.

257 Ephesians 6:7: 'Render service with enthusiasm, as to the Lord and not to men and women, knowing that whatever good we do, we will receive the same again from the Lord, whether we are slaves or free'.

258 Ezekiel 18:5, 9: 'If a man is righteous and does what is lawful and right [...] such a one is righteous; he shall surely live, says the Lord God'.

259 2 Corinthians 5:10: 'For all of us must appear before the judgement seat of Christ, so that each may receive recompense for what has been done in the body, whether good or evil'.

260 Jeremiah 25:14: 'I will repay them according to their deeds and the work of their hands'.

Vnd vſs kettinen in das rych
noch ein ſpruch weiß ich
Der ſtadt im bůch der Stryter
vnd iſt der beſt / loß nun wyter *2. Mach. 12*
Es iſt heylig vnd gůt
[Eii^r] das man den todten nach thůt
Hör nun mee was Paulus ſag
der ſpricht das des Herren tag *1. Cor. 3.*
Eins yeden werck jm fhür probier
was ſol ich mee inhar fürn?
Ich hab dir zeigt der ſprüch ſiben
ſag an / was iſt nun vſs bliben /
Das ich dir nit an tag hab thon /
laß hören / was redſt du daruon?

Ioß Hechelzan.
Gnad herr Fritz wo farſt du har
du haſt hie nun gantz vnd gar
Mit keim ſpruch nüt probiert
der das Fägfhür anrürt
Dann all ſprüch die du dar haſt thon
wöllend vff das letſt gricht ſton
On einr / ghört nit in dTablatur
das weiß ich wol / vnd bin ein pur
Der ſelb nun in dem Strytbůch ſtadt *2. Mac. 12*
kein krafft er by den Iuden hat
Was gadt vns Machabeus an?
er hets ouch vſs gůtduncken thon
Das er thon hatt macht vns kein gſatz
ouch kam das gelt in gotz ſchatz
Man hatt do nit Vigilg noch Mäſs
fraß todten nit wie mans yetz fräſs
Ouch was kein bätt für dſelen noch bitt
vnd wüßd man von keim Fägfhür nit
Es iſt ſidhar vom bapſt erdacht

1931 1. Cor. 5. *CDF* 1932 probiern *CDF* 1943 gon *CDF* 1956 keim] dem *CDF*

and out of our chains into the kingdom.[261] I know another verse also, which is in the book of the Maccabees. And it's the best; listen to it now: 'It is holy and good to make atonement for the dead'.[262] Now hear also what Paul says, when he states that the Day of the Lord will test everyone's works in the fire.[263] What more do I need to refer to? I've shown you seven verses. Tell me, what have I missed out, that I haven't made known to you? And tell me, what do you think of it?

Joß Hechelzan

Good Sir Fritz, where have you come from? You haven't proved anything to do with purgatory in even a single verse, for all the verses you've referred to have to do with the Last Judgement. Except for one, which isn't part of the canon: even a farmer like me knows that.[264] That's the one from the Maccabees: that book has no authority at all with the Jews, so what has Maccabaeus to teach us? He did what he thought was right; but what he did is no law for us to follow. And none of his money went into the Treasury of Merit. At that time there weren't any vigils or Masses devoted to eating the dead, as there are now; nor were there any prayers or requests on behalf of the dead, and people knew nothing of purgatory. That was invented later by the Pope.

261 Cf. Ecclesiastes 4:14: 'One can indeed come out of prison to reign, even though born poor in the kingdom'.

262 2 Maccabees 12:45: 'But if he was looking to the splendid reward that is laid up for those who fall asleep in godliness, it was a holy and pious thought. Therefore he made atonement for the dead, so that they might be delivered from their sin'.

263 1 Corinthians 3:13: 'The work of each builder will become visible, for the Day will disclose it, because it will be revealed with fire, and the fire will test what sort of work each has done'.

264 Zwingli's refusal to countenance the canonicity of the Apocrypha was indeed well known (although it did appear in the first Zurich Bible of 1530).

[Eii^{v}] hett es dir als wenig bracht
Als du gibſt in ablas kaſten
dſeelen müßtind lang faſten
Du gäbiſt nit ein pſalmen dryn
vnd müßtind lang on pſalmen ſin
darumb der ſpruch Machus machab
wäriſt da gſin do mans gelt gab
Du hettiſt zwar da nit gfyret
ouch für dſeelen ein reckbein glyret
Das bůch iſt angnon von der Kilch
der ſpruch allein gibt dir milch
Sag mir noch ein druß den du kündiſt
on ein bůch / gelt wo du ein findiſt?
Darumb far mit dem ſpruch gen Genff
vertuſch jnn an ein lägel mit ſenff
So heſt du ſenff zun ſeelen zeſſen
vnd heiß dir nun wol meſſen
Zum erſten den du an heſt zogen
vſs Mattheo / den haſt du ouch bogen *Math. 25.*
Das er möcht zerſprungen ſin
das züg ich mit ſant Auguſtin
Der ſpricht ſelb das er well
diſer ſpruch der dien in dhell
Da einer eewig in müß ſin
on end da blyben vnd lyden pin
So wil Chryſoſtomus darneben
der kercker ſyg hie jrdiſchs läben
Ambroſius ein leerer thür
der meint es ſyg das Fägfhür
Es ſind nun hie der leerer dry
[Eiii^{r}] lůg was eins yeden meinung ſyg
Man hats all dry für heilig man
nun welcher iſt denn recht dran?
Fält einr ſo hat der ander recht
ſo ſind die zween nun kurtz vnd ſchlecht
Vnrecht dran / das fält ſich nit
der ſpruch ſich von jm ſelbs gitt

And if it had brought you in the same small amount of money as you yourself have put into the indulgence chest, then the souls of the dead would have had to fast for a long time: you wouldn't put in even a single Psalm's worth, so they'd have been out of Psalms for a long time now. Hence the saying: 'Machus machab'.[265] If you'd been there (in Maccabaeus's time) when money was being given, you certainly wouldn't have rejoiced, or moved a muscle to help the dead souls. This book was accepted by the Church, but it only has this one verse that you can milk. Quote me any other verse that you know from it off by heart. Where can you find one? So go off to Geneva now with that verse and exchange it for a pot of mustard.[266] Then at least you'll have mustard to eat on behalf of the dead souls. And I ask you now to think carefully. First of all, the verse you quoted from Matthew[267] you bent about so much that it almost burst. I can attest this with reference to St Augustine, who himself says that this verse means hell, where you have to stay and suffer permanently. Chrysostom, on the other hand, argues that the prison here means life on earth, whereas Ambrose, an excellent teacher, says it means purgatory.[268] So here you have three teachers: see what their opinions are. All three are considered holy men, but which of them is right? It's the case that if one is right, the other two are completely and utterly wrong. But it isn't really like this, since the verse provides its own interpretation,

265 A pun which works (slightly) better in German. The translation would be something like 'take out, take off'.

266 This proposed exchange can only be plausibly accounted for by the fact that 'Genf' rhymes temptingly with 'Senf'.

267 Matthew 5:25 is meant.

268 This statement about the differing interpretations of these Church Fathers is in essence true: see Augustine, *Speculum de scriptura sacra: De Evangelio secundum Matthaeum,* V (*Patrologia Latina* XXXIV, 971); Chrysostom, *Homilia super Matthaeum,* XVI, 13; Ambrose, *Expositio Evangelii secundum Lucam* (*PL* XV, 1739–40).

Wenn man bſicht was vorhar gadt
das im ſelben capitel ſtadt
So lert vns Gott vo*n* einigkeit
ee einer ſin gab zum alter treyt
Vnd heyßt man ſöll einhällig ſin
vnd tröuwt vns mit der hellſchen pyn
Der text vom fägfhür ſeyt hie nüt
Chriſtus allein vns friden büt
Er ſpricht: Du ſolt einhällig ſin
mit dim widrigen ſo du gaaſt hin
Vff dem wäg dich eben verſün
er wirt dich ſuſt dem richter gen
Der richter gibt dich denn dem knecht
der leit dich in kercker ſo gſchicht dir recht
Denn wölcher hie nit nach wil lon
dem wirts (wie Chriſtus ſeyt) ergon
So all menſchen Gott wirt richten
mit fröud vnd fhür einander ſchlichten
In fröuden wirt der grecht wol bſton
der Gottloß můß in kercker gon
Da wirt ſin hülen vnd zänklaffen
wär dahin kumpt dem wirt zſchaffen
Das keiner me vaſt vßhar ficht
[Eiii[v]] wee dem der von Gott dar wirt gricht
Wir ſind all brüder hie vff erden
mit fygenden müſſend wir eins werden
Ouch vnſren ſchuldnern hie nachlon
ſo wir wend mit einander gon
Widrumb in des vatters rych
iſt not das einer dem andren wych
Sol nun din meinung fürſich gon
wie du den text haſt dar thon
So gwünn ich recht vnd du nit
ein Byſpil merck / da züg ichs mit
Wenn wir mit einander giengen

1997 von] vor *AE*

if you look at what comes before it in the same chapter: you will see that God is teaching us about unity. He says that, before we lay our gifts upon the altar, we should be at peace with one another, and he threatens us with the pains of hell if we don't do this. The text says nothing at all about purgatory. Christ alone offers us peace. He says: 'You should be at peace with your adversary when you go before the altar. On your way there you should be reconciled to him. Otherwise he will deliver you to the judge, and the judge will deliver you to his servant, who will put you in prison' – and deservedly so. For he who does not forgive here on earth will not be forgiven (as Christ says), when God comes to judge all men. He will judge them with fire. The righteous man will live joyfully forever, but the godless man will have to go to a prison where there will be wailing and gnashing of teeth. Whoever goes there will have to see to it that no one fights his way out. Woe to him who is judged by God! We are all brothers here on earth, and we must be reconciled with our enemies and forgive our debtors. If we want to go together into the kingdom of God, we must submit to one another. But even if the way you expounded the text were valid, I'd still be right and you'd be wrong. Let me prove my point with an example. If you and I were walking along

vnd der glychen anfiengen
Vnd kämind beid für Gottes gricht
wir wurdind von einandren gſchlicht
Ich käm in kercker / vnd du daruon
wie wurd es gon hie loß nun
Müßt ich nun im kercker ſin
biß das ich bzalte vnd lyden pin
So mag denn Iopp nit für mich ſton
noch Daniel wie du dar haſt thon
So můß ich ſelbs burde tragen *Galat. 6.*
ſo hilfft mich nüt das ſeelen klagen
Ouch ſprichſt / es helff nit Noes fürbitt *Iero. lib. 3.*
ſo hilfft kein gůthat dſeelen nit *ſup. illud*
Wenn yeder ſin burde tragen můß *Gallat. 6.*
ſo hilfft für dſeelen nun kein bůß *Ioann. 3.*
Wenn wär nit gloubt der iſt ſchon gricht *Marc. 16.*
der ſpruch allein die din all bricht *Ioan. 3.*
Der wirt nit gricht der an jnn gloubt
[Eivr] des ewigen läbens nit beroubt
Du züchſt ein andren ſpruch ouch yn
Der wirt gantz wider dich ſin
Wir müſſend vor dem richtſtůl ſton
vnd Gott mit vns rechnen lon
Vmb gůtz vnd böß gott rechnung geben *2. Cor. 5.*
diſer ſpruch der fügt mir eben
Der zeygt an das nun zween wäg ſind
lůg wo man denn das fägfhür find
Er ſpricht / wir müſſind all da ſton
ſo ſind wir nie all zemen kon
Sind wir denn nit noch all da gſin
ſo far nun mit dem fägfhür hin
Wir all müſſend zemen kummen
die gůten werdend vßgnommen
Darnach gfürt ins Paradiß
die böſen in einer andren wyß *Math. 25.*

2043 Gallat. 6.] *om. CDF*

and had a disagreement, and we both came before God's court of judgement and were separated one from the other, such that I went into the dungeon and you escaped, what would happen? Listen now. If I had to be in the dungeon until I had paid, and had to suffer pain, then Job couldn't stand before God on my behalf, and nor (as you said) could Daniel, but rather I would have to carry my own burden.[269] People's laments for my soul wouldn't help me. You also say that neither Noah's interceding nor any good deeds could help my soul. Because if everyone has to carry his own burden, no penance on behalf of dead souls can do any good:[270] he who does not believe is already condemned.[271] That verse alone shatters all of yours. Anyone who believes in him will not be condemned, and will not be deprived of eternal life. You also brought to bear a second verse, which again actually argues dead against you. We must stand before God's judgement seat and let God weigh us in the balance; we must give an account before God for our good and bad works.[272] This verse too works in my favour. It shows that there are two paths. Have a look, can you find any mention of purgatory? He says that we must all stand there, but in fact we have never come together. If we haven't all been there together, then feel free to go away and believe in purgatory. But in fact we do all have to come together: then, the good people are separated out and taken to paradise, but the evil ones go off in a different direction.

269 Galatians 6:5: 'For all must carry their own loads'. The marginal reference to Jerome's commentary on Galatians (*Commentarium in Epistolam ad Galatos Libri tres, PL* XXVI, 425–38) achieves nothing beyond pointing superficially to Eckstein's (or perhaps Joß Hechelzan's) learning. Certainly Jerome makes no reference to Job, Daniel, or Noah in this context.

270 John 3:18: 'Those who believe in him are not condemned; but those who do not believe are condemned already, because they have not believed in the name of the only Son of God'.

271 Mark 16:16: 'The one who believes and is baptized will be saved; but the one who does not believe will be condemned'.

272 2 Corinthians 5:10 (see above, n. 259).

Die gůts hand thon ins ewig läben *Ioann. 5.*
den böſen wirts hellſch fhür ggeben
Hörſt da wirt kein mittel ſin
ouch fürſt ein andren ſpruch yn
Der iſt nun gantz wider dich
darumb den text bas bſich
Hör zů nun wie der text ſag
er zügt ouch vff den Iüngſten tag *1. Corin. 3*
Eins yeden werck wirt offenbar
durch fhür probiert / ſo blybt zwar
Sälig der lyb / das werck nun brennt
das iſt Sant Pauls Argument
Des herren tag iſt noch nit gſin
[Eiv^{v}] ſo iſt kein werck durchs fhür hin
Probiert biß vff den hüttigen tag
darumb der ſpruch nüt zügen mag
Zeyg mir ein werck das da ſy probiert
im fhür wie Paulus ynhar fürt
Stünd er wie du ſeyſt daruon
ſo wär kein ſeel noch zgnaden kon
Vnd müßtind dſeelen lyden pyn
der jüngſt tag iſt ye noch nit gſin
Můß mans im fhür denn vor probiern
ſo wirſtus hüpſchlich vßhar fürn
Můſt warten biß zuns herren tag
die ſeelen wol verdrieſſen mag
Drumb ſag ich dir min Doctor Fritz
das fägfhür hat noch kleine hitz
Du magſt mit dinem tandt nit bſton
ich můß mich bas an dich lon
Hör zů was Chriſtus ſelbs lert
fürwar ſag ich / der min wort hört *Ioan. 5.*
Vnd gloubt dem der mich hat gſendt
der wirt ewig von mir nit trendt
Vnd wirt ouch für das gricht nit kon *Ioan. 3.*

2089 zů des *CD*, ans *F*

Those who have done good works go to eternal life, whereas the evil ones receive the fires of hell.[273] Listen: there will be no middle way. You also cite another verse which works completely against you. Consider the text better; hear what it really says. It too is about Judgement Day: 'Everyone's works will be revealed and tested by fire'.[274] So the body remains unharmed; it's the works that are burnt. That's St Paul's argument. The Day of Judgement hasn't yet come, so, up to now, no work has yet been tested by fire. So that verse doesn't say what you want it to. Show me a work that has been tested in the fire in the way St Paul speaks of. If what you say were true, no soul would ever have come into grace, and the souls would be suffering pain. The Last Day hasn't yet happened. So do you have to test your soul in the fire before that Day comes? You'll have to argue that very prettily! Or do you have to wait until the Day of the Lord? That's the reason, good Doctor Fritz, why purgatory hasn't yet been heated. You won't win the argument with your sophistries: I must instruct you better. Listen to what Christ himself teaches: 'Truly I say to you, he who hears my Word and believes him who has sent me will never be separated from me and will not come into judgement,

273 John 5:28: 'For the hour is coming when all who are in their graves will hear his voice and will come out – those who have done good, to the resurrection of life, and those who have done evil, to the resurrection of condemnation'.

274 1 Corinthians 3:13 (see n. 263 above).

darzů vom tod ins läben gon
Er ſpricht: Wär hört das wort min
der wirt des vrteyls ledig ſin
Vnd vom tod gon ins läben
hörſt da wirt kein vrteyl ggeben
Welcher denn ſin wort nit hört
den nechſten er in dhell fert
Das vrteyl treyt er mit jm drin
[Ev^{r}] da můß er ewig inn ſin
Hör was Chriſtus wyter ſag
die gſchrifft ligt heyter an dem tag
Ich bin das läben vnd die vrſtend *Ioann. 11.*
ſtirbt einer vſſz diſem ellend
Das läben wirt jm widergeben
gloubt er / jm wirt das ewig läben
Er ſpricht: Wölcher gloubt in jn
wie köndiſt nun darwider ſin?
Wider Ioannem ſolt nit ſtreben
gloubſt du nit du haſt kein leben *1. Ioann. 5.*
Der da gloubt wirt nit geurteylt werden
der nit gloubt iſt gricht vff erden
Das ſind doch nun völlige wort
darzů aller glöubigen hort
Das ich weyß wenn ich gloub in ſun
ſo darff ich nit zwyflen nun
Ich hab gwüß das ewig läben
über mich wirt kein vrteyl geben
So darff ich nit ins fägfhür
Chriſtus hat mich erkoufft thür *I. Cor. 6.*
Das ich jnn im hertzen trag
vnd nit fürcht den böſen tag
Denn was ſin iſt das iſt ouch min
durch jnn tring ich durch all pin
Müßt ich bzalen ins fägfhürs not
was hulff mich denn ſin blůt rhot?

but will go from death to life'.[275] He says: 'He who hears my Word will be free from judgement, and will go from death to life'.[276] Listen: no judgement will be given. He who does not hear his Word will take his neighbour with him into hell. He carries the judgement with him there, and he must be there for ever. Hear what Christ goes on to say (the Scriptures clearly show this): 'I am the resurrection and the life. If someone dies in this vale of tears, his life will be restored to him if he believes: he will receive eternal life'.[277] He says: 'Whoever believes in him'. How could you be against that? You shouldn't strive against St John. If you don't believe, you won't have life; but he who believes will not be condemned. He who does not believe is judged on earth. Those are now all the words you need, and it is a treasure to all believers, to know that if I believe in the Son, I do not need to doubt; I will certainly have eternal life, and no judgement will be given against me. So I don't have to go into purgatory: Christ has purchased me at a great price,[278] so that I might carry him in my heart and not fear the evil day. For what is his is mine also; and because of him I can pass through all troubles. If I had to pay for everything in the pain of purgatory, how would his red blood help me then?

275 John 5:24: 'Very truly, I tell you, anyone who hears my word and believes him who sent me has eternal life, and does not come into judgement, but has passed from death to life'.

276 John 3:16: 'For God so loved the world that he gave his only Son, so that everyone who believes in him may not perish but may have eternal life'.

277 John 11:25: 'I am the resurrection and the life. Those who believe in me, even though they die, will live, and everyone who lives and believes in me will never die'.

278 1 Corinthians 6:20 (see n. 219 above).

Er hat zalt für die gantzen welt *1. Ioann. 2.*
vnd gibt vns gnad er darff kein gelt
er hat vmkert der hellen zelt

[Ev[v]] **Weybel Schwynbeltz.**
Gnad min herr Gugel frantz
wie gfalt dir der ſeelen tantz
Du haſt hie kleine kundſchafft ghan
kein bůchſtaben nye zeiget an
Der da vff ein fägfhür ſag
iſt das nit ein groſſe klag
Das du ſeyſt das nit iſt
dauon vns büt der Endchriſt
Diewyl vns Gott dauon nüt büt
wie ſind jr denn ſo gytig lüt
Das jr hand darus gmacht ein bott
vß üch ſelb / vnd nit vſſz Gott *Eſaie. 30.*
Nun ſinn ein yeder frummer Chriſt
diewyl von Gott nit botten iſt
Das man für die todten bitt
ſo dient man jm vergeben mit *Eſaie. 29.*
Thůnd wir denn das er nit hat botten *Matth. 15.*
vnd volgend ye den pfaffen rotten
Gebend wir jn vil / ſo hands des me
das thůt den ſeelen nit wol noch wee
Es kumpt allein den pfaffen wol
jr hüſer ſtäckend ſeelgrädt vol
Hand acht ſo einer jarzyt hat
vnd ſiner vordren dächtnuß bgadt
Man můß zů allen altren gon
wär gibt es denn der vnderthon?
Wäm kumpt es baß denn jm allein
das opfer treyt er mit jm heym
Sy läbend ouch zun zyten wol

2135 bzalt *CDF*   2154 29] 92 *CDF*

He has atoned for the whole world,[279] and he gives us grace. He needs no money for this: he has already defeated hell.

Weybel Schwynbeltz

Greetings, Lord Gugelfrantz:[280] how do you like the dance of the souls? You haven't given us much of a message, and haven't shown us a single word that talks about purgatory. Isn't that a great pity? In saying things that aren't true, you bring us the message of the Antichrist, whereas God doesn't say anything about it. How come you are such greedy people that you've had to invent a command of your own about purgatory which isn't from God?[281] Now all faithful Christians should consider that it is not commanded by God that we should pray for the dead. You're serving him in vain if you do that.[282] If we do what he hasn't commanded[283] and continue to follow the pack of priests, we'll give them loads of money – then they will get still richer, but we won't be doing either good or harm to the dead souls. It's only the priests who benefit from it. Their houses are full of wills and documents endowing Masses.[284] They take care to note when the anniversaries of people's deaths fall and their relations are commemorating this. Then they have to go and wait at all the altars. Who then offers his services? And whom does all this benefit but the priest? He brings the collection home with him, and has a good time on it.

279 1 John 2:1–2: 'But if anyone does sin, we have an advocate with the Father, Jesus Christ the righteous; and he is the atoning sacrifice for our sins, and not for ours only, but also for the sins of the whole world'.

280 'Gugelbube', 'Gugelfranz' and 'Gugelweit' are all recorded by the *FWB* (VII, 630–2) as mocking names for clerics.

281 Isaiah 30:1: '"Oh, rebellious children", says the Lord, "who carry out a plan, but not mine"'.

282 Cf. Isaiah 29:13: 'The Lord said: "Because these people draw near with their mouths and honour me with their lips, while their hearts are far from me, and their worship of me is a human commandment learned by rote; so I will again do amazing things with this people, shocking and amazing"'.

283 Cf. the quotation from Isaiah recorded in Matthew 15:8–9.

284 'Seelgerät' translates the Latin term *testamentum ad pias causas*, though in the later Middle Ages it tended to be used in particular for Masses celebrated *ad remedium anime*, for the healing of the (dead) soul. See *SI* VI, 1622.

[Evi[r]] denn wirt Caplan vnd ſigriſt voll
Als bald der imbiß nun iſt vß
ſo machend ſy im Quatterduß
Fahend an ſpilen vnd karten
vnd mögend kum biß morn warten
Das man denckt eins andren todten
nun me har / das iſt verſchroten
So bald ſy kömmend in*s* ſigental
einer klagt dem andren ſin vnfal
Vnd fahend an denn ſuffragieren
der ein den andren wil Cittieren
Ouch richtends biderblüt vß
es wär zfil im frouwen huß
Das iſt jr lotzdienſt vnd ouch bitt
gibt man jnen Preſentz nit
So zürnend ſy von ſtundan
hand ein für ein böſen zinßman
Wirt eim nit me denn zween ſchillig
ſo iſt er nit als gůt willig
Als wenn man jm ein batzen gitt
pur kumm nun on gelt nit
Alſo verkouffend ſy das brot
vnd ſagend heyter / es ſyg Gott
Wie er am crütz ghanget ſy
doch gelt müß ſin allein daby
Iudas hat das eineſt thon *Marc. 15.*
vnd bracht kein haller nie dauon
Er hat ye wider geben das gelt *Luce. 23.*
wo findt man in der gantzen welt
Ein / der ein haller widergeb?
[Evi[v]] vnd vſſz ſiner eignen arbeit leb
Nun iſt der Iudas frümmer gſin
der warff das gelt doch wider hin *Math. 27.*
Vnd bkant das er vnrecht hatt thon
vnd mocht denocht nit zgnaden kon

2175 in *AE*

Both chaplain and sexton do themselves well; and as soon as they've finished eating they start shouting 'quatre deuce',[285] gamble, and play cards. They can hardly wait for the next morning, when it's time to commemorate some other dead person. Scarcely has someone died but they already find their way into the document chest. Once there, one complains to the other of his misfortune, and then they start to squabble and issue citations to one another. And they tell decent people that there was too much going on in the whorehouse. This is what their service of God and their prayer is all about; and if you don't give them presents, they'll soon get angry and reckon you're a poor payer. If a priest doesn't get any more than two shillings, he's not as well disposed towards you as if he'd been given a batzen: 'Don't come to me without money, you farmer'. And so they sell us bread, happily telling us that it's God, who hung on the cross for us. It seems money just has to be involved, as it once was for Judas.[286] But he didn't earn a single penny from it: he gave the money back.[287] Where in the whole world nowadays can you find someone who'd hand back even that much, and live instead by his own labour? But Judas was holier than people today: after all, he threw the money away and admitted his wrongdoing, even though he did not come into grace because of it.

285 A term from backgammon.

286 Judas's acceptance of money to betray Jesus is recorded in Matthew 26:14–16; Mark 14:10–11; and Luke 22:3–6.

287 The distraught Judas's return of the 30 pieces of silver to the High Priests is in fact recorded only by Matthew (27:3).

Gieng hin erhanckt ſich mit eim ſtrick
ich fürcht es gſchech noch offt vnd dick
Einer wüſſz das dMeſſz kein opffer ſy
dennocht bhalt jnn der gyt daby
Nun iſt es ſchwär alſo ſünden
da einer nit kan in jm finden
Das dMeſſz doch mög ein opffer ſin?
die ſelb ſünd nimpt kein opffer hin *Hebre. 10.*
Da einer weyßt daß vnrecht iſt *2. Petri. 2.*
thůts nüt deſtminder zů aller friſt
Gott erlücht ein yeglich hertz
das man nit alſo mit jm ſchertz
Vmmballe wie ein katz die Mus
gouglen ghört ins füllhuß
Da man von tiſch zů tiſch vmb gadt
Gotslyb ſich nit radbrechen ladt
Er iſt vf gen himmel gfaren
jm dienend all engel ſcharen
Er laßt ſich nit ins pfaffen hand
wie ein hergott an der wand
Alſo hab yetz min red ein end
Gott vns vſſz allem jrthumb lend.

Herolt.
Gnediger Doctor herr Laurentz
[Evii^{r}] biſt von Chur oder von Valentz
Nimm ouch hie etwas zhanden
du biſt lang gnůg müſſig gſtanden
Sag vns von der Bicht vnd Bůß
gen dir ſitzt hie Hans Ofenrůß

Doctor Laurentz.
Ich bin nit darumb har kon
das ich von dir bring gſpött daruon
Ich bin yetz meng jar Doctor gſin

2213 erlüchte *CDF* 2224 wend *CDF*

He went and hanged himself with a rope. I fear that nowadays it happens all the time that someone knows that Masses aren't sacrifices, but still continues celebrating them out of greed. It's a serious thing to sin in this way, since no one can prove that the Mass is actually a sacrifice. People should not accept any offerings for it:[288] but even though they know it's wrong, they still do it all the time.[289] May God enlighten everyone's heart, so that we don't play around with him, like a cat with a mouse. Trickery like this belongs in a house of gluttony, when people are going from table to table. God's body can't be broken on a wheel: he has ascended into heaven, where all the companies of angels worship him. He doesn't let himself be taken down from the wall and put into a priest's hand like a crucifix. My speech is now at an end. May God lead us away from all error!

Herald
Gracious doctor Sir Laurentz: if you're from Chur or Valens, take up something here too; you've spent long enough doing nothing. Tell us about confession and penance. Hans Ofenrůß is here sitting opposite you.

Doctor Laurentz
I haven't come here to be mocked by you. I've been a doctor these many years now,

288 Hebrews 10:11–12: 'And every priest stands day after day at his service, offering again and again the same sacrifices that can never take away sins. But when Christ had offered for all time a single sacrifice for sins, "he sat down at the right hand of God"'.

289 2 Peter 2:21: 'For it would have been better for them never to have known the way of righteousness than, after knowing it, to turn back from the holy commandment that was passed on to them'.

der weybel weyßd wol wär ich bin
Frag jnn darumb das er dirs ſag
warumb ich das rot hütli trag

Herold.
Ich ſpott din nit min lieber Lentz
biſt du denn nit von Valentz?
Ich hab dich für ein Doctor ghan
villicht bin ich nit recht dran
Du ſichſt eben wie ein papiſt
ſag an du weybel wär er iſt

Weybel
Er ſyg von Chur oder von Valentz
jch wän er ſyg Doctor Laurentz
Vnd ſyg von Fäldkilch vſs der ſtatt
zů Baden yetz ein pfrůnd hatt
Iſt ouch vor zyten Zürich gſin
jm gieng da nit vil opffers yn
Drumm zoch er vff ein beßre pfrůnd
[Evii^{v}*]* wie all Fägſhür heitzer thůnd
Sin kunſt hat ouch kleinen athen
jſt Doctor gmacht vom Legaten
So wol thůt jm die doctorſchafft
jſt klein / aber ſunſt mannhafft
gadt gern wol bkleydt in wadt vnd ſyden
hat gar nüt vff pfaffen glyden
Iſt einigs läbens wie Helias /
hat ouch etwan mit dirnen quies
Iſt ouch am erſten Lutriſch gſin
biß das jm nüt me gon wolt yn
Vnd man nüt hatt vff ſiner kunſt
do vergieng jm der Lutriſch dunſt
Vnd nam das trüb wider zhanden
jſt lang vff Hochenkräyen gſtanden
Dahar kumpt jm ſin Doctorat
er wurde lieber ein Legat

and the Weybel knows perfectly well who I am. So ask him to tell you why I'm wearing this red hat.

Herald
I'm not mocking you, my dear Lentz. Aren't you from Valens then? I thought you were a doctor, but perhaps I'm wrong in that. You certainly look like a papist. Tell me, Weybel, who is he?

Weybel
Whether he's from Chur or Valens,[290] I think he's Doctor Laurentz and comes from the city of Feldkirch. He now has a benefice at Baden, and previously was at Zurich. The collections weren't great there, though, so he moved to a better job, as all the heaters of purgatory fire do. His learning is pretty short-breathed, too. Papal legates made him a doctor, and his doctorate does him a lot of good:[291] he's small but manly, and is keen to go about well dressed in cloth and silk. In some ways he's like Elijah. He sometimes takes his ease with whores. At first he was a Lutheran, until he found that it didn't pay and that people didn't think much to his learning. Then he returned to the trough, and was for a long time at Hohenkrayen. That's where his doctorate comes from, though he would really rather have been a legate.

290 The relevance of the toponyms mentioned in this speech to Laurentius Merus is not always clear, but they are doubtless intended to point to the peripatetic nature of his career, and hence to his perceived inconstancy of character. Collectively they encompass various different parts of Switzerland: Chur is in the Canton of Graubünden, Valens in that of St. Gallen, Huttwil is near Berne, and Hohenkrähen is on Lake Constance.

291 Vasella plausibly suggests (n. 2, p. 44) that this sentence might mean that Merus enjoyed papal support during his studies, and indeed that he took his degree at the University of Rome, rather than at a German institution.

Er darffs werden in kurtzer yl
ja ſturb der Biſchoff zHutwyl
Da halt yetz ein biſchoff hus
da der bachof hangt über dmur vs
Drumb min Lentz laß dich nit duren
wir hend hie wie all puren
Nüt in Rhetorica gläſen
wir redend hie nach pürſchem wäſen
In vnſerem tal iſt es ſitt
das man ein irret nitt
Er ſyg Doctor oder bader
drumb du nit anfach erſt ein hader
Vnd ſag vns recht hie von der Bůß
[Eviii r] loß im du Hans Ofenrůß

Doctor Laurentz.
Ich wil ja von der Bycht ſagen
das jr üch nit mögind klagen
Ich ſye hie nun hädrig gſyn
hie far ich mit ſant Marxen yn
Als dIuden ſind an Iordan ggangen
den touff von ſant Iohans empfangen
Habend ſy bychtet ire ſünd *Marc. 3.*
als ich ouch in Mattheo find *Matth. 3.*
Da ſtadt es klar: Nun beßrend üch.
ſant Iacoben ich ouch ynhar züch
Der heißd eins dem andren bychten *Iacobi. 5.*
da har iſts kon biß an dgwychten
Diewyls ſant Iacob gheiſſen hett
ſo wärs nit gůt das mans nit thät *Auguſti.*
Der meinung ſind all leerer gſyn *ſuper Ioan*
die bycht mindre vns die pyn *nem tra*
Habend vil von der bůß gſchriben *ctatu. 124.*
bycht iſt vil hundert jar bliben *Ambroſi.*
Das mans hett gthon by dem bann *li. 2. de pe*
yetz bychtet weder wyb noch mann *nit. ca. 5.*

He might indeed soon become one. The Bishop of Huttwil died, and he now has a bishop's house with the oven hanging out over the wall.[292] So then, my good Lentz, don't delay. Those of us here, like all farmers, haven't studied rhetoric, and so speak in a rustic way. It's the custom in our valley not to stand on ceremony with anyone, whether you're a doctor or a barber. So don't start a quarrel, but tell us straightaway about penance. Listen to him, Hans Ofenrůß.

Doctor Laurentz

As to confession, I want to say that you've nothing to complain about. I'm not being quarrelsome here, but am coming to you with St Mark. When the Jews went up to the Jordan to be baptized by St John, they confessed their sins[293] – as I find also in Matthew. There it's clearly stated: 'Now amend your life'.[294] I can also bring St James to bear: he commands people to confess their sins to each other.[295] From there it has come to mean that you should make your confession to ordained priests. But since St James has commanded it, it wouldn't be good not to do it. All teachers have been of the opinion that confession reduces our suffering. They've written a lot about penance: confession has been going on for many hundreds of years, when people have been doing it in fear of the ban. But nowadays no one goes to confession,

292 An obscure image, though 'bachof' (oven) can also mean 'big (or loud) mouth', and a carnival float from Zurzach, where Merus spent some of his career (see *SI* IV, 291). Maybe also 'mur' is a play on his surname?

293 Mark 1 (*sic*): 4–5: 'John the baptizer appeared in the wilderness, proclaiming a baptism of repentance for the forgiveness of sins. And people from the whole Judean countryside [...] were going out to him, and were baptized by him in the river Jordan, confessing their sins'. See also Matthew 3:1 and 5.

294 Matthew 3:2: 'Repent, for the kingdom of heaven has come near'.

295 James 5:16: 'Therefore confess your sins to one another'. The marginal references that follow this one in the German text (from l. 2299) are presumably intended to point to Merus's pride in his learning. His referencing is somewhat hit-and-miss: Isidore of Seville's *De summo bono*, II, 13 is indeed a chapter on 'De confessione peccatorum', but St Gregory's *Moralia in Job* does not have a chapter (or section) 49 in its fourth book. The other citations are genuine enough: Augustine discusses the efficacity of penance in the thirty-third of his *In Ioannis Evangelium Tractatus CLXXIV* (*PL* XXXV, 1650–1), and Ambrose in his *De poenitentia libri duo* (not least in II, 5 – *PL* XVI, 504–7).

Es gfallt den puren vaſt wol
das man nit mee bychten ſol *Grego. 4.*
Ich hab es von mengem ghört *mo. ca. 49.*
wölt Gott das bychten wär erweert *Iſido. li. 2.*
Das ich nit mee bychten ſött *de ſum. b.*
Gott hett erhört jr bätt *cap. 13.*
Thůt es gůts / Ich will gern ſehen
[Eviii^{v}*]* Es ſol in miner pfarr nit gſchehen
Die puren müſſend all jar bichten
darnach ſol ſich ein yeder richten
Es iſt ein gůte gwonheit
das einr ſin ſünd dem pfaffen ſeyt
So wirt eim ggeben rechte Bůß
das ſag ich dir Hans Ofenrůß

Hans Ofenrůß.
Die ſprüch die du all dar haſt thon
find ich alſo (wie du ſagſt) ſton
Das ſy aber bichtet habind
wie wir zů den pfaffen trabind
vnd heimlich gſagt ire ſünd
zeig an wo ich das ſelb find

Doctor Lentz.
Du grober filtz ſol ich dichs leeren
weiſt noch nit was iſt Confiteri?

Hans Ofenrůß.
Confiteri heyßd mir bkennen
man mag es ouch für ſchwätzen nemmen
Ouch mag es heyſſen lobſagen
aber wo heißds dem pfaffen klagen?
Das einer hat heimlich gthon
jch finds nun gar an keim ort ſton
Die Iuden hand ouch bichtet nit
wie wir yetz thůnd / es was nit ſitt

2324 trabttind *CDF*

either women or men. The farmers really like not having to confess any more. I've heard many people say: 'I wish to God there wasn't such a thing as confession, so that I didn't have to do it any more'. Their prayer has been answered. I'm willing to see whether it does any good – but it won't happen in my parish. There, farmers have to go to confession every year. Everyone should do this: it's a good habit to tell your sins to a priest; that way, you're given proper absolution. That's what I have to say to you, Hans Ofenrůß.

Hans Ofenrůß
I too can find all the Scriptures you've mentioned. But that these people confessed to a priest as we do, and told him their sins in secret – tell me where I can find that.

Doctor Laurentz
You great fool, do I have to teach you that? Don't you know what 'confiteri' means?

Hans Ofenrůß
To me, 'confiteri' means to confess. You can also define it as talking to somebody. It can also mean to praise. But where does it mean 'to bemoan your sins to a priest'? I can't find it written anywhere that someone did this in secret. The Jews also didn't confess as we do; it wasn't their custom.

Hettinds bichtet wie wir hand thon
[Fi^{r}] war kam Ioannes mit dem lon?
Sy hand zwar kein gelt mit inen bracht
die Bycht iſt erſt vom Bapſt erdacht
Denn hettinds bychtet wie du ſeyſt
wär es eineſt gſchehen aller meyſt
Wir puren müſſend all jar kon
zweymal vor der Communion
Der Bapſt ouch nun von eim mal ſeyt
der tüfel das ander hat zůtreyt
Was iſt nun gůtz von beyden kon?
den puren habend irs gelt abgnon
Vnd hands quittiert zur ſelben ſtund
ſind on ſünd gſyn / wie ein hund
On flöch im Ougſten vmmhar loufft
die gnad Gots hat man inen abkoufft
Ouch kumpſt du mit ſant Iacob har
der gſchriben hat der Iüdſchen ſchar
Ee die bäpſt die bycht erdächten
hat er gſchriben den zwölff gſchlächten *Iacob. 1.*
Die da warend wyt zerſtröuwt
ſant Iacob nun nüt vom bychten ſeyt
Vnd wär es ſchon wie du ſprichſt
Lůg obd nit wider dich ſelbs fichſt
Sölt einer dem anderen bychten dſünd
als ich nit in der Epiſtel find
So müßt ein pur dem anderen bychten
vnd kämind nit für üch gwychten
Denn do ſant Iacob gſchriben hatt
do was weder pfaff noch blatt
Wie Iacob ſchrybt / wil er damitt
[Fi^{v}] das einer für den andren bitt
Vnd yetlicher ſich ſchuldig gäb
einer fründtlich mit dem andren läb
Ouch kumpſt du mit Ioannes bůß
jch hör das ich dich leeren můß
Was Ioannes zbůß hab ggeben

If they had confessed as we do, where would John the Baptist have got his reward? They certainly didn't bring any money with them on that occasion. No, confession was first invented by the Pope. Because if the Jews had confessed as you say they did, it wouldn't have happened more than once. We farmers have to go to confession before Communion twice a year. The Pope says only once; the devil has added the second occasion to it. But what good has come from doing it twice? You've relieved farmers of their money and given them a receipt for it at the same time; but they've been without sin, like a dog might run around in August without fleas. God's grace has been bought from them. And you come at us with St James, who was writing to the Jewish people before the Pope had thought up the idea of 'confession'! He was writing to the twelve tribes who were widely scattered.[296] Now St James isn't saying anything about confession (as we now understand it); and if what you say were true, you'd better be careful not to argue against yourself. Because if one person were to confess his sin to another (which I don't myself find written in the epistle), then surely one farmer would confess to another farmer, and wouldn't present himself before you ordained ones. Because when St James was writing, there was neither priest nor certificate. What he wants to achieve by writing this is that one should pray before another and each confess his sins, and that all should live in harmony with each other. You also come at us with John's penance. I see that I've got to teach you about what John gave as a penance.

296 James 1:1: 'James, a servant of God and of the Lord Jesus Christ, To the twelve tribes in the Dispersion: Greetings'.

loß mir zů / jch ſag dirs eben
Ioannes bůß die iſt gſyn
als glychßner kamend / dIuden mit in
Zů Ioanſen an Iordan
do zeigt jnen Ioannes an
Wie Chriſtus nun zůkünfftig wär
brächt gnad fürs gſatz / das wäre ſchwär
Die ax wär gſetzt nun an den ſtamm *Matth. 3.*
ſy ſöltind nit den Abraham
Im hertzen für ein vatter ſagen
wie ſy hattend gſagt all jr tagen
Damit er jnen gab zůuerſton
es müßt nun anders zůgon
Vnd ſyg nit gnůg mit läfftzen ſagen
man müß es ouch im hertzen tragen
Gott bkanten dIuden nun mit mund
das kam nun nit vſſz hertzen grund
Daruf denn Gott gar nüt wil han
er ſicht kein fleiſchlich gſchlächt an
Die bůß ward gſetzt den Iuden yn
ſy ſöltind / wie Abraham glöubig ſyn *Ioan. 8.*
Das thett denn nit das Iüdiſch gſind
drumm hatz Chriſtus fürs tüfels kind
Noch dryerley bůſſen iſt
[Fii^{r}] als Lux ſchrybt der Euangeliſt
Da heyßd Iohans die gmeinen ſcharen *Lucæ. 3.*
heig einr zween röck / ein laß er faren
Einem der da kain rock hab
zum andren den zolnern er zbůß gab
Eim yeden offnen amptman zimpt *Lucæ. 3.*
das er nit mee / denn im ghört / nimpt
Do fragtend jnn ouch die kriegslüt
was ſöllend wir thůn / das ſelb vns büt?
Ir ſöllend für gůt an ſölden han *Lucæ. 3.*
vnkümbret laſſen yederman

2379 an den Iordan *CDF* 2382 wäre nit ſchwär *CDF* 2409 Lucæ. 3.] *om. CDF*

Listen to me, I'll tell you: John's penance was given when hypocrites came, along with the Jews, to him in the Jordan. John showed them how Christ was about to come and put grace before the law. That was a difficult thing for them: the axe was now set beside the tree trunk.[297] They were no longer to say in their hearts that Abraham was their father, as they had done all their days. Rather, he gave them to understand that things had to be different from now on, and that it wasn't good enough to say things with their lips; rather, they had also to carry them in their hearts. The Jews confessed God with their mouths, but it didn't come from the bottom of their hearts. And God has no regard for this: he doesn't look upon anything fleshly. Penance was imposed on the Jews so that they might be faithful, like Abraham.[298] The Jewish people didn't then do it, which is why Christ thought they were the devil's brood. There are three kinds of penance, as the Evangelist Luke writes. There, John tells the common people that, if anyone has two coats, he should give one to someone who doesn't have any.[299] Secondly, he told the tax collectors as a penance that it is right that no official should take any more in taxes than he is supposed to.[300] Then the soldiers also asked him: 'What should we do? Tell us'. 'You should be content with your wages and do violence to no man'.[301]

297 Matthew 3:10 (see n. 83 above).

298 John 8:39–40: 'If you were Abraham's children, you would be doing what Abraham did, but now you are trying to kill me, a man who has told you the truth that I heard from God. This is not what Abraham did'.

299 Luke 3:11: 'Whoever has two coats must share with anyone who has none; and whoever has food must do likewise'.

300 Luke 3:13: 'Collect no more than the amount prescribed for you'.

301 Luke 3:14: 'Do not extort money from anyone by threats or false accusation, and be satisfied with your wages'.

Der glychen bůß hand jr nie brucht
habend nun thon / das üch gůt ducht
Ir wüſſend nit was recht bůß iſt
vnd wänend was üch füll die kiſt
Das ſyg recht bůß / ſicht man wol
drumb ſteckt die gantz welt ſünden vol
So groſſes gſchicht nit in der welt
nun kumm zum pfaffen / bring gelt
So ſpricht der pfaff / Nun ſtifft ein Mäſs
wilt du das Gott der ſünd vergeſs
Das iſt denn nit die recht bůß
einer in ſich ſelbs gon můß
Vnd haſſen was er böß hat thon
das ſelb von hertzen rüwen lon
alſo möcht man zů Gott kon.

Amma Krůg.
Die Lüſelbycht hat gar kein grund
das wirt durch all propheten kund
[Fii[v]] Die heiſſend vns allein Gott bychten
gedenckend nun keiner gwychten
Gott hat vns zůgſagt manigfalt
das er vns wöll in der gſtalt
Selbs gnädig vnd barmhertzig ſyn
ſin ſun vns gſetzt zů pfand yn
Welcher dran nit gnůg wil han
der ist doch ein torecht man
Hör zů was Eſaias ſagt
keer zů mir / denn ich hab veriagt *Eſaie. 44.*
Wie ein wolchen dine ſünd
jch hab dich erlößt / du biſt min gſind
Hat er denn nun dſünd veriagt
ſo ſyg es Gott immer klagt
Das ich nit hab langeſt zů jm keert
die pfaffen hand nit ſömlichs gleert

2418 pfaffen vnd bring *CDF*

You have never given a penance like that: you've just done what you wanted; you don't know what true penance is, and think a proper penance is what fills your chests. So you can see that the whole world is full of sin. When nothing much is happening in the world, just go to the priest and bring your money with you. The priest will say: 'If you want God to forget your sin, pay for a Mass to be said'. But this isn't true penance. Rather, you should examine yourself, hate the evil you have done, and repent of it in your heart. That's the way to come to God.

Amma Krůg

There's no point in auricular confession. This is clear from all the prophets. They tell us to confess to God alone, and don't think of our doing it before an ordained priest. God has told us in many places that he himself wishes to be gracious and merciful towards us; and he has given us his Son as a pledge. Anyone who thinks this isn't enough is a fool. Hear what Isaiah says:[302] 'Turn to me, for I have driven away your sins like a cloud; I have saved you, you are my people'. If, then, God has driven our sins away, we should lament to God that it is a long time since we turned to him: the priests didn't teach us to do such a thing.[303]

302 Isaiah 44:22: 'I have swept away your transgressions like a cloud, and your sins like mist; return to me, for I have redeemed you'.

303 Cf. Isaiah 1:4: 'Ah, sinful nation, people laden with iniquity, offspring who do evil, children who deal corruptly, who have forsaken the Lord, who have despised the Holy One of Israel, who are utterly estranged!'.

Bůß iſt das man rein blyb *Eſaie. 1.*
böße dancken vſs dem hertzen tryb *Mathe. 5.*
recht wandlind vor dem Herren Gott *Mich. 6.*
vnd ſtyff haltind ſine gbott *Ioann. 15.*
Böß thůn ſöllend wir vfhören
vns hüten vor menſchen leeren
Die dem Gotz wort widrig ſind
denn ſo ſind wir Gottes kind *Ioann. 1.*
Wir ſöllend liebhan die grechtigkeit
zů allen zyten ſin bereyt
Dem vndertruckten zhilff kon
witwen vnd weyſen byſton
Denn wil er vns gnädig ſin
vnd nemmen all ſünd von vns hin
[Fiiiv] Das vordret gott nun von vns allen
jm wirt ouch ſuſt kein opffer gfallen
Ouch verſpricht er vns darzů
wir werdind läben hie mit růw *Eſaie. 1.*
Vnd wärind dſünd wie ein rhot tůch
darumb ſich ein yeder růch
Sy werdend gwyßt wie der ſchnee
vnd wil jr nit dencken me *Eſaie. 43.*
Ich bin der erſt / der letſt darzů
tilck dſünd ſelb ab / ich gib üch růw
Iſt das nit gnůg wenn ers ſelb thůt?
ich laß mich dran vnd hab vergůt
Hat ers abthon ich darffs nit büſſen
ich mocht nie thůn das pfaffen hieſſen
Wenn das jar nun vmmhar kam
die alten bůß ich fürhar nam
Vnd ſeyt dann: Herr ich ha*b*s nit thon
dry Mäſſen můßt ich leſen lon
Wenn ich denn ſprach: Wem ſol ichs gen?
ſo ſeyt er denn: Gib ich wils nen
Vnd nam mir ab min armen ſchweyß

2475 hahs *A* 2478 Gibs *CDF*

Penance is to remain pure,[304] to drive evil thoughts out of your heart, to walk justly before the Lord your God,[305] and to stick rigidly to his commands.[306] We should cease doing evil and guard against human teachings which are contrary to God's Word. Because, since we are God's children,[307] we should love justice and always be ready to come to the aid of the oppressed, and to support widows and orphans. For God wishes to be gracious to us and to take from us all our sins. God demands this from all of us, and no other sacrifice will please him. He also promises us that we shall live here in peace, and that if our sins were like a red cloth[308] and caused us great distress, they would become as white as snow. 'And I will not remember them; I am the First and the Last, and I myself will wipe out your sins and give you peace'.[309] If he does it himself, isn't that enough? I will depend on that and accept it. If he has wiped out my sin, I don't need to do penance for it; I don't need to do what the priests tell me. If, when a year was done, I took up my old penance again and said: 'Sir, I haven't done it. I've got to have three Masses read', and if I then said: 'Whom should I go to?', the priest would say: 'If you give me the money, I'll take it'. And he would take from me the very sweat of my poor brow.

304 Cf. Matthew 5:8: 'Blessed are the pure in heart, for they will see God'.

305 Micah 6:8: 'Has he told you, O mortal, what is good; and what does the Lord require of you but to do justice, and to love kindness, and to walk humbly with your God?'

306 John 15:10: 'If you keep my commandments, you will abide in my love, just as I have kept my Father's commandments and abide in his love'.

307 John 1:12: 'But to all who received him, who believed in his name, he gave power to become children of God'.

308 Isaiah 1:18: 'Though your sins are as scarlet, they shall be like snow; though they are red like crimson, they shall become like wool'.

309 Cf. Isaiah 43:10–11: 'Before me no god was formed, nor shall there be any after me. I, I am the Lord, and besides me there is no saviour'.

mengs gitze gab ich von miner geyß
Das ich ſolt ſelber zogen han
gab ich denn für den Mäſſz lan
Eins mals vff Sant Vlrichs tag
min höuw vff der matten lag
Es was lang rägenwetter gſin
vnd was do ſchon / ich trůgs yn
Am abent do ich heim kam
der pfaff den banſchatz von mir nam
[Fiii^{v}] Vnd fieng mir an darzů tröuwen
gelt pur ich well dich leren höuwen
Gib mir har den banſchatz
ich bſchick dir ſuſt ein Citatz
Ich ſtallt jm für ein anckenballen
die was nit groß / wolt jm nit gfallen
Er ſprach: Du můſt wol bas dran
jch ſeyt: Ir ſöllend vergůt han
Sprach: Min herr nun thůnd das beſt
vff dfaßnacht ich ein ſuw meſt
Dauon wil ich üch würſt geben
der pfaff da ſprach: Es iſt mir eben
Zog vſſz dem huß mit der ballen
vnd was ſchier ein beyn abgfallen
Also was er vollen wyn
den gantzen tag im wirtzhuß gſin
Darzů verſpillt was er hatt
vnd dacht / du lyſt wol im katt
Doch ſinnet ich jm ſo vil nach
der pfaff lag / hatt Sant Villtis rach
Vnd dacht / ſoltu im wirtzhuß lappen
vnd ich höuwen mit lärer kappen
Darzů dir ouch geben das min
ſpilen möcht wol ſünder ſin
Denn höuwen an ſant Vlrichs tag

2491 Gib mir har] denck das du mir gebist *CDF* 2492 oder ich schick dir *CDF*
2507 Doch] Do *CDF*

I've given away many of my goat's kids, which I should have raised myself, in payment for Masses. Once, on St Ulrich's Day,[310] my hay was on the meadow: the weather had been rainy for a long time and it had grown quickly, so I harvested it. In the evening, when I came home, the priest took the ban money[311] and started threatening me about it: 'I'll teach you to make hay, farmer; you'd better give me the ban money or I'll send you a citation'. I put a ball of butter before him. It wasn't very big, and he didn't like it. He said: 'You've got to do better than that'. I said: 'You should accept it. I'm doing my best, Sir: I'm fattening a sow for Shrove Tuesday, and I'll give you some sausage from that'. Then the priest said: 'That's all right with me'. He left the house with his ball of butter, and almost fell and broke his leg: he'd been so full of wine in the tavern all day and gambled away all he had. I thought: 'You're lying in the shit'. I thought a lot about this. The priest was lying there, and St Vitus had had his revenge.[312] And I thought: 'Should you be knocking it back in the tavern while I'm out haymaking with empty pockets,[313] and then have to give you what's mine? Gambling might just be a worse sin than haymaking on St Ulrich's Day.

310 14th July.

311 A payment made to the Church in order to escape (or have lifted) a ban (generally 'minor excommunication', involving exclusion from the sacraments). See *SI* VIII, 1658–61; *FWB* II, 1912–13.

312 'St Vitus' Dance' (properly 'Sydenham's Chorea') is a neurological disorder associated with various involuntary, uncoordinated movements which can resemble the symptoms of drunkenness.

313 Literally, an empty coat (or cap).

nit das ich den ancken klag
Mir iſt allein vmb jren bſchiß
ich gib nit me / iſt er wol gwüß

[Fivr] **Hans Ofenrůß.**
Nachpur Lentz / bona dies
hör was me ſpricht Eſaias
Ich bin Gott kein ander mer *Eſaie. 45.*
der gantz erboden zů mir ker
Denn on mich iſt kein andrer Gott
ich mach ſelig / vnd hilff vß not
Er rüfft hie allen gemeyn
vnd ſpricht: Ich bin gott allein
Wir ſöllind all zů jm keren
ghörſt? er ſelb wil vns gneren
Wie kanſt du mir nun nach lon
wenn du ſelb (was ich) haſt thon
So ſind wir nun beyd ſünder
du machſt mir min ſchuld nit minder
Vnd biſt darzů als kranck als ich
wie möchteſt denn gſund machen mich?
Wär nam dem Dauid ſin ſünd ab?
Nathan nit / darfür ichs hab *2. Reg. 12.*
Was wol als heilig als du biſt
dſünd nachlon / gots allein iſt
Weyſt wie man in dem Pſalm findet?
Herr / dir allein hab ich gſündet *Pſalm. 50*
Dauid bychtet keim propheten
das wil ich mit eim pſalmen löten
Ich hab dir min ſünd kund gmacht *Pſalm. 31.*
din grechtigkeit nit veracht
Min ſchalckeit hab ich dir dar thon
herr gott / vnd du haſts nachglon
Der iſt ſelig / wirt nit erklupfft
[Fivv] dem gott ſin ſünd nit vfrupfft

2530 beyd groß ſünder *CDF*

Not that I'm bothered about the butter. It's just the dishonesty that gets me'. I won't give him anything again – he's in no doubt as to that.

Hans Ofenrůß

Good day, neighbour Lenz.[314] Hear more of what Isaiah says: 'I am God, and there is no other.[315] The whole earth should turn to me, for there is no other God but me. I bless you and help you in trouble'. Here he's calling to everyone when he says: 'I alone am God'. We should all turn to him. Do you hear? He himself wants to heal us. How can you absolve me from something that you and I have both done? We're both sinners: you don't make me any less guilty, and are as weak as I am. How then can you make me well? Who relieved David of his sins? Not Nathan, it seems to me.[316] He was certainly as holy as you are; but forgiveness of sins belongs to God alone. Do you know what we find in the Psalms? 'Lord, against you only have I sinned'.[317] David isn't making his confession to any prophet. I'll confirm this with another Psalm: 'I have made my sin known to you and have not despised your justice. I have laid my iniquity before you, Lord God, and you have forgiven me'.[318] The man whose sins God does not pluck up is blessed, and will never be afraid.

314 Latin greetings such as this are used much more sparingly in Eckstein's dialogues than in many – where, again unlike here, they are used exclusively by the clergy. This can be seen as another example of Eckstein's much more thoroughgoing dialogicity, and of the considerable level of intellectual ability he ascribes to his farmers.

315 Isaiah 45:5, 7: 'I am the Lord, and there is no other; besides me there is no god [...] I form light and create darkness, I make weal and create woe'.

316 The interview between David and Nathan following the former's murder of Uriah the Hittite is in 2 Samuel 12:1–15.

317 Psalm 51:4: 'Against you, you alone, have I sinned, and done what is evil in your sight'.

318 Psalm 32:5: 'Then I acknowledged my sin to you, and I did not hide my iniquity'.

Dann ſo ers uns wölt fürleſen *Pſalm. 129.*
herr Gott wär wölt vor dir gneſen?
Ghörſt hie nun Laurentz?
gott allein iſt remittens
Er vergibt vnd nit der pfaff
als wenig ein ſuw iſt ein aff
Hör wie lieblich Gott ſelb ſag
wenn ein můter vergeſſen mag *Eſaie. 49.*
Irs kinds / des ſy ſich nit erbarm
vnd wär ſchon ein můter als arm
Das ſy der frucht jrs lybs nit dächt
ſo wirſt von mir doch nit verſchmächt
Ich wil dinen nit vergeſſen *Eſaie. 49.*
da mag ein yeder Chriſt ermeſſen
So er alſo denckt ſins gſinds
wie ein můter jrs kinds
Das er vns frylich ſälig macht *Epheſ. 2.*
vnd keiner wercken nit acht
Er darff der gůten wercken nit *Pſalm. 15.*
vnd wil allein das man jnn bitt *Roma. 12.*
Vmb ſin gnad vnd barmhertzigkeyt *Pſalm. 33.*
jm lob vnd danck werd allweg gſeyt
Das ſind eins gůten Chriſten frücht
das er all werck vff glouben richt
Vnd was nit vß dem glouben iſt *Rom. 14.*
dauor hüt ſich ein yeder Chriſt
Wie wirt nun aber das probiert? *Deut. 12.*
wenn einer kein werck ynfürt
Denn die da gſetzt ſind in der Bibel
[Fv^{r}] thůt er die ſelben er fart nit übel
Sprichſtu: Der werck ſind mengerley
welches iſt nott das ich denn heyg?
Můß ich die gantzen Bibel han *1. Cor. 7.*
nein / bſchnydung gadt dich nüt me an
Ouch Gott vſopffren vihiſch blůt

2560 Eſaie. 49.] *om. CDF*

Because if he did take account of our sins – who could stand before you, Lord God?[319] Are you listening to this, Laurentz? God alone is 'remittens', he alone remits sins, it is he who forgives – and not the priest, any more than a sow is an ape. Hear how lovingly God himself says: 'Even if a mother forgets her child[320] and does not have compassion on him, even if a mother were so poor that she did not consider the fruit of her womb, I will not despise you'. From that a Christian can judge that he thinks of his people as a mother does of her children, so that he might freely save us, taking no account of works.[321] He doesn't need good works,[322] but wishes only that we should ask for his grace and mercy.[323] May he always receive thanks and praise![324] These are the fruits of a good Christian, that he directs all his works towards faith; and every Christian should guard himself against anything that doesn't spring from faith.[325] How can you prove that?[326] Well, if someone performs only those works that are laid down in the Bible, he will not go wrong. You say: 'But there are many works. Which ones must I do? Do I have to obey the whole Bible?' No: circumcision need no longer concern you,[327] and nor need sacrificing the blood of cattle to God;

319 Psalm 130:3: 'If you, O Lord, should mark iniquities, Lord, who could stand?'

320 Isaiah 49:15: 'Can a woman forget her nursing-child, or show no compassion for the child of her womb? Even these may forget, yet I will not forget you'.

321 Ephesians 2:8: 'For by grace you have been saved through faith, and this is not your own doing; it is the gift of God – not the result of works, so that no one may boast'.

322 Cf. Psalm 16:1–2: 'Protect me, O God, for in you I take refuge. I say to the Lord, "You are my Lord: I have no good apart from you"'.

323 Presumably Romans 12:1: 'I appeal to you therefore, brothers and sisters, by the mercies of God, to present your bodies as a living sacrifice'.

324 Psalm 34:1: 'I will bless the Lord at all times; his praise shall continually be in my mouth'.

325 Romans 14:23: 'For whatever does not proceed from faith is sin'.

326 Deuteronomy 12:28: 'Be careful to obey all these words that I command you today, so that it may go well with you and with your children after you for ever, because you will be doing what is good and right in the sight of the Lord your God'.

327 1 Corinthians 7:19: 'Circumcision is nothing, and uncircumcision is nothing; but obeying the commandments of the Lord your God is everything'.

das blůt Chriſti all opffer hinweg thůt *Hebr. 9.*
Flyß dich allein Chriſti botz *Ioann. 15.*
dem gloub das iſt ein werck Gots
Chriſtus ward ouch von Iuden gfragt
was ſöllend wir thůn? hater jn gſagt *Ioan. 6.*
Das iſt ein recht werck nun
das jr gloubind an Gots ſun
Vnd wie ein boum gůt frucht bringt
on gheyſſen / das man *jnn* nit zwingt
Alſo ouch ein yetlich Chriſt *2. Cor. 8*
zů gůtem ſol ſin allweg grüſt *Galat. 6.*
Man darff eim gůten boum nit ſagen *Epheſ. 4*
du ſolt mir ſo vil öpffel tragen
Vnd wenn mans ſchon lang ſeyt
eins öpffels er nit me treyt
Welche Gottes kinder ſind *Roma. 8.*
die fürt der geiſt Gots gſchwind
Die würckend gůts nach jrer natur
lond ſich vff Gott wie ein mur
Vnd wie ein boum ſin eigne frucht *1. Cor. 13.*
jm ſelbs nit bhalt / darzů nit brucht
Alſo ouch ein yetlich Chriſt
vmbs nächſten nutz ſorgen iſt *Roma. 6.*
Was er denn gůts thůt iſt nit ſin
[Fv^{v}] ſunder des der jms gibt yn
Wie ein räb nit vßtrybt *Ioann. 15.*
ſo ſy nit an dem ſtock blybt
Alſo wir nit on Gott mögen
das aller kleinſt glid rögen
Darumb min Lentz / nun bſinn dich baß
da der rych man in der hell ſaß *Luce. 16.*
Vnd hellſche pyn drinn můßt erarnen
weyſt wär vns dauor ſol warnen?
Moyſes vnd propheten allein

2591 jnn] *om. AE* 2605 Roma. 7 *AE*

the blood of Christ has done away with all other sacrifices.[328] Seek only to perform Christ's commands and to have faith in him.[329] That is the work of God. Christ was also asked by the Jews: 'What should we do?' He said to them: 'It is now a true work of God that you should believe in his Son'.[330] And just as a tree brings forth good fruit without being commanded or forced to,[331] so every Christian also will always be equipped to do good.[332] You can't say to a good tree: 'You've got to bear me so many apples'.[333] And if you did say it, it wouldn't bear a single extra one. And those who are God's children are guided straightaway by God's Spirit.[334] They do good deeds naturally, and lean on God as on a wall. And just as a tree neither needs nor keeps its fruit for itself, so every Christian is concerned for the welfare of others.[335] The good that he does is not his own, but belongs to him who gives it to him.[336] Just as a grape cannot bear fruit unless it remains on the vine, so we cannot move the least of our members without God.[337] So, my dear Lentz, think better of it: do you know who should warn us against being the rich man sitting in hell suffering hellish torments?[338] Only Moses and the prophets,

328 Hebrews 9:12: 'He entered once for all into the Holy Place, not with the blood of goats and calves, but with his own blood, thus obtaining eternal redemption'.

329 John 15:10 (see n. 306 above).

330 John 6:28–9: 'Then they said to him, "What must we do to perform the works of God?" Jesus answered them, "This is the work of God, that you believe in him whom he has sent"'.

331 2 Corinthians 8:8: 'I do not say this as a command, but I am testing the genuineness of your love against the earnestness of others'.

332 Galatians 6:10: 'So then: whenever we have an opportunity, let us work for the good of all, and especially for those of the family of faith'.

333 The relevance of the marginal reference to Ephesians 4 is not clear to us.

334 Romans 8:4 (see n. 230 above).

335 Cf. 2 Corinthians 13:11: 'Put things in order, listen to my appeal, agree with one another, live in peace'.

336 There is here perhaps an echo of Romans 6 (*sic*), with its concept of our having been crucified with Christ and now living with him (verses 5–7).

337 John 15:4: 'Just as the branch cannot bear fruit by itself unless it abides in the vine, neither can you unless you abide in me'.

338 Luke 16:29: 'Abraham replied: "They have Moses and the prophets; they should listen to them"'.

die wyſend vns zů Gott hein
Der Moſes vns die bycht nit wyßt
noch all propheten ſo man ſy durch lißt
So můß ſy nit vß Gott ſin
dann gott hats vns nit gſetzt yn
So iſt nit not das man ſy halt
ob ſchon dem bapſt der buch ſpalt
Zeig mir ein heilgen der gmartret ſy
da einer hab bychtet daby
Du zeygſt mir kein mit warer gſchrifft
drumb iſt die bycht von bäpſten gſtifft
Vnd ſtecket voll glychßner gifft

Weybel.
Nun loß mir ouch min doctor Lentz
jch ler dich / was iſt Penitentz?
Es heyßt in ſich ſelbs gon
die boßheyt vnderwegen lon
Das ſelb im hertzen anfacht
vnd wirt von Gott ins hertz bracht
[Fvi^{r}] Weyſt wie Hieremias ſagt *Hiere. 8.*
ſy hand der ſünd all nach gjagt
Wie ein hengſt loufft in ſtryt
der vogel bkennt ſin zyt
Es iſt nun keiner der ſich klagt
was hab ich thon / in jm ſelb ſagt
Hörſts? ſich ſelb bkennen iſt die bůß *Ezech. 18*
ſünden man vfhören můß
Wenn das gſchicht / ſo volgt härnach
das Gott der herr halt inn die rach *Hiere. 18.*
Die er ſuſt über vns ließ gon
wil ouch von ſim fürnemmen ſton
Gott denn ſelber bůß thůt *agam &*
das iſt / er endret ſin můt *ego*
Wie er gſeyt hat das er thůn wölt
wenn ſich der ſünder abſtellt
Vnd kert ſich von ſim böſen wäg

who direct us towards God. Moses doesn't commend confession, and nor do all the prophets, even if you read them all the way through. So it can't come from God, because God hasn't instituted it; and so you don't have to do it, even if saying that makes the Pope's belly burst open. If you show me an account of a saint who was martyred after having made confession to a priest, you won't be showing me a true report. So confession was instituted by the Pope, and is full of hypocritical poison.

Weybel

Now listen to me also, Doctor Lentz. I'll teach you what penitence is. It means examining yourself and leaving aside evil. This all begins in the heart, whither God brings it. Do you know what Jeremiah says? 'They have all pursued sin like a horse rushing into battle.[339] The bird knows its appointed time, but there is no one who laments or says to himself: "What have I done"'? Do you hear? Penance is admitting your sin[340] and ceasing to commit it. If we do this, the Lord God will hold back the vengeance that he would otherwise have poured on us and will stand back from his intention.[341] God himself repents, then – that is, he changes his mind, as he has said he would do, if a sinner repents,

339 Jeremiah 8:6–7 (see n. 16 above).

340 Ezekiel 18:21: 'But if the wicked turn away from all their sins that they have committed and keep all my statutes and do what is lawful and right, they shall surely live; they shall not die'.

341 Jeremiah 18:7–8: 'At one moment I may declare concerning a nation or a kingdom, that I will pluck up and break down and destroy it, but if that nation, concerning which I have spoken, turns from its evil, I will change my mind about the disaster that I intended to bring on it'.

vnd volget nach dem gotzſtäg *Pſalm. 36.*
Vnd flyßt ſich das er frumm ſy
kert ſich von abgöttery *Ierem. 18.*
vnd laßt dem nechſten ſin wyb *Deuter. 5.*
mit zytigen frouwen nit můtwil tryb *Leuit. 20.*
Vnd bkümbret ouch ſin nechſten nit *Matth. 3.*
dem ſchuldner ſin pfand wider gitt *Deut. 24.*
Darzů nyemant ſtilt das ſin *Leuit. 19.*
vnd fürt die hungrigen mit jm hin *Eſaie. 58.*
Darzů den nackend ouch bkleyt *Matth. 25.*
ſin gelt ouch nit in wůcher leyt *Pſalm. 14.*
Lůg das er nach gotz bott fecht
welcher das thůt der iſt grecht
[Fvi^{v}] Sömlich bůſſen wil Gott han
von allen menſchen wyb vnd man
Er hat nüt vff der pfaffen bůß
das einer ein hund vmbtragen můß
Oder geben ein meſſzgwand
ſo einer in eim frömbden land
Hat gſtolen ſim nechſten lyb vnd gůt
büßt nit ſo ers in dkilchen thůt
Der glychen bůſſen ſind noch vil
ein Türck hats für ein faßnacht ſpil
Das ein todſchleger vmm dkilchen gadt
der pfaff vnder der thüren ſtadt
Vnd mit der růten dflöch jagt
das heyßt die armen ſeelen klagt
Noch eins thůt die pfäffiſch ſchar
ſchickt zů den heilgen hin vnd har
Als ob gnad in den kilchen ſteck
man findt darinn me hundstreck
Vnd ſo man lang vmmloufft

2653 Pſalm. 36.] *om. CDF*

turns away from his evil path,[342] and follows God's ways: striving to be faithful, turning from idolatry,[343] not coveting his neighbour's wife,[344] not consorting with loose women,[345] not troubling his neighbour,[346] and returning pledges to his debtors.[347] Also he will not steal what belongs to anyone else,[348] but will take the hungry into his house,[349] clothe the naked,[350] not lend his money at interest,[351] and see to it that he struggles to carry out God's commands. Anyone who does these things is a just man. This is the penance that God wants from all people, both women and men. He has no regard for the 'penance' of the priests, which makes you carry a dog around with you – or give a Eucharistic robe. If you've stolen life and goods from your neighbour in a foreign country, you don't have to atone for it if you've done so in a church. There are all kinds of such penances. A Turk would think he was seeing a Shrovetide Play[352] if he knew that a murderer might go about a church while, behind the doors, the priest is hunting for fleas with a stick – in other words, is tormenting poor souls. Another thing the priests do is to send you away to see the saints, as if you could find grace through being in certain churches. In fact all you find there is more dog shit, and however much you run around,

342 Cf. Psalm 37:27: 'Depart from evil, and do good; so you shall abide for ever'. Also Jeremiah 18:11: 'Turn now, all of you from your evil way, and amend your ways and your doings'.
343 Jeremiah 18:15: 'But my people have forgotten me, they burn offerings to a delusion'.
344 Deuteronomy 5:21: the Tenth Commandment.
345 Leviticus 20:10–21 describes a range of sins involving sexual acts.
346 A false attribution to Matthew 3: Eckstein may have in mind Matthew 5's passage about burying the hatchet (verses 23–5), or Luke's account of John the Baptist's words of instruction for tax collectors and soldiers (3:12–14).
347 Deuteronomy 24:13: 'You shall give the pledge back by sunset, so that your neighbour may sleep in the cloak and bless you; and it will be to your credit before the Lord your God'.
348 Leviticus 19:11: 'You shall not steal; you shall not deal falsely'.
349 Isaiah 58:6–7: 'Is not this the fast that I choose: [...] to share your bread with the hungry, and bring the homeless poor into your house?'
350 Matthew 25:36, 38, and 43 refer to clothing the naked.
351 Psalm 15:5: '[...] who do not lend money at interest, and do not take a bribe against the innocent. Those who do these things shall never be moved'.
352 Presumably, 'would consider it farcical' (or 'topsy-turvy'?).

nüt denn müde beyn man koufft
Vnd kumpt mit lärem ſeckel heym
es nützt die pfaffen nun allein
Der gytzdienſten ſind noch vil
deren aller Gott nit wil
Da bringt menger blůt zapff
ſant Velltis kopff in eim napff
Ein ſtück von ſant Wendels teſchen
den ryemen von ſant Otmars fleſchen
Damit bättlet er ein groſſe ſumm
vnd loufft von huß zhuß vmm
[Fvii^r] Einer iſt zum heilgen grab gſin
der ander by ſant Katherin
Der dritt vſs Venus berg kumpt
damitt wirt nun dem ſeckel grumpt
Das alles hand pfaffen erdacht
die puren vmb das jr bracht
Vnd übernützt den gmeinen man
wir hands nit anderſt wöllen han
Dſünd laßt ſich nit abkouffen
man darff nit gen Rom louffen
Ouch nit gen Hieruſalem
zů welcher ſtund der ſünder käm
Vnd bkent ſich Gott ſiner ſchuld
ſo gwünnt er gwüſs Gottes huld
Hat er ſchon nüt mit jm bracht
ſiner ſünden wirt nimmer gedacht *Hiere. 18.*
Ich gloub Gottes zůſag
vnd bycht jm alſo alle tag
So dick ichs Vatter vnſer bätt
jch darff ſunſt keins der mich verträtt
Denn jnn allein / den wil ich han
er bgärt das wir jm hangind an
Eins wir in Ioanne findend
ermant er vns das wir nit ſündend

2705 Rom drumm louffen *CDF*

you don't get anything but tired legs and come home with an empty purse. This is only any use to the priests. Still other things are done in the service of greed, none of which God wants. People bring taps to shed blood, St Valentine's head in a bowl, a piece of St Wendelin's bag,[353] the strap of St Otmar's barrel,[354] which he used to beg a large sum and run around from house to house. One man has been to the Holy Sepulchre, another has gone to see St Catherine,[355] a third has come back from the Venusberg.[356] And with all that purses have been emptied. Priests thought up all of this, and have done farmers out of what was their own, and exploited the common man. Formerly we didn't want it to be any different. But you can't have your sins bought off you. You can't run off to Rome for that reason, or to Jerusalem. But whenever the sinner comes and confesses his sin to God, he will win God's favour, even if he hasn't brought anything with him. His sins will not be remembered.[357] I believe God's promise, and so confess to him every day, whenever I pray the Lord's Prayer. I don't need anyone else to act as my representative, save God alone: he's the one I want, and he wishes us to abide in him. We find a verse in St John, where he exhorts us not to sin,

353 Wendelin's standard attribute was a shepherd's bag.

354 Otmar was a Swiss saint, the first Abbot of St. Gallen (c. 689–c. 759). His dead body is said miraculously to have prevented a wine barrel used by thirsty sailors' from becoming dry. Hence such a barrel was his most common attribute.

355 For certain St Catherine of Alexandria, to whom various popular shrines and altars were established in the Middle Ages.

356 A reference, presumably, to the penitent Tannhäuser's pilgrimage to Rome following his escape from the clutches of Venus – as related in the many fifteenth-century versions of the legend (and later by Wagner). See also the introduction, p. 56.

357 The idea of God forgetting sin is not explicitly mentioned in Jeremiah 18; presumably the author is thinking of God's 'repentance' of the harm he has been intending to do to sinners, as described in verses 7–8 (see n. 341 above).

Ob wir aber ſündind damitt
habend wir Chriſtum / der vns vertritt *1. Ioan. 2.*
Er iſt der Ablaß aller welt
heißd vns zů jm kummen on gelt *Eſaie. 55.*
Darumb die ſiben Sacrament
habend pfaffen vff iren nutz gwendt
[Fvii^{v}] Vnd iſt keins in der gantzen welt
man hats von pfaffen koufft vmb gelt
Das iſt nun mächtig wider Got
vnd ouch wider Chriſti bott

Herold.
Doctor Gryff im langen rock
hie ſitzt gen dir Claus Rebſtock
Sag jm hie von dem Sacrament
vnd bring kein heidiſch argument
Sag wie es der text innhab
ob Gott doch ſtig von himmel ab
Vnd kumm zum pfaffen in der Mäſs
das er ſin blůt vnd fleiſch eſs
Es iſt nun der gröſt ſpan
worden / vnderm gmeinen man
Das niemant weißd woran man iſt
einr hats für den lyb Ieſu Chriſt
Der ander für des lybs zeichen
das mag ein andern nit erreychen
Dann ſo es nun ein zeichen iſt
vnd nit der lyb Ieſu Chriſt
So ſolt man es nit bätten an
allein nun für ein zeichen han
Iſt es denn ſin fleiſch vnd blůt
ſo ſol man es han in groſſer hůt
Iſt es nun ein zeichen des lybs
laſs hören wär bricht vns des kybs

2721 1.Ioan.1. *CDF* 2725 A (only) repeats this line at the top of Fvii^{v} 2746 der ſelbs lyb *CDF* 2748 ein] des lybs *CDF*

but says that, if we do sin, we have Christ who will intercede for us. He remits the sin of the whole world,[358] and asks us to come to him without money.[359] But the priests have turned the seven sacraments to their advantage, and now there isn't a single one in the whole world that you can't buy for money from priests. This goes strongly against God and against Christ's commands.

Herald

Doctor Gryff, in your long robe, Claus Rebstock is sitting here opposite you. Tell him here about the sacrament, and don't give us any heathen arguments: say what the text contains, about whether God descends from heaven and comes down to the priest at the Mass, so that he eats and drinks his flesh and blood. It's now become the greatest source of contention amongst common men that no one knows what they're eating: one thinks it's the body of Jesus Christ, and the other thinks it's a symbol of that body. These two things aren't compatible; because if it's only a symbol and not actually the body of Jesus Christ, then you shouldn't venerate it, but think of it only as a sign. But if it really is his flesh and blood, then you should take great care of it. If it is only a symbol of his body, then tell us who can put an end to our quarrel.

358 1 John 2:1–2 (see n. 279 above). The phrase 'Er ist der Ablaß aller welt' could also be translated, tellingly, 'he is the indulgence for the whole world'.

359 Isaiah 55:1: 'Ho, everyone who thirsts, come to the waters; and you that have no money, come, buy, and eat!'.

Dann ſo man all leerer bſicht
[Fviii[r]] einer wider den andren ficht
Darumb fach an min Doctor Gryff
allein blyb by dem text ſtyff

Doctor Gryff.
Ir herren es iſt ein groſſe ſach
vnd bſorg wenn ich ſchon lang mach
Ich ſyg nit gnůg darzů gleert
vnd hab yetz von mengem ghört
Der Aſinus von Rotterdam
möchte wol (ſye aber lam)
Schryben von dem Sacrament
das es nun ſyg ein Teſtament
Die läme er von gaaben hat
Penſion jm all jar yngadt
Vnd bſorgt wenn er dawider ſchryb
das jm ſyn Penſion vſs blyb
Vnd yederman hat vff jnn acht
er hat am erſten redlich gmacht
Sin gmächt iſt kon in all welt wyt
vnd machti noch / wär nun der gyt
Der hat jm ouch ſin hertz durch rennt
er weißt vaſt wol vom Sacrament
Vnd ſchrib er nun den halben teyl
dMäſs gult nit vil / hett mans ſchon feyl.
Der Luther vnd der Pomerantz
die ſind beyd glych eins tantz
Sy ſchrybend beyd ich weiß nit was
doch Pomerantz der gfalt mir baß
Der Luther ſchrybt in einem bůch
jm Deuteronomij man das ſůch
[Fviii[v]] Da *er* leert wie man thier ſöll eſſen
da hat er dſach wol gnůg ermeſſen *Deute. 14.*
Vnd ſpricht daſelbs in ſinem Comment

Lines 2760–81 are very different in C, E, and F. See the appendix, p. 466.

Because, when you look at what all the teachers have written, they're at odds with each other. So, then, Doctor Gryff, begin; but stick rigidly to the text.

Doctor Gryff

Sirs, this is a great matter, and I am worried that, if I treat it at length, I shan't be learned enough to cope with it. Yet I have heard from many people that the Ass of Rotterdam[360] is intending to write about the sacrament (but isn't well enough to do so) that it's a kind of testament. He's only pretending to be ill: he has an annual pension, and is worried that, if he writes against the Mass, he'll lose it. But everyone listens to him, and at first he did some very good things: his achievements[361] were known throughout the world, and would be so still if it weren't for the greed that has penetrated his heart also. He knows all about the sacrament, and if he were to write down even half of it, the Mass wouldn't count for much any more – they'd already be selling it off. Luther and Pomerantz[362] are in the same boat on this one; I don't know what they've written, but I prefer Pomerantz. Luther writes in one of his books that we are taught in Deuteronomy what animals we should eat, and he understands it well:[363] he states in a commentary

360 Erasmus, whose reluctance to state his position on the Mass was a source of frustration to many in the 1520s: he fully clarified his allegiance to the doctrine of transubstantiation only as late as 1530, in the dedicatory preface to his edition of Alger of Liège's *De sacramentis corporis et sanguinis Domini.*

361 A pun, no doubt: 'das gemächt' was also used to refer to the male genitalia (see *FWB* VI, 802–5).

362 Eckstein's (and Luther's) name for Johannes Bugenhagen (1485–1558). It reflects Bugenhagen's origins in Pomerania. Bugenhagen was particularly important in this context in that his *Contra novum errorem de sacramento corporis et sanguinis Domini* (1525), written in response to Zwingli, was the first text that clearly highlighted the differences between the Lutheran and Zwinglian positions on the Mass – and especially on Christ's words of institution (does 'est' mean 'really is' or 'signifies'?). See Gummelt, pp. 189–201.

363 Deuteronomy 14:3–9 is a list of clean and unclean creatures. As far as we can ascertain, Luther's only brief discussion of this passage is in his preface to the first part of his translation of the Old Testament, published in 1523 (*WA, Deutsche Bibel* 8, 10–30, especially p. 26). His fullest and liveliest treatment of the question is in *Von Menschenlehre zu meiden* of 1522 (*WA* 10, II, 73–92).

mit glouben eſs man das Sacrament
Nun *hab* der gloub nit beini zän
ſo ſagt ouch Pomerantz dar gen
Das blůt Chriſti allein die trenck
die all zyt ſygind yndenck
Das Chriſtus für ſy hin ſyg geben
vnd iſt nun war / ſagt ouch darneben
Sin fleiſch man ouch nit anderſt eſs
ſo man all zyt gloubt / vnd nit vergeſs
Man mög jnn ouch anderſt nit nieſſen
denn ſo man gloub Chriſti blůt vergieſſen
Vnd wär des ſelben nit vergeſs
der ſelb im geiſt das fleiſch recht eſs
So ligt das eſſen nun am dencken
man darff gotz blůt in kelch nit ſchencken
Dann trinckt man es nun allein im geiſt
das blůt nit ſelbs / wie du wol weyſt
So ſind wir all vnrecht dran
vnd wyt gfaren von der ban
Man meint es ſye ſin lyb gſin
wie er ans crütz ſyg geben hin
Vnd ſyg ſin blůt vnd fleiſch nun gwüſs
ſo ichs denn hin vnd wider miſs
So find ichs in dem text ſton
das iſt min lyb / da eſſend von
Hörſts? er ſagt clar: Das iſt min lyb
vnd iſt der text daby ich blyb
[Gi^{r}] Sölt ich hie von dem text gon
vnd mich nun an die gloß lon?
Das kan ich nit in mir finden
die wort ſind ſchlecht / lond ſich nit winden
Das iſt min lyb. Die wort ſtond eben

Super Euangelium: Caro mea uere eſt cibus.

Lucæ. 22.

2788 hat *AE* 2793 vnd… war] gefallt mir nit *CDF* 2800 ligt] läg *CDF* 2801 man darff] vnd dörft man *CDF* 2802 truncke *CDF* nun] *om. CDF* 2804 ſind] wärend *CDF* 2806 man meint] ich gloub *CDF* sye] iſt *CDF* 2814 von dem text] nun vom text *CDF* 2817 ſchlecht] klar *CDF* 2818 Die wort ſtond] ſtadt nun *CDF*

on this chapter that one should eat the sacrament with faith. Now faith does not have teeth made of bone. Pomerantz says, against this, that only those should drink Christ's blood who always remember that he gave himself for them. But that's not true.[364] He also says that you shouldn't eat his body unless you believe in the shedding of Christ's blood, and that whoever remembers this truly eats his flesh in the spirit. So on this basis eating has to do only with thinking, and you shouldn't pour Christ's blood into the chalice, because you would only be drinking it in the spirit, and would only be eating bread and not flesh. And if this is the case, then we're all wrong and have strayed far from the right path. But people think it *is* his body, as he gave it for us on the cross, and it certainly is his flesh and blood, even if I from time to time do not take it. I find it in the text: 'This is my body, eat of it'. Do you hear? He says clearly: 'This is my body'; and if that's the text then I'll stick to it. Should I depart from the text itself at this point, and rely only on the gloss? I can't find it in me to do that. The words are clear, and can't be turned about. 'This is my body', that's what it says,[365]

364 Coming from Doctor Gryff, these words of course imply that Eckstein and Zwingli *did* prefer (or had preferred) Bugenhagen's views to Luther's. Gummelt (pp. 198–9) reinforces the likelihood of this by referring to Zwingli's *Responsio ad epistolam Ioannis Bugenhagii* of 23rd October 1525. Here the reformer argues that, in his *Interpretatio in librum Psalmorum* of 1524, Bugenhagen had himself given a tropological interpretation of the words of institution that, in essence, agreed with Zwingli's.

365 Luke 22:19: 'Then he took a loaf of bread, and when he had given thanks, he broke it and gave it to them, saying, "This is my body, which is given for you. Do this in remembrance of me"'.

der für üch hin ſol werden geben
Das iſt min blůt / ſprach er deßglychen *Marc. 14.*
da wil ich bſton / vom text nit wychen
bringſt mich daruon / du můſt baß kychen

Claus Rebſtock.

Der glychen ſprüch findt man noch me
da Moyſes ſchrybt von dem Phaſe *Exod. 12.*
Heyßt vff tütſch der überſchritt *Leuit. 23.*
jſt noch by den Hebreeren ſitt *Num. 9.*
Da ſtadt noch klar das iſt Phaſe *Deut. 18.*
jſt langeſt hin / kumpt nimmermee
Vnd heißt darumb der überſchritt
das Iſrael ward plaget nit
Am abent ee der Vßgang was
gmein volck das phaſe vorhin aß
Vnd bſtrichend türen mit dem blůt
das was namlich darzů gůt
An welchem huß das blůt wurd ſton
der engel Gotz ſolt da für gon
Das nit getödt wurd Iſrael
do hieß Gott das man fürhin ſöll
In eewigkeit das lemlin eſſen
deß überſchritz nit vergeſſen
Das iſt nun wol den Iuden kund
[Giv] ſy eſſends noch vff diſe ſtund
Alle jar vff das Oſterzyt
vnd wenn man fragt was es bedüt
So ſprechend ſy: Es iſt phaſe
do Gott vns in der alten Ee
Hatt vſs dem land Egypten gfürt
behüt das vns die plag nit brürt
Die überging Egypten land

2819 ſol werden geben] wirdt hin gegeben *CDF* 2821 om. *CDF* 2822 daruon] drab *CDF*. After this line, *CDF* have 285 additional lines. See the appendix, pp. 466–82 2823 om. *AE*

'which is to be given for you'. Likewise he said, 'This is my blood'.[366] I'm going to stick at that and not budge from the text. If you're going to make me shift my position, you'll have to argue better.

Claus Rebstock[367]

You can find plenty more sayings of this kind when Moses writes about the 'pasach'.[368] In German this is called 'der Überschritt', the Passover.[369] Even though it's still the Hebrews' custom to celebrate this,[370] it's clearly written that it's 'pasach': it has passed over, it happened a long time ago, and won't come again.[371] It's called the Passover because Israel was spared the plague. On the evening before the Exodus, the common people first ate the Passover meal, and then smeared their doors with the blood suitable for the purpose. God's angel was to pass by any house on which there was blood, so that the Israelites might not be killed. For this reason God commanded that henceforth the Passover lamb should always be eaten and the Passover itself not forgotten. The Jews know this well, and they still eat the lamb to this day at Eastertide. And when you ask what it means, they say: 'It is Passover, when, in the Old Testament, God led us out of the land of Egypt and saw to it that the plague did not touch us. It passed by the land of Egypt,

366 Mark 14:24: 'This is my blood of the covenant, which is poured out for many'.

367 No change of speaker is indicated here in A, but the words which follow are plainly Rebstock's.

368 More normally 'Pesahim' or 'Pesach'. Exodus 12:1–27 contains an account of the Passover.

369 Leviticus 23:5: 'In the first month, on the fourteenth day of the month, at twilight, there shall be a passover-offering to the Lord'.

370 Numbers 9:1–14 has numerous regulations concerning the Passover.

371 The intended marginal reference is almost certainly to Deuteronomy 16:1–8; chapter 18 has nothing on the Passover.

Gott vns erneert mit ſiner hand
Es iſt phaſe / der Iud gwüſs ſeyt
wenn er das lämlin zůbereyt
Nun iſt es nit der überſchritt
vnd mags nit ſin / das fält ſich nit
Nach Iüdſcher wyß ouch Chriſtus redt
am abent / als er das Nachtmaal hett *Luc. 22.*
Sin lyb hatt er da yngeſetzt
an ſtatt des lamms / do er ſich letzt
Hat vns all gſprengt mit ſinem blůt *1. Petr. 1.*
drumb vnſere ſeelen ſtond in hůt
Vnd wir ſöllend fürhin yndenck ſyn
ſines tods / hat er vns gſetzt yn
Drumm doctor Gryff von hohen Sinnen
blybſt du bym text / du wirſt innen
Das nit da wirt ſin Chriſti lyb
vnd nüt denn brot allein da blyb
Vnd Chriſti blůt da nit wirt ſin
wolan wir wöllend ann text hin
Als er nun hargnon hatt das brot *Matth. 26.*
brach er das / vnd dancket Gott
Sprach: Nemmend hin das ich üch gib
[Gii^{r}] vnd eſſends / dann Das iſt min lyb
Der für üch ggeben werden ſol
die wort allein ermiſs du wol
So er ſpricht: Der für üch wirt ggeben *Luce. 22.*
was noch nit gen / verſtand mich eben
So hand die junger Chriſtum ggeſſen
vor ſym tod / magſt du wol ermeſſen
Was er denn noch in tod nit ggeben
ſo hatt er ye gwüſs ſin läben
Do er inen gab brot vnd wyn
dann er mocht noch nit crützget ſyn
Vor ſinem tod (bim text ich blyb)
ſo eſſend wir den tödten lyb

2869 an *CDF* 2876 Luce. 22.] *om. CDF* 2881 ye noch gwüſs *CDF*

and God saved us with his own hand'. 'It is Passover', the Jew will certainly say, when he is preparing the lamb. But this is not and cannot actually be the Passover. Now Christ also spoke in this Jewish fashion on the evening when he held the Last Supper.[372] He gave his own body instead of the lamb's. When he was wounded he sprinkled us all with his blood,[373] so that our souls might always be protected. He gave it so that, henceforth, we might always remember his death. This is what he has set down for us. So then, my high-minded Doctor Gryff, if you stick to the text you will learn that nothing but bread remains, and that Christ's body and blood are not in it. Come now, let's look at the text: 'When he had taken the bread, he broke it, gave thanks to God and said: "Take what I give you and eat, for this is my body, which is to be given for you"'.[374] Just think about the words properly. When he says: 'Which will be given for you', this means (understand me now) that it hadn't yet been given. So the disciples ate Christ before his death. Judge well now: if he hadn't yet been given in death, then he was certainly still alive when he gave them bread and wine. Because he could not very well be crucified before his death. I'm sticking to the text here. If we ate the dead body of Christ,

372 Luke 22:19 (see n. 365 above).

373 1 Peter 1:2: '[To the exiles], who have been chosen and destined by God the Father and sanctified by the Spirit to be obedient to Jesus Christ and be sprinkled with his blood'.

374 Matthew 26:26: 'While they were eating, Jesus took a loaf of bread, and after blessing it he broke it, gave it to the disciples, and said: "Take, eat; this is my body"'.

So můß das eſſen zwifalt ſin
das erſt / ee Chriſtus ward ggeben hin
Am abent hand djünger Chriſtum gnoſſen
ee er ſin blůt noch hatt vergoſſen
Hett do der lyb denn djünger gnützt
was hat er denn ſyn blůt verſchwitzt?
Nun magſt du nit dar wider ſin
on tod das fleiſch nam dſünd nit hin *Ioan. 12.*
Es was nun not das Chriſtus litt *Lucae. 9.*
für dſünd nützt vns ſin läben nitt *Marc. 8.*
Er můßt durch tod zum vatter gon
ſunſt wär der heilig geiſt nit kon *Ioann. 16.*
Denn wär es Gott müglich gſin
wir wärind gſälget on ſuns pin
Sag an / iſts brot am crütz ghangen
das djünger hand am abent empfangen?
Sagſt du nein / es hieng nit dran
[Gii^{v}] wie wilt du denn by dem text bſton?
Denn er ſprach: Das wirt für üch geben
hats brot in der hand / merck nun eben
Iſt denn das brot nit geben hin
ſo iſt es nit ſin lyb gſin
Vnd do er ſprach: Das wirt hin geben
meint er ſyn lyb der käm vmms läben
Sprichſt du / der iſt im brot ouch gſin
ſag ich / für kundſchafft darumm yn
Wie mocht der todt lyb ſin jm brot
er läbt ye noch / vnd was nit todt
Gott büt vns nit das wir ſöllind glouben
das man jnn ſech / wie pfaffen touben
Nun ſagt Ioannes der zwölff bott
kein menſch hab nie gſehen Gott *Ioann. 1.*
Sicht man denn Gott nit hie vff erden *1. Ioan. 2.*

2888 Am abent hand] Hettind *CDF* 2898f. Es ist vns vnmüglich geſin / ſelig werden on des ſuns pin *CD;* Vns ohn marter des Sohns fürwar / ſelig zu werden vnmüglich war *F* 2912 todt] *om. CDF*

then we would have had to eat him twice; and the first occasion would have been before he was actually given up. If the disciples had eaten Christ before he had shed his blood and the body had been of any use to them, why did he then go on to sweat out his blood? You can't deny that, without his having died, his flesh would not have taken away our sin.[375] It was necessary for Christ to die.[376] His life was of no use to us in respect of our sins: he had to go back up to his Father through death.[377] Otherwise, the Holy Spirit wouldn't have come.[378] Because if it had been possible for God to do it, we would have been saved without his Son having to suffer. Tell me: did the bread that the disciples ate on that evening hang from the cross? If you say 'no, it wasn't hanging there', how can you be true to the text? For he said, with bread in his hand: 'This will be given for you'. Now look, if the bread hadn't been given up, then it wasn't his body. But when he said 'this will be given for you', he meant that his body would die. If you say 'he was also in the bread', I will say to you, so that you know: 'How could his body be in the bread? He was still alive, he wasn't dead'. May God grant that we might never believe we can see him, as priests claim to. The apostle John says that no man has ever seen God.[379] So if you can't see God on earth,

375 Presumably John 12:24: 'Unless a grain of wheat falls into the earth and dies, it remains just a single grain; but if it dies, it bears much fruit'.

376 Cf. Luke 9:23 (as n. 38 above).

377 Closest to Mark 8:31: 'Then he began to teach them that the Son of Man must undergo great suffering, and be rejected by the elders, the chief priests, and the scribes, and be killed, and after three days rise again'.

378 John 16:7: 'It is to your advantage that I go away, for if I do not go away, the Advocate will not come to you'.

379 John 1:18 and 1 John 4 (*sic*): 12: 'No one has ever seen God'.

ſo mag kein oblat Gott werden
Noch eins das ichs nit vergeſs
kämind wir zů einer Mäſs
Vnd hüb man vf das Sacrament
ein ander pur käm ouch gerent
Der fragte: Was iſt da bſchehen
habend jr vnſeren Herrgott gſehen?
Ia ſprächeſt du / on allen ſpott
ſo lügt Iohannes der xii. bott
Der ſpricht: Gott hab niemant gſehen *Ioan. 1.*
wie darfſſt du denn darwider yehen? *1. Ioann. 2.*
Vnd mit dem blůt deßglychen
můſt du ouch vom text wychen
Sag an / iſts tranck vſs ſim lyb gfloſſen
[Giii[r]] daß djünger hand am abent gnoſſen?
Sprichſtu nein / als es ouch ist
wie trunckends denn das blůt Iesu Chriſt?
Er ſprach nun klar: Das wirt vergoſſen *Luce. 22.*
nun ist nit wyn vßhar gfloſſen
Nüt anders habend djünger gnoſſen

Doctor Gryff.
Nun nempts sant Paul ouch Chriſti lyb *1. Cor. 11.*
liß wie er den Corinthern ſchryb
Do er ſy ſtrafft vmb jrn mißbruch
vnd meint ſy fulltind nun den buch
Wenn ſy zů einander kämind
vnd des Herren mal nämind
Das Capitel lut in der wyß
wie ich in Euangeliſten lyß *Luce. 22.*
Vnn ſpricht: Wär des herren lyb nit entſcheyt *Math. 26.*
das vrteyl er jm ſelb vfleyt *Marc. 14.*
Ghörſt nun? er ſeyt des herren lyb
vnd als offt man das eſſen tryb

2928 Ioan. 1.] *om. CDF* 2929 1. Ioann.2.] *om. CDF* 2930 blůt ouch deßglychen *CDF*

then no Eucharistic host can become God. And here's another thing, lest I forget: if we went to a Mass and someone elevated the sacrament, and some other farmer came running along and asked: 'What's happened here? Have you seen our Lord?', you would say 'yes', quite seriously. If that were the case, then the apostle John would be lying when he says that no one has seen God. How can you speak against that? And it's the same with the blood: again, you would have to depart from the text. Tell me, on that evening, did the disciples take a drink which had flowed from his body? If you say 'no', as indeed is correct, how could they be said to have drunk the blood of Christ? He stated quite clearly: 'This will be shed'. But the wine didn't flow from him, and that wine is what the disciples drank.

Doctor Gryff

But St Paul also calls it the body of Christ: read what he says to the Corinthians[380] when he is scolding them for their abuse of it and saying that, when they come together and take the Lord's Supper, they are merely filling their bodies with it. The chapter reads as the Gospel does, when it says: 'He who does not properly discern the Lord's body brings a judgement upon himself'.[381] Can you hear this now? He says: 'the Lord's body' and 'as often as you eat it,

380 1 Corinthians 11:20, 27: 'When you come together, it is not really to eat the Lord's Supper. For when the time comes to eat, each of you goes ahead with your own supper, and one goes hungry and another becomes drunk [...] Whoever, therefore, eats the bread or drinks the cup of the Lord in an unworthy manner will be answerable for the body and blood of the Lord'.

381 Cf. Matthew 26:29: 'I tell you, I will never again drink of this fruit of the vine until that day when I drink it new with you in my Father's kingdom'.

Söll man des herren tod verkünden
biß das er kumm / anders ich nit finden

Claus Rebſtock.

Das iſt eben ein ſpruch für mich
den letſten verß nun bas bſich
Er ſpricht: So offt jr eſſind das brot
ſöllend jr verkünden des herren tod
Des glychen: ſo offt jr trinckend den wyn
ſöllend jr ſins tods yndenck ſin
[Giii[v]] Hie nempt ers brot vnd nit den lyb
den kelch ouch wyn (bym text blyb)
Vnd ſpricht: Als offt jr das brot eſſen
des herren tod ſöllend jr nit vergeſſen
Wie lang? nun biß das er kumm
ſtoß du mir diſen ſpruch vmb
Iſt er von himmel kon ins brot?
ſo iſt fürhin kein dencken not
Denn ſo ich ſpräch: Du ſolt min dencken
biß ich kumm / wil ich dir ein guldin ſchenken
So bald ich denn käm wider zů dir
den guldin wölteſt han von mir
Denn wurd die dächtnuß ouch vß ſin
es wär dir nit lenger bunden yn
Alſo ſag ich ouch / iſt der herr kon
ſo ſol man von dem dencken lon
Er iſt noch nit kon / weyßt man wol
drumm man ſinen für vnd für dencken ſol
Biß er kumpt zů den letſten gricht
das ſelb vns Paulus hie bericht *Matth. 26.*
Denn eſſend wir in ſinem rych
ein ſpyß die deren iſt vnglych
Die wir in ſiner dächtnuß nyeſſen
es iſt nun ein zeychen ſins blůts vergieſſen
Gott laßt ſich nit in dmuren bſchlieſſen.

you will proclaim the Lord's death until he comes'. I can't find it saying anything else.

Claus Rebstock

But those words actually support my case. Look at that last verse more carefully. He says: 'As often as you eat the bread, you will proclaim the Lord's death'. In the same way: as often as you drink the wine, you will remember his death. It's bread that he's taking here, and not Christ's body; and it's also a cup of wine. Stick to the text. It says: 'As often as you drink the blood, you will not forget the Lord's death'. And for how long? 'Until he comes'. Just turn this saying the other way around for me: has he come down from heaven into the bread? If so, there's no need to remember him from now on. Because if I said: 'You should remember me until I come back, and then I'll give you a gulden', as soon as I came back to you, you would want me to give you the money. Then remembering me just wouldn't happen any more, you'd no longer be bound to do it. In the same way I say that if the Lord came back, then we should stop remembering him. But he hasn't come back, as we well know, and for that reason we should remember him all the time, until he returns for the Last Judgement. This is what Paul is telling us. Because in his kingdom we shall eat a food that is unlike the one we have eaten in remembrance of him, which is only a sign that his blood has been shed. God doesn't let himself be confined within walls.

Doctor Gryff.
Wolan ich hab all min tag
gmeint / wenn man dMuſtrantz vmm trag
So ſyge Gott gwüß ſelb im glaß
[Givr] vnd gwänt der gloub erfülle das.

Claus Räbſtock.
Der recht gloubt füllt den glöubigen gnůg
gang vnd trinck waſſer vß eim krůg
Vnd gloub daby es ſyge wyn
rücht es dir denn ins houpt yn
Louffſtu denn vmb als ſygiſt truncken
ſo iſt recht gſin din gůt tuncken
Nun biſtu ye ein torecht man
das du ſichſt brot für fleyſch an
Wie kanſtu nun brot für fleyſch haben
meinſtu Gott laß ſich eſſen dſchaben?
Er laßt ſich nit in krätzen bſchlieſſen
man můß jn allein im geiſt nyeſſen
Darumb min Gryff ich ſag dir das
Den tüfel bſchweert man in ein glas
Ich habs gredt / vnn hat mich nit gruwen
man mag Gott hie kein huß buwen
Der himmel iſt nun Gottes huß *Eſaie. 66.*
darinn wachßt weder katz noch muß
Das ertrich ein ſchemel iſt ſiner fůß
lůg wo man jnn denn ſůchen můß
Man weyßt nit wo gott hab ſin růw
es kumpt kein läbendig menſch darzů
Sprichſtu: Er mag ouch by vns ſin
glych ich der ſelben meinung bin
Er iſt by vns / man ſicht jnn nit
fah an vnd zell jm ſine ſchritt
Mit ſiner krafft wonet er vns by
[Givv] ſich vmb dich wo ſin menſcheit ſy

3006 vnn] *om. CDF*

Doctor Gryff
Well now, all my days I've believed that, when people carry the monstrance around, God himself has been within the glass; and I've thought that faith made this happen.

Claus Rebstock
True faith makes plenty of things happen for the faithful man. If you go and drink water from a jug and believe that it's wine, it'll go to your head – you'll stagger about as if you were drunk. Because you think it *is* wine. But you really are a foolish man to see bread as flesh. How can you regard bread as flesh? Do you think God wants you to eat him all up? He doesn't let himself be shut up in enclosed spaces. You have to eat him only in the spirit. I tell you this, my good Gryff, because the devil lets himself be conjured into a glass. I've already said, and haven't regretted doing so, that you can't build God a house here. Heaven is God's home,[382] and no cats or mice live there. The earth is his footstool. Look, then, where you must seek him. We don't know where God has his ease: no living man can go there. If you say 'he might also be with us', then I share your opinion. He *is* with us; but we can't see him. Start counting his footsteps! It's his power that abides with us: look around you, and see where his humanity is.

382 Isaiah 66:1: 'Heaven is my throne and the earth is my footstool; what is the house you will build for me, and what is my resting-place?'

Sprichſtu / es ſtadt Matthei gſchriben
ich wird biß zend der welt by üch blyben *Matth. 18.*
Es iſt alſo / er by vns blybt
ja wie Ioannes dauon ſchrybt
Als prieſter kamend zů jm gon
gſant von der ſtatt an Iordan
Sin touff er jnen da vßleyt
zů den prieſtren er ouch ſeyt *Ioann. 1.*
Es ſtadt mitten vnder üch einer
den jr nit wüſſend / ſo gſach jn keiner
Alſo wonet er vns ouch by
hör wie Matthei ein ſpruch ſy
Wenn üwer zwen einhällig werden
einer ſach hie vff erden
Vnd das in minem namen bgeren
fürwar min vatter wirt üch gweren
Vnd wo üwer zwen werdend ſin
ich mitten vnder üch bin *Matth. 8.*
Hörſts? er iſt yetz by vns hie
vnd hand jnn noch gſehen nye
Sin menſcheit mögend wir nit ſehen
vnd Chriſtus hats ouch ſelb gjehen
Wir werdind jnn nit allweg han
die wort betracht nun yederman
Wil er nit allweg by vns ſin
war wilt mit dem Sacrament hin?
Dann diſer ſpruch wil nit zůlon
das allweg in muren werd gott ſton
Denn dwort ſind klar vnnd heyter gnůg
[Gv^{r}] ein yetlicher nun dem text lůg
So findend wir wie es iſt gangen
ee ſin lyden hat angfangen
Do Chriſtus in Bethania was
mit Simon dem feldſiechen aß
Vnd Magdalen da mit der ſalben
den herren ſalbet allenthalben
Die jünger entſatztend ſich darab

You say: 'It says in St Matthew: "I will remain with you to the end of the world"'.[383] That's true; he *does* remain with us. As John writes: 'When priests came to him [John the Baptist], sent from the town on the Jordan, he gave them his baptism. He also said to the priests: "There stands among you one whom you do not know and whom no one has seen"'.[384] In the same way he dwells with us. Hear how Matthew gives us this saying: 'Where two of you agree in a matter here on earth and you ask for it in my name, my Father will indeed grant it to you; and where two of you are, there am I with you'.[385] Do you hear? He is with us here and now, yet we have never seen him. We cannot see his humanity, and Christ himself has also said that we will not always have him with us. Let every man consider these words: if he is not going to be with us always, what do you want to do with the sacrament? These words of Christ won't allow for God being all the time within walls. For the words are clear and lucid enough. Let every man look at the text, and we will find what happened at the start of his Passion, when he was in Bethany and was eating with Simon the Leper, when Mary Magdalene anointed him all over with her oils, and the disciples were outraged by this.

383 Matthew 28 (*sic*): 20: 'And remember, I am with you always, to the end of the age'.

384 John 1:26–7: 'Among you stands one whom you do not know, the one who is coming after me; I am not worthy to untie the thong of his sandal'.

385 Matthew 18 (*sic*): 19–20: 'If two of you agree on earth about anything you ask, it will be done for you by my Father in heaven. For where two or three are gathered in my name, I am there among them'.

hör wie inen Chriſtus ein antwurt gab
Das wyb ſöllend jr vnkümbret lon
ſy hat ein gůt werck an mir thon
Ir werdend allzyt han die armen *Math. 28.*
deren jr üch mögend erbarmen *Marc. 14.*
Ir werdend mich nit allweg han *Ioann. 12.*
der ſpruch rürt hie das fleyſch an
Als hett er gſagt: Das lond yetz hin
ich wird nit ſin wie ich yetz bin
Nach mym tod wird ich clarifficiert
mit fleyſch von üch in himmel gfürt
Sitzen zů mins vatters rechten hand
hörzů wie es im glouben ſtand
Er iſt vf gen himmel gfaren
das ſprechend all Chriſtenlich ſcharen
Zů richten iſt er wider künfftig
nun ſinn jm nach / biſtu vernünfftig
Er iſt ye noch nit widerkon
zerichten ouch nit zhanden gwon
Iſt er nit kon / hat noch nit gericht
der gloub hie mich vnd dich ſchlicht
ſin lyb jm kein pfaff nit bricht

[Gv^{v}] **Doctor Gryff.**
Iſt denn ſin fleyſch nit vnſer ſpyß
das ſag / vnd mich daruß wyß
Er ſpricht: Ich bin das läbendig brot
vom himmel kon herab von Gott
Wär min fleyſch ißt / vnd min blůt trinckt
dem ſelben nimmerme mißlingt
der text hie mich vaſt tringt

Claus Räbſtock.
Liß du den text biß an das ort
ſo ſeyt er allein vom gotzwort
Vnd nempt das fleiſch / wie du weyſt
er ſpricht zeletſt: Min wort ſind geyſt

Hear how Christ answered them: 'You should not trouble the woman, for she has done a good work upon me. The poor you will always have with you, and you may have pity on them; but me you will not always have'.[386] These words touch the matter of his flesh; it is as if he had said: 'Now leave this be, for I will not always be as I am now; after my death I will be transfigured, and my flesh will be taken from you up to heaven, and I will sit at my Father's right hand'. Hear what it says in the Creed: 'He has ascended into heaven'. And all the Christian throngs say: 'He will come again to judge'. So remember him if you are sensible. He hasn't yet returned and hasn't yet taken it in hand to judge us. And if he has not come and has not yet judged, then our confession of faith settles the matter between us: no priest breaks his body here on earth.

Doctor Gryff

Is his flesh then not our food? Tell me, and instruct me. He says: 'I am the living bread who has come down from God in heaven. He who eats my flesh and drinks my blood will never come to harm'. This text presses hard on me.

Claus Rebstock

If you read this text to the end, you will see that he is speaking only of God's Word, and calls this his 'flesh' – as you know. At the end he says: 'My words are spirit'.

386 Recorded, with almost identical wording, in Matthew 26 (*sic*): 10–11; Mark 14:6; John 12:7.

Das wirt nun klar an einem ort
er ſpricht: Ich bin der welt hort
Das lebendig brot vom himmel kon
meint er ſyge warer Gottes ſon
Das fleyſch iſt nit von himmel kommen
hats erſt vff erden angnommen
Nun magſtu yetz vaſt wol verſton
der geiſt der iſt von himmel kon
Der ſelb dſeel ſpyßt / vnd gibt jrs leben
ſin fleyſch iſt drumb ans crütz ggeben
Das er hie an ſich gnommen hatt
vnd iſt da ghangt an des flůchs ſtatt *Galat. 3.*
Denn Gott der vatter hat gethon *Deute. 27.*
daß fleyſch můßt für dſünd hin gon *Eſaie. 53.*
Das ſelb fleiſch dörffend wir nit eſſen
vnd eſſends nit / hab dich vermeſſen
[Gvi^{r}] Dſeel ſpyßt nit was zum mund yngadt
ein geiſtliche ſpyß die ſeel hat
Das iſt das lebendig gotzwort
das iſt allein der ſeel hort
Vnd wie brot iſt ein vffenthalt
des lybs / das er nit in hunger falt
Alſo iſt das wort gots ein vnderhab
der ſeel / vnd wirt nit verdrüſſig drab
Das magſt aber bas verſton
Gott wil ſich nit in ein kadtbuch lon
Wär ſin fleyſch ißt / der ſelb nit ſtirbt
in ewigkeit ouch nit verdirbt
Ghörſt? hettind djünger ſin recht fleych geſſen
ſo lebtinds noch / magſt wol ermeſſen
Die wyl ſy aber gſtorben ſind
wie ich in göttlicher gſchrifft ſind
So ward dozmal nit gſpyßt der lyb
die ſpyß allein der ſeel blyb
Die hat nit zän / vnd ißt nit brot
jr thůt ouch hie kein meſſz not
So bald der Herr hatt ſin red volbracht

That becomes clear elsewhere, when he says: 'I am the world's treasure'. When he says that the true bread has come from heaven, he means that he is the true Son of God: his flesh hasn't come down from heaven; he took it upon himself only on earth. Now you can very well understand that his spirit came down from heaven, and that this is what feeds the soul and gives it life. For this reason the flesh which he had assumed here on earth was given over to the cross and was hanged there instead of the curse[387] which God had sworn, to the effect that flesh must be offered up for our sin.[388] We can hardly eat this flesh, and indeed we don't: you have been arrogant. The soul is not fed by what goes into the mouth. The soul has a spiritual food, namely the living Word of God; that alone is the soul's treasure. And just as bread sustains the body, so that it does not fall into hunger, so the Word of God sustains the soul, and does not tire of doing so. But you can understand this better: God won't let himself enter into a shitty stomach; and whoever eats his flesh will not perish and will not see corruption in eternity. Do you hear? If the disciples had eaten his true flesh, you might very well think that they would still be alive today. But because they have died, as I see in the divine Scriptures, their bodies can't have been fed at that time; only their souls were. And souls don't have teeth and don't eat bread. You don't need a Mass here. As soon as the Lord had finished his speech,

387 Galatians 3:13–14: 'Christ redeemed us from the curse of the law by becoming a curse for us – for it is written, "Cursed is everyone who hangs on a tree"'.

388 Cf. Deuteronomy 27:6–7: 'You must build the altar of the Lord your God of unhewn stones. Then offer up burnt-offerings on it to the Lord your God, make sacrifices of well-being, and eat them there, rejoicing before the Lord your God'. The Isaiah 53 reference could suggest verse 6 (see n. 55 above), and/or verse 12: 'He poured out himself to death, and was numbered with the transgressors; yet he bore the sin of many'.

Petrus der ſpyß recht nach dacht
Do Chriſtus ſagt: Wend jr ouch von mir gon? *Ioann. 6.*
Seyt Petrus: herr war ſönd wir vns lon?
Du haſt die wort des ewigen leben
ſprach nit / wie mag er ſin fleiſch vns geben
Wie dIuden hattend die red verſtanden
Petrus nam den geyſt zhanden
Daruf du ouch dich můſt gründen
der glychen wir me ſprüch finden
[Gvi^{v}] Das man ſeyt: Das iſt / vnd iſts nit
wenn yetz ein bott gegen vns ritt
Vnd wär in wyß vnd ſchwartz bekleyt
das iſt Baſel / man denn ſeyt
Wenn nun der rock dſtatt Baſel wär
ſo gieng mit ding der Bott nit lär
Oder käm yetz ein bott gangen
vnd hett an jm ein büchß hangen
ein gantz rhot fäld / ich frag: was bdüts?
ſprichſtu zů mir / es iſt Schwytz
nun iſts nit Schwytz / vnd hats doch gſeyt
dann kein Bott Schwytz allein treyt
Nimm dir für noch ein exempel
kämiſt yetz gen Ulm in tempel
vnd fundiſt da vil bilder ſton
ſo ſprichſt: Das iſt ſant Baſtion
Sant Martin / vnd ouch ſant Vicentz
ſant Peter vnd ſant Laurentz
Vnd wenn du lang zellſt / ſo ſind es bilder
ein hummel am faden der iſt wilder
Denn all Götzen die da ſtond
ins antlitz ſy dflügen ſchyſſen lond
Sy wüſchend nit ab ein flügen dräck
nun ſinn was krafft denn drinn ſtäck
Man findt ouch in der heylgen gſchrifft
deßglychen das me antrifft
Das Chriſtus ſelb hat gnempt ein ding
vnd nit da was verſtaaſtu ring *Math. 16.*

Peter understood this food properly. When Christ said: 'Will you also go from me?', Peter said: 'Lord, to whom should we go? You have the words of eternal life'.[389] He didn't say: 'How can he give us his body?', which the Jews had understood his statement to mean. Peter seized the idea of the spirit; and you too must base your views on it. We find many more of these statements where people say 'it is', but it isn't. If a messenger were to ride up to us now dressed in black and white, someone would say: 'That's Basle'; and if the tunic was indeed the City of Basle, the messenger would not go empty away. Or if a messenger came and had a box hanging from his shoulder with a big red area painted on it, and I asked you: 'What does it mean?' You would say: 'Switzerland'. Now, even though you've said it's Switzerland, it actually isn't: because no messenger can carry Switzerland on his own. Consider another example: if you went into the temple at Ulm and found lots of pictures there, you would say: 'That's St Sebastian, St Martin, St Vincent, St Peter, and St Laurence'.[390] But however long you went on enumerating them, they would still be pictures. A bumble-bee perching on your braid is livelier than all the idols that are there. They're quite happy to let flies shit on their faces, and never wipe away the droppings. Now see what power lies in that. In the holy Scriptures too you find many other similar things, where Christ himself has named something that doesn't actually exist. Do you understand a little?

389 John 6:66–7: 'Many of his disciples turned back and no longer went about with him. So Jesus asked the twelve: "Do you also wish to go away?" Simon Peter answered him: "Lord, to whom can we go? You have the words of eternal life"'. The discussion follows Jesus's description of himself as 'the bread of life' (verse 35), rather than the Last Supper (the Johannine tradition has no institution narrative).

390 Assuming that Eckstein was indeed a Swabian, this could be seen as an example (perhaps the only one in these texts) of local patriotism. One suspects, though, that fame especially of the remarkable later fifteenth-century choir stalls of Ulm Cathedral, on which these saints are depicted along with over ninety others, had anyway spread into Switzerland by 1525. On the Ulm carvings see for example Herbert Pée, *Jörg Syrlin d. Ä. Das Ulmer Chorgestühl 1468–1474* (Stuttgart: Reclam, 1963).

Ich wird dir dſchlüſſel geben er ſprach
kein ſchlüſſel man da nit ſach
[Gvii[r]] So ſinds nit wie wir hand / ſchlüſſel gſin
die inn bläch gangind vs vnd yn
Vnd hat doch hie von ſchlüßlen gſeyt
nit die man an gürtlen treyt *Matth. 4.*
Wie hat ſant Peter menſchen gfangen?
er iſt nit mit netze vmbgangen
Die man in ein waſſer ladt
das fahen mit leer zůgadt
Von menſchen fiſchen ſagt er hie
vnd warff darzů kein garn nie
Er hat da jrdiſch glychnus geben
das man geiſtlichs verſtünd darneben
Das Sacrament ouch ein zeichen iſt
deß eineſt gſtorbnen Ieſu Chriſt
Als wölt er ſagen: Menſch das jſs
min lyb wirt hin gen für dich gwüſs
Als offt du nun das brot wirſt eſſen
ſolt du mins tods nit vergeſſen
Gloubſt ich ſye für dich gſtorben
vnd heig dir damit gnad erworben
So biſt ein erb in mynem rych
vnd jſſeſt min blůt täglich
Die wyl du nit vfhörſt glouben
mag dich der ſpyß niemand brouben
Du blybſt in Gott / vnd er in dir
vnd ſichſt jnn nit / das gloub mir
Allein im glouben wirt er gſehen
das iſt ouch mit Abram gſchehen *Ioann. 8.*
Der ſach ouch des Herren tag
nit im fleiſch / fürwar ich ſag
[Gvii[v]] Das iſt / er gloubt wie Gott hat gſeyt *Roma. 4.*
ſin ſomen wurde wyt vßbreyt
Einer ſölt vſſz ſinem ſchlächt vffton *Deut. 18.*
der wurd der gantzen welt vorgon
das volck ſölt erlöſen von ſünden

‘I will give you the keys’, he said,[391] but no one saw any keys there. So he didn’t mean keys as we have them, the keys made of metal that we see around the place, and he wasn’t talking about keys you carry on your belt. And how could St Peter have caught men?[392] He didn’t go around with nets like the ones you put into the water. He did this kind of fishing with doctrine. No, here Christ is speaking of fishing for men, and Peter never threw any nets into the sea for that purpose. He was giving an earthly parable by means of which you might understand something spiritual. The sacrament is likewise a symbol of Jesus Christ, who once died. It is as if he wanted to say: ‘Man, eat this; my body will certainly be given for you, and as often as you eat this bread you will not forget my death, but believe that I died for you and have thereby earned you grace, so that you are an heir in my kingdom. And if you drink my blood daily and do not cease to believe, no one will be able to rob you of this food, and you will abide in God and he in you – even though you will not see him. Believe me in this: he is only seen by faith’. This happened also with Abraham,[393] who saw the day of the Lord, but not in the flesh. What happened, I tell you for sure, is that he *believed* God had said that his seed would be sown widely,[394] that one from his lineage would rise up and go before the entire world,[395] and save the people of Israel from their sins,

391 Matthew 16:19 (see n. 120 above).

392 Matthew 4:19: ‘And he said to them, “Follow me, and I will make you fish for people”’.

393 Cf. John 8:56: ‘Your ancestor Abraham rejoiced that he would see my day; he saw it and was glad’.

394 Romans 4:3, 18: ‘Abraham believed God, and it was reckoned to him as righteousness [...] Hoping against hope, he believed that he would become “the father of many nations”, according to what was said: “So numerous shall your descendants be”’.

395 Deuteronomy 18:15: ‘The Lord will raise up for you a prophet like me from among your own people; you shall heed such a prophet’.

vnd von jm kon on zal kinden
Dem zůſag hat Abraham gloubt
wolt ſich ſines ſuns han broubt
So ſtyff vnd veſt hieng er an Gott
ſin ſun er jm vfopffren wott
Gott an ſim willen hatt für gůt
ließ nit vergieſſen Iſaacs blůt
Alſo ſöllend wir anhangen gott
ſo eſſend wir das himliſch brot
Andreſt mag man jnn nit nieſſen
dann ſo man gloubt ſin blůt vergieſſen
So eſſend wir das recht Phaſe
mit zänen jßt man gott niemer mee

Herold.
Gnad herr Doctor Stroubutz
hie ſitzt gen dir pur Eigennutz
Der wolt gern wüſſen wie es käm
das man noch Zins vnd Zähend näm
Vnd meint gang rent vnd gült nit ab
das menger wider vmbhin trab
Vnd läbe nach dem alten gſatz
biß das krägend wärd ein katz
man můß doch geben was man erkratz

[Gviii^{r}] **Pur Eygennutz.**
Sag an min Doctor Stroubutz
was iſt vns nun das gotswort nutz
das wir hand ghört yetz lange zyt
vnd man nüt deſt minder Zins git
Dauon ich meint wir wurdind fry
Gelt wo ich Euangeliſch ſy
Můß ich noch gen das ich vor gab
das ich fürwar nit ghoffet hab
Ich meint all ding die wurdind gmein
wo einer käm / wär er da heim
Vnd dörfft man fürhin nüt mee zinſen

and that from him would come children beyond number. Abraham believed this promise, and was willing to rob himself of his own son. So strongly and fixedly did he trust in God that he was prepared to sacrifice his son to him. But God rewarded his willingness and did not let Isaac's blood be shed. In the same way we should trust in God, so that we might eat the bread of heaven. You cannot eat him other than by believing in the shedding of his blood. This is how we eat the true Passover: God can never be eaten with our teeth.

Herald

Grace be with you, Doctor Stroubutz. Pur Eygennutz is sitting here opposite you, and he would like to know how it came to be that interest payments and tithes are still being taken. He also thinks that rents and taxes haven't been abolished, but that there are still lots of them around, and that we'll carry on living according to the old law until cats start crowing. You've still got to give away whatever you can scratch together.

Pur Eygennutz[396]

Tell me, good Doctor Stroubutz, what use is God's Word to us now? We've been hearing it for a long time, but we're not paying any less interest. I thought we'd be free from payments like these. Now that I'm an Evangelical, do I still have to pay what I paid before? That certainly isn't what I'd hoped for: I thought all things would be held in common, that you'd be at home wherever you were, and that you wouldn't have to pay any more interest –

396 For a discussion of this debate between Eygennutz and Stroubutz see the introduction, pp. 46–51.

weder wyn / korn / erbs / noch linſen
Dacht ouch als bald die Mäſs ab näm
das nüt mee gen ouch naher käm
Vnd hett ich gwüßt das ich yetz weiß
jch wölt recht vff dem alten kreyß
Hingfaren ſyn biß in min grab
wee das ich ye geuolget hab
Min pfaff ſagt mir es wär nit recht
das man Zinß näm / nun kurtz vnd ſchlecht
Vnd Chriſten gang kein Zähend an
vnd zimm ouch nit eim Chriſten man
Das er ſin gelt vßlich vmb Zinß
daruon nüts hoff / nit groß noch kleinß
Ich dacht das kumpt dir nun vaſt wol
wenn man von gelt nit zinſen ſol
Ich ſol all jar wol zwentzig pfund
Ach Gott erläbt ich nun die ſtund
Das ich fürhin nit zinſen ſött
[Gviiiv] wölt Gott das man nun růffte wett
Es wär für mich ein eben ſpyl
jch nimm nüt yn / vnd ſol nun vil
Darzů hand mir die Töuffer gſeyt
ein Chriſt dörff keiner Oberkeyt
Gott ſy ſelb ein Herr ob allen
darab hatt ich ein wol gfallen
Dann ſo kein gwalt wär in der welt
ſo hulff menger jm ſelbs vmb gelt
Der ſtercker wär / näm dem ſchwachen
vnd wurd man alle ding gmein machen
denn möcht der arm mann wol bachen

Doctor Stroubutz.
Hör hie zů ein yetlich Chriſt
was nun des puren meinung iſt
Er hat mee vff zytlichem gůt
dann was der ſeel not thůt
Vnd ſpricht: Was jnn das gotswort nütz

in the form of wine, corn, peas or lentils. I also thought that when the Masses went away, the day when we didn't have to pay anything would also be near. If I'd known then what I know now, I'd have wanted to carry on in the old way until my dying day. Alas that I ever followed the new way! My pastor told me quite simply that it wasn't right for people to take interest, that tithes shouldn't affect Christians, and that it wasn't fitting for a Christian man to lend money at interest, or to hope for any profit, big or small, from it. I thought you'd be all for it if people didn't have to pay interest on money. I owe twenty pounds every year. O God, that I might live to see the hour when I don't have to pay any more interest; would to God they'd call it quits! I'd think it was fair enough if I didn't have any income, but also didn't owe much. Also the Anabaptists told me that a Christian needs no worldly authority, and that God himself is Lord of all. I liked this, because if there weren't any powers that be in the world any more, many a man could help himself to money.[397] Whoever was stronger could take from the weaker, and all things would be held in common. Then the poor man really could bake his bread in peace.

Doctor Stroubutz

Let all Christian men listen to what this farmer thinks. Worldly goods are more important to him than the needs of the soul. He asks what use God's Word is to him

397 'The *Concilium* and *Rychsztag* do not deal with the Radical Reformation directly, but they do blame the teaching of Radical Reformers for the popular uprisings of 1525' (Love, 'Dialogue', p. 99).

müß er verzinßen was er bſitz
Vnd wänt das gotzwort mach jnn fry
von allem das er ſchuldig ſy
Von fryheit der ſeel / Gotswort redt
ſo wär der pur von Zins gern wett
Das möcht wol eewig helliſch ſin
louffen durch gſchrifft alſo hin
Gotzwort verſton nit nach dem geyſt
wie es denn gſchicht yetz allermeyſt
Vnd gſchehen iſt in diſem jar *Anno M.*
es koſtet mengen hut vnd haar *D. XXV*
[Hi^{r}] Der ouch iſt diſer meynung gſyn
das gotzwort näme all Zins hin
Daruf hands Schloſs vnd Klöſter durch loffen
darinn ſich vollen wyn gſoffen
Menger hat darinnen gnummen
das nit von jm iſt dryn kummen
Darzů hands mengerley zergengt
meng koſtlich gmächt ann himmel ghenckt
Daruor man wol hett mögen ſyn
es gilt nit alſo nemmen hin
Da einer nüts hat dar gethon
man ſol eim yeden ſins lon *Matth. 7.*
Er wil das wir zů jm keerind
nit das wir vns mit dem ſchwärt weerind *Ioann. 18.*
Ein Chriſt hat ouch geiſtlich waaffen *2. Cor. 10.*
ſol ſich laſſen / wie Gott wil ſtraaffen
Dann wir hands bſchult mit vnſren ſünden
Gott mag vns wol dauon entbinden
Von aller bſchwärd lybs vnd der ſeel
wie er erlößt hat Iſrael *Exod. 14.*
Darumb min nachpur Eygennutz
das gotz wort iſt der ſeel bſchutz
vnd fryet nit von Gült vnd Rent
jr puren ſind damit verblent
Gotzwort verbüt nit Oberkeyt
vnd felſcht die gſchrifft der anders ſeyt

if he has to pay interest on what he owns, and believes that God's Word sets him free from all his obligations. But God's Word speaks of the freedom of the soul. If the farmer was indeed free from having to make payments, he could still end up in hell eternally. They ride roughshod over God's Word, not understanding it according to the spirit. This now happens most of the time, and certainly it happened this very year. It cost the lives of many people who also took the view that God's Word would take all their financial obligations away. On this basis they ransacked castles and monasteries and made themselves drunk with wine. Many took away things which they hadn't brought. On top of that they've destroyed many things and hung up many a costly item[398] in the sky.[399] This might well have been prevented. It isn't right to take away things that you haven't brought: you should let everyone have what is his.[400] God wants us to turn to him, and not to defend ourselves with the sword.[401] A Christian has spiritual weapons,[402] and should rely on God to punish. We are guilty because of our sins. God can free us from all troubles of body and soul, as he saved Israel.[403] So, neighbour Eygennutz, God's Word protects only the soul, and does not free you from payments and rents. You farmers are blinded by this. God's Word does not forbid temporal authority, and anyone who says otherwise is falsifying the Scriptures.

398 Or 'male member'.

399 At least in the Swiss context, this is a rather exaggerated and overly pathetic account of the farmers' uprising: 'The Peasants' Revolt of 1525 that tore across Germany did not leave the lands of Zurich untouched, though the damage was minor. In April peasants stormed the Praemonstratensian abbey in Rüti and then the houses of the Knights of St John at Bubikon and the Dominicans in Töss [...] the mediation of magistrates and peasant leaders averted loss of life' (Gordon, p. 66). Given his origins in and geographical proximity to Swabia, however, Eckstein will certainly have known that things were much worse there.

400 Cf. Matthew 7:5: 'First take the log out of your own eye, and then you will see clearly to take the speck out of your neighbour's eye'.

401 Presumably a reference to the story of Peter and Malchus in John 18:10–12.

402 2 Corinthians 10:4: 'For the weapons of our warfare are not merely human, but they have divine power to destroy strongholds'.

403 The chapter describes the Israelites' miraculous crossing of the Red Sea.

Die heilig gſchrifft vfnet den gwalt
das man eim yeden recht halt
Darzů bſchützt witwen vnd weyſen *Eſaie. 1.*
Gott heißt vns nit in krieg reyſen
[Hiv] Verwüſten darzů dach vnd gmach
von Eygnem nutz entſpringt die ſach
Denn wär jr anſchlag für ſich gangen
ſy hettind gröſſers ouch angfangen
Kein huß wär bliben on erſůcht
ſy hattend wie ein hůr verrůcht
Das was nun alles wider Gott *Pſalm. 25*
er haſſet ein vfrürig rott *Matth. 5.*
Vnd wil das man im friden läb *Pſalm. 61.*
vnd rychtumb nit im hertzen kläb *Collo. 3.*
Ein Chriſt hab acht / was ob jm ſy
ſo er denn macht die gwüßne fry *Ioann. 8.*
So lydet der lyb was man jm thůt *Hebre. 11.*
vnd hat nüt vff zytlichem gůt
So man eim Chriſten nimpt den rock *Matth. 5.*
er lydet es alles wie ein ſtock *1. Cor. 13.*
Den mantel gibt er ouch darzů *Lucæ. 6.*
damit man frid hab / vnd ouch růw
Das iſt eins rechten Chriſten art
ob man jm ſchon vsroufft den bart
Das tringt jnn von Gots liebe nit *1. Cor. 13.*
er trüwet Gott / der anders gibt
Das hand jr puren nit gedacht
vnd üch ſelbs in gros vnglück bracht
Wärind jr nun rüwig gſin
vnd gdacht / Ach Gott ich kum wol hin
Mine vordren hand ouch Zins ggeben
es hindret nit das eewig läben
Můß ich denn alſo ſin verſetzt
mit ſünden hand wir Gott geletzt
[Hiir] Von Gott kumpt vns ſömlich ſtraaff *Danie. 13.*

3321 was] iſt *CD*

The holy Scripture tells the authorities to be just towards all, and to protect widows and orphans.[404] God doesn't command us to wage war or to destroy roofs and chambers. That comes from selfishness. And if their campaign had gone on, they'd have started doing worse things: no house would have been left unmolested, and they'd have acted like whores. Now all this goes against God: he hates marauding mobs,[405] and wants people to live in peace[406] and not cling to riches in their hearts.[407] A Christian should pay attention to things that are above,[408] so that his conscience might be free. His body should suffer whatever is done to it,[409] and he should have no regard for worldly goods. If somebody takes away a Christian's coat, he should suffer it as if it were nothing, and give away his cloak also,[410] so that people might live in rest and quietness. That is the way of a true Christian. Even if you pluck out his beard, that doesn't separate him from God's love. Someone who gives to others is trusting in God. You farmers forgot this, and brought great misfortune upon yourselves. If you'd only been peaceable and thought to yourselves: 'O God, I will manage. My forebears also paid their dues, and doing so certainly doesn't hinder eternal life. If it hurts to do it, well, we have wounded God with our sins, and it's from him that the punishment

404 Isaiah 1:17: 'Learn to do good; seek justice, rescue the oppressed, defend the orphan, plead for the widow'. This principle will form the basis of Salomon's arguments in the *Rychsztag* (see below, pp. 391–5).

405 Psalm 26:5: 'I hate the company of evildoers, and will not sit with the wicked'.

406 Cf. Matthew 5:9: 'Blessed are the peacemakers, for they will be called children of God'.

407 Psalm 62:10: 'Put no confidence in extortion, and set no vain hopes on robbery; if riches increase, do not set your heart on them'.

408 Colossians 3:1: 'So if you have been raised with Christ, seek the things that are above, where Christ is, seated at the right hand of God'. The gospel idealism of this speech may indicate the influence of Erasmus, who advocates a similarly high standard of behaviour and morality (notably in his *Enchiridion*).

409 See the account of the sufferings of the heroes of the faith in Hebrews 11:32–8.

410 Matthew 5:40: 'If anyone wants to sue you and take your coat, give your cloak as well'. Luke 6:29: 'From anyone who takes away your coat do not withhold even your shirt'. The reference to 1 Corinthians 13 presumably refers in a general way to that chapter's discourse on love.

das wir verſthürind küe vnd ſchaaff
Der Iopp was frümmer denn ich bin
dem nam er gůt / wyb / vnd kind hin *Iopp. 1.*
Im ward mee dann er vor hatt ghan *Iob. 14.*
alſo můß thůn ein Chriſten man
So jm Gott gibt / danck er darumb
nimpt er jm denn / mache smul nit krumm
Denn ein Chriſt můß all gſchöpfft verlon
von Gott ſur vnd ſüß für gůt han
Gott gibt vnd nimpt / wie es jm gfalt
jn ſiner hand ſtadt aller gwallt
Vnd alles das vns zhanden gadt
das ſelb Gott alles zůladt
vnd er iſt grecht in aller tadt

Pur Eygennutz.
Wenn rüfft man denn ouch ein mal wett
das allweg geben ein end hett
Wie dIuden hand vor zyten thon
man ſolt das ſibend jar fry lon *Deut. 15.*
Wir hand im nüwen Teſtament
geſchriben / das all wůcher blendt
Man ſöl lihen on widergelt *Matth. 6.*
wo gſchicht es in der gantzen welt?

Doctor Stroubutz.
Das du vſſz Moſe haſt anzeigt
jſt allein den Iuden gſeyt
Das gadt die Chriſten nüt me an
[Hii^{v}] du gibſt ein gůten gſatz man
Wo man dir gäb / das hört man wol
din hertz das ſteckt nun nemmen vol
Loß was mee im Capitel ſtadt
wie wyter Moyſes botten hat *Deute. 15.*
Wenn du haltiſt Gottes bott
ſo wärd dich gſegnen din Herr Gott
Werdiſt herſchen über dHeyden

of paying tax on cows and sheep comes.[411] Job was more devout than I am, and God took away his goods, wife, and children.[412] But he ended up getting more than he had lost.[413] This is what a Christian man should do: if God gives him something, he should be thankful, and if God takes it away again, he shouldn't pull a face. Because a Christian must leave behind all created things and accept both sweet things and sour from God's hand. God gives and takes away as it pleases him; all power is in his hands, and all that comes into our hands is granted us by him. And he is just in all his doings.

Pur Eygennutz
When is somebody finally going to call it quits, so that there might be an end to this endless giving? We should make every seventh year a jubilee,[414] as the Jews did in earlier times. In the New Testament it is written that all usury blinds, and that you should lend without interest.[415] But where, anywhere in the world, does that happen?

Doctor Stroubutz
What you cited from Moses was said to the Jews alone. It no longer has anything to do with Christians. It's easy to tell that you're very good at laying down the law when it comes to other people giving things to *you*. Your heart is set on taking. Hear what it says later in the chapter, what Moses goes on to state:[416] 'If you keep to God's command, your Lord God will bless you, and you will rule over the heathen.

411 Presumably Daniel 13:23 (in the Greek version): 'I choose not to do it; I will fall into your hands, rather than sin in the sight of the Lord'.

412 Job's misfortunes are listed in chapter 1, verses 13–19.

413 Cf. Job 42:10: 'And the Lord restored the fortunes of Job when he had prayed for his friends; and the Lord gave Job twice as much as he had before'.

414 A year in which debts are released. Deuteronomy (15:1–11) states that this should happen every seven years, Leviticus (25:8–38) every fifty.

415 Matthew 6 is cited in the margin, but we can see no obvious correspondence.

416 Deuteronomy 15:5–6: 'If only you will obey the Lord your God by diligently observing this entire commandment that I command you today. When the Lord your God has blessed you, as he promised you, you will lend to many nations, but you will not borrow; you will rule over many nations, but they will not rule over you'.

dich wärd ouch kein fyend bleyden
Vnd werdiſt lihen aller welt
von niemand nit entlehnen gelt
Diewyl du denn entlehnet heſt
ſo biß nun gwüſs / das iſt der präſt
Du haſt nit ghalten ſine bott
wie dich hatt gheiſſen din Herr Gott
Weiſt was me im Moſe ſtadt /
das Gott der Herr verheiſſen hat?
Wenn du nit höriſt was Gott ſag *Deut. 28.*
ſo wärd dir Gott ſchicken all plag
Du gangiſt vs oder yn
der flůch Gots wärd by dir ſin
So wirſt vff din acker gon
der flůch gots wirt dich nit verlon
Gott ouch verflůcht din ſchaaff vnn rinder
die frucht dins lybs ouch nüt minder
Peſtilentz wirt ouch dich angon
denn Gott der wirt nit nachlon
Gſchwulſt / hitz / gſchwär / vnd ouch kaltwee
wirt dich verlaſſen nimmer mee
So lang biß du verdorben biſt
[Hiiir] nun loß was me im text iſt
Der himmel wirt Eri werden
darzů yſin die gantz erden
Für rägen wirt abfallen ſtoub
äſchen ouch / fürwar mir gloub
Du wirſt vor dinen fygenden fliehen *Leuit. 26.*
an ſiben orten abziehen
Mit menger plag wirt dich gott ſtraffen
din eygen wyb ein andrer bſchlaffen *Deut. 28.*
Gott wirt dich plaagen mit torheyt
das iſt allen gottloſen gſeyt
Die werdend blind zů mittentag
kein artzet jnen helffen mag
So ſchon der Gottloß buwt ein huß
ein frömbder wirt jnn tryben druß

No enemy will harm you, and you will lend to all nations, but not borrow from anyone'. Your error, you can be certain of this, is that you have borrowed. You have not obeyed the command that your Lord God gave you. Do you know what Moses also says, about what God has promised you?[417] 'If you do not listen to what God says, God will send all manner of plagues upon you, and whether you go out or in, God's curse will be on you. So if you go into your field, God's curse will not leave you: God also curses your sheep and cattle and (no less so) the fruit of your loins. Pestilence will also come upon you, for God will not let up. Swellings, fevers, ulcers, and cold-sickness will never depart from you until you have been destroyed'. Now read what the text also says: 'The heavens shall be brass, and the whole earth shall be iron, dust and ashes will fall as rain and, believe me, you will flee from your enemies and withdraw from them in seven directions.[418] God will punish you with many plagues, another man will lie with your wife, and God will plague you with madness'. This is said to all godless people: 'They will go blind at midday, and no doctor will be able to help them. As soon as the godless man builds a house, a stranger will drive him out of it;

417 This quotation, and the next two, represent a generally accurate version of Deuteronomy 28:15–30. In the light of his earlier rejection of Mosaic Law, it is significant that Stroubutz nevertheless applies so much material from it. In doing so he reveals the extent to which he has become the mouthpiece of Eckstein (and indeed of Zwingli, whose reliance on the Hebrew Bible far exceeded that of other Reformers).

418 This is still really part of the quotation from Deuteronomy 28. Leviticus 26:14–24 contains broadly similar material, but does not (for example) have the motif of fleeing from the enemy in seven directions.

Pflantzet er ein wyngarten
der frucht wirt ein ander warten
Es wirt jm ouch darzů kommen
jm werdend ſchaaff vnd rinder gnommen
Vnd wirdt ſinen fygenden ggeben
pur Eigennutz du merckſt eben
Das iſt den puren zhanden gangen
do man vfrůr hatt angfangen
Denn Gott ſpricht klar an diſem ort *Deut. 28.*
wo man nit läb nach ſinem wort
So werd vns kon vil böſers zhand
denn hie in dem Capitel ſtand
So wir thůnd das Gott hat gſeyt
wir kämind zů der fryheyt
Vnd wurdind wůchren aller welt
[Hiii^{v}] von vns wurd niemant wůchren gelt
Gott hats den Iuden do erloubt
damit die Heyden wurdind broubt
Vnd was zů einer ſtraaff erdacht
damit der Heyd wurd vmb ſins bracht
Weyſt wie es offt gieng?
ſo bald das volck anfieng
Nit hören wolt gottes wort
ſo warends gfürt an frömbde ort
Wie ſy hattend den Heyden thon
das můßt ouch über ſy ſelb gon
Vnd warend in Babilon gfürt *4. Reg. 25.*
hand in Egypten pflaſter grürt *Exod. 1.*
Do namends lützel wůcher yn
můßtend mit lyb vnd gůt gfangen ſyn
Von jren ſünden kam jnn das
weyſt wär jr erlöſer was?
Ders dryn gfürt hatt der fůrts ouch druß
ſy zucktend nie kein ſchwärdt vß
Für ſy ſtreyt ſelb jr herr Gott
alſo ſolt ouch die püriſch Rott
Schryen zů Gott biß das er käm

if he plants a vineyard, another will tend it. It will also come to pass that his sheep and cattle will be taken away and given to his enemies'. Notice, Pur Eygennutz, that this is what happened to the farmers when they began their revolt. Because God states clearly at this point that, if we don't live according to his Word, many worse things will soon come upon us than are spoken of here in this chapter. Doing what God has commanded is the way to freedom. Then, even if the whole world were full of usurers, no one would extort money from us. God allowed the Jews to do it in order that the heathen might be robbed, and it was conceived as a punishment that the heathen should be relieved of their money. Do you know what often happened? As soon as the people started not to want to listen to God's Word, they were led into a foreign land. What they had done to the heathen was done to them, and they were led into Babylon.[419] In Egypt they worked with mortar.[420] They took little in usury, and their bodies and worldly goods were held captive. This happened because of their sins. Do you know who was their Saviour? He who had led them thither also led them thence, and they never drew a sword. The Lord God himself fought for them. In the same way you pack of farmers should cry to God until he comes

419 2 Kings 25:11: 'Nebuzaradan the captain of the guard carried into exile the rest of the people who were left in the city and the deserters who had defected to the king of Babylon – all the rest of the population'.

420 Exodus 1:13–14: 'The Egyptians became ruthless in imposing tasks on the Israelites, and made their lives bitter with hard service in mortar and brick and in every kind of field labour'.

vnd jnen alle bſchwärd ab näm
Gott iſt mechtig als er ye was
hat er thon den Iuden das
Vnd ſy erlößt vß allen nöten
für vns zů letſt ſin ſun lan tödten
Er wirt vns frylich ouch nit lon
nun lond vns frölich zů jm gon *Hebr. 4.*
Lond vns nit vndultig ſin
[Hivr] lyb vnd gůt fart ſchnäll dahin
Sůchend nun das ewig iſt
wir müſſend all zyt ſin gerüſt
Das wir vnſers brütgams warten
gots rych ſtadt nit in äcker noch garten
Sůchen Gott zů aller zyt
das ſelb vns me anlyt
Denn zinß kumpt nun vß gottes zorn
ſo wir denn darzů ſind erborn
Das vns Gott wil mit zinſen plagen
ſo ſöllend wir nüt darwider ſagen
Dann biſt ein Chriſt / es jrrt dich nit
gottgeb was plag gott vff dich ſchütt
Vnd wenn du biſt ein rechter Chriſt
ſo man dir ouch zinß ſchuldig iſt
Gibt man dir nüt / du zürneſt nit
nimpt man dir ſchon das din damit
So ſinneſt jm nit wyter nach
du weyſt das gott zůghört die rach *Rom. 12.*
Nach dem gſatz möchtiſts klagen
vnd einer Oberkeyt ſagen
Darumb ſag ich ein yetlich Chriſt
wyt über alle gſatz iſt
Ein Chriſt thůt me denn das gſatz büt
vnd engt jnn diſer ſpruch nüt
Das man ſöll lihen vergeben *Math. 6.*
der ſpruch iſt den Chriſten eben *Luce. 6.*

3481 Rom. 12.] *om. AE*

and takes from you all your troubles. God is as mighty now as he ever was. If he did this for the Jews and saved them from all their troubles, then in the latter days he let his Son be killed for us. And he will indeed not leave us. Now let us go to him rejoicing,[421] let us not be impatient: our bodies and our worldly goods soon disappear; so let us seek that which is eternal. We must be prepared at all times to receive our bridegroom. God's kingdom is not a matter of fields or gardens. The same reason bids us to seek God at all times. For interest payments come only from God's anger, and if we are born with the idea of God plaguing us with them, we should not complain. Because if you are a Christian, this will not harm you, let God visit any plague he chooses upon you. And if you are a true Christian you will not be angered if someone owes you money and doesn't give it to you. And if he also takes something of yours, you won't hold a grudge against him: you know that revenge belongs to God.[422] By law you can make a complaint and bring it before the authorities. For this reason I say that every Christian is far above all laws. A Christian does more than the law requires, and is not restricted by the statement that one should write off loans.[423] This statement also is apt for Christians,

421 Hebrews 4:16 (see n. 187 above).

422 Romans 12:19: 'Beloved, never avenge yourselves, but leave room for the wrath of God: for it is written, "Vengeance is mine, I will repay", says the Lord'.

423 Whilst the reference is not wholly clear, Eckstein appears to be drawing on the principles of Luke 6:34–5 and/or Matthew 18:27–33.

Die widrend ſich darwider nit
ein Chriſt ſin lyb vnd gůt gitt
Wenn man jm ſchon vnrecht thůt
[Hiv[v]] das man jm nimpt ſin houpt vnd hůt
So mags die liebe als erlyden *1. Cor. 13.*
das gfürdret werd gmeiner friden
Er weyßt das er in gotz hand ſtadt
wie man mit jm vmbgadt
Vnd wirt darumb nit hön noch frech
begärt nit das er ſich rech
Was man jm nimpt das laßt er hin
zů Gott allein ſtadt jm ſin ſinn
Vnnd ſpricht: Herr gott es iſt alles din

Pur Eigennutz
Ich hör das ich noch kein Chriſt bin
denn ich nimm gern / gib wenig hin
Ich wond wir hettind fryheit
was Gott hett den Iuden gſeyt
Das ſölt vns Chriſten ouch zůſtan
anders ich nit gwänt han

Doctor Strouwbutz.
Das iſt ouch eben das ich ſag
gott der wil noch hütt by tag
Halten was er zů hat gſeyt
wenn man ſin bott im hertzen treyt
Das er vns mit den zinſen plagt
hand wir durch vnſer ſünd erjagt
Mit hoffart vnd mit trunckenheyt
ſähiſt wie wan yetz gwand treyt
Das nun nit zimpt der Chriſten kilch
die puren tragend nit me zwilch
[Hv[r]] Wend all Sammat vnd ſyden han
das iſt gmein vnder yederman

3518 man *CDF*

and they do not resist it:[424] 'A Christian gives his body and his goods, even if others do him wrong and seek to kill him'. Love can suffer all things,[425] in order that the common peace might be promoted. He knows that he is in God's hands, however people treat him, and for this reason he becomes neither angry nor insolent: he does not wish to avenge himself, and lets go of everything that is taken from him. He thinks of God alone and says: 'Lord God, it is all yours'.[426]

Pur Eygennutz

I hear that I'm not yet a Christian, because I like taking and give little. I thought we had freedom. What God said to the Jews should also apply to us – I've never thought otherwise.

Doctor Stroubutz

That's precisely what I'm saying. God will still today keep what he has promised, if you carry his commandment in your heart. His plaguing us with interest is something that we have earned by our sin, by our arrogance and drunkenness. You see how in these days people are wearing clothes that are not fitting for the Christian Church.[427] Farmers are no longer wearing twill; they all want velvet and silk. It's common amongst everyone

424 Likely to refer to Luke 6:34–5: 'If you lend to those from whom you hope to receive, what credit is that to you? Even sinners lend to enemies, to receive as much again. But love your enemies, do good, and lend, expecting nothing in return'. Eckstein might also have had in mind verses 27–31, Jesus's instructions to do good to those who hate one.

425 1 Corinthians 13:4–7: 'Love is patient; love is kind; love is not envious or boastful or arrogant or rude. It does not insist on its own way; it is not irritable or resentful; it does not rejoice in wrongdoing, but rejoices in the truth. It bears all things, believes all things, hopes all things, endures all things'.

426 Here Eckstein, through Stroubutz and like Zwingli, seems to employ a different hermeneutic from the one he uses when discussing matters of faith and religious practice, no longer insisting on a clear biblical mandate. In temporal, especially economic matters he seems content to permit anything that the Bible does not forbid and that does not hinder eternal life. See Demandt, *passim.*

427 As this sentence and the previous one imply, Eckstein sees this section on modish clothing as having spiritual significance: in that current fashions reflect the sin of arrogance. A similar point is made by Stricker, p. 17.

Sich bkleyden gantz nach Welſchem ſitten
röck / paret / vnd dhoſen / zerſchnitten
Es můß als ſin nach Welſcher art
ein yetlich ſchnudernaß zücht ein bart
Gibt ein kronen vmb ein paret
ein filtzhůt jm ſin gnůg thet
Macht darzů ein langen rock
der wyter iſt denn kein glock
Henckt darzů groß ermel dran
gäbind ein rock eim armen man
Die zerhouwt er / nun gůt tůch
treytt wie ein tägel vßgſchnitten ſchůch
Ein lang ſchwärdt hanget ouch daby
als ob er ein hencker ſy
Deßglychen thůnd die wyber ouch
tragend ſchwentz am gwand wie ein gugouch
machend köpf wie ein ſtockhüwel
das iſt vor Gott ein groſſer grüwel
Ouch machend ſy die ſtuchen gelb
hand rhot backen wie ein felb
Vnd ſehend vß den ſtuchen wie
ein ſtuckfleyſch vß einer gelwen brye
Ouch tragend ſy vßgſchnitten röck
das man jnen ſicht die milchſeck
Dröck hangend über die achßlen ab
das man ſech wo eine gſchräpffet hab
Vnd ſicht man jnen durch die arm
ſy bſorgend jnen wurde zwarm
[Hv^{v}] Darumb ſo müſſend ſy han lufft
menge hat ein dürre krufft
Das kum jr gwand daran kleb
dſchultren ragend für wie ein miſtkreb
Der rock iſt ouch mit ſammat bſetz
dar durch ein arm menſch wirt verletzt
Vnd nackend vor der thüren ſitzt
gantz von armůt blůt ſchwitzt
On zal ſuſt in vppikeit

to dress just like the French, with tunic, beret, and hose. It all has to be in the French style. Every snotty-nosed kid[428] grows a beard and pays a crown for a beret. A felt hat would suffice. He also wants a long tunic, which is broader than any bell,[429] and he hangs great sleeves on it. If you gave a tunic to a poor man he would just cut it up, and wear good cloth like a piece of half-shoe. He would also carry a long sword by his side, as if he were an executioner. And the women do the same. They wear trains on their dresses like cuckoos' tails, and have heads like owls. That is truly loathsome to God. They also make their veils yellow and have cheeks as red as plush, and they look out from below their veils as a piece of meat might from out of a yellow broth. They also wear low-cut dresses, so that you can see their udders. And the dresses hang over their shoulders, so that you can see where they've been bled; you can see right through their arms. They're obviously worried they'll get too hot, and so they have to have air. Many a woman has a body so skinny that her dress can hardly stick to it, and her shoulders jut out like rakes. Her dress is trimmed with velvet, something which has caused a poor man to suffer, so that he sits naked at people's doors sweating blood out of poverty. In countless other cases too, the whole world – women and men, young and old – are now clothed in vanity,

428 See the definition of 'Schnudernasen' in *SI* IV, 801.

429 Presumably at the bottom.

iſt ietz die gantz welt bkleyt
Wyb vnd man / ouch jung vnd alt
ſündet wider gott manigfalt
Darumb vns Gott zůſchickt vil plag
hör was vns Eſaias ſag
Nimm war din herr gott der kumpt *Eſaie. 3.*
der alle zierd von dir hin rumpt
Du haſt gegen gott din houpt erhebt
all din tag wider jnn ouch glebt
Darumb din herr gott nimpt von dir
all krafft vnd ſterck / ouch ſylbergſchir
Er nimpt von dir die zierd diner ſchůch
vnd bkleydt dich mit härinem tůch
Ein glatz wirt dir für din krußhaar
denn wirt din boßheit offenbar
Dine ſterckſten fallend ouch im ſtryt *Leuit. 26.*
vnd werdend mit flucht verſtröuwt wyt
Meinſtu nit es ſyge yetz gſchehen?
man hats leyder wol gſehen
An allen orten vmb vnd vmm
darzů iſt yetz kein pur ſo krumm
[Hvi[r]] Einer dem andren yetz zůtrinckt
das yetwedrer wie ein vaß ſtinckt
Was volgt darnach? nüt denn ſchweeren
mit flůchen / leſtren gott den herren
Das thůt ein yeder puren klotz
der ſchweert denn by dem lyden gotz
Ouch by ſinen wunden vnd macht
darzů denn yederman lacht
Vnd ſo es lang vmbhar gadt
das gſoffen er wider von jm ladt
Holifernes was ein houptman *Iudith. 13.*
in den ouch zfil wyn ran
Darumb ſin houpt jm nam ein wyb
ſin läger man ouch gar vertrib
Er hat ſich vollen wyn gſoffen
wär gern zů der Iudith gſchloffen

and they are sinning in many ways against God. For this reason God sends us many plagues. Hear what Isaiah says:[430] 'Behold, the Lord your God is coming, who will remove all your adornments from you. You have lifted up your heads against God and lived against his will all your days. So the Lord your God will take from you all your strength and might, and all your silver vessels; he will take from you the ornaments of your shoes, and clothe you with a hair shirt; you will have a bald head instead of your curly hair, for your evil will be made known. And the strongest amongst you will fall in battle, and you will flee to all corners'.[431] Don't you think this is what has been happening recently? I'm afraid we've seen all of this, in all places. Also, farmers are now so twisted that one drinks the health of another, and both end up stinking like a beer barrel. And what comes of that? Nothing but swearing, cursing, and blaspheming. All peasant oafs do that: they swear by God's passion and by his wounds, so that these things are made into a laughing stock; and so they carry on until they part company, drunk. Holofernes was a captain[432] who also drank too much wine, so that a woman cut his head off and his camp was destroyed. He had made himself drunk with wine, and wanted to sleep with Judith;

430 What follows is by way of a paraphrase of Isaiah 3:18–25.

431 There are no specific verbal parallels to Leviticus 26, but Eckstein is probably thinking in general terms of the account of God's punishment of Israel in verses 14–39.

432 The story of Judith and Holofernes begins as early as Judith 10:17.

Das mocht er vor völle nit *Iudith. 14.*
ſin houpt on den lyb ritt
Gen Hieruſalem vff die muren
alſo gſchicht ouch üch puren
Denn wo jr ſind zamen kommen
hand jr andren lüten das jr gnommen
Darumb hand üch die fygend gjagen
leyder üwer vil ztod gſchlagen
Ir hand ouch praſſet tag vnd nacht
gottes daby lützel dacht
Pur eygennutz das ſag ich dir
in eim wyten huß hat man vil gſchir
Eins brucht man zů eeren
mit eim andren můß man weeren
[Hvi[v]] Das ful fleyſch nit nemm überhand
weyſt warumb es yetz übel ſtand?
Gott hat vns kinder zfürſten geben
wir fürend als ein ſündig läben
Denn künig vnd volck iſt eben glych
darumb nemmend ab alle rych
Die fürſten müſſend das volck plagen
ein küng nach des andren küngrych jagen
Vnd můß man böß mit böſem ſtraaffen
grechtigkeyt iſt gar entſchlaaffen
da hilfft nüt für / brucht man ſchon waffen

Pur Eygennutz.
Iſt denn böſer gwalt von Gott?
das er plag die püriſch rott
Ich hab gwänt wir ſygind fry
was der geyſt Gots ſy
Vnd dörff man keiner oberkeyt
das hat mir ein Töuffer gſeyt
Ich hatt mich gantz darnach gericht
vnn meint zinß / rent vnd gült wär gſchlicht

3630 vnn] *om. CDF*

but he couldn't do this in his drunkenness, with the result that his head rode into Jerusalem without the rest of him.[433] The same thing is happening with you farmers. Because when you have banded together, you have robbed other people of their possessions, so that your enemies have hunted you down. You have also boozed night and day, and thought little of God in doing so. I tell you, Pur Eygennutz, in a big house there are many vessels. One you should honour, and another you should use to defend yourself, so that your rotten flesh does not get the upper hand. Do you know why things are so bad at this time? God has given us children for princes,[434] and we are all leading sinful lives. Kings are the same as the common people. So all kingdoms are in decline. The princes plague the people, one king is always after another one's kingdom, and people seem to have to punish evil with evil. Justice is sound asleep. There is nothing else for it but to take up arms.

Pur Eygennutz

Do evil authorities which plague the farmers come from God, then? I thought we were free, as the Spirit of God is free, and no longer needed authorities. An Anabaptist said that to me, and I've gone completely by what he said. I've thought that interest payments, rents, and taxes were over and done with.

433 Judith 13 (especially verses 6–10) describes the death of Holofernes. His head is actually placed on the walls of Bethulia, not Jerusalem (see Judith 14:11).

434 Presumably a reference to Emperor Charles V, who was however twenty-five when the *Concilium* first appeared. This is the first example of Eckstein criticizing the behaviour of princes or kings, something he was to do in a much more concerted way in the *Rychsztag*.

Doctor Strouwbutz
Aller gwalt kumpt von oben ab
weyſt wie Chriſtus ein antwurt gab
Pilato / der jnn wolt richten?
der text wird din fraag ſchlichten *Ioan. 19.*
Du hettiſt kein gwalt über mich
käm er dir nit vſſz vatters rych
Hörſt hie? Pilatus hatt nit gwalt
[Hvii^r] dann von oben ab in der gſtalt
Wie jm von Gott was vergundt
hie wirt by diſem text kund
Das aller gwalt kumpt von Gott
über gůte vnd böſe rott
Thůſt du gůts ſo biſt wol fry *Roma. 13.*
vnd magſt dem gwalt wonen by
Groſſes lob dardurch erlangen
ſo ein dieb můß am galgen hangen
Das gſatz iſt nit dem grechten gſetzt *1. Tim. 1.*
der hencker dieben vnd mördren netzt
Es iſt ouch darzů Gottes will
das gmartret werdind heilgen vil
Allen menſchlichen gſchöpfft biß vnderthon *1. Petr. 4.*
hat dir ſant Peter zletze glon *1. Petri. 2.*
Ouch hat vns ſant Paulus gleert
das Oberkeit von vns werd geert *Tit. 3.*
Hör was wyter Paulus ſpricht
der ſelb dich ab dym whon richt
Sind allem gwalt vnderthon
dem gwalt ſolt du nit widerſton *Roma. 13.*
Wär ſich nit vnderen gwalt ladt
der ſelb Gots ordnung wider ſtadt
Wilt du nit fürchten den gwalt
thů gůts / vnd dich frummcklich halt
Der gwalt ein diener Gottes iſt
gib yedem das du ſchuldig biſt
Darumb gibt man Sthür vnd Zoll
das der gwalt vſſehen ſol

Doctor Stroubutz

All power comes down from above. Do you know how Christ answered Pilate, when he wanted to judge him? This text will settle your question:[435] 'You would have no power over me unless it came to you from my Father's kingdom'. Do you hear this? Pilate has no power other than what comes from above, in the form that God has granted it to him. This text makes it clear that all authority over both good and bad people comes from God. If you do good, you will indeed be free,[436] and if you uphold the powers that be, you will be greatly honoured for it. A thief has to hang from the gallows. The law is not made for the just:[437] it is thieves and murderers that the hangman hurts. It is also God's will that many saints should be martyred. 'Be subject to all human creatures',[438] St Peter says in his last chapter.[439] St Paul has also taught us that we should honour the authorities.[440] Hear more of St Paul, who can guide even you away from your bad habits: 'Be subject to all authorities. You should not resist authorities.[441] He who does not place himself under authority lives contrary to God's order'. So if you don't wish to live in fear of the authorities, do good and behave honourably. Worldly authority is a servant of God. Pay what you owe to everyone. It is for this reason that one pays taxes and dues, which the authorities are to oversee.

435 John 19:11: 'Jesus answered him, "You would have no power over me unless it had been given you from above"'.

436 Romans 13:1: 'Let every person be subject to the governing authorities; for there is no authority except from God, and those authorities that exist have been instituted by God'.

437 1 Timothy 1:9: 'The law is laid down not for the innocent but for the lawless and disobedient, for the godless and sinful, for the unholy and the profane'.

438 The marginal reference may be to 1 Peter 4:12–19, with its statements about the desirability of Christians sharing in Christ's sufferings; or, if 'the last chapter' is indeed meant, Eckstein may have in mind the exhortation to 'humility in your dealings with one another' which appears in 1 Peter 5:5.

439 1 Peter 2:13: 'For the Lord's sake accept the authority of every human institution'.

440 Titus 3:1: 'Remind them to be subject to rulers and authorities, to be obedient, to be ready for every good work'.

441 Romans 13:2: 'Therefore whoever resists authority resists what God has appointed, and those who resist will incur judgement'.

der zů eeren iſt / ſolt du eeren
[Hvii[v]] der zfürchten / ſolt förchten / dich nit weeren
Du ſolt niemand nüts ſchuldig ſin
denn dliebe ſyg dir pflantzet yn *Liebe.*
Hörſt? dliebe dienet aller welt
ſicht nüt an / weder gůt noch gelt
Vnd ladt eim yeden ſins blyben
ſy haſſet nit / vnd kan nit kyben *1. Cor. 13.*
Sy bläyt ſich nit / vnd wirt nit hön
gſchicht jr böß / ſy thůt gůtz dar gen
Gloub vnd hoffnung nun empfacht *Gloub.*
dliebe würckt / gar niemand verſchmacht *Hoffnung*
Man wirt durch glouben Gott vereint
nun hör zů / wie er das meint
Wir ſind all ſünder von natur
dern manglet Gott / iſt on ſünd pur
Wie mögend wir vnd gott eins ſin?
ſo er dſünd nimpt gar von vns hin
Die vns allen iſt an boren
gott ladt vns nach / enthalt ſin zoren
Vnd ſtraafft vns nach gerechtigkeit
wenn das ein menſch ouch dultig treyt
So lidend wir / vnd er laßt nach
nimpt vff ſich ſelbs all vnſer ſchmach
Die ſünd in ſinem blůt verſchwindt
by gott alſo man friden findt *Rom. 5.*
Vnd Gott der vatter hat für gůt
das ſigel iſt ſines ſuns blůt *Galat. 4.*
Das iſt die fryheit / daruon du ſeyſt *2. Cor. 3.*
vnd wirt allein gfryet der geyſt
Nun haſtu klarlich gnůg gehört *Ioann. 8.*
[Hviii[r]] wie dich die Liebe gottes leert
Was du ſchuldig bist eim yeden / gib
nit wider die ſtraaff gots kyb
Biß dir gott ſendt ein ſölich zyt
das er dir himliſchs vmb jrdiſchs gitt
Der ſeelen heyl iſt über gold *Eccleſ. 30.*

You should honour what is to be honoured, and fear what is to be feared; you should not resist doing this. You should owe nothing to anyone, for love should be planted in you. Do you hear? Love serves all, has no regard for possessions or money, and lets everyone keep what is his. Love does not hate, cannot quarrel, does not puff itself up, is not angered when bad things befall it,[442] but repays evil with good. Receive now faith and hope, practise charity, and despise no one. 'By faith you are united with God'.[443] Listen to what he means by that. We are all sinners by nature, but God is not: he is pure and free from sin. So how can we and God be one? By him completely removing from us the sin we are all born with. God pardons us, withholds his anger, and punishes us according to his justice. We suffer what a man is able patiently to bear, and he spares us. He takes upon himself all our shame, and our sins disappear in his blood. So one finds peace with God,[444] and God the Father accepts the seal of his Son's blood. That's the freedom you're talking about:[445] you are freed only in your spirit.[446] Now you've heard clearly enough[447] how God's love teaches you: give what you owe to everyone; don't quarrel with God's punishment, until God sends the time when he will give you heavenly things in exchange for earthly ones. The soul's salvation is more than gold,[448]

442 1 Corinthians 13:4–7 (see n. 425 above).

443 Uniquely in the early editions of Eckstein's dialogues, a pointing hand draws the reader's attention to this line, 'a classic statement of Evangelical soteriology that shows just how closely theology and politics are intertwined in Eckstein's thinking' (Love, 'Dialogue', p. 251).

444 Cf. Romans 5:18: 'Therefore just as one man's trespass led to condemnation for all, so one man's act of righteousness leads to justification and life for all'.

445 Galatians 5 (*sic*) : 1: 'For freedom Christ has set us free'.

446 2 Corinthians 3:17: 'Now the Lord is the Spirit, and where the Spirit of the Lord is, there is freedom'.

447 We can see no obvious connection to John 8; indeed, as the *Concilium* nears its end, the accuracy of its Bible references seems to decline somewhat.

448 Cf. Ecclesiasticus (*sic*) 30:15: 'Health and fitness are better than any gold, and a robust body than countless riches'. Also 31:5: 'One who loves gold will not be justified; one who pursues money will be led astray by it'.

allein ſo dir din gott iſt hold
Des lybs heyl über all Zins iſt *eodem*
ein rechter menſch ſich allwäg rüſt
Das er behalt was jm gott ſag
der wirt wol bſton am jüngſten tag
Darumb thů hie das dich gott leer
das ſich gott dört nit von dir keer
nüt anders wil hie gott der herr

Pur Eigennutz
Wol an / alſo verſton ichs nit
mir iſt allein das man gitt
Zähend / Zins / rendt / vnd gült
damit man müſſigenger fült
Můß das ouch von gott ſin
das ich inen geb das min hin?
ſag ob ich recht dran bin

Doctor Strouwbutz.
Du haſt gnůg diſen tag ghört
Chriſtus hat geben / da by vns glert
Was vns dien zů gmeinem friden
wir ſöllind ergernus myden
Dann Chriſtus ſelbs vnſer Herr
[Hviii^{v}] ſchickt Petrum biß an das Meer
Petrus dem gheyß Gots nachgieng
ein fiſch er vſs dem Meer fieng
In ſinem mul fand er gelt
damit er nit ergrete dwelt
Gab er für ſich vnd Chriſtum zol
ein yeder Chriſt deßglychen ſol
Sich hüten vor ergernuß
dann Chriſtus hats nit gſagt vmb ſuſs
Ouch vorzyten dIuden kamend *Matt. 22.*
Herodis knecht mit inen namend
Fragtend do den Herren eben
ſol man dem Keyſer Zins geben?

and if God is faithful to you, the salvation of your soul is more important than any payment. A just man always ensures that he does what God tells him, and he will abide at the Last Day. So, then, do here what God teaches you, so that God will not turn his face from you in heaven. The Lord your God wants nothing else from you here.

Pur Eygennutz
Very well, but I don't understand things that way. All that concerns me is that we give tithes, interests, rents, and taxes to enrich lazy wasters. Does it also come from God that I should have to give them what's mine? Tell me if I'm right.

Doctor Stroubutz
You've heard enough about this for today. Christ paid his dues, and taught us in so doing what serves the common peace. We should avoid giving offence. Because Christ our Lord himself sent Peter to sea; Peter followed this command, and caught a fish in the sea in whose mouth he found money which enabled him not to cause offence to the world. He gave it to pay his own and Christ's dues. Every Christian should do the same and take care not to give offence. Because Christ did not say this in vain:[449] 'In earlier times also the Jews came, took Herod's servants with them, and asked the Lord whether tribute should be paid to Caesar.

449 Matthew 17 (*sic*): 24–7 is accurately summarized over these two quotations.

Der Herr fragt eim pfennig nach
als bald er die bildtnus ſach
Sprach er: Weß iſt die übergſchrifft?
hör wie er dglychßner wider trifft
Des Keyſers / ſprachend ſy zum Herren
darwider wolt er nit leeren
Waſs Keiſers iſt / gebend dem Keiſer
das hortend wol Herodis reyſer
Was Gott zů ghört / das gebend Gott
alſo leert er die Iüdſchen rott *Matt. 17.*
Von Zinß vnd Sthür das Capitel ſeyt
den Zoll hat Petrus zůtreyt
Wie wol das erdtrich Chriſti was
nüt deſt minder hieß er das
Damit er vns gäb zůuerſton
das man den Gwallt ſol vor ougen han
Einer vor zyten ouch ſprach
[Ii^{r}] do er vnſeren herren ſach
Meyſter / minem brůder ſag *Lucæ. 12.*
das er ſich mit mir vertrag
Vnd das erb mit mir teil
do ſprach Chriſtus der ſeel heyl
Wär hat mich üch gſetzt zů richter?
ghörſt? er wolt die zween nit ſchlichten
Sagt ouch ſinen jüngeren darby
hütend üch das keiner gytig ſy
Hie magſt du aber wol verſton
er hat nit wider den gwalt thon
Darumb Eer ouch die Oberkeyt
din hertz zů friden ſyg bereyt *Matthe. 5.*
Gib yedem das du ſchuldig biſt
denn magſt du ſin ein rechter Chriſt
Din läben richt nach der ſchnůr
vnd hüt dich vor vfrůr
Biſt du ſchon mit Zinſen bſchwärt

3762 zum *CDF*

The Lord asked for a penny and, as soon as he saw the picture on it, he said: "Whose is this superscription?"' Again, hear how he deals with the hypocrites: 'The Emperor's', they said to the Lord. He didn't want to say anything against this: 'Give to the Emperor what is the Emperor's'. Herod's servants heard this well. 'Give to God what is God's' – thus he taught the Jewish crowd. The chapter speaks of payments and taxes; and Peter also paid his dues. Even though the earth was Christ's, he nevertheless commanded this, so as to give us to understand that we should respect the powers that be. Somebody also said in earlier times, when he saw Our Lord: 'Master, tell my brother[450] to do a deal and divide the inheritance with me'. To this Christ, our souls' Saviour, said: 'Who has made me a judge over you?'. Do you hear? He didn't want to mediate between the two of them, and at the same time he said to his disciples: 'Take heed that none of you is covetous'. Here again you can well understand that he did not go against the authorities. So, honour authority; may your heart be ready to make peace;[451] and give to everyone what you owe. Then you can be a true Christian. Lead your life this way, and refrain from rebelling. If you are already burdened with payments,

450 Luke 12:13: 'Someone in the crowd said to him, "Teacher, tell my brother to divide the family inheritance with me". But he said to him, "Friend, who set me as a judge or arbitrator over you?" And he said to them, "Take care! Be on your guard against all kinds of greed; for one's life does not consist in the abundance of possessions"'.

451 Possibly a further reminder of 'blessed are the peacemakers' (Matthew 5:9); but also reads like a 'summary of the Law' of the kind found in verses 17–20.

din vordren hand ſich ouch erneert
Vnd gabend mee denn du gäbiſt
lůg das du wie din vordren läbiſt
Die liebe mags alles ertragen
ſichſt wie vil yetz ztod ſind gſchlagen?
Die woltend ouch nit zinßbar ſin
yetz iſt lyb vnd gůt dahyn
Hettind ſy ſich wol bedacht
jn dwelt hand wir gar nüt bracht
Ouch nackend müſſend wir druß gon
wir wend dem gwalt nit widerſton
So blybend wir by wyb vnd kinden
[Ii[v]] wir hands bſchult mit vnſren ſünden
Denn rennt vnd gült kumpt nienen von
ſo man Gott nit wil vor ougen han
Vnd bſchwärt vns Gott mit eim joch
das man nit alſo mit jm boch
Den Iuden gſchach es vor zyten
můßtend frömmden küngen zhoff ryten *2. Par. 12.*
Inen darzů bringen rennt vnd ſthür *2. Par. 28.*
es iſt by vns kein abenthür
Sy woltend nit mee Gottes ſin
vnd ſchrüwend nach eim Künig hin *1. Reg. 8.*
Den gab inen Gott / ſagt ouch daby
was eins Künigs grechtigkeit ſy
So lyde dich nun du biderman
diewyl es Gott alſo wil han
Dem willen gotz nit widerſträb
gib das dir Gott ouch gäb
Vnd wenn man ſchon glych wild thůt
es iſt ein teyl erkoufft gůt
Iſt es verheiſſen von den alten
ſo ſöllends die erben billich halten
wenn man die ſach wol durchloufft
vil gůter werdend näher koufft

3782 wol bedacht] vorhin alſo gedacht *CDF*

remember that your forebears also had enough to eat, yet gave more than you do. See to it that you live as your forebears did. Love can bear everything. Do you see how many have now been put to death? They also didn't want to pay up, but now they've lost both their lives and their goods. If only they'd thought beforehand: 'We've brought nothing into the world, and we shall also have to leave it naked; we don't want to resist authority, and so we'll stay with our wives and children. We've brought it upon ourselves by our sins'. Because rents and taxes come only from our not respecting God: God burdens us with a yoke, so that we might not be stiff-necked. It happened to the Jews in earlier times. They had to ride to the courts of foreign kings to pay them rents and tributes[452] – it's not a new adventure for us. They didn't want to be God's subjects any more, and clamoured for a king.[453] God gave them one, but told them at the same time what the nature of a king's justice would be. So be patient now, my good man, because this is the way God wishes it. Don't resist the will of God, but give what God himself gave you. And even if you are mad about it, remember that if goods were promised by ancestors, they have in part been bought, and the heirs are quite entitled to keep them. If you go into this matter properly, you find that many goods are bought more easily

452 The two Chronicles references cannot be found with any confidence.

453 1 Samuel 8:4: 'Then all the elders of Israel gathered together and came to Samuel at Ramah, and said to him, "You are old and your sons do not follow in your ways; appoint for us, then, a king to govern us, like other nations"'.

Wenn man findt das Zins druff ſtadt
näher der gantz kouff zůgadt
Man lycht offt gelt vmb Zinß vs
das bhalt den armen by ſym hus
Sprichſt du denn / Das ſelb iſt waar /
wenn vmbhar kämind zwentzig jar
Denn ſolt das gůt ouch ledig ſyn
[Iii^{r}] das vmb zwentzig pfund wär gſetzt yn
Sag ich das ſelb wär Chriſtenlich.
wo findt man aber des glych?
Ich gloub das er vff erd nit leb
der dir yetz zwentzig pfund geb
Darzů beytti zwentzig jar
nüt von dir nem gantz vnd gar
Er lebt in diſer welt nit
der ſin gůt alſo vßgitt
Ir puren haltend ſuſt nit vil
wenn nun eins jars lang iſt das zil
Magſtu aber einen finden
der jm das laſſe ynbinden
So nimm jn an / verſchmach jnn nit
wenn er dir zähen guldin git
Vnd das zwentzgeſt jar vmmhar kumm
das denn wett ſyg die houpt Summ
Diewyl du aber dich verſchrybſt
den Lehman ſelb darzů trybſt
Das gelt ſolt jm ouch zinſen fry
jm darumb thůn das gnůg ſy
Denn ſprächiſt dem Lehman
hör was ich yetz im ſinn han
Das gelt das du mir nun gibſt
mit lieb nimmer von mir trybſt
Er ſpräch der tüfel lihe dir
pur kumm nimmerme zů mir
Wiltu nüt geben / ouch nüt enpfach

3822 beytti] borgete *CDF*   3841 lieb es nimmer *CDF*

if interest payments are attached to them – this means the purchase happens more quickly. Often people lend money for interest, and this enables the poor person to stay in his house. If you then say, 'Here's something true: after twenty years goods bought for twenty pounds should be freed from interest payments', I'd say that was a Christian thing. But where can you find anything like that? I believe that there's no one alive now who would give you twenty pounds, and then just wait for twenty years without taking anything from you at all. There's no one living in this world who would give away his possessions for nothing. You farmers don't think much about it if it's only a matter of a year. But if you find somebody who would allow himself to be tied in like that for twenty years, then accept and don't despise him if he gives you ten gulden and comes back in the twentieth year because the principal is due. You're driving your creditor to do what you won't do yourself. If his money is to be free from interest, then do what's right by him. If you said to him: 'Hear what I have in mind now. You're not going to get back the money you're now giving to me', he would say: 'May the devil lend to you then, farmer; never come to me again. If you're not willing to give anything, you won't get anything –

ſo louffend dir nit güldten nach
Sprichſtu: Ich mag nit on ſin
[Iii[v]] ſag ich / ſo gib ouch Zinß hin
Dann was du wilt das dir ouch gſchech *Matth. 7.*
deßglychen man ouch von dir ſech
Wenn du hettiſt zinßlüt
wöltiſt das ſy dir gäbind nüt?
So ſolt inen ouch nüt geben
ſprichſt du denn: Das wölt ich eben
Du lügſt pur wie ein dieb
kein haller lieſſiſt nach mit lieb
Pur Eygennutz zürn es nit
nüt nachlon dir jm hertzen ligt
Du haſt es vor ouch ſelbs gſeyt
dich fröuwe ſo man dir zůtreyt
Haſt du denn Gotzgaaben ggeben
oder die dinen merck mich eben
So begär iren von hertzen nit
ob man dir ſchon nüt wider gibt
Dann es iſt ein verſprochne gaab
dIuden habend ein grüwel darab
Spricht man: Das iſt verſprochen Gott *Marci. 7.*
vnd was dennocht nun menſchen bott
Das von Gott verworffen was
Gottes bott halten gfalt jm baß
Es iſt ein recht gottes gebott
das man neere die leerend rott
Das iſt den / der dir Gotzwort ſeyt
darumb man Zähenden zamen leyt *Deut. 14.*
Den gib mit luſt on vorteyl
ſo gibt dir Gott glück vnd heyl
Dann es iſt darumb erdacht
[Iiii[r]] wär jnn nit gibt gotz bott verſchmacht
Sprichſt: Was gadt mich Zähend an?
ich bin ein Chriſten man

3865 hattend *CD* 3866 Spricht man] So man ſprach *CD* 3872 dirs *CDF*

gulden won't come running after you that way'. If you say: 'But I can't get by without them', then I say: 'So then, pay your interest, do as you would be done by'.[454] If you had debtors, would you want them not to give you anything? You wouldn't give them anything if they didn't. If you answered 'Indeed I would' to my question, then, farmer, you'd be lying like a thief. You wouldn't willingly let them have a single heller. Don't get angry about this, Pur Eygennutz, but letting off debts just isn't in your nature. You said yourself just now that you are pleased when someone gives something to you. Is it the gifts of God you have given, or your own? Listen to me: don't desire them in your heart, whether or not you are given anything in return. Because these are gifts that have been promised. The Jews hated it when people said: 'This has been promised to God, but was offered to men'.[455] God rejected this: he is more pleased by people keeping his commands. It is a true command of God that one should feed those who teach – that is, him who teaches you God's Word. Tithes are gathered in for this reason:[456] give them willingly and without respect of persons; then God will give you happiness and salvation. This is the reason why they were thought of. So anyone who doesn't give his tithe holds God's command in contempt. You say: 'What have tithes to do with me? I'm a Christian man,

454 Matthew 7:12: 'In everything do to others as you would have them do to you; for this is the law and the prophets'.

455 Most obviously a reference to the Pharisees rebuking the disciples for eating with defiled hands in Mark 7:1–7.

456 Deuteronomy 14:27: 'As for the Levites resident in your towns, do not neglect them, because they have no allotment or inheritance with you'.

Chriſten iſt nit Zähenden botten
das man geb den pfaffen rotten.
Sag ich / du biſt ein böſer Chriſt
vntrüwer denn ein Iud iſt
dIuden denen prieſtern gabend
denen Leuiten / als wir habend
Die lertend nun des lybs heyl
ouch ghört den armen ein teyl
Vnd du wilt nit Zähend geben
dem der dir zeygt ewigs leben
Was mag dir doch nützers ſin
ſo dir erſchötzt gott korn vnd wyn
Das du ein prieſter züchſt daruß
der gotzwort leert in eim gotzhuß
Als wöltiſt ſprechen: Sichſtu Herr
dir ſyg pryß / danck / lob vnd eer
Wyl du mir erſchötzeſt die frücht
iſt billich das ich mich verpflicht
Du macheſt wachſen / weyß ich wol
daruß der menſch leben ſol
Iſt das gwechß denn nit von mir
ſo iſt ouch billich das ich dir
Drumb dancke / vnd ouch verjech
das es on min verdienſt gſchech
Frucht vnd ertrich / das iſt din *Deut. 12.*
alles das wachßt / korn vnd wyn *& 14. 26.*
So iſt von nöten das ich geb
[Iiii^{v}] dem der mich lert / das ich ewig leb
Darumb den lerer trülich neer
es iſt Gots vnd Sant Pauls leer *1. Cor. 4.*
Wenn es dir ſchon nit botten iſt *1. Tim. 3.*
gib jnn nüt deſtminder frummer Chriſt *Galat. 6.*
Abraham ouch Zähenden gab
dem Melchzedech von ſiner hab
Do zmal noch kein gſatz was
vſſz gůter trüw thett er das
Von jm ſelb on das bott gotz *Gene. 14.*

and giving tithes isn't required of Christians for them to end up giving them to packs of priests'. I say: 'You're a bad Christian, you're less faithful than a Jew. The Jews gave to those priests, those Levites who (so we are told) taught only the salvation of the body; and a part also went to the poor. And now you don't want to pay tithes to the person who points you towards eternal life. What could serve you better, you who grow God's corn and his wine, than to choose someone as a priest who might teach God's Word in God's house? It is as if you wanted to say: 'To you, Lord, be praise, thanks, glory, and honour, for it is you who make my fruit grow. It's right that I should plant the seed, but you cause those things to grow which are necessary to life. I well know that. So if their growth isn't down to me, it is right that I should thank you, and also affirm that it's not happened through any achievement of my own. The earth and its fruits are yours, everything that grows, both corn and wine.[457] So it's necessary that I should give from them to him who teaches me, so that I might live eternally'. For this reason you should faithfully feed your teacher. This is God's and St Paul's teaching. Although it isn't commanded of you, you should nevertheless give to him, faithful Christian.[458] Abraham also gave tithes out of his possessions to Melchizedek, even before there was a law. He did that out of his great faithfulness, on his own initiative, not needing God's command.[459]

457 The key verse would seem to be Deuteronomy 14:22: 'Set apart a tithe of all the yield of your seed that is brought in yearly from the field'. Also Deuteronomy 26 (*sic*): 11: 'Then you, together with the Levites and the aliens who reside among you, shall celebrate with all the bounty that the Lord your God has given to you and your house'.

458 Galatians 6:6: 'Those who are taught the word must share in all good things with their teacher'. The relevance of 1 Corinthians 4 may be Paul's assertion in verse 6: 'I have applied all this to Apollos and myself for your benefit, brothers and sisters, so that you may learn through us the meaning of the saying, "Nothing beyond what is written"'. The relevance of 1 Timothy 3 is unclear.

459 Genesis 14:20: 'And Abram gave him [Melchizedek] one-tenth of everything'.

ſo gib du ouch grober klotz
Sprichſt: Ich gib den pfaffen geren
aber nit weltlichen herren
Wirt mir lützel / ich gib nit vil
mit pfaffen ich vßkommen wil
Daran kumpt nit der weltlich gwalt
erfrürt der wyn im winter kalt
Erſchlacht der hagel ouch das korn
gwalt wil nit han ein haller verlorn
Sag ich: Es wär gůt Chriſtenlich
das es ſitt wär in allem rich
Wenn gott die armen lüt angriff
das man ſy denn nit überlüff
Ob ſchon der Pur käm denn zmal lär
das man jm ouch gnädig wär
Es wirt den herren übel gon
vor gott dem herren nit wol bſton *Pſalm. 31.*
Die alſo freſſend die armen
vnd ſich deren nit erbarmen
Acht ſy nit du biderman
[Iiv^r] Diewyl du magſt din narung han
Vnd mit frummkeyt überkummen
wirt dir ſchon hie abgnommen
Die ſeel man dir nit nemmen mag
din bſchwärd allein Gott klag
Der vns ſelb ſetzt in ſölich gfär
denn wir ſind all gotzforcht lär
Wenn wir aber zů jm kerend
vnser trähen vor jm rerend *Pſalm. 49*
Vber vns erbarmt er ſich
er iſt der hirt / wir ſind ſin vych *Ioann. 10.*
Denn wie das vich ſich weyden ladt
vnd in des hirten gwalt ſtadt
Alſo ſtond wir in Gottes hand

3917 grober klotz] wo es thůt not *CDF* 3918f. Sprichſt [du *F*] denn: Den pfaffen die leren gib ich gern / nit weltlichen heren *CDF* 3922 welt *CDF* 3925 gwalt] er *CDF*

You too should give in this way, you great clot. If you say: 'I'll willingly give to the priests who teach, but not to secular lords. If I don't have a lot, I won't give much, but I want to get on well with the priests. It doesn't matter to the powers that be if my wine freezes in the cold winter and hail destroys my corn – they won't lose a heller by it'. Then I will say to you: 'It would be truly Christian if it were the custom in every kingdom that, when God struck the poor people, their lords didn't punish them; that, even if the farmer had nothing left, lords would still be gracious towards him. It will go ill for those lords (they will not be able to stand before God) who eat up the poor and do not have mercy on them.[460] Pay no heed to them, good man, for as long as you have food, and your faith will bring you victory. Even if they take away your goods, no one can take away your soul; make your complaint to God alone, who himself places us in such danger. For we have forgotten the fear of God. If, though, we turn towards him and weep our tears before him, he will have mercy on us.[461] He is our shepherd and we are his flock.[462] For just as the sheep can graze safely under the shepherd's authority, so we are in God's hands,

460 Possibly a reference to Psalm 35 (*sic*): 10: 'You deliver the weak from those too strong for them, the weak and needy from those who despoil them'.

461 More likely to refer the Penitential Psalm, 51. Cf. verse 1: 'Have mercy on me, O God, according to your steadfast love; according to your abundant mercy, blot out my transgressions'.

462 John 10:11: 'I am the good shepherd'.

der löß vns vf all vnſer band
Vnd mach vns fry an lyb vnd ſeel
als er thett dem volck Iſrael
Gott vns in ſinem rych zel

Herold.
Ir thüren Chriſten jung vnn alt
hie hat man ghört in was gſtalt
Die prieſterſchafft hat vns verfürt
wirt klar durch offne that probiert
Denn damit wir hand dienet Gott
kam wol allein der gſchmirbten Rott
Der glychen dienſt wil Gott nit han
damit man ſchindt den armen man
Keins andren gůts Gott nit bgärt
[Iiv^{v}] denn das zů jm allein wärd kert
In allem kumber vnd trübſal
es ſyg des lybs oder ſeel fal
Da wil er ſelber mit vns ſin
findt man in aller gſchrifft durch hin
Der Dauid ſpricht im Pſalmen bůch
das man by Gott all zůflucht ſůch *Pſalm. 70.*
Ouch ſpricht gott / wär nun hofft in mich
allein den ſelben erlöſen ich *Pſalm. 90.*
Vnd bhüt jnn drumb das er mich bkent
wär zů mir ſchrygt der wirdt nit gſchent
In kumber wil ich mit jm ſin
von aller bſchwärd erlöſen jnn
Ouch die da ſind eins trübten hertzen *Pſalm. 33.*
denen iſt Gott nach / trybt vß all ſchmertzen *Pſalm. 50.*
Ein kümbret hertz verſchmacht er nit
on das hilfft nüt was man jm gibt *Prouer. 23.*
Allein das hertz begäret gott
vnd das wir haltind ſine bott
So wir jm gend das hertz allein

3958 prieſterſchafft hat] pfaffen vns habind *CDF*

and he will liberate us from all our bonds and make us free in body and soul, as he did for the people of Israel. May God count us worthy to be numbered amongst the members of his kingdom.

Herald

Dear Christians, both young and old, we've heard here how the priests have led us astray. This has been demonstrated clearly and openly by their deeds. For that with which we served God has benefited only the greasy pack of priests. God doesn't want the service of such as these, who would skin the poor man alive. God wishes for no other wealth than that we turn to him in all things and tell him of sorrows and troubles, whether of body or of soul. He desires to share these with us. We can see this throughout the whole of Scripture. David says in the book of Psalms that we should seek all our refuge with God.[463] God also says: 'He who hopes in me I will save, and I will protect him, so that he knows me. He who cries out to me will not come to harm. I will be with him in his sorrow and save him from all trouble'.[464] Also God looks after those who are distressed in their hearts;[465] he drives away all their pain. He does not despise a troubled heart,[466] but apart from that nothing that we can give him can help: God desires only our hearts, and that we should keep his commandments.[467] If we do but give him our heart,

463 Psalm 71:1: 'In you, O Lord, I take refuge; let me never be put to shame'.

464 Psalm 91:14–16: 'Those who love me, I will deliver; I will protect those who know my name. When they call to me, I will answer them; I will be with them in trouble, I will rescue them and honour them. With long life I will satisfy them, and show them my salvation'.

465 Psalm 34:18: 'The Lord is near to the broken-hearted, and saves the crushed in spirit'.

466 Psalm 51:17: 'The sacrifice acceptable to God is a broken spirit; a broken and contrite heart, O God, you will not despise'.

467 Proverbs 23:26: 'My child, give me your heart, and let your eyes observe my ways'.

das on ſin geist iſt vnrein
Wenn es vom geiſt denn reyn wirt gmacht
denn hat man ſiner botten acht
vnd flyſſend vns was er vns büt
ſo darff man menſchen ſatzung nüt
Ich mein nit drumb all menſchen bott
wir haltend vil das nit büt gott
Vnd was ſim bott nit vnglych iſt
das halt nun ſtyff ein yeder Chriſt *Eſaiæ. 10.*
Wee dem der büt vngöttlich bott
[Iv[r]] vnrechts fürſchrybt der armen rott
Damit der arm wirt vndertruckt
der witwen / weyſen klag geſchmuckt
Wie wirt der ſelb vor Gott nun bſton
am letſten gricht ſo er wirt kon?
Was iſt der geyſtlich ſtand ſuſt gſin?
beſchwären mit gſatz durch all welt hin
Den lyb hand ſy beſchwärt mit gſatz
die ſeel verblendt mit menſchen gſchwatz
Denn all jr ſünd ſind wider Gott
vnd hand kein grund in gottes bott
Nun ſinn jm nach du armer Chriſt
wenn du thůſt das ſin bott nit iſt
So gfaltz jm nit wie hüpſch es glyßt
denn er mit ſim gheyß das nit wyßt
Nun denck jm nach wär dich hab gmacht *Deut. 4.*
er wil / ſin bott / nit wärd veracht
Vnd büt dir nit deß Bapſts recht
halt nun ſin bott das wil er ſchlecht
Was denn in ſinem bott nit ſtadt
das ſelb vns Chriſten nüt angadt
Er wil der menſchen ſatzung nit *Matt. 15.*
vnd wirt geert vergeben mit
Denn was er redt dem gadt er nach
haltſtu das nit / ſo wart der raach *Deute. 18.*
Was volgſtu eim der dir iſt glych?
jm blybt ſelb weder volck noch rych

which without his Spirit is impure, he makes it clean – by his Spirit. For if we take heed of his commands and seek to do what he has laid down, we need no human laws. By that I don't mean all the commands of men: we keep to a great deal that God has not commanded; and what is not at odds with his instructions, all Christians should adhere to rigidly. But woe to him who issues godless commands and prescribes unjust behaviour to the impoverished horde, so that the poor man is oppressed and the lament of the widow and the orphan ignored. How will such a person stand before God at the Last Judgement?[468] What have the clerics done apart from burdening the whole world with laws? They have encumbered our bodies with laws and blinded our souls with human chatter. For all their sins are against God and have no basis in God's commands. Now think of him, you poor Christian man: if you do something other than follow God's commandments, this doesn't please him, however prettily it glistens, because he has not ordained it.[469] Think of him who made you: he does not wish his instructions to be despised. Yet he does not command you to keep the Pope's laws. He simply wants you to keep *his* commandments – and anything that is not in these commandments is of no concern to us Christians. He doesn't want human laws,[470] and it is in vain that you seek to please him by obeying these. Because he keeps to what he says; and if you go against this, vengeance will come.[471] Why should you obey someone who is just like you? Such a person has no lasting kingdom or subjects,

468 Isaiah 10:1–3: 'Ah, you who make iniquitous decrees, who write oppressive statutes, to turn aside the needy from justice and to rob the poor of my people of their right, that widows might be your spoil, and that you make orphans your prey! What will you do on the day of punishment, in the calamity that will come from far away?'.

469 Deuteronomy 4:2: 'You must neither add anything to what I command you nor take anything away from it, but keep the commandments of the Lord your God with which I am charging you'.

470 Matthew 15:3, 6: 'And he answered them, "And why do you break the commandment of God for the sake of your tradition? [...] So, for the sake of your tradition you make void the word of God"'.

471 Deuteronomy 18:19: 'Anyone who does not heed the words that the prophet shall speak in my name, I myself will hold accountable'.

Vnd wartet ſelb des todes zil
er můß noch gon da er nit wil
Für dich mag er vor gott nit bſton
[Iv^{v}] denn wirſtu den ſun gotz nit han
Der dir iſt ggeben zů eim pfand
on jnn vor Gott wirſtu zů ſchand
Wenn du nun kumpſt für gotz angſicht
ſin zorn dir denn kein bapſt nit bricht
Haſt dienet Gott dir wirt der lon
ja wenn du haſt (das er heißt) thon
Gůt duncken wirt fürwar nit gelten
was gott nit heyßt / das gfalt jm ſelten *2. Reg. 6.*
Oſa vor zyten was ein man
der růrt die Arch Gots an
Als ſy gegen jm wolt gfallen ſin
die hend er vßſtrackt gegen jr hin
Als die rinder ſtruchtend vor dem wagen
ward er mit gähem tod gſchlagen
Gůt duncken hatt jn ouch verfürt
er ſolt ſy nit haben angrürt *Iosue. 3.*
Gott gibt vns damit zů verſton
was er verbüt das ſöllend wir lon
Vnd thůn allein des er vns büt
vnſer krafft gegen jm gilt gar nüt
Küng Saul thet ouch das Gott nit hieß *1. Reg. 15.*
darumb Gott jnn von ſym rych ſtieß
Er opffret wider gottes bott
das thůt ouch yetz des Bapſts Rott
Die opffrend Gott / das gfalt jm nit
mit Mäſſzhan / vnnd der heilgen fürbitt
Von himmel heilgen ich yetz ſag
die hörend nit der menſchen klag
Sy ſind nun in der ſäligkeyt
[Ivi^{r}] Gott hat den wäg jnen vor bereyt
Inen ligt nit an das vns hie briſt
Gott ſelb ein houpt der Chriſten iſt
Vß jm in vns flüßt all gſundtheyt

and he himself will die; then he will have to go where he doesn't want to go.[472] He can't stand before God on your behalf, because then you wouldn't have the Son of God, who has been given you as a pledge. Without him, you will be put to shame before God when you come before his face. Then no Pope will be able to appease his anger for you. If you have served God, then you will get your reward – if you have indeed *done* what he has ordered (good intentions won't be valid). What God does not command seldom pleases him. In earlier times Uzzah was a man who touched the Ark of the Covenant.[473] When it was about to fall against him, he stretched out his hand towards it, and as the oxen pulling its cart were stumbling, he was immediately struck down dead. His good intentions had led him astray: he shouldn't have touched the Ark.[474] By this God gives us to understand that we should leave aside what he has forbidden us to do, and only do what he has commanded us. Our strength against his is worth nothing at all. King Saul also did what God hadn't commanded, and for that reason God drove him out of his kingdom.[475] He made sacrifices contrary to God's command. The Pope's lot do that now: they sacrifice God (and he doesn't like it) with their Masses and prayers to the saints. I'm speaking now of the saints in heaven. They don't hear the laments of the people, because they are now in paradise. God has prepared the way for them. What we lack here doesn't matter to them: God himself is the head of all Christians, and all health of body and soul flows into us from him,

472 An ironic echo of Christ's words to Peter in John 21:18.

473 2 Samuel 6:6: 'When they came to the threshing-floor of Nacon, Uzzah reached out his hand to the ark of God and took hold of it, for the oxen shook it. The anger of the Lord was kindled against Uzzah; and God struck him there because he reached his hand out to the ark; and he died there beside the ark of God'.

474 Joshua 3:4: 'Yet there shall be a space between you and it, a distance of about two thousand cubits; do not come any nearer to it'.

475 The account of Saul's disobedience and his rejection by God occupies all of 1 Samuel 15.

in lyb vnd ſeel / hat er ſelb gſeyt
Was haſtu denn das er nit gitt?
die Mäſſz büt er dir ouch nit
Die hat allein der gyt erdacht
vnd allen nutz den bſchornen bracht
All rendt vnd güldt ſind daruf gſtifft
das ſtrebt alles wider göttliche gſchrifft
All wellt die můß ee zſchyter gon
ee wůcher werde nachlon
Dem armen wirt gar lützel gſchenckt
noch meng huß wirt an himmel ghenckt
Vnd werdend vil vatterloſer kind
ee man vßrüt das tüfliſch gſind
Das iſt der bſchoren vnnütz hufen
thůnd tag vnd nacht nüt denn Suffen
Das fägfhür hand ſy all anzündt
on gotzwort / dauon man nüt findt
Die bycht hat ouch jr Penſion
kein pur darff lär zum pfaffen kon
Als bald man gelt hat zůhin bracht
fragt der pfaff / Pur was haſt dacht
Oder all din läbtag thon?
gib gelt / ich mag dirs nachlon
Ich ſitz hie ſelb an Gottes ſtatt
das im Gott nit empfolhen hat
Kein menſch mag gotz ſtatthalter werden
[Ivi[v]] Gott ghört zů aller gwalt vff erden *Math. 28.*
Ein rechte bycht hat er vns glert
wie man im Vatter vnſer hört
Vatter vergib vns vnſere ſchuld *Macha. 6.*
ſo wir denn hand allein ſin huld
Vnd er vns vnſer ſchuld vergitt
täglich der pfaff das ouch bitt
Der iſt wie ich ouch ſünden vol
drumb gfalt gott teglich bycht wol
Also hand wir mit Gott ein pundt
der ſünder kumm zů welcher ſtund *Ierem. 18.*

as he himself has said. What, then, do you have that he doesn't give you? He doesn't command you to say any Masses: avarice invented those, and gave all the benefit from them to the tonsured ones. All the monies and payments that are given for them go all against the divine Scriptures. The whole world will be destroyed before usury comes to an end. Very little will be given to the poor, many a house will be blown to the skies, and many children will be made fatherless before that devilish rabble, the useless tonsured throng, are wiped out. Every day they do nothing but booze. And they've all lit purgatory's fire without any help from God's Word – where you can't find anything about it. Penance is also an earner for them. No farmer can approach a priest empty-handed, and as soon as you've brought him your money the priest asks: 'You farmer, what have you been thinking or doing all your life? Pay me and I'll let you off. I'm sitting here as God's representative'. God has not asked him to be so – no man can represent God, and all power on earth is God's.[476] He has taught us true confession in the Lord's Prayer, where we say 'Father, forgive us our trespasses'.[477] The priest prays that every day as well, because he too is full of sin, just as I am. God wants us to confess daily, because that creates a bond between him and us. The sinner should come at whatever hour,[478]

476 Matthew 28:18: 'And Jesus came and said to them, "All authority in heaven and on earth has been given to me"'.

477 The version of the Lord's Prayer in *Matthew* 6:9–13 is of course meant.

478 If he is citing the right book, then Eckstein can only have in mind Jeremiah 3:12–13: '"Return, faithless Israel," says the Lord; "I will not look on you in anger, for I am merciful", says the Lord. "I will not be angry for ever. Only acknowledge your guilt, that you have rebelled against the Lord your God"'.

Wenn jn ſin that von hertzen rüwt
Gott wil jr dencken nimmer nüt
Diewyl denn Gott der ſünd nit denckt
vnd vns ſin ſun für eigen ſchenckt
Der vnſer ſünd ſelb tragen hat
was hilffts das man zun pfaffen gadt?
Deren huß vnd hof iſt roubes vol
mit hůren bſetzt / weyßt mencklich wol
Ouch londs nüt nach man geb denn gelt
das iſt nun kund in aller welt
des glychen ouch das Sacrament
in muren ſtadt / als ſygs verpfennt
Es hat ſin kouff wie wyn vnd brot
das iſt verbotten als von gott
Ach frummer Chriſt ker dich nit dran
gott geb was dir ſag yederman
So ficht allein nach gottes bott
hüt dich vor der gſchmirbten rott
Vnd ker dich nit an menſchen leer
[Ivii^{r}] darinn nit gſůcht wirt Gottes Eer
Vil leerer yetz vff erden ſind
die hand eins ſchůchs dick noch den grind
Vnd leerend vaſt vff iren nutz
vnder der kapp ſtecket der butz
An irer leer kennt man ſy wol
Ir hertz ſteckt münchſcher tücken vol
Nüt gůtz ye von den münchen kam
ob mans ſchon wol hat gfangen an
Da ligt nit an / man můß nun bharren *Matth. 10.*
die Kutt verlaßt nit gar den narren
Drumb hat die kapp ein gugel ſpitz
wär ſy an treyt / der manglet witz
Es zücht kein münch die kutten ab
das er fürhin nit etwas hab
Das ſich nit ziech vff glychßnery

4102 roubens *CF*

when he is sorry from his heart for what he has done; God will never remember these sins. For God does not remember sin but, instead, has sent us his own Son, who himself has borne our sin. What's the point of going to a priest? Their houses and courts are full of robbing, and you know well that many are liberally provided with whores. And they don't let you off giving them money. This is now known through all the world. Similarly also the sacrament is placed within walls, as if it were being pawned. It's sold, like bread and wine. All this is forbidden by God. O, devout Christian, do not turn towards all this, whatever anyone may say to you. Struggle only to obey God's command, beware this greasy mob, and don't turn towards any human teaching which doesn't seek to honour God. Nowadays there are many teachers in the world who have neither sense nor substance, and who teach very much for their own gain. They are fools under their caps. You can tell them by their teaching: their hearts are full of monkish cunning. Nothing good ever came from monks. It doesn't matter if you've started well; you have to persevere. A fool's habit never entirely leaves him: that's why his cap has a tip. Anyone who wears it doesn't have all his wits. No monk ever takes off his habit – this would mean he wouldn't have anything that enabled him to carry on his devious ways.

man ſichts an irem wandel fry
Was man in ſagt / ſo gfalt inen baß
das ſitt in irem kloſter was
Glych wie ein wyb / dem ſtirbt der man /
ein andren nimpt von ſtunden an
Was jr der ander man gůts thůt
hat ſy nit wie vom erſten für gůt
Was ſchon der erſt nit wärdt eins manns
ſo ſpricht ſy / Das thett nit min Hans
Vnd wirt Hans erſt gůt wenn er ſtirbt
alſo vnkrut ouch nit verdirbt
Drumb acht ſin nit du frummer Chriſt
das man alſo zwyträchtig iſt
Es ſtadt alſo in Luca gſchriben
[Ivii[v]] zwey werdend wider drü kyben *Luc. 12.*
Sprichſt du / Man ſolt aber eins ſin *Matth. 10.*
ſag ich das Gots wort hats nit in
Es macht wol einigkeit im geyſt
friden im hertzen allermeyſt *Roma. 5.*
Dann geyſt vnd fleiſch ouch nit eins ſind *Gallat. 5.*
als ich zů den Galatern find
Sprichſt / Es ergeret aber mich
wenn ich die Gleerten kyben ſich
Sich / Luther vnd der Karrenſtatt
vff denen ich nun vil hatt
Die kybend wie zwo Badermätzen
nun könnends beyd gnůg ſchwätzen
Es hippet einer den anderen vß
wie hůren in eim frouwen huß
Der Luther nempt den Carrenſtatt
ein ſuw die im bantzer gadt
Sagt jm ouch Frouw Hulden daby
nun lůg ob das Chriſtiſch ſy
Das ergret vaſt den gmeinen man

4159 wie frouwen in eim hůren huß *CF*

You can easily see that in the way they live. Whatever you say to them, they always prefer what used to go on in their monasteries. It's just like a woman whose husband dies and who immediately takes another. She doesn't appreciate the good that the second husband does for her as much as she appreciates her first one. She says: 'My Hans didn't do that'. But Hans has only been any good since he's been dead; and, like weeds, he doesn't wither. So see to it, pious Christian, that you don't cause division. It says in Luke: 'Three will fight against two'.[479] If you say 'but we should be one', I tell you that God's Word doesn't have that in it.[480] It can certainly create unity in the spirit and peace in your heart – but that's the most it can do.[481] For spirit and flesh are not as one, as I read in the letter to the Galatians.[482] If you say: 'But it bothers me to see the scholars quarrelling with one another. Look at Luther and Karlstadt – I don't think much of them.[483] They're bickering like a pair of washerwomen. They can't get enough of slagging each other off like a couple of whores in a brothel: Luther calls Karlstadt a sow in armour, and also calls him Lady Hulde.[484] Just think about whether that's Christian. This really annoys the common man,

479 Luke 12:52: 'From now on, five in one household will be divided, three against two and two against three'.

480 Cf. Matthew 10:34: 'Do not think that I have come to bring peace to the earth: I have not come to bring peace, but a sword'.

481 Romans 5:1 (see n. 192 above).

482 Galatians 5:17: 'For what the flesh desires is opposed to the Spirit, and what the Spirit desires is opposed to the flesh'.

483 'Eckstein's treatment of Luther differs from the pattern established in other so-called "Reformation dialogues", where solidarity or qualified sympathy for the *Causa Lutheri* are the norm [...], arguably reserving greater vehemence for Luther than for Faber and Murner' (Love, 'Dialogue', p. 153).

484 This passage is largely based on Luther's *Wider die himmlischen Propheten, von den Bildern und Sakrament* (1525). Here he breaks, apparently definitively, with Karlstadt, now described as his 'worst enemy' ('unser ärgster Feind', *WA* XVIII, 62). The latter is called a pig who eats pearls ('eine Sau, die nu die Perlen frisst', p. 80), and is associated with the supernatural matriarch Holda via their perceived common use of 'natural reason' ('natürliche Vernunft', p. 94) and adherence to the devil.

der ſpricht: Wo iſt man yetz dran?
Sag ich du armer biderman
was gadt vns der Luther an
Wir Chriſten ghörend Chriſto zů
jn dem wir allein habend růw
Der Luther vnd der Schwindelgrind
yetz widerumb eins worden ſind
Die Bantzer ſuw iſt wider hein
Frouw Hulden ich yetz mein
ſy iſt lang gſyn von wyb vnd kinden
[lviii^{r}] hat nit mögen ſtallung finden
Der Luther metzget ſim hußgſind
all jar ein ſuw vnd ein rind
Der ſchwyntod iſt in Saxen gſin
der Luther hatt diß jars kein ſchwyn
Es iſt jm ſins in Eichlen gſtorben
hat nach der Bantzer ſuw gworben
Damit er nit on ſchwyn můß ſin
yetz wirt ſin ſpruch erfüllt ſyn
Ir torheit wirt allen menſchen kund *2. Tim. 3.*
der ſpruch iſt gredt vſs Paulus mund
Den ſchrybt der Luther vff ſin bůch
vff ſym Haderbůch man jnn ſůch
Hang du an Gott du frummer Chriſt
der fält dir nit / biß allweg grüſt
Das du haltiſt ſine bott
keer dich nit an Münchiſche rott
Gott gibt vns gſatz vnd botten gnůg
daruf ein yeder Chriſt wol lůg
Denn was nit ſtadt in Gottes leer
dauon din gemüt abkeer
gott vns allen ſin gnad meer
AMEN

Utz Eckſteyn.

For the 69 lines which conclude the text in *CDF* see the appendix, pp. 482–4.

and he says: "What are they up to now?"'. I say to you, poor good man: What's Luther got to do with us? We Christians belong to Christ, and it's in him that we find our peace. Luther and old Swindle-Scab have now come to an agreement again, and the Sow has gone back home in her armour[485] – Lady Hulde, I mean: she's been away a long time from the wife and kids and hasn't been able to find a stall. Every year Luther butchers a pig and a cow for his household; but this year the piggy plague has hit Saxony badly. Luther hasn't had any pigs this year, since his died up in Eisleben. So he's been trying to get the Pig-in-Armour, so as not to be entirely swineless.[486] The saying 'Their folly is known to all men' has now been fulfilled. Those words come from Paul's mouth.[487] Luther wrote them in one of his books; we saw them in his Book of Quarrels. Depend on God, good Christian, he will not let you down. Always be ready to keep his commands, and don't turn towards the monkish mob. God gives us enough laws and commands, and all Christians should take heed of them. Because you should turn your mind away from whatever isn't written in God's teachings. May God increase his grace towards all of us.
AMEN.

Utz Ecksteyn

485 Following his expulsion from Saxony in 1524, Karlstadt had repaired to Rothenburg ob der Tauber; but he returned in the early October of 1525. The various references to his armour hint at his perceived support for the violence of the Peasants' War.

486 Luther's half-hearted, ham-fisted (and initially unsuccessful) attempts to encourage Karlstadt to return to Saxony took many forms in the first half of 1525. See Barge, vol. 2, pp. 312–18.

487 The allusion is doubtless to the hypocritical opponents of the Gospel who are mentioned in 2 Timothy 3:8–9: 'As Jannes and Jambres opposed Moses, so these people, of corrupt mind and counterfeit faith, also oppose the truth. But they will not make much progress, because, as in the case of those two men, their folly will become plain to everyone'. For all that the last phrase is emphasized in the German *Concilium* by the use of large print, however, we can find no instance of Luther himself discussing the verse in any detail.

Edition and translation of the *Rychsztag*

[Ai^r] **Rychſztag. Der Edlen vnd Pauren (bricht vnd klag / **zFridberg ghandlet auff dem Rychßtag.

	{Edlen	{Iuncker Ludeman Pfefferſak
Bottschafft der	{Pauren	{Hans Aygennutz
	{Gaiſtlichen.	{Doctor Murnar.

Handlung.
Es zimpt aim yeden Christenman
Das er ain Oberkayt ſöll han
Nach ordnung Gwallts ſol er Zinſen
Weyn / Korn / Erbs / vnd Linſen
Iarzeyt gſetzt von freyer hand
Zů geben kain Christ widerſtand.

Utz Eckstein.

[Ai^v] **Der Adel ab Hohenzorn.**

	{ Ludeman Pfäfferſack.
Iuncker	{ Hans Butz den winckel.
	{ Rüdi Schütt den Bütel.
	{ Claus durch den Buſch.

The Diet

The Diet of noblemen and farmers: a report and record of the events of the Diet at Fridberg.[1] The representative of the nobility is Juncker Ludeman Pfeffersack, of the farmers Hans Eygennutz, and of the clergy Dr Murner.

The action[2]
It is right that every Christian man should have someone in authority over him, and that, in the interests of order, he should freely pay that authority every year wine, corn, peas, and lentils. No Christian should resist this.

Utz Eckstein

The nobility from Hohenzorn:[3]
{ Ludeman Pfeffersack[4]
Juncker { Hans Butz den Winckel[5]
{ Rüdi Schütt den Bütel[6]
{ Claus durch den Busch.[7]

1 There is a ruined castle known as the Friedberg in the village of Meilen on Lake Zurich; but this is likely (also) to be a descriptive name, meaning 'peace mountain (or town)'.

2 One of the early hints (see also R 26/315, 98/319) that this dialogue might be regarded (also) as a play. Such hints cease so soon, however, that one assumes Eckstein is tantalizing his audience's expectations, rather than making a significant statement about his work's genre.

3 Literally 'high anger': a play on the name 'Hohenzollern', a noble and later imperial family based in Baden-Württemberg.

4 A 'luderman' is a scoundrel, or one given to vice. 'Pfäffersack', 'sack of pepper(s)', could imply the vices of wrath, lechery, or both.

5 'Butzen' here probably means 'to haunt' (see *SI* IV, 2009). A 'winckel' is literally the corner of a field, though with overtones of rest, seclusion, and sanctuary (see *SI* XVI, 675–83).

6 The surname means 'shake (or empty) the purse'.

7 'Claus [pulled] through the bush'. The last three named aristocrats do not take part in the subsequent discussion, but another, much more positively named one

Purſchafft von Kybberg.

Hans Eygennutz.
Frantz Lätzkopff.
Kilian Haderman.
Veltin Kybig.
Vyt Hack den Tüfel.
Cleywe Hässig.
Fridrych Hußman
Rüde Brasser.
Gilg Follbuch.
Küni Schnaphan.

Doctor Murnar iſt ouch hie
Kein ſpil zergieng on ein münch nie
Er klagt der Geyſtlichen anſprach /
Die volgt der puren bricht nach.

[Aii^{r}] **Uorred.**

Nun hörend zů vnn ſchwygend ſtill /
welcher ye vernemmen wil
Warumb es yetz als übel ſtand
wider vnd für durch alle land
All vnrůw die man yetzund ſicht
vſs keiner andren vrſach gſchicht
Denn das vns Gott zů diſem zyt
ſyn wort vßſäyet in all welt wyt
Vſs welchem ſich ein yeder flyßt
das er daruß / was jm gfallt / lißt
Vnd brucht man gotswort zů eim deckel

The peasantry from Kybberg:[8]

Pur Eygennutz	Cleywi Hässig[9]
Frantz Lätzkopff[10]	Fridrych Hußman[11]
Kilian Haderman[12]	Rüde Brasser[13]
Velti Kybig[14]	Gilg Vollbuch[15]
Vyt Hack den Tüfel[16]	Küni Schnaphan[17]

Dr Murner is here too: you can't have a play[18] without a monk. He is arguing the clerics' suit, which follows after the farmers' account.

Prologue

Now be silent and listen, anyone who wants to hear why things are now in such a bad way, throughout all the lands. All the tumult we now see has no other cause than that God is at this time spreading his Word into all the wide world. But everyone is making sure to take what he wants from the Word, and is using it as a cover

---

does ('Bernhart Erenuest', i.e. 'steadfast in honour'). Eckstein therefore appears to be misleading his audience deliberately as to the presentation of the aristocratic position they should expect.

8 This might refer to Kyburg-Buchegg, near Solothurn. 'Kyb', originally 'Chyd', means a cleft or ditch, but also a division or quarrel. One suspects the toponym was chosen by Eckstein mainly for its figurative meaning.

9 'Hässig' is close in meaning to NHG 'gehässig', 'spiteful, malicious'; but it also has overtones of NHG 'hässlich', 'ugly'.

10 A 'Lätzkopff' is a fool.

11 'Hußman' normally means no more than a householder. The absence of a clearly negative name is reflected also in this character's speeches, which reveal him to hold moderate views that are probably quite close to Eckstein's own.

12 'Hadern' is to quarrel.

13 A 'Brasser', or 'Prasser' is an extravagantly gluttonous person.

14 'Valentine Quarrelsome'.

15 The surname means 'full belly'.

16 'Vyt Chop-the-devil'.

17 A 'Schnapphahn' is a highwayman or robber, though the *SI* (II, 1309) states that the term can also mean a gun.

18 Or 'a game'. The ambiguity is for certain deliberate.

allein darzů / wär voll min ſeckel
Gott geb denn was ein andrer hett
alſo vſs eim ernſt macht man ein gſpött
Ob man ſchon leert gotswort im geyſt
ſo ſůcht man dennocht allermeyſt
Daß dem lyb allein kumm wol
vnd gibt man nit gern Sthür vnd Zol
Vnd wär man gern wie Adam fry
Alſo Eygennutz ſteckt allwäg darby
Wir wärind gern wie Adam was
lufftfry / ee er mit Eue as
Den öpfel in dem Paradyß
er aß den tod an diſer ſpyß
Ward dardurch vſs der fryheyt triben
on den bitz wär er drinn bliben
Do er kam vſs dem Paradyß
[Aiiv] mocht er nit in glycher wyß
Thůn vnd lon wie vor har
ſchůff das die fryheyt vßwar
Hett er ghalten das Gott hieß
ee er jnn vß der fryheit ſtieß
So wär er bliben fry ob allen
darzů thon das jm hett gfallen
So wir menſchen yetz nun thettind
gots gheyß / einander lieb hettind
Wurdind wir fryer denn Adam was
allein Adam in wolluſt ſaß
Des lybs / im jrdiſchen Paradyß
wir wurdind in einer andren wyß
Im rych Gottes mit Gott ewig leben
vnd weder Sthür noch Zinß geben
So wir aber nit anders wellend
vns alſo wider Gott ſtellend
So ſetzt vns Gott in ſölich gfaar
das wir verbochend hut vnd haar
Wie es yetzund leyder gſchicht
der Pur ſich wider ſin herren richt

for the sole purpose that it might give him what belongs to another (would that my own purse were full!). In this way, people turn something serious into a mockery. Although they teach God's Word in the spirit, they nevertheless try to make absolutely sure that the body alone benefits. And if someone doesn't like paying his taxes and customs dues, and wants to be as free from them as Adam was, then self-interest[19] is always louring nearby. We'd like to be as Adam was, as free as the air – before he ate the apple with Eve in paradise. With that meal he also tasted death, and so was deprived of his freedom. If it were not for that bite, he would have stayed there. Yet after he left paradise, he couldn't any longer do what he wanted, as he had before. He had ensured that his freedom was lost. If only he had done as God had commanded, before he deprived him of his freedom, Adam would have remained totally free to do exactly as he pleased. In the same way, if we people of today would only do as God commands and love one another, then we would be freer than Adam was. Adam pursued fleshly lusts in his earthly paradise, but we would live in a different way, in God's kingdom with God for ever, and would pay neither taxes nor interest. But since we don't want things to be different from the way they are, and set ourselves against God, he is placing us in such danger that we're losing everything.[20] This is already happening. The farmer sets himself against his lord,

19 The various references to Adam in this part of the *Rychsztag* forge a link between it and Eckstein's earlier *Dialogus mit Adam* which does not obtain in the case of the *Concilium.*

20 Literally, 'hair and skin'. The same idiom is translated 'all of him' (the abbot) on p. 347 below.

Des glychen dherren wider Puren
denn můß von not ſin klag vnd truren
Es wachßt allein all krieg vnd zanck
wo die liebe ligt tod kranck
Wie ſy als ich bſorg yetzund lyt
ſy hat ein kranckheyt heyßt der gyt
Das ſelb ein ſöliche kranckheyt iſt
hett einer die gantz welt / dennocht briſt
Ein gytig hertz erfüllt man nit
[Aiii^{r}] biß das man erdtrich druf ſchütt
Wie dem groſſen Alexander
wir ſind all gytig miteinander
Das wirt an gmeiner Purſchafft kund
wie man wirt hören vff die ſtund
Eygennutz iſt vß dem Wäntal kon
wie er dryn kam / kumpt er daruon
Sin meinung was gar nüt mee zinſen
nit zehenden weder Erbs noch Linſen
Darzů hat er nit mögen glangen
das verkündt er ſinen anhangen
hie mit das ſpil wirt angfangen.

Als Pur Eygennutz von Kybberg was heym kummen ab dem Concili im Wäntal ghalten / ließ er im verſamlen den Weibel Lätzkopff ein Gmeynd / deren zů verkünden den vßgang vnd bſcheyd verhandleter ſachen / ſprechende / wie nachfolget.

Pur Eygennutz.
Lieben frummen biderben lüt
es iſt der dritt tag hütt
Das ich in dem Wäntal was
der Abſcheyd iſt eben das
Vnd ſag üch allen kurtz vmm
das jch lär wider har kumm
All Puren ſind da obglegen

78 wider die Bawren *F*   85 dennocht] jhm doch *F*

and the lord against the farmer. And so mourning and lamenting are inevitable. War and unrest are the only things that grow when love lies dying – as I fear is the case now. Love has a sickness called greed. Its symptoms are such that, even if someone had the whole world, this wouldn't seem enough. A greedy heart is never filled until you shovel earth over it – as happened to Alexander the Great.[21] We are greedy, one and all. We can see this with the common farmers, as we'll soon hear: Eygennutz has come back from the Wäntal; just as he went down there, so now he's back. His view was that we shouldn't have to make any more interest payments, or tithe any more peas or lentils. He failed to win the argument, so now he must explain this to his fellow farmers. And with that the play begins.

When Pur Eygennutz of Kybberg came home from the Council held in the Wäntal, he asked Weybel Lätzkopff to gather together an assembly, before which he might explain the conclusions and decisions reached at the Council concerning the subjects discussed there.[22] He spoke as follows:

Pur Eygennutz

Good, faithful, and honourable people, today is the third day since I left the Wäntal.[23] The outcome was, as I'll tell you all briefly, that I've come home empty-handed. All the farmers who spoke were successful

21 There has been much speculation over the centuries that one of the causes of Alexander's sudden and premature death in 323 BC was excessive alcohol consumption.

22 For a discussion of this section of the text and the influence on it of contemporary Swiss communal consultations see the introduction, pp. 35–6.

23 Eygennutz's return to the village and subsequent mission to Fridberg represents more action than is contained in the whole of the *Concilium*. The *Rychsztag* is in various respects a less static text.

on ich allein hab nit mögen
[Aiii[v]] Sigen / in dem Wäntal
ich hatt nun groſſen vnfal
Ich erbarmbt da nye kein Puren
ſy ſagtend all / wir wärind luren
Die ſach hatt ich gnůg darthon
es halff alles nüt / ich mocht nit bſton
Stroubutz kam allweg mit der Bibel
ſprach / wir verſtündind gſchrifft übel
Als bald ich ein ſpruch dar thett
darzů kum halb hatt vßgeredt
Sprach er zů mir: Bſich was vorſtadt
vnd was dem ſententz nach gadt
Daruf hatt ich denn nit gſtudiert
er ſprach: Ir Puren ſind verfürt
Vns puren gfiel allein die gſchrifft
die nun vnſeren nutz antrifft
Denn wärind wir recht biderblüt
wir ſöltind vns nun widren nüt
Zalen das wir von recht ſöttind
jnn wundret was wir damit wettind
Vnderſton / das kein bſtand möcht han
es zymme wol eim Chriſten man
Das er geb was man jm heyſch
ein Chriſt lebe Gott vnd nit dem fleyſch
So man ein ſchon gar vmbkeer
es zymme nit das er ſich weer
Ein Chriſt ſöll keim durchs huß louffen
er ſöll ſich ee laſſen rouffen
Sagt ouch: es ſye Gotts will
das man fridſam leb / vnd ſtill
[Aiv[r]] Vnd das man ſůch das himmliſch ſy
denn ſo werdind wir recht fry
So wir vns zů Gott kerind
Schloſſz vnd Klöſter nit zerſtörind

114 Da war kein erbarmung der Bawren *F*

apart from me. I wasn't able to win in the Wäntal: I had very bad luck. I failed to win any sympathy for us farmers: they all said we were a bunch of oafs. Try as I might to represent our cause, it was no good. I couldn't win. Stroubutz kept coming back at me with the Bible, saying that we misunderstood the Scriptures. As soon as I quoted a verse, and had hardly finished speaking, he would say: 'Look at what comes just before and after that verse'.[24] I hadn't studied those parts. He said: 'You farmers have been led astray'. According to him, we farmers only like those Scriptures that serve our interests. For if we were really people of honour, he said, we wouldn't rebel, but rather pay what we rightly owe. He wondered what of any lasting value we wanted to achieve by it. It's right, he thinks, that a Christian should give what he is told to: a Christian lives for God, not for the flesh. And even if someone turns you on your head, it's not right to defend yourself. A Christian shouldn't ransack anyone's house, but rather should let himself be beaten. Stroubutz also said that it's God's will that we should live peaceably and quietly, and should seek after heavenly things. For we shall be truly free if we turn to God, rather than destroying castles and monasteries.

24 In the *Concilium*, Stroubutz has actually said very little about biblical interpretation; but this whole speech by Eygennutz, which is a reasonable summary of his discourse with Stroubutz in C 3269–954/255–97, indicates that he has already begun to learn his lesson.

Klöſter gangind ſelb wol ab
vnd ſye not das man Oberkeyt hab
Sy ſitz in Schlöſſern oder Statt
denn Gott ſy ſelb geordnet hatt
Vnd der einr Oberkeyt widerſträb
der ſelb nit nach Gotz ordnung leb
Batt vns vaſt / wir ſöltind vns lyden
vnd bylyb vfrůr myden
Darüber han ich appelliert
den Abſcheyd mit mir har gfürt
Daruf mögend jr üch bſinnen
mir iſt es wär noch wol zgwünnen
So wir kartind in ein Statt
die nit Parthyig lüt hatt
Ich dörfft vff min trüw wetten
wir fundind noch in Rychſtetten
Mengen frummen biderman
der ſich ouch näm vnſer not an
Denn vnſer kriegen ſol gar nüt
jr ſehend wol die Edellüt
Mögend vns wol vßwarten
vnd ſitzend růwig / ſpilen vnd karten
Lönd vns ſtreyffen vmb vnd vmm
ſo lang biß vnſer zyt kumm
Höuwen louffend wir denn hein
wo jnen wirt denn einer allein
[Aiv^{v}*]* So lönds nit nach er můß ſterben
vnd on alle gnad verdärben
Vnd ſo wir ſchon hand gſchnitten yn
ſo mögend wir nit růwig ſin
Der Adel kumpt denn mit dem brand
vnd verbrennt vns alle ſand
Also verdirbt denn wyb vnd kind
darzů nimpt man vns roſſz vnd rind
Zů letſt werdend wir erſchlagen

158 kartind] gleich giengen *F* 163 ouch] *om. F*

Monasteries are dissolving by themselves. And we still need some kind of authority over us, whether it's located in castles or in a city, for that is what God himself has ordained. And anyone who fights against that authority isn't living according to God's divine order. He has told us to be patient and, at all costs, to avoid rebellion. About all these things I made my appeal, and have come back to let you know the resolution of the matter, so that you can all consider it. I think we can still win this argument, if we take it to a place where people aren't biased against us. Upon my word, I daresay we might still find somewhere in the imperial free cities some godly and honourable men who would take our suffering to heart. For our wars are useless; you can see that the nobility are going to bide their time. They're sitting idly by, gambling and playing cards, letting us fight here and there, until our time has come. Then they'll beat us and we'll run home. And when they find one of us alone, they'll make sure that he dies, and that without mercy. And now that we've taken a first stab at them, we can't be at ease. The lords are coming with fire to burn us all. So women and children will die, and our horses and cattle will be taken. Finally we ourselves will be slain,

als geſchehen iſt in kurtzen tagen
Vor ſölichem man wol mag ſin
ſo wir von ſtundan kartind hin
Da wir vnſer not erklagtind
wär weyßt was wir erjagtind
Ich weyß ein ſtatt vff diſe ſtund
die iſt mir nun vaſt wol kund
Vnd heyßt Fridberg mit dem namen
da kumpt yetz der Adel zůſamen
Die ſelb ſtatt ligt im Richtal
wolan jr hand nun die wal?
Gfalt es üch das ich dar kumm
Weybel Lätzkopff frag drumm

Frantz Lätzkopff.
Was radſtu Kilian haderman
denn die ſach trifft dich ouch an
Meinſt ſol man den Eygennutz ſchicken
oder das mans laß erlicken?
Din meynung gib vns zů verſton
ſol er blyben oder gon?

[Av[r]] **Kilian Haderman.**
Ich bin yetz wol als vollen kyb
ee ich wölt das er hie blib
Ich wölt ee ſelb gon in mym koſten
lönd by lyb dſach nit erroſten
So wir yetz nit thůnd darzů
wir kummend nymmer me zů rů
Drumb lönd vns nit han růw noch raſt
denn zinſen bſchwärt vns mechtig vaſt
So ich noch ein jar zinſen ſött
ich wurd von huß vnd hof wett
Nach dem vnd mich dſach anſicht
bottſchafft man bald hinweg richt
Diewyl er doch hat Appelliert
ſin trüw man gwüß darinn probiert

as has been happening in recent days. We thought we were safe from this when we first went there. But who knows what we have brought upon ourselves by complaining about our plight? I now know a place – very well indeed – called Fridberg; the lords are gathering there now. This town is in the Richtal.[25] So now it's up to you: do you want me to represent you there? Ask them, Weybel Lätzkopff!

Franz Lätzkopff
What do you advise, Kilian Haderman? After all, this matter affects you too. Do you think we should send Eygennutz there, or should we let the matter rest? Give us your opinion: should he stay or should he go?

Kilian Haderman
I'm so angry that, rather than see him stay here, I'd go there myself, at my own expense, so that the matter shouldn't just stand and rust. If we don't do something about it now, we'll never get any peace. So let's not sit and wait, for our interest payments are weighing heavily on us. If I had to pay interest for another year, I'd lose my house and farm. As far as I'm concerned, I think we should send a representative right away. And since he's already made one appeal on our behalf, his loyalty has been proven.

25 This could conceivably refer to the 'Zürichtal' in the Canton of that name, or to Richenthal near Lucerne; but one suspects that Eckstein has invented the toponym, which means 'valley of judgement'.

Denn es dunckt mich nimmer recht
by mym eyd nun kurtz vnd ſchlecht
Das wir alſo bſchwärdt ſöltind ſin
ee wölt ich es ſchlüg dſtraal drin
Nun gang das der boden krach
fyr nun nit vmb kein ſach
Sölt ich lyden das yetz eynr käm
vnd mir alſo das min näm
Das ich mit übel zyt überkumm
einer zug mir lieber den Galgen vmm
Sölt ich eim laſſen mantel vnd rock
thorechter wär ich denn ein geyßbock
Es iſt eins bocks natürlich art
ſo man jm vßroufft den bart
Mag er nit baß er ſchrygt doch mä
[Av^{v}*]* gelt wo ich mich nit blä
So mich yetz einr an backen ſchlüg
ee ich jm ein haarrupff vertrüg
Das ichs litt / käm mir nit in ſinn
ich hüw ein daß dſonn durch jnn ſchinn
Chriſtus hin / Chriſta har
gelt wo ich nun ein ſtreych ſpar
Sölt ich thůn das Chriſtus hyeß
mich ſelb / wyb vnd kind verließ
Vmb all min gůt käm ich gantz
vnd zů letſt gar an bättler dantz
Ich můß ſunſt geben an ein pfrůnd
vil zinß wie jr ouch all thůnd
Vermag kum das ich gang ins bad
nützt dſeelen nüt / vnd iſt mir ſchad
Geyſtlichen ſtand Purſchafft neert
der pfaff thůt ſelb nit das er leert
Er büt vns Puren reynigkeyt
ſin källerin nun all jar treyt
Ander Eebrecher vmb gelt er ſchirt

246 ſtand die Bawrſchafft *F*

Because, upon my word, and to put it bluntly, it seems to me quite wrong that we should be burdened in this way. I'd rather that lightning came and split the earth in two than I'd suffer, for any reason, someone coming and taking away what's mine. And I'd sooner go to the gallows than suffer hard times. If I let someone have my coat and tunic, I'd be sillier than a billy goat. With a goat it's only natural: if someone tries to tear his beard out and he can't do anything about it, he'll just cry all the louder. But I can say without puffing myself up that, if anyone struck me on the cheek, even before tearing out any hair, it wouldn't occur to me to tolerate it: I'd cut him up such that the sun could shine through him. Christ is neither here nor there when it comes to striking somebody or not. And if I did as Christ commanded and forsook myself, my wife and children, I'd lose everything I own and end up doing a beggar's dance. And I also have to pay a lot of interest to the parish, as you all do: so much so that I can hardly get by. And all of this doesn't help the souls of the dead at all, whilst doing me great damage. The clergy are fed by the common farmers. And the priest doesn't practise what he preaches. He demands purity from us farmers, but goes at it with his housekeeper all the year long. He badgers other adulterers for their money,

vnd ſitzt ſelb wie ein hůrenwirt
Ich wird jm nit hold nimmer mee
er nemm denn dhůren zů der Ee
Im wirt all jar ein banckhart
mich luſte wol das ich ein fart
Spräch: Pfaff nun werck als wol als ich
der tüfel nemm din hůr vnd dich
Er iſt mir gar ein überburde
wölt gott das wir ſin on wurde
Vnd bſorg wir kummind ſin nit ab
[Avi^{r}] denn ſo man jnn läbendig vergrab
Ich opffrete jm ein Guldin dſtür
vnd wär noch gelt vmb mich ſo thür
Wir müſſend vnglückhafft lüt ſin
mit eym ſölichen herlin
Er ſtäcket böſer dücken vol
wyl er hie iſt ſo gadts nit wol
Hettind wir jnn vertriben lengſt
was ſol vns nun der Grüſchhengſt?
Vergiß ſin nit vff dem Rychßtag
laß nit / etwas von jm ſag
Das iſt min radt yetz zmal
dran zbinden vich vnd ſtal
wir ſitzend in groſſem vnfal.

Weybel Lätzkopff.
Haderman du haſt gnůg thon
yetz ſol es an Velti kybig kon
Drumb kybiger Veltin / ſöllend wir tagen
vff dem Rychßtag vnſer not klagen?
Hans Eygennutz wils dar tragen

Velti Kybig.
Wölt Gott das ich ſelb zyehen ſött
wär ich nun ein kleyn baß beredt
Fürwar ich zuge tag vnd nacht
das dſach nun wurde vßgmacht

while he himself behaves like a pimp. I won't ever respect him again, unless he decides to marry his whores.[26] He begets a bastard every year. I'd really like to say to him some time: 'Now, priest, do some work, like me. The devil take your whore and you: it's too much of a burden for me'. Would to God we could get rid of him. But I doubt that we can, short of burying him alive. I'd donate a gulden for that, even if money was very tight. We must be very unlucky people to have such a lordling. If only we'd driven him out long ago! What good is the stinky stallion to us? Don't forget about him at the Diet. Don't let it go, say something about him! That's my advice for now. Also to secure your livestock and stables: we're going through a great disaster.

Weybel Lätzkopff
You've said enough, Haderman. Now it's Velti Kybig's turn. So, grouchy Velti, should we go to the Diet and make our complaints known? Hans Eygennutz wants to take our case there.

Velti Kybig
Would to God I could go there myself! If I were even a little gifted with eloquence, truly I'd travel day and night to see our case resolved.

26 Given what we know of Eckstein's biography (see above, pp. 14–17), some of his inveighing against low sexual morals can seem hypocritical. The evidence suggests, however, that he himself did marry his concubine not long after the possibility of clerical marriage was made available to him.

Denn mir iſt wie dem Haderman
jch wag ouch hut vnd beltz dran
Sind nun dſeelen nit im Fägfhür
[Avi^{v}] vnd nimpt man nüt deſt minder dſthür
So denn nüt nützend dMäſſen
ſolt man das gelt nemmen ouch vergeſſen
Man hat die Mäſs gnůg abthon
man darff nüt über dGreber gon
Das mag recht ſin / denn ichs nit ſchilt
jch meint aber ſo keins nüt gilt
So ſolt man ouch nit nemmen preſentz
jch gſich aber wol ſy nemmentz
Nun wolt ich gern daruon verſton
ob ſy es möchtind mit Gott han
Denn wölt ich mich nit widren drab
jch meint aber ſo dMäſs kein krafft hab
So ſölt ouch abſin das Seelgrät
diewyl man nüt mee darumb thät
Drumb Eygennutz ich bitt dich drumb
on ein bſcheyd darinn nit wider kumm
Denn das zinſen iſt vns zſchwär
wölt Gott das er in der Hell wär
Der Mäſs vnd Fägfhür hat erdacht
vnd am erſten in dwelt bracht
Diewyl ich hab min hof gehabt
ſo nimpt mir ab all jar min Abt
Kernen vnd haber dryſſig Schöffel
vnd er iſt ein rechter Gynöffel
Brächt jch jm eins Vierteyls minder
er ließ nit nach der puren ſchinder
Ich für ims zhuß mit wagen vnd roſs
in ſin Kloſter erbuwen wie ein Schloſs
Darinnen ſitzt er wie ein Fürſt
[Avii^{r}] mir wirt chum ztrincken ſo mich dürſt
Denn ſo klag ich etwan min not
gradts wol mir wirt ein ſpendt brot
Wirt mir denn der Abt in kluppen

For I agree with Haderman: I'd bet my life that there aren't actually any souls in purgatory. Yet they take our money all the same. If these Masses are a waste of time, then they should also forget about taking our money. A lot of Masses have been done away with, and you mustn't trample on graves. They might have been fine, and I don't scold, but I thought that, if they served no purpose, then no money should have been taken for them. But they still do that. I'd like to know how they've squared this with God. If they had done, I wouldn't complain. But I think that, since the Mass has no power, the whole system should be done away with. But nothing's being done about it. So, Eygennutz, I ask you not to come back without some decision. For our interest payments are too heavy for us. Would to God that whoever dreamed up Mass and purgatory and first brought them into the world was in hell now! For as long as I've had my farm, my local abbot has taken 30 bushels of grain and oats every year – he's a real greedy-guts. If I brought him even a quarter less, he wouldn't let it rest, that scourge of farmers. I'd have to take it to him with my wagon and horse, to his monastery, built like a castle, where he sits like a prince. I scarcely get anything to drink there, even if I'm thirsty. Then sometimes, if I bemoan my fate and all goes well, he'll give me some bread set aside for the poor. And if he gets into a fix when talking to me,

ſo bitt ich jnn vmb ein ſuppen
So heißt er mir denn eine gen
jm louffend nach ein hund oder zween
Sunſt vil louffend in der Kuchin vmm
ob ich den Koch ſchon ankumm
Er gibt mir ſchwader mit der kellen
offt hands dhund nit eſſen wellen
Nun gadt es mir alſo fürwar
vnd ſo ich wider heim far
Bim thorhüßlin lůg ich zum fenſter yn
jch gugget nie vergeben dryn
Ich fand mit langen zöpffen brüder
ſungend heyters tags finſtre lieder
Darzů ſungend dNolhart den Baſs
den langen wäg man zů der Mette ſaß
Vnd ſchlůgend mit dem gugel dMenſur
ſprachend denn zů mir: Kumm pur
Löß den Ablaß by der Schatten
vnd ſo ſy gnůg gſungen hatten
Der ſchnatten ward allein Preſentz
die ſang in einr ſtund dry ſequentz
Durchs thorhuß fůr ich für mich hein
denn ſprach ich: Tüfel nimm hut vnd bein
Himmel ſchüß ſchwäbel / hartz / vnd bäch
das ich nit Kloſter noch münch mee ſäch
Das hellſch fhür zünd dhofrellig an
[Avii^v] drumb helff vnd radt yederman
Das man die Lotzhüſer vßrüt
es iſt ſünd was man dryn gibt
Sy ſchindend vns die groſſen ſchälck
es wär zyt das mans ouch melck
Das inen die ſpan adren krachtind
vnd ſy nit alſo mit vns machtind
Wir gebend inen vnſren ſchweyß
allein on allen gotsgheyß
Klöſter buwen hat Gott nit botten
wärind dMünch all in öl verſotten

I'll ask him for some soup. Then he'll get one of his people to give me some, with a dog or two running behind him. There are lots more of them running around the kitchen, and if I get to see the cook, he gives me some slurry with his ladle which, as often as not, the dogs have refused. That's how I'm treated. And when I'm on my way home, I'll look in again at the gatehouse window. I've never looked there in vain: I once found long-haired brothers singing dark songs there in broad daylight: moreover some lay brothers were singing bass and beating time with their cowls all the way down to where Mass was being said. And they said to me: 'Leave your money with the slag there, peasant'. And when they had done their singing, all the money went to the woman, and she sang three sequences in an hour. I headed home through the gatehouse and said: 'The devil take the lot of them! May heaven pour down sulphur and pitch, so that I never get to see an abbey or a monk again! May they all burn in hellfire'. So help and advise everyone to tear down these houses of Lot.[27] What goes on in them is sinful: they skin us alive, the great scoundrels. It's about time someone milked their teats until they hurt, rather than them doing it to us. We give them the sweat of our brows, even though God hasn't commanded us to. God never demanded that people should build monasteries. I'd like all monks to be steeped in oil,

27 A translation persuasively suggested by Vögelin (n. 6, p. 153), on the basis of Lot's association with the depravities of Sodom.

Hey das ichs verbrennen ſött
wüſs gott wie ich inen fhüren wett
Denn ich red vff min Eyd
Klöſter ſind des Tüfels beſte weyd
Vnd ee ichs noch ein jar well lyden
ee wil ich wyb vnd kind myden
Vnd bitt dich min Eygennutz ſtrych
nun blyb nit / far ſchnäll für dich
Gott geb was dir ſag yederman
denn vns ligt nit ein kleyn dran
Der gwalt gibt den pfaffen gſtand
den münchen ouch in ſtetten vnd land
Daß ſy hůren by inen habind
vnd mit Milchzinß zum Biſchoff trabind
Es treyt den Biſchoffen vil nutz
das Biſtumb / mit namen Fudutz
Nun ſinn ein yetlich Chriſten man
wie möcht es immer wol ſton
Wenn nun einr yetz vff die ſtund
[Aviii^{r}] zween hund vff ein andren fund
Er wurd ſy von einandren tryben
vnd ſölich hůry laßt man blyben
Allein wir puren müſſends ziehen
vmb vnd angen / darzů bſchühen
Drumb iſt yetz fürwar min radt
man thü darzů / es wirt ſunſt zſpaat
man tritt vns puren gar ins kadt.

Weybel Lätzkopff.
Cleywe häſſig leg von dir dſeck /
din meynung vns ouch hie entdeck
Radt das beſt / es zimpt dim ampt
du biſt vogt über vns all ſampt
Weyſt wie übel wir habind verlorn
von den Edlen ab Hohenzorn?
Denn ſölt es vns wie vormals gon
wir dörfftind vmb lyb vnd gůt kon

so that I could set fire to them! God knows how I'd like to set them on fire – because I can state on oath that monasteries are the devil's favourite pastures. And I'd rather be without my wife and children than suffer the monks for another year. So, good Eygennutz, I ask you to go and not to tarry – get yourself there quickly. May God give you the words to speak before everyone, since this matter concerns us not a little. The authorities support the priests, and the monks too, in town and country – so that they can have their whores with them and go to the bishop with the interest they've milked from us. The diocese called Fudutz[28] serves the bishop's interests. Now let every Christian man think how he would react if, at this moment, he were to find two dogs mounting another one. He would drive them away; yet such whoring is allowed to go on. We farmers alone must support it, give to it, even keep them in shoes. So my advice is this: we must do something before it's too late. They're treading us farmers in the muck.

Weybel Lätzkopff
Cleywi Hässig, put your sacks away. Advise us what is best, as befits your office as Vogt over us all. Do you know how badly we lost at the hands of the Hohenzorn nobility? For if we are treated again as we were before, we may well lose both life and property.

28 Presumably Vaduz, in Liechtenstein, which was a staunchly Catholic area.

Meinſt du ob wirs ſöllind waagen?
du haſt wol hören vmbfraagen
Weyſt beſſers denn du noch haſt ghört
ſo wirt von allen din radt gmeert
Drumb nimm all din witz für dhand
es iſt dir nun vaſt wol bkandt
Wie man vſs der ſach käm
daß die ſchindery ein end näm
Wo in der ſach nit radt wirt funden
wär vns weger läbendig gſchunden
jch gloub der Tüfel ſye entbunden.

[Aviii[v]] **Cleywe Häſſig.**
Nun helff was ſtab vnd ſtang trag
das wir ſchickind vff den Rychßtag
Wir habend zyter nie ghan
wölt Gott vnſer not wüßt yederman
Ach was müſſend wir doch erlyden
von pfaffen / münchen / vnd kloſter glyden
Denn üch allen iſt wol kund
wir ſöllend inen wol tuſent pfund
Wölt Gott das es darzů käm
daß der Tüfel Nunnen vnd Zinß näm
Wir mögends dlenge nit erharren
jch fürcht wir ziehind hie am karren
Vnd dört an des Tüfels wagen
hettind wirs langiſt ztod gſchlagen
Was ſol des Tüfels faſel hie
mich wundret ob es Gott nit mü?
Wie mag er doch ſo lang zůſehen
das er laßt ſo vil boßheyten gſchehen?
Ich gloub ſo ich an ſiner ſtatt ſäß
das ich gwüſs mich ſelbs vergäß
Vnd den himmel abfallen ließ
das ich alle wurmnäst vßſtieß
Wie mag er doch so gütig ſin
das er nit wirfft ſtül vnd benck dryn?

Do you think we should risk it? You have heard the consultation; if you know a better argument than the ones we have heard, your advice will be greatly esteemed by all of us. So bring all your cleverness to bear. Do you know how to get out of this situation, how to end this maltreatment? If we don't get some good advice, then we'd be better off being skinned alive. I think the devil has been let loose.

Cleywi Hässig

May anyone who bears the rod or staff of office help us to send someone to the Diet, something we haven't done before. Would to God that everyone knew our plight! O, what we still have to suffer at the hands of priests, monks, lay brothers, and monastery officials! For as you know, we owe them at least a thousand pounds. Would to God the devil would take both nuns and payments, but we can't wait that long. I fear that here we're pulling a cart, but there the devil's wagon. If only we'd destroyed it long ago, what would the devil's spawn be able to do here now? I wonder whether it bothers God or not. How can he look on for so long, and allow so much evil to be done? I think that if I were in his position I'd forget about myself and let the heavens cave in, so that I might destroy all the worms' nests. How can he be so generous that he doesn't hurl down his throne and bench?

Waß fröuwt doch Gott an irem hülen
damit ſy den armen das jr abgylen?
All jr Gytzdienſt tag vnd nacht
gantz weder kalt noch warm macht
Ir hülen achtends für ein bitt
[Bi^{r}] was ſy bättend verſtond ſy nit
Ir bätt vor Gott vil minder gilt
dann ſo einer ein korb mit waſſer füllt
Vnd jnn wil tragen voll ins huß
wiewol das waſſer ründt daruß
Erlernt der torecht menſch darby
daß beſſer in gelten tragen ſy
Noch můß ich ein exempel geben
jr ſingen das ermant mich eben
Als ſo einer mit eim welſchen gadt
der nit ein tütſch wort verſtadt
So man jm flůcht / es gilt jm glych
als ſo einer ſpräch / Gott ſchend dich
Oder Gott grüß dich biderman
nimpt er ſich eins wie des anderen an
Alſo haſplends vmb in pſalmen
verſtonds minder denn die ſchwalmen
Das Schwalmen gſang vil me nützt
deren die vnderem tach ſitzt
Man kennt doch by deß Schwalmen gſang
ob rägen wätter am himmel hang
Nunnen gſang nützt zů keinen dingen
vnd wenn ſy ſchon jr läbtag ſingen
Drumb wirt inen Gott eben lonen
als ſunginds: Gang mir vſs den bonen
Denckend lieben biderben lüt
was nützts das wir thůnd das Gott nit büt
Vſs den örden iſt entſprungen
das ſy vns puren hand arm gſungen
vnd verderbt den gmeinen man
[Bi^{v}] ſy kläbend noch wie äglen an
Vſs vns puren ſugends jr ſpyß

What can possibly please God about their caterwauling, as they appropriate the things of the poor? All they do day and night in the service of greed[29] doesn't make anybody either warm or cold. They think their howling is prayer; but they don't understand what they're praying for. In God's sight, their prayer is less effective than someone filling a basket with water and then trying to carry it indoors even though the water is leaking out of it. The foolish man learns from this that it's better to carry water some other way. I must give another example; their singing compels me to do it. It's like walking with a foreigner[30] who doesn't speak a word of German. If you curse him, he doesn't mind. Whether you say 'God damn you' or 'God bless you, my good fellow', he takes both the same way. This is the way they gabble their Psalms, which are harder to understand than the song of swallows. Indeed, swallow song is much more useful to people sitting underneath the roof that the birds are on: you can tell from it whether rain is coming. But the songs of nuns are totally useless, even if they sing all the days of their lives. Therefore God will reward them just as if they had sung 'Come away from my beans'. Think about it, dear good people: what's the good of doing things that God has never commanded? The monastic orders have sung us farmers into poverty and have destroyed the common man. They still cling to us like leeches, sucking their food from us.

29 'Gytzdienst' permits a neat play on 'Gotzdienst', 'service of God'.

30 'Welsch' is a generally derogatory term to describe someone from the Romance lands.

kläbend vns in der hut wie filtzlüß
Der Tüfel hat erdacht das gyren
ich wölt lieber hören lyren
Nun ſing*t in* aller tüflen namen
wölt Gott ſy müßtind allſamen
Mit Fäldſiechen klaffen vmm ryten
gelt ſy müßtind mir denn beiten
Vnd nemmen das ich willig geb
wöll Gott das ichs bald erleb
Du Eygennutz kumpſt ins Richtal
laß nit du ſagiſt überal
All vnſer not die vns truckt
wir hand vns warlich lang gſchmuckt
man hat vns wie die Reyff buckt.

Weybel Lätzkopff.
Ob yemand anders radten well
fürhar iſt yenen ein gůt gſell.

Fridrych Hußman.
Hettind wir yetz zmal recht růw
wir kummend gwüß vmb kalb vnd ků
Denn der Pundt von Hohenzorn
hat vns vormal gnůg gſchorn
Ich radt das Eygennutz hie blyb
vnd nit wider gotzſtraaff kyb
Ich kan nit anders in mir finden
wir hettind böſers bſchuldt mit ſünden
[Bii^r] Gott hat vns ſelb in die not gſetzt
vnd bſorg vns werd gſchorn on gnetzt
Denn ſo jr ſchon yetz all ziehend
gloub ich das jr waſſer fliehend
Vnd werdind zletſt mit fhür verbrennt
ich han üch Puren lang kennt
Ir namend dſach vormals zhanden

472 ſingend *B*

They stick to our skin like lice. The devil dreamed up their greed, but I'd rather listen to a lyre. They sing the names of all the devils. Would to God that they had to ride about and talk to lepers! Then they'd have to wait for me and take what I'd willingly give. Would to God I'll experience this soon! You, Eygennutz, go to the Richtal. Don't give up telling everyone about the sufferings that are weighing us down. We've been cowering for long enough, and they've trodden on us as if we were frost on the ground.

Weybel Lätzkopff
If anyone else would like to give advice, please do so: we'll all think you're a good fellow.

Fridrych Hußman
Even if we had real peace right now, we would still for certain lose cows and calves: the Hohenzorn's league of nobles[31] have already taken enough of them from us. I advise Eygennutz to stay here, and not to fight against God's punishment. I can't find any other advice in me; we would only load worse sins upon ourselves. God himself brought these dire straits upon us, and I'm worried that we are being punished without mercy. For now that you're all for going away, I'm afraid you'll be fleeing from water and end up being destroyed by fire. I've known you farmers a long time. You've taken up this cause before,

31 A reference to the Swabian League, which was heavily involved both in the Swabian (or Swiss) War of 1499 and in putting down the farmers' uprising of 1525. The League is doubtless associated here with the Hohenzollerns not least because of the major role played in it by the Hohenzollern Casimir, Margrave of Bayreuth (1481–1527).

üwer anſchleg aber ſind nit bſtanden
Darumb das es nit was vſs Gott
jr ſind ein vaſt kybige rott
Vnd wo man alſo kybig lebt
der Tüfel ſelb damit ſtrebt
Der hetzt üch all fürwar ich gloub
jr thůnd eben als ſygind jr toub
Vnd gſchäch üch ſchon als jr bgären
ſo möcht es doch nit lang wären
Vnd růffte man ſchon yetzund wett
biß znacht einer mee denn der ander hett
Vnd ſo man yetz all zinß vfhieb
wär es üch nit biß zjar lieb
Ir mögend nit on entlehnet ſin
ee ſatztind jr huß vnd hof yn
Es iſt kein bott das man zinß mach
zinſen kumpt vſs der vrſach
Ir ſitzend tag vnd nacht bym wyn
ſuffend vnd wütend wie die ſchwyn
Vnd mögend nit han růw / noch raſten
als ein bſchloßne muß in eim brotkaſten
Ir wellend voll ſin ſtädt vnd ſtyff
denn ruffend jr wie ein Sackpfyff
[Bii^{v}] Ir tönend nit jr ſygind denn voll
das beſt gſang iſt nüt denn troll
Vnd das iſt üwer gmeyner ſitt
füllen / das man mit ſtiflen drinn knitt
All voll all voll / vnd ſelten wan
lärt den ſeckel / vnd füllt den man
Sprechend denn / Wirt tryb vns nit vß /
das bringt üch vmb matten vnd huß
Lieſſind jr nach das wölt ich radten
trunckind waſſer / äſſind erbs für braten
Was üch denn Gott gibt / Můß vnn Linſen
denn wurde man üch müſſen zinſen
Vil Zinß macht man nach gmeiner art
wo man nit trinckt vnd zamen ſpart

but you didn't succeed because it wasn't of God. You're a very quarrelsome lot, and the devil himself strives against those who, like you, live quarrelsomely. He's the one who's stirring you all up, I think. You're acting like you're deaf. And even if what you want came to pass, it wouldn't be long before you were competing against each other, and one would still end up with a lot more than the other. And even if all your debts were written off, you still wouldn't be happy come the end of the year. You can't live without borrowing: you'd soon mortgage your houses and farms. No one commands that you must be charged interest; it happens because you sit day and night with your wine, drinking and raging like boars. You can't abide peace or rest, like a mouse shut up in a bread bin. You want to be full and bloated all the time – and then you howl like bagpipes. You don't make any noise unless you're full. Your best song is no more than foolishness. This is what you usually do: you fill yourselves up so full that you'd burst if anyone stepped on you with a pair of boots. Full, full, never empty. Empty the purse and fill the man! Then you say: 'Don't kick us out, landlord'. It's that sort of thing that does you out of your meadows and houses. My advice would be to hold back. Drink water. Eat peas instead of meat, eat the things God gives you: porridge and lentils. Then you'd be owed money by other people. You can make money if you don't drink, but save instead.

Thůt man aber wie jr thůnd
da bſchüßt nüt / hett ſchon yeder ein pfrůnd
Alſo vertrinckend jr das üwer
ſack vnd ſeyl / kern vnd ſprüwer
Vnd ſo jrs als in wyn vernetzend
denn jr huß vnd hof verſetzend.

Hie redt jm einer dryn mit zorn / vnd ſpricht alſo:

Rüde Braſſer.
Dilema däle hat höuw feyl
die zinß ſind der merteyl
Gmacht / ee wir ſygind born
vnd ouch der Pundt von Hohen zorn
Du weyſts grad als wol als ich
[Biii[r]*]* wir werdend gſchunden wie das vich
Ir rychen mögends wol erlyden
jr gond har in Sammat vnd ſyden
Wir ziehend die küe / jr eſſend dmilch
jr tragend lünſch / vnd wir den zwilch
Vch rychen darff man nit lang borgen
jr dörffend nit Martini ſorgen
Das man üch huß vnd hof vergante
der dich nit ſo wol kante
Meint ich doch dir wäre ernſt
man weyßt wol wo du das lernſt
Du bringſts mit dir vß der Abty
wenſt das vns wie dir ſy?
Lang biſt des Apts Hoffmeyſter gſin
ee man dich nam ins kloſter yn
Du hatteſt weder rendt noch güllt
vor rychtag du nit mee dienen wilt
Nun biſt ſelb herr / haſt darzů gnůg
vnd haſts nit gwunnen mit dem pflůg
Man gab dir do nit ſo vil zlon
nach dem du gůt haſt überkon
Du haſt ein ſumm gellt wie ein fürſt

But if people act like you, it's no good – even if you all had an income, you'd spend it on drink, every last penny, every little bit.[32] And since you waste it all on wine, you then have to put up your houses and farms as collateral.

At this point someone interrupts him angrily, saying:

Rüde Brasser

But, you fool,[33] we do sell our hay! And most of the interest payments were agreed before we were born. As for the Hohenzorn's League, you know as well as I do that they're skinning us like cattle. You rich men have no problem going about in velvet and silk. We raise the cow, you drink the milk. You wear wool, and we wear twill. We're not able to borrow from you rich folk for very long: you can't wait until St Martin's Day[34] to get your hands on houses and farms. If I didn't know you so well, I might think you were serious. But we know where you learned all this. You brought it back with you from the abbey. Don't you know that you're no different from us? You've been the abbot's steward for ages. Before you were taken into the monastery, you didn't have a pension or any other kind of income. You obviously don't want to serve at the Diet any more: you've become a lord yourself and have enough, even though you didn't earn it with the plough. It's true that no one gave you so much money before you'd done so well for yourself. You get a princely sum

32 Literally, 'sack and rope, kernel and chaff'.

33 See the *SI*'s interpretation of the phrase 'Dilema däle' (XII, 1424).

34 11th November. Traditionally a day for carnivalesque feasting, preceding a period of penitence; but also a day on which labourers were hired, and bills and wages paid.

all jar von Zinß das dich nit dürſt
Ietz ſprichſt / Zinſen kumm nyena har
ſo man wyn lapp / vnd nüt ſpar
Wie offt hab ich dich ſehen lappen
mit dinem Apt in der kappen
Das du dich fulteſt wie ein ků
ich ſchanckt dir yn / vnd lůgt dir zů
Drumb din gůt haſtu nit erſpart
[Biii^{v}] ouch nit gwunnen mit der kart
Ich ſach dich allweg by dem Apt
da haſtu tag vnd nacht glapt
Man ißt im kloſter kein gůten bitz
das din gnad nit darby ſitz
das alles iſt der puren ſchwitz.

Hie bricht aber einer harfür vnn ſprach zum Hußman vor gantzer Gmeynd alſo:

Gilg Vollbuch.
Sol ich dir ſagen Hußman
dir ligt nit vnſer not an
Du haſt gnůg / gang dir wie es well
vnd magſt wol ſin ein gůt gſell
Du biſt ouch ein Hofknab
daß dir din ſpiß nit brünnt ab
Du ſorgſt ſo das kloſter abgang
ſyg es dins vnglücks anfang
Denn werd dir din huß durchloffen
dfeſſer im käller vßgſoffen
Forchtiſt dir nit du wäriſt kecker
nun thůſt wie all täller ſchläcker
Du haſt allein den Apt in huld
vnd gnüſt ſin / das iſt dſchuld
Wenn ich hundert jar hie ſäß
er ſchanckte mir nit ein käß

592 nit vnſer not] vnſer noht wenig *F* 595 ein feiner Hoffknab *F*

every year from the interest you get, and so you don't have to go thirsty. And now you're saying: 'Interest is what you get when you drink too much wine and don't save'. How often have I seen you lapping it up with your abbot in his habit, and filling yourself like a cow! I poured the wine for you myself and watched you at it. So you haven't gained your wealth by saving, and you haven't won it at cards either. I used to see you with the abbot all the time. You lived in the abbey day and night. They never eat a nice piece of food in the monastery unless Your Worship is there to share it with them. And it all comes from the sweat of the farmer's brow.

At this point, someone else interrupts and says to Hußmann before the whole assembly:

Gilg Vollbuch
Shall I tell you, Hußmann, that you don't care about our situation? You've got enough, whatever happens to you. You may well be a good fellow, but you're also a fine courtier who makes sure that your own interests are looked after.[35] You're worried that if the monastery is dissolved, your misfortunes will begin: your house will be ransacked and the barrels in your cellar will be drunk up. You wouldn't be worried if you were braver. Now do as all the flatterers do. You've only got the abbot's favour, and you make the most of it. That's what's caused it. If I sat here for a hundred years he'd never give me a cheese

35 Literally, 'that your end isn't burnt off'.

Wie er üch Schmorotzern ſchickt
wölt Gott jr wärind dran erſtickt
[Biv[r]] Gnuſſind jr der klöſter nit
Ir jähind / Tüfel mimm den Apt mit
Hut vnd haar / nun wart nit lang
das in dſchyß jm Ougſt an gang
Kerend üch nüt dran lieben gſellen
laſſend vns klöſter abſtellen
Ich gloub wir dientind Gott mit
lüg ich das mich der ritt ſchütt
Eygennutz far hin / nun blyb nitt

Weybel Frantz.
Vit Hack den tüfel radt ouch hie
wie man doch der ſach thie
So kumpt man mit der ſach ans end
radſt du das man bottſchaft ſend?
Gwunnind wir denn / das käm vns wol
du weyſt wie vns der Apt roll
Wurd vns nun der halb teyl nachglon
wir wöltind wol vergůt han
ſöllend wir blyben oder gan?

Vyt Hack den tüfel.
Es iſt ein kyde blůt ſchand
das wir vns alſo würgen lond
Wir ſöltind tag vnd nacht nit fyren
vßjagen / mit pfleglen nahin lyren
Was wellend wir der Otterzucht?
ſy hand ſo gar nit ein ducht
Die ſich nach dem geyſt gots ziech
hey das ſy gott ewig verflüch
[Biv[v]] Tüfel nemm den Apt vnd Conuent
wär hat doch all ſin läbtag kent
Das Chriſtus hab ein orden ghan

626 wol vergůt] ein vergnügen *F*   629 ein kyde] fürwar ein groß *F*

like the ones he sends to you spongers. Would to God you all choked on the cheese! If you didn't enjoy the abbey so much, you'd say: 'The devil take the abbot, all of him!'. It won't be long before the August shits get him.[36] Don't let that bother you, good fellows: let's get rid of the monasteries. I think we'd be serving God if we did. May the fever get me if I'm lying! Go, Eygennutz, don't delay!

Weybel Frantz
You advise us too, Vit Hack den Tüfel, as to how we should deal with this case. To bring the case to an end, do you think we should send a representative? If we won, it'd be good for us. You know how the abbot is punishing us. If we got only half of what we wanted, that'd be good for us. Shall we stay or go?

Vyt Hack den Tüfel
It really is a terrible shame to let ourselves be throttled. We shouldn't rest day and night, but hunt them down and beat them with our flails. What do we care about that brood of vipers? They don't have so much as the wick of a candle to draw them towards God's Spirit. May God curse them for ever! The devil take the abbot and his monastery! Who in his entire life has ever heard that Christ had an order,

36 Maybe a reference to the so-called 'Summer diarrhoea', an unpleasant form of gastroenteritis.

vnd in eym kloſter wyb vnd man
Das iſt im orden Saluatoris
vaſt an galgen mit jnen foris
In eim kloſter ſind dryzehen man
zwölff můß man für xij botten han
Der dryzehend iſt an Chriſti ſtatt
hey das mans nit all krützgen latt
Denn iſt vnſer Frowen orden
wo iſts doch ye erhört worden
Daß Maria hab ein orden ghan?
ich finds nun an keim ort ſtan
All jar man klöſter viſitiert
wärinds all an dböum gſchnyert
Barfüſſer hand ein Prouincial
ſchlach hagel / donder / blitzg vnd ſtral
Lützel frouwen klöster ſind
da man nit ein Bychtiger in find
Der můß jr Penitentzer ſin
vnd er wirt nimmer lär von wyn
All tag er ſich voll trinckt
das er wie ein Elſes bättler ſtinckt
Er ligt tag vnd nacht im lůder
wie ein voller Etſch brůder
Wir gebend jnen darzů täglichs brot
wie möcht nun ſölichs gfallen gott?
Vber das alles hand ſy erdacht
mit glychßnery darzů bracht
[Bv^{r}] Das man ſy müß vor ougen han
ſölt vnſer einer für ſy gon
Das er nit ſpräch / gnad herr / gnad frow
ſpräch man / was touben menſchen / ſchow
Darzů můß ich jnen geben das min
ſy herren / vnd ich knecht / ſin
Sölt es wären noch als lang
vnd lenger han ein fürgang
Es käm darzů das ſy ſich fliſſind
den arswüſch hieſchinds ſo ſy ſchiſſind

or put men and women in a monastery? But the Order of the Redeemer – take them forth to the gallows! – have thirteen men to a monastery. Twelve they must have for the twelve apostles, and the thirteenth takes the place of Christ.[37] If only they could all be crucified! Then there's the Order of Our Lady.[38] But where have we ever heard that Mary had an order? I can't find it written down anywhere. You have to visit monasteries every year. May they all be tied to the tree! The Franciscans have a Provincial who strikes hail, thunder, and lightning. It's rare to find a nunnery without a confessor. He has to give them absolution, but he's never free of wine. All day long he fills himself to the brim with drink, so that he stinks like an Alsatian beggar.[39] He lies about dissolutely all day like a real beggar from the Adige.[40] We're the ones who give them their daily bread. How can this be pleasing to God? And they've also dreamed up the custom – and brought it about by their scheming – that we've got to go and see them. And when one of us comes before them, we've all got to say 'my Lord' or 'my Lady' to them, haven't we? 'Look, what fools!', you'd say. But then I also have to give them what belongs to me. They get to be the lords, and I'm their servant. If this went on for as long as it has up to now, or even longer, they'd be ordering us to wipe their arses when they shit.

37 He means the Carthusians, the original model for whose communal life this is.
38 i.e., the Carmelites.
39 See *SI* IV, 1838.
40 i.e., the Southern Tyrol. See *SI* V, 418.

Was kumpt nun von den klöſteren gůts?
nüt / denn ſy zechend gůts můtz
Ir werck iſt hünen vnd ſingen
ſuffen / braſſen / einandren bringen
Vnd hand damit ſo vil erhünet
huß / äcker / matten / überginet
Darumb ich vff min Eyd yetz radt
wir ſchickind hin nun ſchnäll vnd tratt
Gen Fridberg / ob vns nach werd glon
wir hand lang gnůg das beſt thon
Nüt beſſers weyß ich by miner trüw
jch gloub nit das es vns grüw
Man findt noch vil barmhertzig lüt
die gſtond dem Ottergſchlecht gar nüt.

Weybel.
Ob yemant beſſers radten wett
denn man noch bißhar ghört hett
Der thüge es / denn es iſt zyt
denn gen Fridberg iſt vaſt wyt
[Bv^{v}] wo iſt einer der ein radt gibt?

Alt Vogt Erhart.
Diewyl ich ouch ein Meyer bin
vnd vor eim jar Vogt gſin
Můß ich ouch hie min radt ggeben
vnd radt / das jr by lyb vnd leben
Hie blybind als lieb üch Gott ſy
denn jr werdend nimmermee fry
Ir ſind wol ſo notwendig lüt
vnd blybend on entlehnet nüt
Ir fahend an das gar nüt ſol
das hört man an üwerem kyb wol
Wie offt ſind jr zů mir kummen
vnd mich vff ein ort gnummen
Mich bätten das ich üch gelt lich
üch ward zů antwurt / Nein ich

What good comes from the monasteries? Nothing, except for monks having a good time eating and drinking. Their work is howling, singing, drinking, feasting, and finding women for each other. And in doing this they've howled themselves into the ownership of so many houses, fields, and meadows! So, on my oath, I advise that we should send as quickly as we can to Fridberg, to see if we can succeed there. We've already been doing our best for long enough; and I know of no better advice, upon my word. I don't think we'll regret it. There are still plenty of merciful people to be found there, who don't belong to the brood of vipers.

Weybel
If anyone dares to offer better advice than what we've heard so far, let him do so – because the time has come. Fridberg is a long way from here. Who will give us some advice?

Alt Vogt Erhart
Because I'm a free peasant too, and was Vogt a year ago, I too must offer my advice here. I advise you, by life and limb, to remain here for the love of God. For you'll never again be free. You're such poor people, and you'll be punished for it. You're starting something you shouldn't, that much is evident from your quarrel. How many times have you come to see me, taken me aside, and asked me to lend you money? I've always given you the answer: 'No,

Ir gebend nüt wider mit lieb
es wär mir lieber / mir ſtäls ein dieb
Denn ichs mit hader ynziehen wett
darnach üch nun zum fygend hett
Sölt ich mit mim gůt fyentſchaft kouffen?
ich finds näher / darff nit wyt louffen
Denn ſprachend jr: Mins bäts mich ergetz
min huß vnd hof ich zpfand ſetz /
Ir klagend man wöll üch nüt me lihen
das walt der Tüfel / man hat ein ſchühen
Ich weyß / gäb man üch yetz ein gbott
daß keiner nüt mee verſetzen ſott
Vnd ſtůnds jm Euangilg Bůch
[Bvi^r] ee irs hieltind / verſatztend jr brůch
Hettind jr huß wie die alten
jch wil üch nun kein har ſpalten
Wärind jr das vorig jar rüwig gweſen
jr hands nit in heilger gſchrifft gleſen
Das man ſölle vfrürig ſin
hettind jr gfolget dem radt min
Das käm üch yetz vil baß
hey wie trüwlich riedt ich das?
Ich ſprach / Lůgend was jr thügind
das jr nit über Oberkeyt ziehind
Ir ſatztend mich von ſtundan ab
do ich üch diſen radt gab
Vnd ſtieſſend mich von der Vogty /
ſprachend: Wir wöllend ſyn gar fry
Ir hand üch wider Oberkeyt gſetzt
all Herren tütſch lands nun vfghetzt
Das üwer vil hand ztod erſchlagen
jch gäb ein ſchweyß vmb üwer tagen
Ir hand üch ſelbs nun letz gſtelt
das man üch für trüwloß lüt zelt
Ich bleib hie / vnd ließ üch ziehen

735 über] wider *F*   746 bliebe *F*

you're never willing to repay any loan, so I'd rather a thief stole my money than have to argue with you to get it back, and always thereafter have you as an enemy'. Why should I buy myself enemies with my own money? I can find enemies enough close at hand; I don't have to go far. Then you reply: 'Do as I ask, and I'll give you my house and farm as collateral'. You complain that no one will lend to you any more. The devil take that! People are afraid to. I know that if you were commanded right now never to pawn anything any more, and even if the command were in the Gospel itself, you'd pawn your breeches rather than keep to it. I won't split hairs with you: if you'd still had houses, as you used to, you'd have been peaceable last year. You haven't read in holy Scripture that you should start a rebellion. If you'd followed my advice, you'd be better off now. How faithfully I advised you! I said, 'Be careful what you do. Don't pull against the authorities'. But you removed me from office as soon as I offered this advice, and told me, 'We want to be totally free'. You set yourselves against authority, and roused all the lords of the German lands against you, so that they killed many of you. I don't give a fig for your conference. The way you've behaved recently has made people think you're untrustworthy. I'll stay here and let you go.

aber jr můßtend wider fliehen
Ir ſprachend zů mir blyb daheimen
du fürchſt man klopffe dir den leymen
Ich ſölte recht gon zum ofen ſitzen
ſpinnen / vnd (wölt ich gern) gufen ſpitzen.
Eygennutz weyſt noch was ich ſprach /
ee die ſchädlich vfrůr ynbrach?
Lůgend nun vnd ſind nit zwyß
[Bvi[v]] jch vörcht fürwar üch byſſind dlüß
Denn ee man das ir wend nach werd lon
jr werdend ee all zſchyter gon
Es zimpt ſich luter den puren nit
vnd was all vnſer tag nie ſitt
Daß ſy ſelb ſöltind Herren ſin
wiewol ich nun der eltiſt bin
Eygennutz du ſagteſt vor eim jar
zů mir es ſtünde heyter vnd klar
Das man vergeben lihen ſött
vnd ſin all ſiben jar wett
Ich ſprach zů dir wo ſtadt es gſchriben?
du hetteſts vſs dem Moyſe kliben
Das ſelb do din antwurt was
ja ſprach ich / gfiel dir das?
So opfrend ſtier wie dIuden ouch
do ſagteſt du ich wer ein gouch
Alſo ziehend jr das Gotzwort
nach des lybs nutz an mengem ort
Wo man denn Gotswort mißbrucht
jſt kein wunder ob man ſtrucht
Min Eygennutz das ſye dir gſeyt
du biſt nun vollen gytigkeyt
Volg mir noch / radt ich allein
das nützt dich vnd die gantz gmein
Doch wilt nit anders / do magst wol gon
aber dir wirt nüt nachglon

767 thetteſt *F*

But you had to flee again. You said to me: ‘Stay at home. You’re just afraid you’ll get a thrashing’. I was supposed to go and sit by the oven, spin and (if I wanted to) sharpen some nails. Do you remember what I said, Eygennutz, before that destructive uprising started? Look now, and don’t be too clever: truly I was afraid that the lice would bite you. Because before you get what you want, you’ll all come to grief. It clearly isn’t right for farmers to be lords, and it’s something that’s never been seen in all our days – even in mine, as the oldest among you. Eygennutz, you told me a year ago that, in Scripture, it was as clear as day that people should lend without expecting anything in return, and that every seven years all debts should be cancelled. I asked you then: where is that written? You pointed to Moses; that was your answer then. I said, ‘Well, if you like that, then you should sacrifice bulls as the Jews did’; and you told me I was a fool. In this way you distort the Word of God in many places, for the good of your own body. If you abuse God’s Word, it’s hardly a surprise if you stumble. Listen to me, Eygennutz: you are full of greed. All I advise is that you should heed me: it’s in your interests and in those of the whole community to do so. But if you won’t have it any other way, then go. You won’t find any mercy, though.

Verſůch ob man dir geben well
das du mögiſt ſin ein gůt gſell
Möchtiſt dHerren darzů bringen
[Bvii[r]] daß müßtind wie du wöltiſt ſingen?
Käm dir wol vnd dinen gſellen
gelt wo man zinſen werd abſtellen
Blibiſt hie das frouwte mich
es gadt fürwar nit fürſich
jr wurdind ſunſt ein jars rych.

Weybel Lätzkopff.
Was dunckt üch all gůt das wir thůgind
radtend jr das wir gen Fridberg ziehind?
Oder wend ir ein botten dar ſchicken
wir puren geltend nit ein wicken
Darumb wöllend jr bottſchafft han
ſo rüſtend jnn by zyt vff ban
So kumpt er ouch by zyten dar
ee der Pundt von einandren far
Vilicht findend wir gnädig Herren
wolan ich wil drumb meeren
Heb vf ſin hand dem es wol gfall
das Eygennutz gen Fridberg wall.

Hie meeret der Weybel / vnn ward mit gemeyner hand das meer man ſölte den Eygennutz hinwäg richten / vnd im empfelhen was er handeln ſölte.

Weybel
Farhin Eygennutz vff den Rychßtag
all not die wir habend / da ſag
Wir ſygind bſchwärt mit Edlen vnn pfaffen
[Bvii[v]] flyß dich vnſeren nutz zeſchaffen
Gott well du bringiſt mit dir har hein
daß du erfröuwiſt die gantz gmein
Frag obs das gotswort innhalt
das ein Chriſt můß han weltlicher gwalt

Try and see if they'll give you something that might make you into a good fellow. If you could make the lords sing the tune you want them to sing, then it'd turn out well for you and your friends – if they'd abolish interest payments. But if you stayed here, I'd be glad. And it really is very far from certain that you'll be rich in a year's time.

Weybel Lätzkopff
What do you all think we should do? Do you advise that we should all go together to Fridberg, or would you rather send a representative? They think we farmers are worthless, so you might prefer to have a representative. So then, help him to prepare for his trip in good time. That way he'll come to Fridberg on time, before the League break up their meeting and go home. Perhaps we'll find gracious lords. Now I'm ready to count. Raise your hands if it pleases you that Eygennutz should go to Fridberg.

At this point, the Weybel counted. And the majority of hands from the community showed in favour of Eygennutz going. And they recommended to him what he should say.

Weybel
Go then, Eygennutz, to the Diet. Explain there all our needs, how we are weighed down by lords and priests. Try your hardest to achieve something that's in our interest. May God will you to bring back some good news to encourage the whole community. Ask if it's written in God's Word that a Christian should be under temporal authority.

Verſůch ob dir doch einiſt gling
tryb dſach als ſye es din ding
das wir fry werdind / daruf dring

Pur Eygennutz.

Ich verſůchs wie einer vff ein zyt
der ſpilt im brätt / vnd gabs zwyt
Er warff nun ein quaterduß
vnd gabs über fünff pündt vß
Sin gſell ſprach / warumb thůſt du das
der gegen jm am Brätt ſaß?
Do ſprach er / was ligt am verſůchen?
Alſo wil ich mich ouch růchen
Verlür ich denn / ich hatt nie mee
jch far da hin mit Gott / alldee

Hie kam Eygennutz gen Fridberg im Richtal glegen / vnd fragt dem Burgermeyſter nach / zů dem ſprach er also:

Pur Eygennutz.

Herr Burgermeyſter Salamon
wüſſend das ich bin har kon
Von Kybberg vmb der vrſach allein
das ich klagen ſöll für die gantz gmein
[Bviii^r] All vnſer fründ ſind ztod gſchlagen
ein teyl von huß vnd hof gjagen
Das alles hand wir von Edlen lüten
hand vnſer gůt vßteylt in büten
Darzů vns huß vnd hoff verbrennt
wyb vnd kind vaſt übel gſchendt
Vil hand müſſen in blůt baden
die läbenden ſind mit ſthür bladen
Das man den Adel nit mee vmbkeer
habend ſy vns gnommen all weer
Wir ſind minder denn wir vor warend
ſy ſchindend yetz daa ſy vor ſcharend
Thů ſo wol / verſamel ein Gricht

See if you can succeed, presenting our case as if it were your own. Insist that we must be free.

Pur Eygennutz
I'll try to do like the one who, once upon a time, was playing dice and was coming second. He threw 'quatre deuce' and paid over five pounds. His friend who was sitting at the table with him asked him, 'Why are you doing that?' He replied: 'Why not give it a go?' I'll try my best too. I've nothing to lose. But I'll go with God's blessing. Farewell.

Then Eygennutz came to Fridberg, which is in the Richtal, and asked to see the Mayor, to whom he said this:

Pur Eygennutz
My lord Mayor Salomon,[41] know that I have come here from Kybberg for the sole purpose of pleading the cause of my whole community. All of our friends have been killed. Some have been chased away from their homes and farms. All this has been done by noblemen, who have divided up our goods as booty. What is more, they have burned our homes and farms. They have done great harm to our wives and children. Many have had to bathe in blood, while those who are still alive are burdened with taxes. And to make sure we can't rise up against the nobility any more, they have taken all our weapons from us. We are fewer than we were before. They're now skinning, rather than just shearing us as before. So please be good enough to summon a court,

41 The introduction of an authority figure with this name who is to engage in dialogue with a peasant character draws the reader's attention to the possibility of correspondences with the carnivalesque Solomon and Markolf tradition. As with the earlier implications that a play is to take place, however, initial expectations are confounded, as Salomon emerges as the genuinely 'wise' one (from Eckstein's point of view). For a comment on Eygennutz's notably drastic account of the events of the 'Peasants' War', see n. 399 on the *Concilium* above.

ſo klag ich inen alle gſchicht
Vnd büt dem Adel ouch darzů
ſo hörends wie ich min klag thů
Ach Salamon hilff vns zerůw.

Burgermeyſter Salomon.
Wolan min Pur Hans Eigennutz
jch thett das beſt ſo es nun bſchutz
Denn man ſol vnfrid abſtellen
jch fürcht du vnd din gſellen
Sygind vrſach diſes kybs
denn jr ſůchend nun den nutz des lybs
Ir achtend nit der ſeel heyl
Damit verbochend jr ſack vnd ſeyl
Wo man nit acht hat vff gotswort
vnd gwalt / ſo gſchehend ſöliche mort
Ir hand ghan ein vnrüwig jar
[Bviiiv] das koſtet mengen hut vnd haar
Wär ſich wider Oberkeyt widret
Erhöcht er ſich / er wirt ernidret
Welcher Oberkeyt widerſtadt
gwüſs er Gott zů eim fygend hat
So einer denn von Gott wirt ghaßd
denn hilfft nüt wie er ſich verfaßd
Vnd was nit gſchicht vſs gotsworts krafft /
da blybt kein anfang ſtandhafft
Erzürnet Gott / er ſchlacht on truren
das hat man gſehen an üch puren
Wär es an der vile glegen
jr hattend ſo vil ſpieß vnd dägen
On zal wie das ſand im Meer
büchßen / gſchütz / on andere weer
Doch hat Gott der Herr nit wellen
ein Oberkeyt laſſen abſtellen
Ietz ſind ir von ein anderen gſtröuwt

867 *marg.* Rom. 13. *F*

and I will plead before you everything that has happened. Invite the nobility to come too; that way they will hear my complaint.[42] O Salomon, help us to find peace.

Burgermeyster Salomon

Very well, farmer Hans Eygennutz. I would do best if I took care of this case now, for one should put down unrest. I fear that you and your fellows caused this quarrel, for you were seeking only the good of your bodies. You were not thinking of the salvation of your soul. That's why you've destroyed everything. When people don't heed God's Word and authority, then this kind of carnage is the result. You have had a year of turmoil, which cost many people their lives. Whoever exalts himself and rises up against authority will be brought down. Whoever resists authority surely has God for an enemy. And if God hates you, no matter how you present yourself, it won't help. Whatever isn't done through God's strength will never stand firm. If God is angered, he will strike people down without mercy, as we have seen with you farmers. If it had been down to numbers, it would have been different – you had spears and swords as numberless as the sand of the sea; guns, ordnance, and other things. But the Lord God didn't want to let authority be overturned. And so now you're being scattered to the four winds,

42 The predominant verb in the negotiations between Eygennutz, Salomon, and the new Weybel is 'klagen', implying a complaint or grievance which needs addressing. The tone is thus considerably more confrontational, and also more formal and juridical than was the case in the preceding village consultation. Moreover there is here an implicit inequality, both of status and of role, between the peasant 'plaintiff' Eygennutz and the aristocrats who answer him.

das üwer wyb vnd kind nit fröuwt
On die vatterloſen kind
deren on zwyfel nun vil ſind
Die werdend yetz mit armůt bhenckt
welcher fürhin daran nit denckt
Der wil ſich doch nit laſſen warnen
yetz můß meng byderman erarnen
Dem ſine güter ſind zergenckt
huß vnd dſchür an himmel ghenckt
Das bringt ein ſölich vneinigkeyt
daß purſchafft gem Adel haſs treyt
Alſo hand dHerren nit gůten frid
[Ci[r]*]* wo vnderthonen tragend nid
Wolan ich lůg möcht man üch richten
vnd wider miteinander verpflichten
Gang an din herberg ſchlaaf mit rů
morn füg dich wider harzů
biß ichs dem Pundt ouch kund thů.

Am morgen ward beyden parthygen fürbotten / vnd erloubt dem puren zeklagen.

Weybel Rychart.

Diewyl es zimpt in diſem zyt
das man all vnfrid vßrüt
Als yetz denn iſt vil kyb vnd ſpan
Zwüſchem Adel vnd dem purſman
Zum erſten klage die ein parthy
die ander geb antwurt daby
Deßglychen ouch der Pundt klag
vnd all anligen frölich ſag
Darumb ſitzt yetz zmal das gricht
Gott well es werde wol gſchlicht
Als es ouch wirt mir zwyflet nüt
wir hand hie wol ſo witzig lüt
Sy namend nye kein ſach zhanden
das ſy darinn ſygind gſtanden

which hardly pleases your wives and children. Quite apart from the orphaned children – of whom I'm sure there are now many – they are now burdened with poverty. Anyone who doesn't think about this in future will be stubborn, because he refuses to heed a warning. Now many a good fellow will have to pay for it, having his goods destroyed, and his house and barn blown to the skies. It causes so much division when farmers show such hatred towards the nobility. Lords have no peace where their subordinates resent them. It's right, I think, that you should be judged, and reconciled to each other. Go now to your lodgings and sleep peacefully. Present yourself here again tomorrow, while I inform the League.

The following morning, both parties were ordered to come before the judge, and the farmers were allowed to speak.

Weybel Rychart
Since it is appropriate to our times that we should put an end to all dissensions, such as the disputes and tensions that exist between the nobility and the farmers, may one party first state its complaint, and then the other respond. The same procedure will be followed for the complaints of the League of the nobility. All requests should be made freely. The court is now sitting here for this purpose. May God grant that it will bring reconciliation, as I have no doubt it will. We have here such clever people. They would never take up a matter unless they were well versed in it.

Darumb ſo ſye eim yeden gſeyt
man wirt nit gſton der Oberkeyt
Nit glimpffen der puren vfrůr
ſunder richten nach der ſchnůr
Vnd wo es wirt not ſin
[Ci^v] puren vnd edlen reden dryn
Das ſelb hie recht vnd billich iſt
nun fach an Eigennutz wo du biſt
klag hie vor allem was dir briſt.

Hie klagt Pur Eygennutz vff beid ſtend / Geiſtlichen vnd Weltlichen: vnnd der Geiſtlich Doctor gibt erſt antwurt nach dem bericht der Edlen vnd Puren.

Pur Eygennutz.
Herr Burgermeyſter Salomon
darumb ich armer Pur hie ſton
Zeklagen für ein gantze gmein
wie man vns ſchinde / iſt nit nein
Wir ſind von zweyen huffen bladen
lydend von beyden groſſen ſchaden
Der ein huf iſt die geyſtlich rott
jr houptmann der Bapſt / vnd jrdiſch Gott
Vber vnſer lyb vnd ſeel regiert
bißhar (wie er hat gwöllen) gfürt
Hat vns mit pfaffen überſetzt
die hand vns mit dem Bann gehetzt
Habend vns ſo vil gſpenſt vfgricht
wie man nun täglich wol ſicht
Mit Mäſs / Vigilgen / vnd Chorjölen
gabend vns für es hulffe dſelen
vnd gfalle Gott im himmel oben
damit richtends vns den kloben
Diewyl man zů dem altar tringt
[Cii^r] vnd das liedlin (Kummüli) ſingt *Quam*
So bald der Olim vß iſt *olim.*
bin ich gwüſs daß puren gbriſt

For this reason, be it said to one and all that we will not side wholly with the authorities, nor condone the uprising of the peasants. Rather, we will judge justly and fairly, and if need be we will interrupt either farmers or nobles, as is right and fair. Now Eygennutz, you begin. Tell all of those present what your problem is.

Here Pur Eygennutz complains about both estates, the lords spiritual and temporal; and the clerical doctor only answers after the accounts of the nobility and the farmers have been heard.

Pur Eygennutz
My lord Burgermeyster Salomon, I, a poor farmer, am standing here on behalf of a whole community, to complain about how we are being mistreated. We are burdened not with one, but with two mobs. The first is the clergy. Their leader is the Pope and earthly god, who until now has ruled over our bodies and souls just as he pleased. He has put priests over us who have persecuted us with excommunications. They've set up a huge amount of spiritual nonsense for us, as we now see on a daily basis, what with Masses, vigils, and requiems. They pretend to us that it'll help our souls and please God in heaven above. In all this they set traps for us. Meanwhile, they throng to the altar, singing the song 'Kümmuli'.[43] As soon as the 'olim' has been sung, I'm sure that farmers start suffering.

43 From the Requiem liturgy: 'Quam olim Abrahæ promisisti et semini ejus' ('as he [once] promised to Abraham and his seed').

Wir ſind ſo offt zůhin trungen
biß ſy vns hand arm gſungen
äcker / matten / vnd was wir hend
iſt das nit ein groß ellend?
Vnd was von pfaffen überblybt
das ſelb der münch vſtrybt
Ee vnd ſy vns etwas lieſſind
vnd nit vnſren ſchweyß nieſſind
Erdenckend ſy all trug vnd bſchiß
ſy kummend nun all jar gwüſs
Was wir den Summer hand für gſchlagen
kumpt der münch im Winter jagen
Vnd jagt von huß zhuß vmm
von käſen vnd fleyſch ein groſſe ſumm
Es kumpt denn nit nun ein Orden
ouch ſind Brůderſchafften worden
Die bringend von Rhom ſölichen gwallt
das ich offt nit ein haller bhalt
Das vnd anders bſchwärt vns vaſt
noch tragend wir ein groſſen laſt
Von der weltlichen Oberkeyt
die vns groß burdinen vfleyt
Die ich nit all mag erklagen
vnd wil yetz nun das gröſt ſagen
Wir müſſend jr lyb eygen ſyn
verzinſen kernen vnd den wyn
So einer denn ſchier gar verdirbt
[Cii^{v}] jſt er nit fry ſo er ſchon ſtirbt
Verlaßt er hinder jm ein ků
von ſtundan gryfft dHerrſchafft darzů
Denn ſo blybt nüt ſinen kinden
dků nemends / ſo ſy nit beſſers finden
Alſo kumpt einer vmb rind vnd roſs
nun wär es vil / bald mit ins Schloſs
Nahin můß der ſun vmblouffen
das Lehen vff ein nüws kouffen
Vnd mee drumb geben / denn es vor galt

We've been dragged into this so often that they've sung us into poverty. Fields, meadows, and all that we have; isn't this great suffering? And whatever is left over by the priests is taken up by the monks. Rather than leaving us anything, or failing to use the sweat of our brows to the full, they dream up all sorts of tricks and deceits. They come now every year without fail. Whatever we worked all summer for, the monks come hunting for in the winter. They hunt from house to house, getting great quantities of cheese and meat. And nowadays it isn't just one order, but confraternities too, which bring such authority from Rome that I've often lost my last heller to them.[44] This and other things weigh heavily upon us, but we also bear another great burden that the temporal authorities lay on us, about which I can't even tell you everything. I only want to speak against the worst things: namely, that we must be their serfs and bondsmen, tithing grain and wine. And if anyone dies doing this, even then he isn't free. If he leaves a cow behind him, then straightaway the nobility will seize it, so that nothing is left to the dead man's children. They take the cow, if they can't find anything better. In this way, you lose your cattle and your horses. Even if you had a lot of them, they go straight to the castle. Afterwards the son whose father's died has to run to and fro to borrow money for a new cow, paying more for it than it was worth to begin with.

44 Confraternities, or congregations, differ from religious orders in that the vows required of their members are 'simple' as distinct from 'solemn', and are in consequence much easier to rescind. Their growth and prominence around Eckstein's time owed much to Pope Leo X's constitution 'Inter cetera' (1521), which made enclosure merely optional for members of confraternities.

alſo vns die Oberkeyt halt
On andre Sthür vnd Oſter eyer
es gadt alles über vns arme Meyer
Do nun Gott den erſten menſchen macht
der vns in diſe not hat bracht
Mit dem das er vnghorſam was
vnd die verbotne ſpyß aß *Genes. 3.*
Do gab jm vnd vns Gott den flůch
das ein yeglich menſch fürhin ſůch
Im ſchweyß ſins angſichts täglichs brot
allein der Purßman lydet not
All ſtend hand ſich vſs dem flůch zogen
drumb wachßt alſo der fulkeyt rogen
Nun trifft der flůch all menſchen an
puren / pfaffen vnd edelman
Mit wercken der Pur all ſtend můß bgon
jm wirt chum täglichs brott daruon
Der Adel mit des Purs gůt ſicht
gelt vmb gelt der wůchrer vslycht
Purſchafft ouch all pfaffen neert
[Ciiir] jn Klöſtern man puren gůt verzeert
Der Burger ſitzt in gůter růw
vnd laßt jm tragen dPuren zů
Ein Kouffman von dem anderen koufft
nun yederman den Purßman roufft
Das vnd anders vns vaſt bſchwärt
drumb hand wir an ein herſchafft bgärt
Das man vns das joch ringer mach
ſo blybind wir by tach vnd gmach
Nun hat der Pundt zſamen gſchworen
das gantz Künigrych Hohenzoren
Durch gantz Tütſch land nun überal
vil zetod gſchlagen one zal
Sy hand vns gjagt von huß vnd hof
darzů helffend inen dBiſchof
Die vnßre hirten ſoltend ſin
jagend ſelbs die Schäflin

This is the hold that the authorities have on us, not to mention other taxes and Easter eggs.[45] All of this weighs down on us farmers. Now when God made the first human, who brought us to this pass because he was disobedient and ate the forbidden fruit, God placed a curse on him and on us,[46] so that, henceforth, all human beings had to earn their daily bread by the sweat of their brows. But it's only the farming man who has to suffer this distress. All the other estates have managed to extricate themselves from the curse. This is the seed from which sloth grows. But the whole curse actually affects everyone: farmers, priests, and nobility. Every estate must live off the work of the farmer, who barely gets his daily bread from it. The nobility fight on the proceeds of the farmers' goods; usurers lend them money in exchange for money. The clergy too are fed by the farming estate; and in monasteries it's farmers' goods that are consumed. The townsman sits at his ease and has the farmer brought to him; one merchant buys from another. But everyone flays the farming man. This and other things bear down upon us, which is why we have wished that the overlords would make our yoke a bit lighter, so that we might get on better. But now the League has sworn together – the whole kingdom of the Hohenzorn and everywhere throughout the German lands; they have slaughtered more of us than we can count. They have chased us from house and farm, the bishops helping them in this; those who should be shepherds have been hunting down the little sheep.

45 One of the many forms, no doubt, that Easter taxes took.

46 Genesis 3:19: 'By the sweat of your face you shall eat bread until you return to the ground'.

Die äbt gebend ouch jr ſthür darzů
vnd was wir gwünnend mit vnrůw
Mit übel zyt hacken vnd rüten
verſöldends ſy den Kriegslüten
Das ſye üch klagt / lieben Herren
wir mögend vns dlenge nit erneeren
Alſo ſind wir nun gar verſetzt
vns hat der Pundt nun übel gletzt /
darzů mengem gſchoren on gnetzt.

Vff ſölliche klag gab Antwurt einer vom Pundt mit namen wie naher ſtadt:

[Ciii[v]] **Iuncker Ludeman Pfefferſack.**
Diewyl der Pur ſo vnuerzagt
an mich vnd an all Edel klagt
Thett vns nöter das wir klagtind
vnd von der puren vfrůr ſagtind
Durch welche ſind vil Clöſter gſchent
vnſere Schlöſſer hand ſy vor verbrent
Darzů nüt gelaſſen on durchloffen
in källeren ſich vollen wyn gſoffen
Ouch fenſter vnd öfen nidergſchlagen
groß gůt mit ſecken vßtragen
Deßglychen iſt nun nye erhört
ſy lieſſend nun nüt on vmbkert
Das klag ich ab der puren rott
ſy forchtend weder tüfel noch Gott
Hettind ſy thon wie jre vralten
vnd ſich fridlich mit vns ghalten
Inen wäre nit gſchehen von vns leyd
ſy wärind noch by wunn vnd weyd
Do ſy aber nit anders wotten
můßtend wir ouch nahin hotten
Vnd erretten vätterlich Erb

1030 übel zyt] groß arbeit *F*   1045 vor] *om. F*

The abbots also have lent their support; and what we had gained with our hard work, hoeing and weeding, they have used to pay mercenaries.[47] This is my complaint, dear lords. We can't go on like this in the long term; the League has damaged us very severely.

A member of the League responded to this complaint, whose name is given below:

Juncker Ludeman Pfeffersack
Since the farmer has complained so boldly about me and all the other nobles, it's all the more important to us to complain and tell of the farmers' rebellion, because of which many monasteries have been damaged. They had already burned our castles, not forgetting to ransack them, and downing their fill of wine in our cellars. They also destroyed windows and ovens, carrying away a great deal of loot in sacks. The like of this has never been known. They left nothing unmolested. This is my complaint against the hordes of farmers. They fear neither the devil nor God. If they had done as their ancestors did, behaving in a peaceful manner towards us, they wouldn't have had to endure this suffering from us. They would still be enjoying their meadows. But since they wouldn't have it any other way, we had to press hard on them, and save the inheritance of our fathers.

47 This statement reflects the ongoing disagreements within Swiss, and especially Zurich society about the lucrative mercenary trade – with its attendant pensions and expectations of loyalty to Rome and the Pope.

vns fröuwt nit das man Puren verderb
Sy ſind ein anfang der vfrůr gſin
vnd vns gjagt über all berg hin
Darzů verbrent klöſter vnd ſchloſſz
drumb hand wir vns gwert zfůß vnn zroſſz
Wir hand vns deſſe nye verſehen
das vns ein ſölcher ſchad ſölt gſchehen
mag ich by der warheyt jehen.

[Civ^{r}] Hie entſchuldiget ſich Pur Eygennutz des ſchadens halb / vnd wendt ander lüt für die ſölichs ghandelt habind / on gunſt deß gemeynen mans / vnd ſpricht alſo.

Pur Eygennutz.
Iſt üch ſchaden widerfaren
ſo iſt es kon von ſundren ſcharen
Die vns nit dienet hand damit
deßhalb ich dſchuld vff ſy ſchitt
Man findt ſunſt wol vnrüwig lüt
da nüt bſchüßt was man jnen büt
Die ſahend ſölich vnfůr an
als denn iſt der Küny Schnapphan
Vnd der Bertſche Hechelbart
Ioß Schlach in hufen ſich nit ſpart
Baſtion tuſend tüfel fyret nit
Broſe Rumsfäld nimpt ee man jm gibt
Die habend üch den ſchaden thon
wir hand nyemant das ſin gnon
mir ward kein haller nye dauon.

Wie ſich Pur Eygennutz entſchuldiget hat mit vnnützen kriegslüten / Deßglychen ſchlacht im Iuncker Ludeman ouch für vnder den reyſigen / damit bezalt man böß mit böſem.

Iuncker Ludeman Pfefferſack.
Wir hand wol ouch der glychen knecht
denen gadt es lieber krumb denn ſchlecht

It gives us no pleasure to see farmers perish, but they were the cause of the unrest. They were the ones who chased us over every mountain, burning down monasteries and castles. This is why we defended ourselves on foot and on horseback. We had never imagined that such damage as this could be inflicted on us. That I can truthfully say.

Here Pur Eygennutz apologizes for the damage, saying that others had acted in this way, but that it was not the will of the common people. He spoke thus:

Pur Eygennutz

If you experienced damage, it was done by other bands of people, who did us no service in so doing. So it's them I blame. Such rebellious people are easy to find, who don't do what they're told. They began this chaos. One of them is Küni Schnaphan,[48] and Bertsche Hechelbart.[49] Joss Schlach[50] is never far from such a group. Bastion Tusend Tüfel[51] never rests. Brose Rumsfäld[52] takes before you can give him anything. These are the ones who have done you wrong. We didn't take anyone's possessions from them; and I didn't gain a single heller from it.

As Pur Eygennutz defended himself by blaming worthless soldiers, so also Juncker Ludemann made the same excuse for the knights, thereby returning evil for evil.

Juncker Ludeman Pfeffersack

We also have reprobates like these, who would rather do what's wrong than what's right.

48 Named at the beginning as one of the peasants who was to participate in the debate. See n. 17, p. 315.

49 A 'Hechel' is a comb-like implement used mainly for riffling flax or hemp. According to *SI* II, 969, however, the term can also be used of a sharp-tongued or quarrelsome woman.

50 A tool used for beating (for example) clay or fire.

51 'Sebastian Thousand-devils'.

52 The surname means 'empty the field'.

[Civ^{v}] Hans Butz den winckel einer iſt
Rüdin Schütt den bütel allweg briſt
Claus durch den buſch all tag vßrüt
das er erſchnapp ein gůte büt
die hand ouch gſtrafft üch Purslüt

Als Burgermeyſter vnnd Rädt wol verſtůndend die vngſchickte beyder parthigen ghandlet / redt Salomon Burgermeyſter zů den Puren alſo vff ir klag.

Salomon Burgermeyſter.
Pur Eygennutz nun laß dir ſagen
du haſt nun din not fürtragen
Vnd dich völlig gnůg erklagt
du ſygist von huß vnd hof gjagt
Mich dunckt daß vmb der vrſach ſy
du wäriſt gern gült fry
Vnd habiſt nit gern Oberkeyt
das ſelb dir nit ſant Peter ſeyt
Denn das die leer Petri iſt
halts / ſo du ein rechter Chriſt biſt *1. Petr. 2.*
Sind menſchlicher ordnung vnderthon
vmb gotzwillen / hie magſtu verſton
So er vmbs herren willen ſpricht
das der Gwalt an Gots ſtatt richt
Was der Gwalt denn ſetzt vnd macht
darinn Gotswort nit wirdt verſchmacht
Biſtu ſchuldig dem nach zegon
dich ſelb / lyb / vnd gůt verlon
[Cv^{r}] Wir hand vergangner gſchichten vil
welcher denen nit glouben wil
Dem gadts wie es inen gieng
vnd wär ye vfrůr anfieng
Der ward ſelber gſtraafft von Gott
alſo gſchach ouch der Choriſchen rot

1111 Denn was der Lehr Petri gmeß iſt *F*

Hans Butz den Winckel is one such, Ruodin Schütt den Bütel is always after something, and Claus durch den Busch is pulling things up all day long, so as to end up with good booty. They in turn have punished you farming people.

The Mayor and Council having understood the misfortunes of both parties, as related here, Mayor Salomon spoke to the farmers regarding their suit.

Burgermeyster Salomon
Pur Eygennutz, hear what I say. You have now explained your situation, and fully stated your complaint; that you are hunted from your house and farm. It seems to me that the cause of this can be found in the fact that you would like to be free not to pay your dues, and don't like having any authorities over you. But this is not what St Peter tells you. For St Peter's teaching (keep to it) is that, if you think that you are a good Christian, then you are to be subject to human authority[53] for God's sake. Here you should understand that, as he is speaking of the Lord's will, he appoints the authorities to rule in God's stead. Therefore, whatever the authorities decide or do, as long as it does not dishonour God's word, it is your duty to follow – even if you should lose yourself, your body, and your belongings thereby. There are many stories from the past that could be told about this, and anyone who doesn't believe them will find that things will go as badly for them as for those who rebelled in earlier times. Anyone who ever began a rebellion has been punished by God. This is what happened to Korah's faction.

53 1 Peter 2:13–14: 'For the Lord's sake accept the authority of every human institution, whether of the emperor as supreme, or of governors, as sent by him to punish wrong and to praise those who do right'.

Chore wider Moyſen facht *Nume. 16.*
biß er ſich ſelb in not bracht *&. 26.*
Chore / Dathan / Abiron
můßtend läbentig in dhell gon *Pſal. 105.*
Denn das ertrich thett ſich vf
do ward verſchluckt der Choriſch huf
Hettind ſy ſich wie ghorſam gſchmuckt
ſy hett das erdtrich nit verſchluckt *2. Reg. 15.*
Alſo gſchach dem Abſolon
der ſtalt nach ſines vatters kron
Er bgärdt das rych ee Dauid ſtarb
zů letſt er an eym Eychboum verdarb *2. Reg. 18*
Vnd ſins volcks ein groſſe ſumm
es kamend zwentzig tuſent vmb
Siba / Iſrael an ſich zoch *2. Reg. 20*
vnd begärdt das küngrych Dauids ouch
Darzů er nit verordnet was
darumb er můßt erlyden / das
Man im hüw das houbt ab
vnd des Dauids houptman gab
Man ſol dem Gwalt nit widerſton *Rom. 13.*
denn Gott hats nye on grochen glon
Gwalt iſt nun allwegen gſin
vnd von Gott ſelb gſetzt yn
[Cv[v]] In Moyſe ſtadt heyter gſchriben
wenn das volck anfahe kiben
Söllind ſy für dRichter kon *Deut. 25.*
nach dem dſünd iſt ghört / jnen ouch lhon
Hatt einer denn nach boßheyt gjagen
er ward in angſicht der Richter gſchlagen
Ouch hand vor zyten heylger lüt
lyb eygen zů ſin / ſich gwidret nüt
Ioſeph ward in Egypten verkoufft *Gen. 39.*
hat nit wie jr puren geroufft
Sinen herren / den künig Pharaon
Gott halff jm vnd den ſinen dauon
Man fiel ouch nit nit in Cayphas huß

Korah fought against Moses[54] until he brought disaster upon himself. Korah, Dathan, and Abiram had to descend to hell alive, for the earth opened wide[55] and Korah's band was swallowed up. If they had adorned themselves with obedience, they wouldn't have been swallowed by the earth. A similar fate befell Absalom, who plotted to get his father's crown.[56] He desired the kingdom before David was dead, and ended his life hanging from an oak tree;[57] and a huge number of his people – twenty thousand – died. Sheba drew Israel to himself[58] and also desired David's kingdom, although he was not entitled to it. Therefore he had to suffer his head being hewn off and given to David's general. You should not resist authority,[59] for God has never allowed such resistance to go unavenged. There have always been authorities, and they were instituted by God himself. In the books of Moses it is written clearly that when people start to quarrel, they should come before judges.[60] Once the sinful act has been tried, it should receive its just deserts. If someone has committed wickedness, he should be punished in the judge's presence. Previously, holy people were slaves, yet did not rebel. Joseph was sold into Egypt[61] but did not fight against his overlord, the Pharaoh, as you farmers have done. For this, God helped him and his people. No one overran Caiaphas's house either,

54 By far the more relevant chapter is Numbers 16, though there is brief mention of Korah, his rebellion, and his sons in Numbers 26:9–11.

55 Psalm 106:17: 'The earth opened and swallowed up Dathan, and covered the faction of Abiram'.

56 Especially 2 Samuel 15:1–12.

57 2 Samuel 18:9–10: 'Absalom was riding on his mule, and the mule went under the thick branches of a great oak. His head caught fast in the oak, and he was left hanging between heaven and earth'.

58 2 Samuel 20:2, 22: 'So all the people of Israel withdrew from David and followed Sheba son of Bichri [...] And they cut off the head of Sheba son of Bichri, and threw it out to Joab'.

59 Romans 13:2: 'Therefore whoever resists authority resists what God has appointed, and those who resist will incur judgement'.

60 Deuteronomy 25:1: 'Suppose two persons have a dispute and enter into litigation, and the judges decide between them, declaring one to be in the right'.

61 Genesis 39 contains a summary of Joseph's successful early career in Egypt, and an account of his dealings with Potiphar's wife.

das man jm roubte ſin gůt druß
dIunger bgärtend nit Herodis gůt
vnd kam jnn nye in jren můt
Hattend ſy ſchon gůter gemeyn
ſo gſchachs von denen nun allein
Deren gůter will es was
in brüderlicher liebe gſchach das
Wärinds in Cayphas käller gloffen
vnd jm den wyn vßgſoffen
Hettinds fenſter vnd öfen zerſchlagen
wie ich hör von üch puren ſagen
Vnd der prieſter hüſer verbrent
das wär gſin des tüfels Conuent
Das iſt nun von keym junger gſchehen
wie man hat von üch puren gſehen
Vnd wie jr dſach hand angfangen
iſt es über üch vßgangen
[Cvi^{r}] Denn wär vff Chriſten blůt ſtellt *Prouer. 1.*
er ſelb zů letſt in blůt fellt
Min Eygennutz das ſy dir gſeyt
der Gwalt das ſchwärdt von Gott treyt
Das man vfrürig lüt mit ſchnid
vnd die fridſamen habind frid
So vil ich vom Gwallt verſton
vnd ee der gwalt werd abgon
werdend jr hut vnd haar lon.

Vff ſölichs ſtadt ein andrer vf im Radt / vnnd redt wyter von Oberkeyt. Alſo ſtraffende die puren irs vnſchicks halb / ſprechende

Bernhart Erenueſt.

So yederman in liebe läbte
nyemant wider den andren ſtrebte
Denn wurd die beſt Pollicy
wir wurdind an lyb vnd ſeel fry *Ioann. 3.*

1166 *marg.* Act. 2. vnn 4. *F* 1185 *marg.* Rom. 13. *F*

or stole his goods from it. The disciples didn't covet Herod's possessions: stealing them never entered their heads. They already held their goods in common, but this applied only to those who did it with goodwill, in brotherly love. If they had ransacked Caiaphas's cellar and drunk up all his wine, or if they had broken windows and ovens, as I hear it said of you farmers, and burned down the priests' houses, they would have been the devil's own men. But not one of the disciples behaved as you farmers have been seen to. And as you started the matter, so it has come back to harm you. For whoever seeks to spill Christian blood,[62] his own blood will be spilt in the end. My dear Eygennutz, let it be said to you that the authorities bear the sword of God, to cut off rebellious people with it, and in order that peaceable people might have their peace. I understand this much about authority: before authority passes away, you will be dead.

At this, another person stood up in the council chamber, and spoke further on the subject of the authorities punishing the farmers for their unruly behaviour, saying:

Bernhart Erenuest

If everyone lived in love, with no-one striving against the other, then the best polity would have arrived. We would be free in both body and soul.[63]

62 Proverbs 1:11, 18: 'If they say, "Come with us, let us lie in wait for blood; let us wantonly ambush the innocent" [...] they lie in wait – to kill themselves! and set an ambush – for their own lives!'.

63 There is no obvious passage in John's Gospel (see the marginal reference opposite) to which these words correspond.

Die wyl nun aber lützel ſind
die da ſygind rechte Gotz kind
So hat Gott ein artzny zůbereyt
das iſt weltliche Oberkeyt
Damit der Gottloß zämpt werd *Rom. 13.*
der grecht frid hab hie vff erd
Die geyſel ye dem Roſſz ghört *Proue. 26*
damit man jm ſin geyle weert *Eccleſ. 33.*
Mit rûten man den Eſel juckt
ob jnn ſchon die burde truckt
Darumb iſt gſetzt das weltlich ſchwärdt
[Cvi^{v}] daß der böß nit thüge das er bgärt
Welcher da iſt ein grecht man *2. Tim. 1.*
den gadt das gſatzt nüts an
Denn ein Chriſt der läbt ſunſt recht
vnd bgärt nit das er widerfecht
Daß von Gott geordnet iſt *Rom. 13.*
vnrechts lydet ein frommer chriſt
Drumb Gwallt iſt nit den gûten gſetzt
die böſen allein das ſchwärt letzt
Nun nim ein glychnus yetz für dich
ſo ich ein bſeßnen menſchen ſich
Den bſchlüßt man in ein gefencknus yn
das er niemants möge ſchad ſin
Man bindt ein Touben nun darumb
das nit gröſſer ſchad von jm kumm
Der rechtſinnig darff gfencknus nüt
wandlet er wie ſunſt witzig lüt
Mit gûter gewüßne ein Chriſten man
das ſchwärdt mag in der hand han *Gene. 14.*
Schwärdt hat brucht ouch Abraham
do er an die Heydiſchen Künig kam
Das ers brucht / was nit wider Gott
er errettet damit ſin brûder Lott
Ouch bruchts der Heylig Dauidt *1. Reg. 17.*
do er Golie das houpt abſchnitt *Danie. 13.*
Zů Babilon ouch Daniel *1. Reg. 15.*

But for as long as there are only a few true children of God, God has prepared a medicine, that is the temporal authorities, to ensure that the godless are tamed and the righteous have peace here on earth. The horse always has a whip,[64] so that its wilfulness can be curbed.[65] The donkey is driven with a bridle even if the burden weighs him down. This is why the secular sword was instituted, so that the wicked might not do whatever they like. If anyone is a righteous man, the law does not bother him.[66] For a Christian lives rightly and does not desire to resist what God has ordained. A good Christian suffers injustice. So authority is not in place because of good people. The sword only wounds the wicked. Now take this as an example: if I see a person possessed, he will be locked away in prison, so that he can't harm anyone. Mad people are only bound up so as to prevent them causing greater damage. The person of sound mind does not need prison, as long as he lives as other sane people do. In the same way, a Christian may bear a sword with a clear conscience. Abraham also used a sword,[67] when he attacked the heathen king. For him to use it was not against God's will – and by it he saved his brother Lot. The holy David also used a sword when he cut off Goliath's head,[68] Daniel did in Babylon,[69]

64 Proverbs 26:3: 'A whip for the horse, a bridle for the donkey, and a rod for the back of fools'.

65 Ecclesiasticus 33:6, 25–6: 'A mocking friend is like a stallion that neighs no matter who the rider is [...] Fodder and a stick and burdens for a donkey; bread and discipline and work for a slave. Set your slave to work, and you will find rest; leave his hands idle, and he will seek liberty'.

66 Cf. 1 Timothy (*sic*) 1:9: 'This means understanding that the law is laid down not for the innocent but for the lawless and disobedient'.

67 Genesis 14:14–15: 'When Abram heard that his nephew had been taken captive, he led forth his trained men, born in his house, three hundred and eighteen of them, and went in pursuit as far as Dan. He divided his forces against them by night, he and his servants, and routed them'.

68 1 Samuel 17:51: 'Then David ran and stood over the Philistine; he grasped his sword, drew it out of its sheath, and killed him; then he cut his head off with it'.

69 Daniel 13:55 and 59 (Greek version) describe Daniel as killing first one, and then the other elder.

deßglychen ouch der Samuel
Erschlůg den Künig Agag *1. Reg. 18.*
Iehu deßglychen ouch pflag
Das thettend nun frumm heylig lüt
[Cvii r] Ioannes verbüt es ouch nüt *Lucæ. 3.*
In dem Nüwen Teſtament
da das gmein volck an Iordan rendt
Kamend zů jm kriegs lüt
niemant zebſchädigen er verbüt
Er was dem gmeinen frid ſo hold
das er ſy hin ließ vff iren ſold
Damit ward geufnet gmeiner frid
vnd vßgerüt der böſen nid
Ouch der frumm Cornelius
ſant Peter ließ jnn nit vmb ſuſs
An ſinem ampt da er ann was
worzů was nun gůt das?
Zů gmeinem friden was es gůt
darumb man die böſen abthůt
Daß die frommen mögind leben
darzů hat Gott den Gwallt ggeben
S. Peter nit ſprach laß daruon *Acto. 10.*
er was nit darumb zů jm kon
Das er jnn näm von ſinem ampt
Cornelius die böſen dampt
Er was vor ein gotzuörchtig man
vnd von Gott ſelb darfür ghan
Vnd hat allein darumb kriegsknecht
das er Vfrůren demmen möcht
kybig puren iſt ein böß gſchlächt.

Růdolff Fürſichtig.
Darumb iſt gſetzt ouch der Gwalt *Eſaiæ. 1.*
das man witwen vnd weyſen ſchirm halt *Hiere. 22.*
[Cvii v] Der Gwallt iſt ein werckzüg Gots

1245 geufnet] gepflanzt *F*

and Samuel[70] smote down king Agag. Jehu did the same.[71] All the people who did these things were good and holy. Neither did John forbid it[72] in the New Testament. When the common people ran to him in the Jordan, soldiers also came to him. He bade them not to do anyone any harm. The common peace was so dear to him that he asked them to be satisfied with their pay. In this way, the common peace was promoted, and the malice of the wicked undone. Also it was not without good reason that St Peter allowed pious Cornelius to remain in office. What was the good of doing that? Well, it was for the good of the common peace. Evil men need to be dealt with in order that the righteous might live; and God has instituted authorities to achieve that purpose. St Peter did not say: 'Get rid of him'.[73] He did not come to Cornelius to remove him from office: Cornelius, who punished evil men, had always been a God-fearing man, and was considered to be such by God himself. He had soldiers only so that he might put down insurrections. Cantankerous farmers are a wicked breed.

Rudolff Fürsichtig
Authority is also instituted[74] so that widows and orphans might be protected.[75] Authority is a tool of God

70 1 Samuel 15:33: 'And Samuel hewed Agag in pieces before the Lord in Gilgal'.

71 1 Kings 19:17 (*sic*): 'Whoever escapes from the sword of Hazael, Jehu shall kill'.

72 Luke 3:14: 'Soldiers also asked him, "And we, what should we do?" He said to them, "Do not extort false money from anyone by threats or false accusation, and be satisfied with your wages"'.

73 The story of Peter and Cornelius occupies the whole of Acts 10.

74 Isaiah 1 (*sic*): 17: 'Learn to do good; seek justice, rescue the oppressed, defend the orphan, plead for the widow'.

75 Jeremiah 22:3: 'Act with justice and righteousness, and deliver from the hand of the oppressor anyone who has been robbed. And do no wrong or violence to the alien, the orphan, and the widow, nor shed innocent blood in this place'.

damit das keiner den andren trotz
Vnd wo das böß vßbrech
daß der Gwallt denn how vnd ſtech
Man ſol ouch kurtz niemants ſchonen *Deut. 19.*
on erbermbd der boßheyt lonen
Doch das man dſchuld wol bſäch
vnd ouch niemants vnrecht gſchech
Gwallt des Erdtrichs Richter iſt *Pſalmo. 2.*
wiewol zů aller zyt ein Chriſt
Glychmäſſig ſinem Chriſto läbt
mit keiner raach wider ſträbt
Ouch iſt es S. Paulus bitt
daß ſich ein Chriſt reche nit *Roma. 12.*
Denn Gott allein ghört zů die raach *Deute. 32.*
Pur Eygennutz nun ſinn jm nach
Was dir Gott für ein crütz vfleyt
von dir wärd nit darwider gſeyt
Wil dich denn Gott in Zinſen han
ſolt du im willig nach gon
Satzte er dich in gröſſer gfar
dennocht ſind zellt all dine haar
Lern darby wie Chriſtus thett *Ioann. 18.*
do er den ſtreych empfangen hett
Mit keiner hand er ſich daa weert
er hatt nit allein den backen keert
Sunder aller ſin lyb
ſtandhafft nach dem ſtreych blib
Er gſtůnd dem herten backen ſtreych
mit ſym lyb er nit ab ſtatt weych
[Cviii[r]] Damit gab er vns zeuerston
das wir thügind wie er hab thon
Nit das man drumb nit reden ſöll
ſo man dich anlügen wöll
Wo es antrifft die recht Eer Gots
vſs liebe gib antwurt / nit vſs trotz *1. Cor. 13.*
Sprichſt / Es iſt ein böſer Gwallt /
ſag ich / drumb du dich recht halt

to prevent one person from treating another with malice and, where evil does break out, to beat and stab its perpetrators. To be blunt, no one should be spared, or wickedness paid back with mercy.[76] So we should consider our own guilt, and not act unlawfully against anyone. Authority is the judge of the earth.[77] A Christian should live at all times as Christ would live, and never resist in a spirit of vengeance.[78] It is also St Paul's request that a Christian should not seek his own revenge.[79] For vengeance belongs to God alone.[80] Now think about him, Pur Eygennutz: consider that, whatever sort of cross God is laying upon you, you should never speak against it. If God wills that you should pay interest, you should do so willingly. Even if he places you in grave danger, nevertheless he numbers every hair on your head. Learn from what Jesus did when he had been flogged.[81] He didn't defend himself in any way: he didn't just turn the other cheek, but his whole body stood firm in the face of the strokes – he didn't move at all. By this he gave us to understand that we should do as he did. Not that we shouldn't speak out against those who would bring false witness against us, or where the true honour of God is involved. But you should give an answer in love, and not in malice.[82] If you say, 'It is a wicked authority', I reply – so that you might behave rightly –

76 Deuteronomy 19:21: 'Show no pity: life for life, eye for eye, tooth for tooth, hand for hand, foot for foot'.

77 Cf. Psalm 2:10–11: 'Now therefore, O kings, be wise; be warned, O rulers of the earth. Serve the Lord with fear'.

78 Cf. the verses from Deuteronomy 32 cited in n. 80 below.

79 Romans 12:19: 'Beloved, never avenge yourselves, but leave room for the wrath of God; for it is written, "Vengeance is mine, I will repay", says the Lord'.

80 Deuteronomy 32:35, 41, 43: 'Vengeance is mine, and recompense [...] I will take vengeance on my adversaries [...] For he will avenge the blood of his children, and take vengeance on his adversaries'.

81 John 19 (*sic*): 1–3: 'Then Pilate took Jesus and had him flogged. And the soldiers wove a crown of thorns and put it on his head, and they dressed him in a purple robe. They kept coming up to him, saying: "Hail, King of the Jews!", and striking him in the face'.

82 1 Corinthians 13:4–5: 'Love is patient; love is kind; love is not envious or boastful or arrogant or rude. It does not insist on its own way; it is not irritable or resentful'.

Gott geb joch wie er böß ſy
ſo du wirſt gůts thůn / biſt du fry
Den Gwallt fürchſt nit vmb ſinentwillen
du můſt die gwüßne ouch erfüllen *Roma. 13.*
Darumb jnn Gott geordnet hat
kein rechter Chriſt jm widerſtadt
Gott mag durch böſen gwallt ſtraaffen
wie er wil / mit fhür vnd waaffen
Was gadts dich an was er mit well
du dich nit wideren gwallt ſtell
Büt man dir ſchon / daß fleyſch nit nütz
bilyb dich nit darwider ſtütz
So dir aber büt der gwallt
wider Gott / das ſelb nitt halt
Sonder biß mee ghorſam Gott *Act. 5.*
Ob dir ſchon nimpt din Herrſchafft ab
was du denn haſt / alle din hab
Das ſelb dem Glouben gar nüt ſchadt
denn dLiebe das alles zůladt *I. Cor. 13.*
Es zimpt dir das du fridſam ſygiſt *Matth. 5.*
vnd nun nüt darwider ſchrygist
[Cviii[v]] Denck das dir Gott hat zůgſeyt
vnd ſye dir ewigs läben bereyt
Ob du ſchon werdiſt hie durchächt *Matth. 5.*
ſo das ein Chriſten menſch dächt
Wurd er zytlichs gůts nit achten
ſunder nun das ewig trachten
Ein frummer Chriſt fürcht nit ſchwärt
wider Gwalt er ſich nit wert
Denn wär den Gwalt wirt verſchmahen
der wirt ſin gricht empfahen
Denn die weltlich Oberkeyt *Roma. 13.*
ſchwärdt nit vergeben treyt
Das ſchwärdt allein die erſchreckt
deren boßheyt wirt entdeckt
Vnd ſtadt daby eim Chriſten zů
das er lyde wie man im thů

that, however wicked God allows it to be, if you but do good, you will be free. Don't fear the authorities for their own sakes; you must also follow your conscience.[83] God ordained them, so that no true Christian can resist them just as he pleases. God may punish whom he pleases by means of wicked authorities using fire and weapons. Is it your business what he wishes to do with them? Don't set yourself against the authorities. If one commands you not to eat meat, for goodness' sake don't oppose this. But if the authorities command you to do something against God, don't do it. Rather, in such a case, obey God instead of human rules.[84] And if the authorities take from you all that you have, all your worldly goods, even this will not damage your faith at all. For love bears all things.[85] It is right that you should be peaceable[86] and not cry out against others. Remember what God has promised you, that eternal life has been prepared for you, even if in this life people despise you. If a Christian thought like that, he wouldn't heed temporal possessions, but strive only after eternal things. A righteous Christian is not afraid of the sword, and does not defend himself against the authorities. For anyone who disdains these will be judged. The temporal authorities do not bear the sword in vain.[87] The sword only strikes fear into those whose wickedness is uncovered; but it's the Christian's business to suffer, regardless of what people do to him.

83 Romans 13:5: 'Therefore one must be subject, not only because of wrath but also because of conscience'.

84 Acts 5:29: 'But Peter and the other apostles answered, "We must obey God rather than any human authority"'.

85 1 Corinthians 13:7: 'It bears all things, believes all things, hopes all things, endures all things'.

86 Matthew 5:9: 'Blessed are the peacemakers, for they will be called children of God'.

87 Romans 13:3–4: 'For rulers are not a terror to good conduct, but to bad. Do you wish to have no fear of the authority? Then do what is good, and you will receive its approval; for it is God's servant for your good. But if you do what is wrong, you should be afraid, for the authority does not bear the sword in vain! It is the servant of God to execute wrath on the wrongdoer'.

Vfrůr kein Chriſten fröuwt
den vnrüwigen Gott ſelbs tröuwt
Darumb batt Dauid der Prophet
das Gott kriegſch volck zerſtröuwen ſött *Pſal. 68.*
Kriegen manglet ſelten roub
als wenig im Meyen nit wachßt loub *1. Cor. 6.*
Ein röuber bſitzt das rych Gotts nit *Eſaiæ. 61.*
ob er den roub in dkilchen gidt *Pſalm. 61.*
Gott haſſets / jnn eert man vergeben mit.

Nach dem ward ouch dem Adel gſeyt vnd verwiſen ir vngſchickte die ſy handletind mit den vnderthonen. Vnd redt Burgermeyſter Salomon alſo:

[Di^{r}] **Salomon.**
Herr Pfefferſack Iuncker Ludeman
diewyl man ye ſol Oberkeyt han
So iſt von nöten daß der Gwalt
allein ſich nach gots ordnung halt
Mit wyßheyt das gmein volck regier
menſchliche ſatzung nit ynfür
Denn wo man nit nach gotswort richt
allein mit gwallt dryn ſticht
So blybt allein der nammen gwallt
ja der Finſternuß / in der gſtalt /
Denn do dIuden in garten kamend
vnd Chriſtum gfencklich annamend
Redt Chriſtus ſelbs vſs ſinem mund
zun Iuden: Das iſt üwer ſtund /
Vnd ein gwallt der Finſternuß
nach dem jm Iudas gab den kuſs
Der ſelb gwallt ouch von Got was
ſy můßtend aber hören / das
Chriſtus offenlich zů inen ſeyt
ſy wärind ein finſtre Oberkeyt *Lucæ 22.*
Darumb daß ſy by nacht kamend
zů jm / vnd wie ein mörder namend /

Rebellion does not please a Christian. God himself threatens the unruly. This is why David the prophet asked God to destroy a warlike people.[88] As a rule, theft follows war as surely as leaves grow in May. But no thief possesses the kingdom of God,[89] even if he gives his spoils to the church.[90] God hates these, and you cannot honour him with them.

After this, the nobility were told and shown the evil things they had done to their subjects. And Burgermeyster Salomon spoke to them thus:

Salomon

My lord Pfeffersack, Juncker Ludeman: while it's true that we must always have authorities, it is also necessary that the authorities follow only the commands of God, ruling the common people with wisdom and not introducing human regulations. For if you don't rule according to God's Word, but only intervene with force, you have only the name of 'authority'. The substance is darkness. For when the Jews came to the garden and took Christ prisoner, Christ spoke to them directly: 'This is your hour. And it is the power of darkness', he said, after he had been kissed by Judas. Now this authority also came from God. But they had to hear Christ telling them openly that theirs was a dark power,[91] since they came to take him away by night, like a murderer.

88 Psalm 68 (*sic*): 30: 'Trample underfoot those who lust after tribute; scatter the peoples who delight in war'.

89 1 Corinthians 6:9: 'Do you not know that wrongdoers will not inherit the kingdom of God?'

90 Isaiah 61:8: 'For I the Lord love justice, I hate robbery and wrongdoing'.

91 Luke 22:52–3: 'Then Jesus said to the chief priests, the officers of the temple police, and the elders who had come for him, "Have you come out with swords and clubs as if I were a bandit? When I was with you day after day in the temple, you did not lay hands on me. But this is your hour, and the power of darkness!"'.

Vnd do er tags by inen war
berůrtend ſy jm nie kein haar
Darumb böße vnd gůte Oberkeyt
ſchwärdt gwüſs von Gott treyt
Es iſt kein gwallt denn von Gott *Roma. 13.*
redt Paulus ſelbs der Gots bott
Darumb wol zimpt dem gmeinen man
[Di^{v}] das er ein Oberkeyt ſöll han
So iſt ouch das die Eygenſchafft
deſſe der ein andren ſtrafft
Das er ſelb vnſträfflich ſy
denn wirt ein rechte Pollicy
So bald der vnderthon erſicht
den Gwalt der über jnn richt
Vnd aber ſelbs präſthafftig iſt
das thůt nit gůt zů keiner friſt
Wie aber ein Oberkeyt ſöll ſin
findt man klar durch all gſchrifft hin *Deute. 18.*
Denn Gott der Herr ſelb Moſe büt
das er vßziehe wyßlüt
Gotsförchtig / darzů warhafft
das iſt des Gwalts eygenſchafft
Gwalt ſol nit Gyt haben *Eccleſ. 20.*
deßglychen haſſen ouch die gaben
Denn ſo der gwalt nach gaben ficht
ſo wirt verblendt gwalts angſicht
Darumb lůg gwalt wie er regier
das er das vrteyl recht für
Denn nach dem als gott ſeyt
ſo můß der Gwalt han wyßheyt
Das der gwalt nach aller krefft
wyßlich vollende gotz gſchefft
Wie vor zyten Ioſaphat *2. Par. 19*
richter in Iudea bſtelt hatt
Empfalch er jnen das ſy ſöttind
lůgen im richten was ſy thätind
Denn richten wär ein gſchäfft des herren

And though he had been among them by day, they had not touched a hair of his head. Therefore, certainly, both good and evil authorities carry the sword on God's behalf. There is no authority except that instituted by God,[92] says Paul, the messenger of God. Therefore it is right that the common man should have authorities over him. This is also why the one who punishes others should himself be above punishment. This would be a good polity. As soon as the subject perceives that the authority which rules over him is tainted, no good will ever come of it. However, the qualities of a good authority can be clearly found throughout all the Scriptures. For the Lord God himself commanded Moses[93] to select wise, God-fearing, truthful people. These are the characteristics needed for an authority. Authorities should not be greedy,[94] hating bribes. For if the authorities seek bribes, their sight will be blinded. Therefore let the authorities consider how they rule, that they make just decisions. For according to what God says, authorities should also have wisdom, so that they might, with all their strength, carry out God's work wisely – as Jehoshaphat once did,[95] when he placed judges throughout Judea. He urged them to consider what they were doing when they were passing sentences, for, since judgement belonged to the Lord,

92 Romans 13:1: 'Let every person be subject to the governing authorities; for there is no authority except from God, and those authorities that exist have been instituted by God'.

93 Deuteronomy 16 (*sic*): 18–20: 'You shall appoint judges and officials [...], and they shall render just decisions for the people. You must not distort justice; you must not show partiality; and you must not accept bribes, for a bribe blinds the eyes of the wise and subverts the cause of those who are in the right. Justice, and only justice, you shall pursue'.

94 Ecclesiasticus (*sic*) 20:29: 'Favours and gifts blind the eyes of the wise'.

95 2 Chronicles 19:5–6: 'He appointed judges [...], and said to the judges: "Consider what you are doing, for you judge not on behalf of human beings but on the Lord's behalf; he is with you in giving judgement. Now, let the fear of the Lord be upon you; take care what you do, for there is no perversion of justice with the Lord your God, or partiality, or taking of bribes"'.

[Dii[r]] ſy ſöltind nit perſonen eren
Denn wie von jnen gricht wurde
alſo vff ſy ſelb käm die burde
Sy ſöltind ſich nach gotswort wenden
mit wyßheyt alle ding volenden
Darumb der Wyßman ſeyt *Sap. 6.*
über all ſtercke iſt wyßheyt
Denn es iſt fürwar nit kleyn
fürgſetzt ſin einer ganczen gmeyn
Wie wol von Gott iſt herren gwalt
hör was Gott künigen fürhalt
Ir Künig der erden loſend vf *Sap. 6.*
üwers volcks iſt ein groſſer huf
Ein wolgfallen habend jr darab
den gwalt von oben ab ich gab
Vwere werck ich erfar
erforſch üwer dancken gantz vnd gar
Do jr warend knecht im rych
habend jr geurteylt vnglych
Ir hieltend nit min grechtigkeyt
vnd thettend nit wie ich hatt gſeyt
Darumb ye mechtiger jr ſind gſin
also größer wirt üwer pyn
Darumb gotzforcht vnd wyßheyt *Prouer. 1.*
zierend wol ein oberkeyt
Vnd wo by gwalt gotßforcht nit iſt
am ſelben ort gwüß wyßheyt briſt
Das iſt volkumne grechtikeyt *Sapien. 19*
Gott kennen vnd thůn das er ſeyt
vnd iſt der grund der vnſterblicheyt.

[Dii[v]] **Bernhart Erenueſt.**
Das iſt wol ein ernſthafft wort
wie Paulus ſeyt an einem ort *Epheſ. 6.*
Da heyßt er / die jr ämpter verwaltind

1429 All ewere Wercke *F*

they were to be no respecters of persons. For just as they judged others, so they would have to bear the same burdens. They should turn to God's Word, and do everything with wisdom. This is why the wise man says[96] that wisdom is greater than all strength. For truly it is no small thing for lords to be at the head of their whole communities, even though their power comes from God. Hear what God says to kings: 'You kings of the earth, listen,[97] your people is a great host. You should take pleasure in this, for I have given you authority from above. I know your works, and search out your thoughts thoroughly. For though you were servants of the kingdom, you have judged unjustly. You have not upheld my justice, and have not done as I said. Therefore, the mightier you have been, the greater will be your punishment'. This is why the fear of God and wisdom[98] well adorn a person in authority. Where there is no fear of God in such a person, wisdom is also surely lacking. This is perfect righteousness,[99] to know God and to do as he says. And this is the basis of immortality.

Bernhart Erenuest

This is indeed a serious word, as Paul says at one point.[100] He tells you who hold office

96 Wisdom 7 (*sic*): 7–8: 'I called on God, and the spirit of wisdom came to me. I preferred her to sceptres and thrones, and I accounted wealth as nothing in comparison with her'.

97 Wisdom 6:2–5: 'Give ear, you that rule over multitudes, and boast of many nations. For your dominion was given you from the Lord, and your sovereignty from the Most High; he will search out your works and inquire into your plans. Because as servants of his kingdom you did not rule rightly, or keep the law, or walk according to the purpose of God, he will come upon you terribly and swiftly, because severe judgement falls on those in high places'.

98 Cf. Proverbs 1:7: 'The fear of the Lord is the beginning of knowledge: fools despise wisdom and instruction'.

99 Wisdom 15:3: 'For to know you is complete righteousness, and to know your power is the root of immortality'.

100 Ephesians 6:9: 'And, masters, do the same for them [slaves]. Stop threatening them, for you know that both of you have the same Master in heaven, and with him there is no partiality'.

das ſy ouch darin glychs haltind
Vnd heyßt ſy darumb halten glych
denn jr herr ſye im himmelrych
Der ſehe nit an die perſon
alſo Gwalt ſol glychem nachgon
Beſſer iſt ein wyſer jünglig *Ecclеſ. 5.*
denn ein thorechter alter künig
Welcher ander füren wil
vnd nit ſelb hat wyßheyt vil
Vnd iſt an witz ſelb präſthafft *Proue. 28.*
allein verfüren der ſelb ſchafft
Ein herr ſol nit ſin wie ein Löw *Ecclеſ. 4.*
das er die vnderthonen zerſtröw
Denn Gott vrteylt des armen ſach *Eſaiæ. 10.*
es zimpt nit das man mit gwalt mach
Vnd den dürfftigen vndertruck *Prou. 22.*
das Gott nit ouch ſin ſchwärdt zuck *Pſalm. 7.*
Welcher künig in warheyt richt
vnd vff die not des armen ſicht
So wirt ſin rich allweg bſton
in ewigkeyt nimmer abgon *Proue. 29.*
Wo man wittwen vnd weyſen bſchützt *Hiere. 5.*
des ſelb herſchen vor Gott nützt *Eſaiæ. 1.*
Denn eben wie der gwalt regiert
ſölich titel er ouch fürt
Gott im alten Teſtament
[Diii^{r}] Fürſten vnd volck Sodomitiſch nennt *Eſaie. 1.*
Warumb hat er das gthon?
ſy woltend gotzwort nit nachgon
Thettend allein das Gott nit hieß
darumb hatt er ab jnen verdrieß *Eſaiæ. 1.*
Sy opffretend jm Wider vnd Kelber
das hieß er nit / ſy thettends ſelber
Darumb er jnen opffren verbüt
vnd ſpricht / er well jn gar nüt
Ir opffer ein grüwel was / vor gotz gſicht

to treat people as equals; and the reason he commands you to treat all equally is that their lord in heaven is no respecter of persons. And so the authorities shouldn't be either. Better a wise young man[101] than a foolish old king. Whoever would lead others, yet does not himself have much wisdom, or many wits,[102] such a one can do nothing but lead others astray. A lord should not be like a lion,[103] making his subjects scatter before him. For God judges the case of the poor.[104] It is not right to do things by force, and to oppress the needy,[105] lest God also draw his sword.[106] If any king should reign in truth, and pay attention to the needs of the poor, his kingdom will endure forever, and never be destroyed.[107] Governance that protects widows and orphans[108] is of value before God.[109] For as the authorities rule, so will their title be. God in the Old Testament calls princes and people 'Sodomites'.[110] Why did he do this? Because they did not want to follow God's word, and did only what God had not commanded. Therefore he was angry with them. They offered sacrifices to him, rams and calves.[111] This he had not demanded; they did it on their own authority. So he forbade them to make sacrifices, and said he did not want them at all. Their sacrifices were an abomination in God's sight.

101 Ecclesiastes 4 (*sic*): 13: 'Better is a poor youth than an old but foolish king, who will no longer take advice'.

102 Cf. Proverbs 28:16: 'A ruler who lacks understanding is a cruel oppressor; but one who hates unjust gain will enjoy a long life'.

103 Cf. Ecclesiasticus (*sic*) 4:30: 'Do not be like a lion in your home'.

104 Isaiah 11 (*sic*): 4: 'But with righteousness he shall judge the poor'.

105 Proverbs 22:16: 'Oppressing the poor in order to enrich oneself, and giving to the rich, will lead only to loss'.

106 Psalm 7:12: 'If one does not repent, God will whet his sword'.

107 Proverbs 29:14: 'If a king judges the poor with equity, his throne will be established for ever'.

108 Jeremiah 5:28: 'They do not judge with justice the cause of the orphan, to make it proper, and they do not defend the rights of the needy'.

109 Isaiah 1:17 (see n. 74 above).

110 Isaiah 1:9–10: 'If the Lord of hosts had not left us a few survivors, we would have been like Sodom, and become like Gomorrah'.

111 Isaiah 1:11: '"What to me is the multitude of your sacrifices?", says the Lord. I have had enough of burnt-offerings of rams and the fat of fed beasts; I do not delight in the blood of bulls, or of lambs, or of goats"'.

hör zů nach welchem opffer Gott ſicht:
Werdend gereyniget vnd ſind reyn
das trifft den gwalt an mit der gmeyn
Hörend vf ſchantlich leben
lernend nach dem gůten ſtreben
Ir ſöllend nach gerechtigkeyt reyſen
recht richten armen witwen vnd weyſen
So wir ſölichs hettind thon
ghörſt was Gott wil von vns han?
Das wir bößthůn vfhörind
vnd wir allein zů jm kerind
Recht richten hört ouch zů dem gwalt
vnd das man ſich wie Gott ſagt halt
Wo das nit gſchicht / ſo ſpricht Gott
dfürſten ſind vß der dieben rott *Eſaie. 1.*
Denn ſy liebend all die gaben
der weyſen ſy nüt acht haben
Denn ein ſchnöder fürſt vnd herr *Prou. 30.*
wirt verglycht eym hungerigen Ber
Oder eym Löwen der da wüt
[Diii^{v}] es iſt not daß ſich ein fürſt hüt
vnd nit fräſs die vnderthonen
denn warlich Gott wird ſin nit ſchonen *Pſal. 13.*
Wo man die vnderthonen frißt *Pſalm. 9.*
dlenge der armen Gott nit vergißt
Es iſt kein gwallt vff erdtrich
der ſich Gottes gwalt verglych *Iob. 4.*
Gott der Herr fürcht niemants nit
eim yeden nach der that er gibt *Pſal. 106.*
ſin zorn er über die Fürſten ſchütt.

Růdolff Fürſichtig.

Edlen / Veſten / Wyſen Herren
darumb daß ſich puren weeren
Gegen üch / das iſt die vrſach

1493 wir] vns *F*

Hear rather what sort of sacrifice God does desire: 'Be cleansed and you will be pure'. This applies to the authorities and to the whole community. Cease your shameful way of life, learn to seek what is good. You should strive after righteousness, judging poor widows and orphans with justice. If we've done this, hear what God wants from us now: that we cease to do evil and turn only to him. Right judgement also belongs to the authorities, as does obeying what God says. Where that doesn't happen, God says that the princes belong to bands of thieves,[112] for they love bribes and pay no heed to the wise. For a base prince or lord is compared to a hungry bear or a raging lion.[113] A prince must guard himself against devouring his subjects, for truly God will not spare him if he does.[114] Anyone who devours his subjects will find that God will not forget the poor for ever.[115] There is no power on earth like God's.[116] The Lord God fears no one, but gives to each according to his deeds. He pours out his wrath on princes.[117]

Rudolff Fürsichtig

Noble, steadfast, wise lords; the reason why the farmers are arming themselves against you

112 Isaiah 1:23: 'Your princes are rebels and companions of thieves. Everyone loves a bribe and runs after gifts. They do not defend the orphan, and the widow's cause does not come before them'.

113 Proverbs 28 (*sic*): 15: 'Like a roaring lion or a charging bear is a wicked ruler over poor people'.

114 Cf. Psalm 14:6: 'You would confound the plans of the poor, but the Lord is their refuge'.

115 Psalm 9:18: 'For the needy shall not always be forgotten, nor the hope of the poor perish for ever'.

116 A summary of Eliphaz's argument in Job 4:17–21.

117 Psalm 107:40: 'He pours contempt on princes and makes them wander in trackless wastes'.

ſy lydend von üch groß vngemach
So nun Gott die ſelben hat geſtraafft
über üch gots zorn darumb nit ſchlaafft
Gott wil üch mit den puren tröuwen
den hund man offt ſchlacht vor dem löuwen
Arm lüt bſchwären hat ein Vee *Math. 23.*
die bſchetzend jr ye lenger ye mee
Es ſye vff land oder in ſtetten
wider üch ſchryend all propheten
Denckend der gſchicht des Roboam *3. Reg. 12.*
der (kybs) vmm ein teyl ſins rychs kam
Allein das er nit wolt nachlon
das vf was gſetzt vom Salomon
Iſt es müglich / laſſend etwas naach
entſitzend doch die gotsraach
[Div^{r}] Denn wo man arm lüt vndertruckt
darzů jre hüſer vnd äcker verſchluckt
Es wirt nit nachglon dlenge von Gott
gott rechet ouch den Naboth
Den Ieſabel das mördriſch wyb *3. Reg. 21.*
valſchlich bracht vmb ſin lyb
Darumb das er nit von jm gab
ſin wyngarten dem künig Achab
Gott rechet ouch deß Naboths ſeel
vnd ward das böß wyb Ieſabel
Gſtürtzt von eim fenſter obenab
die da was gſin ein hußfrouw Achab
Dhund fraſſend das wyb Ieſabel *4. Reg. 9.*
jn dem acker Ieſrael
Hörend was Iſaias ſpricht
Wee dem der böße gſatz vfricht *Eſaiæ. 10.*
Vnd ſchrybende ſchrybt vngrechtigkeyt /
das iſt allen gwaltigen gſeyt
Die mit gſatzten vndertruckend
daß ſich witwen vnd weyſen ſchmuckend
O wie übel werdend die bſton
ſo der tag jrer ſtraaff wirt kon

is that they are suffering great adversity at your hands. Now that God has punished them, his wrath is not slumbering in your case either. God wants to warn you through the peasants. Often the dog is slaughtered before the lion: oppressing the poor has a cost.[118] More and more of you are guilty of this, whether in the countryside or in towns. But all the prophets cry out against you. Think what happened to Rehoboam,[119] whose fighting lost him part of his kingdom, simply because he wouldn't follow what Solomon had set in place. If it's possible, cut the farmers some slack, and fear God's wrath. For oppressing the poor and swallowing up their houses and fields won't be tolerated by God for long. God also avenged Naboth, whom that murderous woman Jezebel falsely cheated of his life[120] because he would not surrender his vineyard to King Ahab. God also avenged Naboth's soul, and the evil woman Jezebel was pushed from an upper window, she who had been Ahab's wife. The dogs devoured the woman Jezebel[121] in the field of Jezreel. Hear what Isaiah says: 'Woe to him who imposes a bad law,[122] writing unrighteousness into law'. This is said to all who are in authority and oppress others with their laws, so that widows and orphans might bow down before them. O, how badly they will fare when the day of their punishment comes!

118 Cf. Matthew 23:4, 12: 'They tie up heavy burdens, hard to bear, and lay them on the shoulders of others [...] All who exalt themselves will be humbled, and all who humble themselves will be exalted'.

119 The story of Israel's rebellion against Rehoboam is in 1 Kings 12:1–24.

120 1 Kings 21:13–14: 'And the scoundrels brought a charge against Naboth in the presence of the people, saying, "Naboth cursed God and the king". So they took him outside the city, and stoned him to death. Then they sent to Jezebel, saying, "Naboth has been stoned; he is dead"'.

121 In 2 Kings 9:36–7 Elijah prophesies: 'In the territory of Jezreel the dogs shall eat the flesh of Jezebel; the corpse of Jezebel shall be like dung on the field in the territory of Jezreel, so that no one can say, "This is Jezebel"'.

122 Isaiah 10 (*sic*): 1–2: 'Ah, you who make iniquitous decrees, who write oppressive statutes, to turn aside the needy from justice and to rob the poor of my people of their right'.

Wo wirt von inen hilff begärt *Eſaiæ. 10.*
ſo ſy ouch vallend in dem ſchwärt?
Denn es wirt von gott erloubt
das der röuber ouch wärde broubt *Eſaiæ. 33.*
Dann wie all Herren ye hand ghuſet
alſo ward inen wider gluſet
Wo man nit nach gotswort richt
am ſelben ort nüt anders gſchicht
[Div^{v}] Denn das Gott zeletſt ſůcht wäg vnd ſtäg
daß Künig vnn volck wärd gfürt hinwäg *4. Reg. 25.*
Es iſt vaſt yetz der Herrſchafft ſitt
man fraget nach dem gotzwort nit
On vrſach es nit übel ſtadt
vnd allen Künigrychen abgadt
Darumb daß dHerrſchafft vnd die lüt
ſchühend ab keinen laſtren nüt
Eebruch iſt gmein by der Herrſchafft
füllery man ouch nit ſtraafft
Das ſind die zwo größten ſünd
mit hoffart / die man nit findt
Straaffte yetz Gott wie vorzyten
er wurde den Eebruch vßrüten
So bald einer Eebruch anfieng
dſtraaff der ſünd glych nachgieng.
Vorzyten kamend in einr Summ
vier vnd zwentzig tuſent menſchen vmm
Das gſchach von wegen vnluterkeyt *Nume. 25.*
Gott ſelb do zů Moyſe ſeyt
Nimm vnd henck dFürſten allſamen
Einer Zamri mit dem namen
hůryet / daß der Moyſes ſach
Der Phinees beyde erſtach *Pſal. 105.*
Das ſelb erſtechen gefiel do gott
Phinees kam in der prieſter rott
Thäte man yetz den Fürſten das

1556 dem] das *F* 1574 nit] auch *F* 1585 der] es *F*

Where will they seek help[123] when they too fall under the sword? For God permits a robber to be robbed.[124] Then, as has happened with all the lords in history, those who have destroyed others will themselves be destroyed. Wherever one does not judge according to God's Word, what happens is that eventually God will seek ways to remove the king and his people. It's now very much the custom of lords not to enquire after God's Word. Not without reason are things in a bad state and kingdoms crumbling, for rulers and people don't shy away from vice of any kind. Adultery is commonplace among the lords, and gluttony too goes unpunished. These are the two greatest sins, along with pride, that you can find. If God punished them now as he used to do, he would root out adultery as soon as someone began to commit it. The punishment would follow the sin directly. Previously twenty-four thousand people died in one go because of their lechery. God himself told Moses:[125] 'Take and hang the princes all together'. One, named Zimri, was busy with a whore, as Moses saw. Phinehas stabbed them both,[126] and his action pleased God.[127] Phinehas was one of the priests. If the princes were to be treated today

123 Isaiah 10:3–4: 'What will you do on the day of punishment, in the calamity that will come from far away? To whom will you flee for help, and where will you leave your wealth, so as not to crouch among the prisoners or fall among the slain?'.

124 Isaiah 33:1–3: 'Ah, you destroyer, who yourself have not been destroyed; you treacherous one, with whom no one has dealt treacherously! When you have ceased to destroy, you will be destroyed; and when you have stopped dealing treacherously, you will be dealt with treacherously'.

125 Numbers 25:1, 4: 'While Israel was staying at Shittim, the people began to have sexual relations with the women of Moab [...] The Lord said to Moses, "Take all the chiefs of the people, and impale them in the sun before the Lord, in order that the fierce anger of the Lord may turn away from Israel"'.

126 That is, Zimri and the Midianite woman in whose company he is found (see Numbers 25:6–8). Phinehas's action causes God to relieve Israel of a punitive plague which (as Numbers 25:9 states) has killed 24,000.

127 Cf. Psalm 106:28–31: 'Then they attached themselves to the Baal of Peor, and ate sacrifices offered to the dead; they provoked the Lord to anger with their deeds, and a plague broke out among them. Then Phinehas stood up and interceded, and the plague was stopped. And that has been reckoned to him as righteousness, from generation to generation'.

wie vorzyten ſitt was
Man hette nit ſo vil Edel lüt
man thůt inen aber gar nüt
[Dv[r]] Gmein volck loufft wie ein ramlige ků *Oſeæ. 4.*
hörend was ſagt Oſeas darzů
Vff erden iſt kein barmhertzigkeyt
keiner dwarheyt dem andren ſeyt
Todſchlag / Eebruch / vnd Diebſtal
hand überhand gnommen überal
Darumb wirt das Erdtrich bkrenckt
all ynwoner mit kummer bhenckt
Ghörſt min Iuncker Ludeman
wo har in dwelt kummt kyb vnd ſpan?
Darumb daß volck iſt glych als prieſter /
ye einer denn der ander läbt wüſter
Dauid mit dem Eebruch ſchůff
das man jm ſine wyber ouch bſchlůff
Vnd můßt krieg han all ſin tag
darumb das er by Berſabe lag *2. Reg. 11.*
Denn welcher bſchlafft eins andren wyb / *Deut. 27.*
jſt verflůcht mit ſeel vnd lyb *1. Cor. 5.*
Hörend wäm vns Gott verglycht
einer hůren die vom bůlen wycht *Hiere. 3.*
Noch ein ſünd iſt ſo grülich
vor gott / die brucht man doch ſo ſchülich /
Das es nit ein wunder wer
ob vndergienge land vnd Herr
Die iſt S. Viltis kranckheyt
Iſt nun ſo gmein wyt vnd preyt
Wo regiert die Füllery
wenig witz geſpürt man da by
Vergeben nit der Wyßman büt
daß dKünig mit wyn ſich füllind nüt
[Dv[v]] Vnd wo da ſye die trunckenheyt *Proue. 31.*
werdind alle heimliche ding gſeyt
Vnd wirt der armen ſach mißhandlet
wo man in füllery wandlet *Eſaiæ. 32.*

as they once were, we wouldn't have so many nobles left. However, we don't treat them like this. Instead, the common people run about like an unruly cow.[128] Hear what Hosea says about this: 'There is no mercy on earth, and no one speaks the truth to his neighbour. Murder, adultery, and theft are common everywhere. This is why the earth is stricken, and all its inhabitants are laden with care'. Juncker Ludeman, do you hear where quarrels and tensions come from? It's because the people have become just like the priests: each lives more dissolutely than the other. The result of David's adultery was that another man slept with his wives too. He was at war all his days because he slept with Bathsheba.[129] For whoever beds another man's wife[130] is cursed in body and soul.[131] Hear whom God compares us to: a whore who has given up whoring.[132] One other sin is as heinous as this in the sight of God, which is committed so often that it wouldn't be a surprise if lords and country fell away because of it. This is St Vitus' dance,[133] which is now so widespread wherever gluttony reigns. There's not much sense to it. In vain the wise man bids the king not to fill himself with wine; and where there is drunkenness,[134] every secret thing will be spoken. The cause of the poor will be mishandled where people live gluttonously.[135]

128 Hosea 4:16: 'Like a stubborn heifer, Israel is stubborn'.

129 The story occupies all of 2 Samuel 11.

130 Deuteronomy 27:20, 22, 23: 'Cursed be anyone who lies with his father's wife [...] Cursed be anyone who lies with his sister, whether the daughter of his father or the daughter of his mother [...] Cursed be anyone who lies with his mother-in-law'.

131 1 Corinthians 5:1, 5: 'It is actually reported that there is sexual immorality among you, and of a kind that is not found even among pagans: for a man is living with his father's wife! [...] you are to hand this man over to Satan for the destruction of the flesh, so that his spirit may be saved on the day of the Lord'.

132 The image of the formerly idolatrous Israel as a semi-penitent whore being invited by God to return to him dominates all of Jeremiah 3.

133 See n. 312 on the *Concilium*, p. 213 above.

134 Cf. Proverbs 31:4: 'It is not for kings, O Lemuel, it is not for kings to drink wine, for rulers to desire strong drink; or else they will drink and forget what has been decreed, and will pervert the rights of all the afflicted'.

135 Cf. Isaiah 32:7: 'The villainies of villains are evil; they devise wicked devices to ruin the poor with lying words, even when the plea of the needy is right'.

Welcher füllery erkennt
ſol nit werden ein fürſt gnennt
Ouch ſol man jnn nit hören
das thůt Eſaias leren
Darumb ſol ein rechten fürſten
allein nach der grechtigkeyt dürſten
Wo wyßheyt iſt / ſo fält es nit
grechtigkeyt iſt ouch damit
Einer ſol nit ſin ein herr
des er ſich ab armen lüten ner
Vnd tuſſe wie ein Löw vff roub *Pſalm. 9.*
arm lüt mißbruch als ſy er toub
Welcher ein röuber frömbds gůts iſt *Proue. 19.*
wie vil er roubet / noch allweg briſt
Micheas der heylig prophet ſpricht
wee dem der nach boßheyt ficht
Vnd trachtet nach böſem anſchlag
der jrret by liechtem heyteren tag
Sy hand mit gwalt dem armen gnon *Mich. 2.*
des er iſt vmb huß vnd hof kon
Engſtend jnn vmb ſin gůt vnd erb
ghörſt was den gmeinen man verderb?
So man jm ſins nimpt mit gwalt
das ſelb für eygen gůt bhalt
Der gadt nit zů dem rych gotz yn *Hiere. 18.*
welcher etwas nimpt mit gwalt hin
[Dvi^{r}] Dauid ouch den Herren fragt
von wäm das rych gotts wurd erjagt
Spricht er / Welcher on mackel hie gadt *Pſalm. 14.*
vnd den nächſten on kümbret ladt
Vnd nit mit bſchiß den nächſten trügt
die warheyt ſeyt vnd nit lügt
Vnd ſin gelt nit an wůcher gibt
der ſelb wie ein berg veſt blybt

1637 tuſſe] lauſter *F*

No one who lives in gluttony should be called a prince, and neither should one listen to him. This is Isaiah's teaching. Therefore a true prince should thirst only after righteousness. Where there is wisdom there is also righteousness, without fail. No one should be a lord who lives off the poor or pursues them like a lion does his prey,[136] violating them even as he rages against them. No one who steals the goods of a stranger, no matter how much he takes, will ever have enough.[137] The holy prophet Micah says: 'Woe to the one who does evil, and strives after wickedness. This one is lost in the clear light of day'.[138] They have taken from the poor man by force, leaving him without home or farm. They worry him about his property and his inheritance. Do you hear what harms the common man? Taking his property by force, and holding it as your own. No one who takes something by force will enter the kingdom of heaven.[139] David also asks the Lord who will attain to the kingdom of God. He replies, 'The one who lives blamelessly,[140] does not trouble his neighbour or deceive him with guile, but rather speaks the truth and does not lie, nor lend his money at usury – he will remain steadfast as a mountain'.

136 Psalm 10:9: 'They lurk in secret like a lion in its covert; they lurk that they may seize the poor; they seize the poor and drag them off in their net'.

137 We cannot discern the relevance of Proverbs 19 here.

138 Micah 2:1–2: 'Alas for those who devise wickedness and evil deeds on their beds! When the morning dawns, they perform it, because it is in their power'.

139 There is no specific correspondence to Jeremiah 18, but much of it concerns God's judgement on his enemies.

140 Psalm 15:1–5: 'O Lord, who may abide in your tent? Who may dwell on your holy hill? Those who walk blamelessly, and do what is right, and speak the truth from their heart; who do not slander with their tongue, and do no evil to their friends, nor take up a reproach against their neighbours; in whose eyes the wicked are despised, but who honour those who fear the Lord; who stand by their oath even to their hurt; who do not lend money at interest, and do not take a bribe against the innocent. Those who do these things will never be moved'.

Dauid leert mit dem pſalmen hie
welcher ſälig well ſin / alſo er thüe
Denn es zimpt nit einer herrſchafft
das ſy regier vß eygner krafft
Das vngrechtigkeit ſye gſatz vnd ſtercke *Sapien. 2.*
ſunder das ſy vfmercke
Vnd regier nach Gottes gheyß
nit das ſy ſtell nach der armen ſchweyß
kein beßren radt ich nit weyß.

Nach dem die Herren des grichts ſich vnderredt habend / vnd beider parth handlung wol entſcheyden / ward der Sentenz geben vnd gleſen von dem Stattſchryber wie nach volget:

Iohann Schydman.
Dieweyl nach Gottes ordnung zimpt
das man nit acht der perſon nimpt *Epheſ. 6.*
Sunder glych rychen vnd armen richt
iſt nun vff vergangne gſchicht
Beyder parth / Edlen vnd Puren
[Dvi[v]] erkennt / drumb laß ſich nyemant duren
Das fürhin ſöll die Purſchafft
an allen orten ſäßhafft
Sich halten gantz nach alter ordnung
vnd zinſen fry nach gwalts fordrung
Deßglychen wie der gwalt anſäch
ſthür vnd Zähenden ouch gſchäch
Vnd ſich ouch by lyb hütind
vnd nit wider gwalt wütind *Exodi. 22.*
Gott der Herr hat ſelb gſeyt
man ſöll nit ſchmähen Oberkeyt
Dem knecht zimpt nit das er ſich ſtell *Prou. 19.*
über den Herren herſchen well
Man ſol ouch Oberkeyt nit ſchaden
oder ſunſt mit ſtreychen bladen *Prou. 17.*
Sunder das man handle mit gedult
dardurch wird gunſt von fürſten bſchult *Prou. 25.*

David teaches with this Psalm, 'Whoever would be righteous, do likewise'. For it isn't right for a ruler to rule in his own strength, for unrighteousness to be the law and power.[141] Rather, he should take heed and rule according to God's commands, not seeking to profit from the sweat of the poor. I know of no better advice.

After the lords of the court had discussed together and decided between the cases put by both parties, the verdict was given and read by the town clerk, as follows:

Johann Schydman[142]

Since God's decree requires us not to be respecters of persons,[143] but rather to judge the rich and the poor alike, the statements of both parties, nobles and farmers, have now been heeded. So let no one complain if, from now on, the farmers stay in their places, living entirely according to the old order, and paying interest according to the demands of the authorities. Likewise, they should pay taxes and tithes as it is fitting for the authorities to receive them, and they should at all events stop themselves raging against them again.[144] God himself has said that we shouldn't scorn the authorities. It's not right for a servant to wish to be above his masters and govern them.[145] Also, you should not harm authority, lest you be punished.[146] Rather, you should be patient in your dealings, for this is how you earn the favour of princes.

141 Wisdom 2:10–11: 'Let us oppress the righteous poor man; let us not spare the widow or regard the grey hairs of the aged. But let our might be our law of right, for what is weak proves itself to be useless'.

142 The name means one who decides or arbitrates, and points to the essential even-handedness of this 'Sentenz'.

143 Ephesians 6:9 (see n. 100 above).

144 Exodus 22 deals with various aspects of social responsibility, and especially the need for restitution when property rights have been infringed; but it is not an obviously relevant passage here.

145 Proverbs 19:10: 'It is not fitting for a fool to live in luxury, much less for a slave to rule over princes'.

146 Cf. Proverbs 17:11: 'Evil people seek only rebellion, but a cruel messenger will be sent against them'.

Welcher iſt mit vndult bladen *Prou. 19.*
der ſol lyden billich ſchaden
Was er denn roubt von hab vnd gůt
billich ers wider an dſtatt thůt
Ir Herren lůgend das jr leerind
das gůt ſye / vnd dem böſen weerind
Darumb ſind jr gſetzt an das ort
das jr richtind nach Gots wort
Ouch darby witwen / weyſen bſchützind
nit nun allein jre güter nützind
Darumb das gott nit zů üch ſag *Hiere. 5.*
ſy bladend ſich nit der witwen klag
Ein Künig der die armen richt
[Dvii^r] vnd des dürfftigen not anſicht
In ewigkeyt ſo bſtadt ſin thron *Prou. 29.*
wie wol wirt der vor Gott bſton?
Darumb jr herren ſind grecht vnd veſt
thůnd den armen lüten das beſt
Sind nit zeſtreng / ruch vnd wütig
ſunder wie künig David gütig
Do jnn der Abſalon durchächt
Semei den Dauid ſchmächt
Vnd ſprach / Alſo gſchicht dir nun *2. Reg. 16.*
das Abſolon din eygner ſun
Geben werde din rych
denn du haſt des glych
Künig Saul von dem rych glupfft
darumb wirſtu ouch verſchupfft
Du biſt ein Tüfliſch blůtig man
des namend ſich Dauids knecht an
Do ſy jnn hortend alſo trouwen
wolt jm einer das houpt abhouwen
Hörend zů wie Dauid ſprach
do er der knechten willen ſach
Lond jnn gon / vnd thůnd jm nüt
denn er thůt das jm gott büt
Diewyl jms denn gott botten het

An impatient person[147] will rightly come to harm.[148] It's right that he should return what he's stolen. You lords, be sure to teach what is good and avoid what is bad. This is why you have been given your position, that you may judge according to God's Word. By the same token you should protect widows and orphans, not simply exploiting their possessions, so that God will not say of you:[149] 'They don't hear the widow's lament'. A king who judges the poor and sees the need of the needy, his throne will be established forever;[150] and how will he stand before God? Therefore, you lords, be just and firm. Do what is best by the poor people. Don't be too strict, rough or angry. Rather, be compassionate, as King David was when Absalom persecuted him. Shimei spoke ill of David, saying: 'Now the same thing is happening to you: Absalom, your own son,[151] will be given your kingdom, because you did the same in taking the kingdom from King Saul. For this reason you also will be deposed. You are a devilishly bloody man'. David's servants were poised to cut off his head when they heard him speak these words. Listen to what David said, although he knew his servants' wishes: 'Let him go, and do not harm him, for he is doing what God commands him. And since God has directed him,

147 Proverbs 25:15: 'With patience a ruler may be persuaded, and a soft tongue can break bones'.

148 Cf. Proverbs 19:19: 'A violent-tempered person will pay the penalty'.

149 Jeremiah 5:28: 'They do not judge with justice the cause of the orphan, to make it prosper, and they do not defend the rights of the needy'.

150 Proverbs 29:14: 'If a king judges the poor with equity, his throne will be established for ever'.

151 2 Samuel 16:8: 'The Lord has avenged on all of you the blood of the house of Saul, in whose place you have reigned; and the Lord has given the kingdom into the hand of your son Absalom. See, disaster has overtaken you; for you are a man of blood'.

wär dörfft fragen warumb ers thet?
Min eygner ſun mich doch durchächt
was ligt denn dran das er mich ſchmächt
Ich hoff das hütt noch gott der herr
die ſchmach in benedyung keer.
Alſo jr herren thůnd des glych
[Dvii^{v}] ſo werdend gmeeret üwere rych
Laſſend den armen lüten nach
ſind nit ſo grimm mit der raach
Denn ſo Gott den Semei hieß
flůchen / vnd David nach ließ
Söllend jr darby billich dencken
gott der werd üch lützel ſchencken
Darby jr Puren denckend ouch
wiewol Semei do entflouch
Der den Dauid geſcholten hat
das bſtůnd ouch biß vff ſin ſtatt
Salomon Künig Dauids ſun
als er ward künig deß rychs nun *3. Reg. 2.*
Gdacht er noch an des vatters ſchmach
hörend was der künig ſprach
Semei / gang heim in din huß
fürhin gangiſt nit mee druß
Denn ſo bald du wirſt druß gon
wirſt du vmb din läben kon
Semei ſprach: Das iſt recht
was min herr büt / ſol thůn ſin knecht
Vnd bleib jm huß ein lange zyt
eins mals er daruß rit
Das ward kund thon dem Salomon
als bald Semei was wider kon
Von Maacha dem Künig Geth
hörend was der Salomon thett
Sprach zů jm: Hatt ich dir nit gſeyt
blyb inn / vnd nit vſs dim huß reyt?
Do ſpracheſt du: Es gfiel dir wol
[Dviii^{r}] vnd haſts nit gthon / darumb yetz ſol

who dares ask why he did this? If my only son can persecute me, what does it matter if this man speaks ill of me?' I hope that the Lord God will still protect those who turn a curse into a blessing. Therefore if you lords do likewise, your kingdoms will be multiplied. Forgive the poor, and don't be so furious in your vengeance. For in the same way that God called upon Shimei to curse, and David forgave him, so you should think that God will give you very little. You farmers, think on this too. Although Shimei escaped after berating David, this lasted only until Solomon, David's son, became king in his father's stead.[152] He still remembered his father's shame. Listen to what King Solomon said: 'Shimei, go back to your house and never leave it again. For as soon as you go out, you will die'. Shimei said: 'What my lord commands is right. His servant will do this'. And he stayed in his house a long time. But once, when he rode out, Solomon was told about it. As soon as Shimei came back from visiting Maacah King of Gath,[153] hear what Solomon did. He said to him: 'Hadn't I told you, "Stay at home, and do not ride out?"'. And you said that this pleased you well; yet you didn't act upon it. Therefore your wickedness,

152 Solomon's dealings with Shimei are described in 1 Kings 2:36–46.

153 Shimei goes to Gath in order to fetch two of his slaves who have fled thither. The king's name is in fact 'Achish son of Maacah' (1 Kings 2:39–40).

Vergolten werden din boßheyt
die dir din eygen hertz ſeyt
Weyſt wie du haſt mim vatter thon?
er můßt erſt daa vmbs läben kon
Alſo boßheit ſich nit verſchlaafft
ob ſchon Gott nitt von ſtundan ſtraafft
Dennocht kumpt zeletſt das zyt
daß eim dStraff vor der türen ligt
Drumb Herrſchafft ſtell vff frid vnn růw
purſchafft du ouch des glychen thů
Werdend ir nit von ſünden lon
ſo wirt Künig vnd volck zgrund gon *1. Reg. 12.*
Darumb Frumme purſchafft
biſt du ſchon Zinßhafft
Es ſchadt dir nit an dim glouben
hüt dich nun fürhin vor rouben
Laſs yedem ſins vnzergenckt
denn es wirt dir von Gott nit gſchenckt
Deßglychen Adel hüt dich ouch
ſpann den bogen nit zehouch
Damitt dir nit zerſchnell die Senn
ſo Gott dich ſtraafft / weyſt ſelb nit wenn /
Denn ſo man zvil vmmtrybt die wyden
der knebel bricht / mags nit erlyden
Nabuchodonoſor ouch was
Ein züg deß zorn Gots darumb / das
jung vnd alt / künig vnd Herr
warend all gotsuorcht lär
Zů ſtraaff ward Nabuchodonoſor gſandt
[Dviiiv] der ſelb Hieruſalen verbrannt *2. Par. 39.*
Was nit ward mit dem ſchwärdt berürt
das ward in Babylonem gfürt
Zů letſt er ſelb erläbt / das *Daniel. 4.*
er höuw wie ein rind aß
Ich ſag üch darumb vor die gſchicht
daß ſich ein yeder darnach richt
Es iſt ſchwär arm lüt beladen

which your own heart bears witness to, will now be atoned for. Do you know what you did to my father?' Only then did Shimei have to die. So wickedness does not fall asleep, even if God does not punish at the very hour it occurs. The time will eventually come when punishment stands at the door. Therefore lords, establish peace and quietness. Farmers, do the same. If you don't stop sinning, king and people will perish together.[154] Therefore, good farmers, if you owe anyone interest, this doesn't damage your faith. From now on, stop yourselves robbing. Leave everyone's possessions undisturbed; they haven't been given to you by God. Similarly, nobles, watch yourselves. Don't overstretch the bow, so that the string breaks on you and God punishes you, you know not when. For if you pull the bow's wood around too much, the stick breaks, and it won't be able to take the strain. Nebuchadnezzar also demonstrated the wrath of God because, young and old, king and lord, no one feared God. So Nebuchadnezzar was sent as a punishment, and he burned down Jerusalem. Whatever wasn't destroyed by the sword was taken away into Babylon. In the end, he himself found out what it was like to eat hay like an ox.[155] I tell you this story so that you might live by it. It's hard to lay burdens on the poor,

154 1 Samuel 12:25: 'But if you still do wickedly, you shall be swept away, both you and your king'.

155 Daniel 4:33: 'Immediately the sentence was fulfilled against Nebuchadnezzar. He was driven away from human society, ate grass like oxen, and his body was bathed with the dew of heaven, until his hair grew as long as eagles' feathers and his nails became like birds' claws'.

Herr ſin mit eines anderen ſchaden
Pur Eygennutz kumpſt du hein
verkünd das diner gmein
Sy ſölle ſich recht yetzzmal lyden
gott bitten vmb gmeinen friden
Der Oberkeyt ouch ghorſam ſin
biß gott nemme all bſchwärd hin
Denn es yetz zmal nit müglich ſy
das man wärde Zins fry
Zinß ſind ſo vaſt yngwürtzt
es wurd ee dwelt gar vmb gſtürtzt
Ee man ſy möcht vßrüten
vnder pfaffen und Edel lüten
Darumb bätte Pur vnd Edelman
daß gott vns welle ſehen an
Mitteylen ſin barmhertzigkeyt
das wir kummind zů der fryheyt
Die gott dem verheyſſen hat
der ſinem gheyß nach gadt /
gott die ſinen nit verladt.

Weybel Rychart.
Wo iſt deß geyſtlichen ſtands bott
[Ei͛] har gſandt von der gwychten rott?
Der thüge ouch ſin klag dar
ee Eygennutz heim far
harfür du Bott der pfaffen ſchar.

Doctor Murnar.
Ein Eſel hat in kurtzer zyt
ein büchlin gſchiſſen das iſt wyt
vßkummen / vnd kund yederman
das bůch er an einer kunckel ſpan
Im ſelben büchlin er begryfft
ſiben Doctor der heylgen gſchrifft
Mit denen hat der Lutriſch keyb
ein faßnachtſpil vnd ſölich töub

to be a lord at someone else's expense. When you go home, Pur Eygennutz, tell your community that it's right for them to suffer at this time, and to pray to God for a general peace. They should also obey the authorities, until God resolves all their complaints. For at this time it isn't possible to be free from interest payments. They are so deeply rooted that the world would have to be turned upside down before they could be dug out from among the priests and noblemen. Therefore let both farmer and nobleman pray that God will look upon us and pour out his mercy on us, that we may come into the freedom that God has promised to those who follow his commands. God does not forsake his own.

Weybel Rychart
Where is the envoy of the clergy, sent here by the ordained mob? Let him also present his complaint before Eygennutz goes home. Step forward, envoy of the priestly band.

Doctor Murner
A donkey quickly shat out a little book that has spread far and wide, and is now known to everyone.[156] This book he span on his distaff. In it he attacks seven doctors of the holy Scriptures. This Lutheran ruffian makes them into characters in a carnival play,[157] and all kinds of madness go out of them.

156 Murner is referring to the *Concilium*, to which he had already published his *Responsio*. Eckstein subsequently uses this accusation of asinine stupidity to his own advantage, by presenting himself in the guise of Balaam's ass – and hence as a 'wise fool' character of the type favoured by Erasmus and other Humanists.

157 The notion of Eckstein's dialogues containing theatrical elements is here briefly revived, and for the only time (in either text) in relation to the *Concilium*. Not that Murner's views are exactly privileged, of course.

Das es gantz iſt über dmut
er iſt ein Kätzer in der hut
Ia er vnd all ſins glychen
die von dem glouben abwychen
Er hats frylich darumb thon
gwänt jm werde antwurt von jnen kon
Der Lutriſch hippenbůb hat gfält
er ſol von mir nit werden zellt
So gleert / das ich jm antwurt geb
vnd ſinem Schyßbůch widerſtreb
Denn er iſt nit wärdt ein mans
das jm nun antwurt geb ein ganß
So ich ſchon lang mit jm ſtryt
kem ich dauon on bſchiſſen nüt
Iſt es nit ein blůtige ſchand
diſe kätzer hand all Tütſch land
[Ei^{v}] Verfürt mit jrem valſchen leeren
wie jr werdend harnach hören
Sy hand nüt vff dem Sacrament
lützel man zů der Mäſſz rent
Die verfürt kätzriſch rott
hat nüt vff der Vätter bott
Sy gebend nüt mee vmb den Ban
für dſeelen wends nit Grebnuß han
Der Heilgen iſt nun gar vergeſſen
nüt denn am Frytag fleyſch eſſen
Sy faſtend nit / vnd wend nit bychten
ouch haſſend ſy all gwychten
Hand nüt vff Wychwaſſer / noch Saltz
nyemant denn dem Tüfel gfaltz
Bilder ſtürmen / zierd verkouffen
vnd einander dhüſer durchlouffen
Das iſt alles Kätzer art
welcher baß mag ſich nit ſpart
Alſo nüt in den Templen blybt
ſiben Sacrament man vßtrybt
der Luthriſch Eſel wider die ſchrybt.

He really goes beyond the pale. He's a living heretic – he and all like him, who fall away from the faith. Of course he did it for the specific purpose that people would answer him. The Lutheran nincompoop[158] was wrong in this. I don't intend to regard him as educated enough to warrant an answer. I'm not going to fight against his book of shit. He doesn't even merit being answered by a goose. Because even if I did fight with him for a long time, I wouldn't get away without being deceived. Isn't it a great shame that these heretics have led astray all the German lands with their false teaching? As you will hear hereafter, they don't care for the sacrament, and don't like going to Mass. The crowd of heretics, having been led astray, pay no heed to the commands of the fathers. They're no more respectful of the ban, and don't want to have funeral services for the dead. They've entirely forgotten the saints. Not only do they eat meat on Fridays, but they don't even fast at all, and won't make confession. They also hate all who are ordained. They don't care for holy water or salt. It pleases no one but the devil to destroy images, to sell off church ornaments, or to ransack other people's houses. All this is typical of the heretics. If anyone can do better, he shouldn't spare himself. So there's nothing left in the temple. They've driven out the seven sacraments. The Lutheran donkey writes against them.

158 Eckstein's Murner consistently carries through the conceit (implied by the title of the *Responsio*) that the author of the *Concilium* was a Lutheran.

Weybel Rychart.
Wo mag nun der ſelb Eſel ſin
der dir alſo vßrüfft den wyn?
Wär er hie das er dir entſpräch
villicht er einanders jäch
Ich gloub es ſy Balaams Eßli
Murnar hett lieber ein Barnößli
Doch ſye gſin wär er well
[Eii^{r}*]* ich wölt wär er ein gůt gſell
Das er yetz an dich käm
ſich diner klag annäm
So ſähe man doch wär er wer
ich gloubte ſchier er ſye nit fer
Eſel wo biſt? dine yſen vſkeer.

Balaams Eſel.
Murnar diewyl du vff mich ſitzſt
wirt dir denn din beyn zerkniſt *Nume. 22.*
Wie ouch gſchach dem Balaam
der ſin gſchäfft wie du zhanden nam
Du biſt ouch zwüſchend dmuren gfürt
ein mur dir din beyn anrürt
Die iſt gwüß buwen von dem gſteyn
dauon keiner keiner kumpt on gletzt heyn
Vnd du wirſt ee zů ſtucken gon
ee dich der Engel werd für lon
Du haſt yetz mengen ſturm ghalten
dmur die blybt noch vnzerſpalten
Du biſt jr vil zů ſchwach in dharr
darumb heyſtu ouch der Muurnar
Riß Eck vnd du thůnd nit wyter
denn wie ein fuler holtzſchyter
Der allein die wecken ſteckt
ſchlacht nit daruf / das holtz nit kleckt
Ir hand die wecken gſetzt yetz lang
gelt wo das holtz vfgang?
Schafft / jr ſchlahend nit vff dwecken

Weybel Rychart
Now where can this donkey be, the one who's called forth all this bile in you? If he were here to answer you, perhaps he'd say something different. I think he must be Balaam's ass, though Murner would rather he was a little farm donkey. But, wherever he may have been, I'd be glad if he would kindly come forward now and address your complaint. Then we'd see who he is. I'm sure I think he can't be far away. Where are you, donkey? Pick up your irons!

Balaam's Ass
Murner, if you insist on sitting on my back, be careful or you'll scrape your legs – as happened to Balaam,[159] who, like you, took his affairs into his own hands. You are likewise being carried between two walls. The wall that's touching your leg is surely made of stone. No one comes away from it unscathed. And you'll be shot to pieces before the angel lets you pass. You've already made many attacks on the wall, but it's still standing.[160] You're far too feeble-minded to knock it down. That's why you're called Murner. Giant Eck[161] and you can do no more than a lazy woodcutter, who only drives a wedge into his wood, but doesn't really hit it, so that the wood doesn't break. You drove your wedge in a long time ago. What does it matter what happens to the wood? Don't bang on the badge, as you would normally do:

159 The episode of Balaam's ass is related in Numbers 22:22–30.

160 Eckstein is playing repeatedly on the fact that Murner's name comprises 'mur', meaning 'wall', and 'nar(r)', meaning 'fool'.

161 Johann Eck: see n. 113 on the *Concilium* (p. 99 above).

ja gieng es vf mit erſchrecken
[Eii^{v}] Das wär üwer beider fůg
neyn / das holtz iſt üch vil zeklůg
Nüt anders thůnd jr denn touben
kätzren all die an Gott glouben
Das iſt üwer gröſte kunſt
die kumpt ouch gwüß nun vß verbunſt
Wie du Murnar vff mich klagſt
darzů mir dieb vnd röuber ſagſt
Nempſt mich ein wild thier on vernunfft
wolan du haſt ein Schölmen zunfft
Ouch vor etlichen jaren gmacht
die ſelb hat mich geurſacht
Denn du hatteſt eines vergeſſen
der iſt dir doch als nach gſeſſen
Do du ſchribeſt fürt er dfäder
trůgend ein par ſchůch von gouch läder
Wie darffſtu mich ein dieb ſchelten?
ich ſol dem Wingersheim nüt gelten
Ouch ſchilltſt du mich Appoſtatam
min läbtag ich nye gen Trier kam
Ich lüff nye vß keiner Prouintz
vnnd bzalt nye mit louffenberger müntz
Du haſt mich ſunſt vaſt übel gſchent
ich darff aber gen Straßburg in din Conuent
Gang mit mir / man vnſer wartet
weyſt wie man dir eineſt gartet?
Din Badſtüblin iſt zerbrochen
gang mit mir / Magdalen můß vns kochen
Wir wöllends dim brůder Hanſen nit ſagen
wir wurdind ſunſt all beyd gſchlagen

1921 verbunſt] vergunſt *F*

no, the wood is far too clever for you. All you can do is to rage and to label as heretics those who believe in God. This is your greatest skill, which surely stems from resentment. Murner, as you complain against me, calling me a thief and a robber, and a wild animal without understanding, don't forget that, several years ago, you yourself created a 'guild of rogues'.[162] It was this book that inspired me, because you'd left someone out, one who was sitting so close to you that, while you were writing, he was holding the pen. He wears a pair of shoes made from fool's leather. How can you call me a thief? I mean nothing to Wingersheim.[163] Also you scold me for being an apostate, but I've never been anywhere near Trier in all my life.[164] I never ran away from any province, and never paid with Lauffenberg money.[165] You've done me much wrong in other ways too, yet I can go to your monastery in Strasbourg.[166] Come with me, they're waiting for us. Do you know how people once treated you? Your bathroom is all broken up.[167] Come with me, Magdalen will cook for us.[168] We won't tell your brother Hans, or we shall both be beaten.[169]

162 'Schelmenzunft': the title of one of Murner's books.

163 A reference to Murner's enemy Hans Wingersheim OFM, who had accused Murner of malpractice when Guardian of the Strasbourg Franciscans, and with whom Eckstein almost certainly did have nothing to do.

164 According to Vögelin (n. 3–4, p. 159), Murner himself *had* spent time in Trier, and had made himself technically guilty of apostasy, in Cracow in 1499, by renouncing his monastic calling in order to read for a bachelor's degree.

165 The precise allusion is unclear, but Lauffenberg (Canton Aargau) was a market town and trading centre, conveniently placed between Zurich and Basle.

166 As Murner was prevented from doing, following the dissolution of the Strasbourg monasteries by the newly reformed authorities early in 1525.

167 An allusion to Murner's *Badenfart*, in which the Church is compared to a bathhouse in which Christians bathe.

168 This person is unidentifiable; but, especially since Murner had no sister of the name, 'Magdalen' inevitably suggests a woman of questionable morals.

169 A reference to a case in January 1522, which culminated in Murner's brother Hans physically attacking the infamous Wolf brothers and three other clergymen in the cemetery of a church in Strasbourg – for having, as he believed, 'designs on a woman he called his kinswoman but whom the Wolfs called his "good little whore"... This notorious case combined clerical concubinage, clerical crime, clerical violence, all protected by the web of clerical immunities

[Eiii r] Ich ſölt ſunſt nit mit dir gon
denn du haſt mir nit darnach thon
Ich will yetz dinen ſchonen
dir nit / wie du verdient haſt / lonen
Wie dorffteſt nun ſo kün ſin
daß du kätzretiſt min büchlin?
Du haſt ein groſſes gſchrey gfürt
aber nie kein ſpruch angrerürt
Biſt du nun ſo hoch geleert
vnd haſt nie keinen vmbkeert
Biſt Doctor trium Lectionum
biß friſch / keer mir nun ein vmb
So wil ich dich für ein Helden han
nun nims an dhand / vnd biß der man
Ia ſprichſt / ich ſye im vil znider
das mir von dir wärd antwurt wider
Das ſelb ich dir vaſt gern gloub /
was ſols aber das einer toub?
Zů aller zyt ein ding nun ſchilt
vnd zügets nit / das ſelb grad gilt
Als da man Chriſtum ſelbs ſchalt
das ſelb ich dir ouch fürhalt
Iſts ſach das ich kätzriſch gſchriben han?
ſo bzüg das yetz / vnd biß der man
Han ich aber recht gſchriben?
warumb haſts nit laſſen darby blyben?
Ia züg ein ſpruch der Kätzeriſch ſy
vnd denn mich für ein kätzer vsſchry
Du wirſt nit abthůn ein Artickel
hettiſt ſchon ein ſtächlinen bickel
[Eiii v] Vnd ſölte dir din madenſack brechen
mit liegen wirſt Gotzwort nit rechen
Denn du trybſt vil vngſchickter wort
die ſetz ich ein teyl vff ein ort
Gott lone dir drumb zů ſiner zyt

1956 linguarum *F* 1971 haſts nit laſſen] laſt dus nicht *F*

Otherwise I wouldn't go with you, because that's not the way you treated me. So I'll spare you now, and not repay you as you deserve. How could you make so bold as to call my book heretical? You've made a great outcry about it, but have never attacked a single word of it. You're so educated, but you haven't converted anyone to your point of view. You're a doctor three times over[170] – so convert someone for me, if you can. Then I'll take you for a hero. So put your hand to it, and be a man. Yet you say I am far too lowly to warrant your answering me. I'm very happy to agree with you in this. But what's the point of raging as you do? You're forever making accusations without backing them up – as indeed people accused Christ himself. I hold this against you. If it's true that I've written something heretical, then prove it now; be a man. But if what I have written is right, why haven't you just let it stand? Show me a proposition that's heretical, and then you can decry me as a heretic.[171] You wouldn't get rid of a single article, even if you had a steel pickaxe to take to it. And if you should break your bones, then you won't avenge God's Word by telling lies with many inept words. I'll put them to one side. May God repay you for them in his own time,

---

and ecclesiastical jurisdiction'. See Thomas A. Brady, '"You Hate us Priests". Anticlericalism, Communities, and the Control of Women at Strasbourg in the Age of the Reformation', in Peter A. Dykema and Heiko A. Oberman (eds), *Anticlericalism in Late Medieval and Early Modern Europe* (Berlin: de Gruyter, 1993), pp. 167–207 (quotation from p. 193).

170 Murner was, by 1526, a doctor of theology, and of both canon and civil law.

171 This challenge is for certain intended to suggest similarities between the donkey's position here and that occupied by Zwingli at the First Zurich Disputation – and indeed by Luther at the Diet of Worms.

ſo mee denn yetz dran ligt
Vnd jr all mine Herren
jch wil mich gern laſſen leeren
Wo ich vnrecht daran bin
Sagends nun / ſchonend nüt min
ſo wil ich fürhin bhůtſam ſin.

Weybel Rychart.
Eſel das iſt die gröſt ſünd
die ich in dinem Bůch find
Daß die Doctores nennſt allſamen
deren man kennt perſon vnd namen
Ouch haſt ſelbs das Concili bſetzt
vnerkannt Puren an Doctor ghetzt
Denn Doctor ſind nit ſelb da gſyn
du haſt wol gfürt jr meynung yn
Vnd der heilgen Vättren ſprüch
ſunſt ſo ich das Bůch durch ſich
So iſts dwarheyt vnd die götlich gſchrift
on eins / das ſelb die Münch antrifft
Die haſt du vaſt übel gſcholten
Murnar hat dirs widergolten
Vnd ſchmächt dich anders denn du jn
er iſt nun vil zewüſt gſin
jch wil ouch yetz an jnn hyn.
[Eiv^r] Nun loß mir ouch min Murneere
zürns nit das dich nit gnad heere
Ein reſpons ſchrybſt du in latin
die wär vil beſſer tütſch gſin
So hett der gmein man ouch erkennt
wie du doch habiſt den Eſel gſchendt
Diewyl du aber das nit haſt gthon
ſo mag mencklich wol verſton
Daß du ſchrybſt allein den pfaffen
die machſt du mit dir zů affen

2006 daß ich dich *F*

when more hangs on them than is the case now. As for you, my lords, I'm open to being taught by you. If I'm wrong about anything, speak now. Don't spare me. Then I will be careful from now on.

Weybel Rychart

Donkey, the greatest sin that I find in your book is this: that you give names to all the doctors, whose persons and identities are therefore known. Also you've filled the places in your 'council' yourself, setting unknown farmers against doctors who weren't actually there. You've written their opinions for them, and also the words of the holy fathers. Other than this, when I look through your book I see the truth and divine Scriptures – with one exception. This relates to the monks. You have scolded them very badly, and Murner has now paid you back for this, and has attacked you differently from the way in which you attacked him. He has been much too rude. I'll now have a go at him too. Hear me now, my dear Murner. Don't be angry that I've not greeted you respectfully. You wrote a response in Latin, but it would have been much better in German.[172] That way the common man could also have seen how you have insulted the donkey. But since you didn't do this, many people may take it that you only write for priests. Thus you make monkeys out of both them and you,

172 This is not an entirely fair criticism, in that Murner had appended to his Latin *Responsio* a summary in German.

Daß ſy wänend was du ſchrybeſt
ſo mans recht bſicht allein du kybeſt
Mit dem ſchatten an der wand
warumm nimpſt nit ouch gotswort zhand?
Die Römſche Vätter ſetz vff ein ort
vnd wider ficht mit gottes wort
Denn du magſt mit dinem touben
nit vßrüten rechten Glouben
Was meinſt das nun din ſchryen gelt?
gang hin durchſůch die gantzen welt
Vnd bring ein mann der vndertruck
der ſiben Articklen nun ein ſtuck
Magſt mit Gotswort erhalten dMäſs
oder das man Gott mit zänen eſs?
So thů es mit gſchrift / ich bitt dich drumm
mit ſölcher die nit vom Bapſt kumm
Magſt du es thůn / nun ſpar dich nüt
was zychſt du dich vnd ander lüt /
Daß du nun ſo lang gſchwigen haſt?
[Eiv^{v}] ja hettiſt in der pfyffen blaſt
Es iſt nun yetz das ſibend jar
daß din gſell Riß Eck zů Lypſig war
Daran gwan er eben als vil
als der da ſchmidet mit eim bäſenſtil
Nit minder du des glychen thůſt
denn das du ein knopff an einr ſchlegelax ſůchſt
Din gſell Rißeck zů Ingoldſtatt
ſo er dſchlacht zů Lypſig verlorn hat
Vnd nit überwunden hat ein Sachßen
wil er an ein Eydgnoſſen wachßen
Iſt vnuernünfftiger denn ein Bär
denn ſo man ein ſticht mit eim ſpär
Vom Bären wirt zum nächſten trungen /
er ſchonet nit ſiner jungen
Aber Riß Eck loufft für vnd für
vnd fund vil näher vor der thür
Welche ſind in Schwaaben land

insofar as they know what you're writing. When you look at it properly, you can see that you're only fighting with your own shadow on the wall. Why don't you also take up God's Word? Put the Roman fathers to one side, and fight on with God's Word. For you can't get rid of true belief by raging. What do you think your shouting is worth? Go out now and search through the whole world. Bring me a man who can defeat a single one of the seven articles.[173] Do you want to retain the Mass on the basis of God's Word, or show that God can be eaten by human teeth? In that case, do it with Scripture, I beg you. And not with the kind that comes from the Pope. If you can do it, then don't hold back. Why do you think so little of yourself and others, that you have been silent for so long? If only you'd been blowing your pipe! It's now the seventh year since your friend Giant Eck was in Leipzig.[174] There he achieved as much as if he'd been hammering at a forge with a broom handle. You're now doing the same, for you're looking for a knob on a mallet. Since your friend Eck the Giant from Ingolstadt lost the battle of Leipzig and failed to conquer a Saxon, he'd be more senseless than a bear if he now wanted to attack a Swiss man.[175] For if you run at a bear with a spear, the bear will attack you, without even always bothering about its young. But Giant Eck runs far and wide, and finding some much closer to his door (in Swabia, that is),

173 One assumes this must actually mean Zwingli's *sixty*-seven articles, of 1523.
174 Disputing with Luther, of course (1519).
175 The bear is a common symbol of Switzerland.

denen er nit thůt widerſtand
Er thůt nit mee denn das er ſchrybt
ſich ſelbs wie ein Eychorn trybt
Sölt er gen Zürich / es wär jm zwyt
denn Bärmůter jnn übel ſchnyt
Darzů iſt jm der Zürich wyn zruch
er fürcht er überkäm Grimmen im buch
Din vnd ſin ſchryben eben nützt
als der ein Schloſs mit knechten bſitz
Die allein im rodel gſchriben ſind
den Ars an viertzig wüſcht ein Find
Vwer ſchwärter ſind ſchwartz von roſt
[Fiʳ] jr ſchieſſend mit eim äſchrigen Armbroſt /
Verblendend dwelt mit menſchen leren
ir ſoltend üch mit Gotzwort weren
Das ſtünde üch vil baß an
vnd wär ouch für den gmeinen man
Darumm laſſend nach / jr ſind jm zſchwach
laſſend frumm lüt reden zů der ſach
Hör du Murnar fürhin daacken
gang (wilt gern) reych bůcher zKraacken
Du biſt wol vormals me da gſin
ich meyn dir ſchmöck hie vſſen der wyn?
Drumb ſetz din ſach recht hie ans gricht
Gott well du werdiſt vnderricht
Das dir wol kumm an diner ſeel
läg ſchon din lyb by ſant Michel
Das wär recht in Harenam gſtigen
da möchtind jr all ſiben gligen
Denn jr ſind die ſiben wyſen
vnd hand vnder üch ein Riſen
On Schmid vnd ander handwercks lüt
üch thettind all tüfel nüt
loß yetz was der Salomon büt.

Salomon.
Doctor Thomma ich kan dir ſagen

he doesn't fight against the Swiss. He does no more than write; he's just like a squirrel. Zurich would obviously be too far for him to come because mother-bears might cut him up terribly. On top of that, he thinks the wine in Zurich is too rough, and that he'd get a tummy ache. Your book and his are about as much use as trying to besiege a castle using knights that only exist on paper. An enemy washes forty of their arses. Your swords are black with rust, and you shoot with a burnt crossbow, blinding the world with human doctrines. You should defend yourselves with God's Word. That would be much better for you both, and also for the common man. So give up: you're too weak. Let holy people speak to the subject. Listen, Murner: you should go and wash and then take your books to Cracow (where you were before).[176] You used to be here a lot more; I guess you like the wine out here? Therefore state your case properly here before the court. May God grant that you be taught doctrine that's good for your soul. If your body were already with St Michael, it would have gone directly down to hell. That's where all seven of you might end up, since you're the seven wise men, and have a giant among your number. If it weren't for Faber and other craftsmen,[177] no devils would harm you. Hear what Salomon will bid you do.

Salomon

Doctor Thomas, I can tell you

176 In the Winter Semester of 1499–1500, to be precise. See Hedwig Heger, 'Thomas Murner', in *Deutsche Dichter der frühen Neuzeit*, ed. by Stephan Füssel (Berlin: Schmidt, 1993), pp. 296–310 (here p. 296). See also n. 164 above.

177 Another pun on Faber's name.

Gott wirts dlenge nit vertragen
Das man nach menſchen ſatzungen leb
vnd nüt vmb ſin heylig wort geb
Du biſt ob Gott wil / darwider nit
man eret jnn vergeben mit *Matth. 15.*
[Fiv] Es thett nye anders kein prophet
denn allein das Gott gheyſſen het
Du kanſt in heylger gſchrifft nit finden
das Gott heyſſe puren ſchinden
Vnd nüſſen der armen lüten ſchweyß
gelt wo es nun nit einer heyß
Hör was ich im Propheten find
jre Wächter ſind nun all blind *Eſaie. 56.*
Sy verſtond nüt vnd ſind ſtummend hund
vnd bällend nit zů keiner ſtund
So ſy ſchon böſe ding ſehend
ſchlaaffend ſy / ouch gar nüt jehend
Ire Hirten hand nun kein verſtand
ſy ſind nit zů füllen all ſamd
Sy jagend all dem gyt nach
eben das iſt denn jr ſpraach
Kummend laſſend vns trincken wyn
laſſend vns hütt vnd morn voll ſin
Vnd alſo für vnd für
lůg ob man das nit bym pfaffen ſpür
Es iſt nun yetz der pfaffen ſitt
darumb ſo du ſchryben witt
Vnd beſtädten der pfaffen rott
ſo ſchryb allein das vns büt Gott
So du ye pfaffen bſchirmen witt
lieber ſag an womit?
Mitt Römſcher gſchrifft gloub ich wol
probiertiſt ein gantzen ſack vol
Du hörſt aber wol / gott wil ſin nüt
er wil das man thüge das er büt

2101 ſtumme *F*

that God will not suffer us much longer to live by human commandments, caring nothing for his holy Word. You'll not go against that, God willing, because you can't honour him that way.[178] No prophet ever did anything but what God had commanded. You can't find in the holy Scriptures any command from God that farmers should be oppressed or the sweat of their brows exploited. Not one of them says that. Hear what I find in the prophet: 'Your watchmen are all blind',[179] 'they understand nothing and are like dumb dogs, that never bark at any time. Although they know there's wickedness going on, they sleep through it and say nothing. Their shepherds are without understanding. They are all insatiable, seeking always their own greedy desire. Their refrain is always: "Come, let us drink wine. Let us fill ourselves, today and tomorrow"', and so on. See if you can find this also in our priests. It is the practice of them all. So, if you want to write in support of the pack of priests, write only what God commands us. Or if you want to protect the priests, please tell us what with. I'm sure you've already tried it with a whole sackful of Romish writings. But hear me well: God doesn't want these. He wants us to do as he commands,

178 Matthew 15:8–9: 'This people honours me with their lips, but their hearts are far from me; in vain do they worship me, teaching human precepts as doctrines'.

179 Isaiah 56:10–12: 'Israel's sentinels are blind, they are all without knowledge; they are all silent dogs that cannot bark; dreaming, lying down, loving to slumber. The dogs have a mighty appetite; they never have enough. The shepherds also have no understanding; they have all turned to their own way, to their own gain, one and all. "Come", they say, "let us get wine: let us fill ourselves with strong drink. And tomorrow will be like today, great beyond measure"'.

[Fii^r] Vnd das man nüts thüge zů ſinem wort
ſo bſtäteſt nit der Römſchen kilchen port
du findeſt des Bapſts gwalt an keim ort.

Bernhart Erenueſt.
Durchläſe man all gſchrifft vmm vnnd vmm
findt man das zwytracht davon kumm
Des kybs iſt yetz die gröſt ſchuld
man fraget nüt nach Gotz huld
Denn wo man / das gott heyßt / ladt
vnd nach menſchen ſatzungen gadt
So wirt das zů den prieſteren gſeyt *Hiere. 10*
ſy gangind vmb mit torheyt
Denn ſy fragind nit nach Gott
darumb ſyginds ein vnwyß rott
Ghörſt woruon torheyt entſpringt?
daruon / ſo man nit zů Gott tringt
Billich denn das volck ouch jrrt
wo nit recht gadt ſelb der hirt
So entblößt Gott die gantz erden
vnd wirt das volck wie pfaff werden *Eſaiæ. 10.*
Der Herr wirt ouch wie der knecht
dfrow wie dmagt nun kurtz vnd ſchlecht
Es ſol alles nüt nun überal
denn es iſt eben vych als ſtal
Nun loß noch einer prophecy
vnd lůg obs yetz nit alſo ſy
Denn alſo ſpricht Ezechiel *Ezech. 34.*
wee den hirten Iſrael
Sy weydend nun ſich ſelbs allein
[Fii^v] vnd ſoltend aber dſchaaff gmeyn
Von den hirten gweydet werden
ſo eſſend dhirten ſelbs die herden
So der pfaff ſich ſelb erneert
wie man vmb vnd vmb hört
So werdend gſchunden dſchaf mit gwalt
das keins nit wollen noch hut bhalt

and to add nothing to his Word. This isn't how to support the gates of Rome's Church, though: you can't find any mention of the Pope's authority.

Bernhart Erenuest

If you read the Bible thoroughly, you will find that disputes come from it. The main reason for our quarrel is that people don't seek after God's grace. For when you forsake God's Word and follow after human ordinances, it's said of the priests that they have made a pact with foolishness,[180] for they don't ask after God. So they're an unwise lot. Have you heard where folly comes from? It comes from not striving for God. Of course the people will also go astray when the shepherds themselves don't follow the right way. So God will uncover the whole earth, and the people will become like the priests,[181] the lord like the servant, and the lady like the maid; all will be in the same bad way. Nothing will be anything any more, since the cattle will be just like the stable. Now hear another prophecy, and see if it too hasn't already been accomplished. For Ezekiel says:[182] 'Woe to the shepherds of Israel! They take only themselves to pasture. And though as shepherds they should also tend the sheep, these shepherds even eat their sheep'. Likewise, the priest feeds only himself, as we hear again and again. Therefore the sheep are shorn by force. Not one of them keeps its wool or its skin.

180 Jeremiah 10:8: 'They are all senseless and foolish; they are taught by worthless wooden idols'.

181 Cf. Isaiah 10:1–2 (as n. 122 above).

182 Ezekiel 34:2–3: 'Ah, you shepherds of Israel who have been feeding yourselves! Should not shepherds feed the sheep? You eat the fat, you clothe yourselves with wool, you slaughter the fatlings; but you do not feed the sheep'.

Ie feyßter / ye ee einer gfreſſen wirt *Miche. 3.*
ſo ein Wolff iſt ſelb hirt
Wo der pfaff leert vmb ſold
vnd dfürſten ſind den gaaben hold
Vnd man vmb gelt wyß ſeyt
da werdend gantz ſtett zgrund gleyt *Ezech. 32*
Wo man arm lüt vndertruckt
darzů die armen ſelen ſchluckt
Vnd man gotz dienſt thůt vmb lon
da můß man vil witwen han
wo iſt nun ein ort in der welt *Verſtand*
da man Gott diene on gelt? *Pfaffen.*
Darumb was da iſt von gſpenſt erdacht
hat pfaffen gyt alles zwegen bracht
Meſſz / Fägfhür / Bycht / vnd dfaſten
gellt geben in Ablaß kaſten
Ouch von dem zun heylgen wallen
ſind pfaffen ſchaaff vnd hüner gfallen
So ein pfaff über alter gieng
eins wegs man opffren anfieng
Er kardt ſich ob dem Altar vmm
Thoma nit laß ouch zů har kumm
Das kam alles vß des Bapſts bott
[Fiii^r] das er bkleyt was wie ein Meerkrott
So man das Meſſzgwand an legt
hend vnd füß harfür ſtreckt
Findt man nit vff gantzer erden
das einer Merkrott mög glycher werden
Denn eben ein pfaff im Mäſsgwand
ſo er vßſtreckt füß vnd hand
Die bkleydung kumpt von Bäpſten har
kein xij. bott hats nye gancz vnd gar
Vnd Chriſtus ſelb hats nit yngſetz
do er ſich mit den jüngeren letzt
Sy iſt ein ſchmach dem lyden Chriſti

The fatter the sheep, the sooner it will be eaten,[183] when the wolf himself is a shepherd. Where the priest teaches for personal gain, the princes are in thrall to bribes, and people prophesy for a fee, whole towns will be laid waste. Where the poor are oppressed[184] and the souls of the poor are swallowed up; where divine worship is offered for money, there you will surely find many widows. Can you name me anywhere in the world where God is served without money? Therefore what has been invented by spirits, the greed of priests has brought about: Masses, purgatory, confession, and fasting, throwing money into indulgence sellers' coffers. Also from going on pilgrimages, many sheep and hens have fallen into the hands of the priests. If a priest, on his way to the altar, turns and sees that people have begun to bring gifts, he immediately moves aside from the altar. Don't give up, Thomas, treat this subject too. All this has come about from the Pope's commands that priests dress up like sea toads. So they put on their vestments, having to stretch out hands and feet in order to do so. You won't find anything on earth that's more like a sea toad than a priest in his vestments sticking out his hands and feet. This clothing comes from the Popes. Not one of the twelve apostles ever wore such a thing. And Christ himself didn't institute it, when he was with them. So it's a blasphemy against the suffering of Christ,

183 Cf. Micah 5:4: 'And he shall stand and feed his flock in the strength of the Lord, in the majesty of the name of the Lord his God'.

184 Cf. a similar condemnation of the princes of Israel in Ezekiel 22 (*sic*): 6–12.

vnd füllt allein den pfaffen kiſten
Gäbend ſy vß als ſy nemmend yn
ſy wurdind all darwider ſin
ſunſt falt dMeſſz nimmer me hin.

Beſchluß der Pricht zwüſchend Geiſtlichen / Weltlichen vnd Puren / wie nach volget / vnd redt der Herold a*l*ſo:

Herold.
Diewyl Gott das vorig jar
üch gwarnet hat / das iſt nun klar
Darby jr mögend wol verſton
werdend jr nit von ſünden lon
Allweg für vnd für ſünden
er wirt üch warlich aber finden
Vberheb ſich nit die herrſchafft
[Fiii^{v}] das Gott allein hat puren gſtrafft
Denn es iſt wol mee gſchehen
das man das volck hatt ſtraffen ſehen
Vnd der künig gſündet hatt
wie in dem dritten Küngbuch ſtadt *3. Reg. 24.*
Ir dry parthygen ſöllend nüt
puren / pfaffen vnd Edel lüt
Ietliche parth krieget darumm
das der ander teyl vmb das ſin kumm
Ir puren wärind nun gern fry
ſo lůgt der pfaff das er ſchry
kätzere frumm lüt tag vnd nacht
das dMeſſz werd widerumb bracht
Denn als bald die Meſſz abgang
ander fröſchmalter das dran hangt
Falle alles eins mals hinwäg
denn dMeſſz iſt aller pfaffen ſtäg
So bald man den ſtäg abwirfft
das der pfaff nit bröti herrgott knürpfft

2194 den] der *F*   2199 aſo *B*

and serves only to fill the priests' money chests. If they had to give money away in the same manner they gather it in, they'd suddenly all be opposed to it. But otherwise the Mass won't fall away.

Here ends the report of the debate between the clergy, temporal lords, and farmers, the herald speaking thus:[185]

Herald

Although (as has now become clear) God warned you last year, so that you might understand his message, you must know that if you don't leave off sinning, and always sinning more and more, truly he will find you out again. May the lords not puff themselves up, thinking that God has punished only the farmers. For it has often happened that the people are punished when the king has sinned, as it is written in the third book of Kings. None of the three parties – farmers, priests, or nobility – should be arrogant. The reason why you're all fighting is that the other parties are being denied what is theirs. You farmers would like to be free, so the priest sees to it that he calls pious people heretics day and night. Let the Mass itself be brought down. For if the Mass were abolished, all the other rubbish that depends on it would also fall away once and for all. The Mass is the stay of all the priests. If that support were removed and priests no longer munched on bready hosts

185 This lengthy closing speech is another occasion where a character seems to take on the role of a spokesperson for Eckstein.

Vnd abgond dMeſſz lieder
ſo gäbind pfaffen gůt Iacobs brüder
Der Edelman des Puren glebt
ſo bald der purßman widerſtrebt
Vnd nit mee gibt rendt vnd güldt
ein bättelſack iſt der Edlen ſchilt
Darumb du herrſchafft denck daby
dem Gwalt hört nit zů ſchindery
Sunder Gwalt iſt ein dienſtbarkeyt
das man ſye yederman bereyt
Die gůten vor den böſen bſchirmen
die böſen mit rad vnd galgen firmen
[Fiv^{r}] Darzů ghört ſchwärdt / fhür / vnd růt
gotzleſteren ghört der laſterhůt
Das ſind rechte inſtrument
damit man vnkrut vßrüt vnd brent
Ein laſter iſt doch yetz als gmeyn
das brucht jung / alt / groß vnd klein
Das iſt Gotzleſterung in aller welt
das ſelb doch Gott als übel gfelt
Das es nit ein wunder wär
ſo der erdbod wurd menſchen lär
Es iſt kein junger ſchnuder klotz
er ſchweert yetz by dem lyden gotz
Kein glid blybt Chriſto on erſůcht
es wirt inſunders jm damit gflůcht
Was der Schwab ſeyt jhenthalb dem ryn
das můß alls by gotz marter ſin
Des glychen by gotz Sacrament
die gſchlächt allein man daby kennt
Wo man hört gotz Marter flůchen
darff man frölich ein Lantzknecht ſůchen
Wo man denn ſchweert by gotz wunden
ein ander volck wirt da empfunden
Darumb alle Nationen
ſoltend gar nyemants ſchonen
Sunder ſchwärdt vnd fhür vaſt bruchen

or sang at Mass, then they would turn to wandering around like pilgrims.[186] The nobleman has been living on what by rights belongs to the farmer. As soon as the farmer resists by withholding rent and taxes, then the nobleman's shield turns into a beggar's sack. Therefore you lords, consider. Mistreating others isn't part of your authority; rather, authority exists to serve others. You should be ready to serve all, protecting the good from the wicked, and correcting the wicked with advice, or else with the gallows. This is what the sword, the fire, and the rod are for. The criminal's hat[187] belongs to blasphemers. These are the right instruments with which to uproot and burn the weeds. And one vice has become common everywhere these days, practised by young, old, big, and small; and that is blasphemy, which is all over the world, and which so displeases God that it wouldn't be a surprise if the whole earth were to be emptied of its inhabitants. Nowadays there's no snotty-nosed kid who doesn't swear by the sufferings of God. No part of Christ's body is left unexamined; it is torn asunder to make people's curses. Whatever the Swabians across the Rhine want to say, it must always be 'by God's suffering!'. The same goes for 'by God's sacrament!'. You can recognize them just from their swearing. If you hear someone swear in the name of God's suffering, you'll know that a soldier can't be far away. But if someone swears by God's wounds, you'll discover a different kind of person. Therefore – in every nation – no one should be spared, but sword and fire should be used.

186 A 'Jacobsbruder' is strictly speaking a pilgrim going to Santiago di Compostella.

187 A 'Lasterhut', suitably inscribed, was, at least during the Middle Ages, worn by criminals in the pillory. See *SI* II, 1788.

ſo vergieng dem gotzleſtrer s*fl*uchen
Das ſelb Gott angnämer wär
denn ſo man wychte vnd blatten ſchär
Wölte gott das es darzů käm
das man jung vnd alt annäm
[Fiii[v]] Wär nun by gots lyden ſchwür
das mans all an Brangen für
Vnd man ein dahin ſtallte
biß jm das Miltz wol erkalte
Gelt man lerte denn gots lyden pryſen
ſo man bruchte das Halßyſen
Darzů vſſatzte den Laſterhůt
denn ſo vergiengs jm gwüſs / das er ſunſt thůt
Das gfiel gott im himmel oben
ſo man bruchte des Henckers kloben
Das heyßt vff recht tütſch der Brangen
daſelbs wirt Wildprät on hund gfangen
Gloub mir drumb du frummer gwalt
das ſölichs voglen gott baß gfalt
Denn ſo man vſſetzt ein Wynbiſchof
damit man vfnet Cayphas hof
Vnd du gwalt nun zwyfel nit
du dieneſt Gott mee damit
Denn ſäſſiſt in einer Carthuß
vnd kämiſt ſchon nimmer daruß
Thätiſt nüt denn bätten vnd faſten
laſs bylyb das Schwärt nit raſten
Du dieneſt Gott damit recht
vnd heyſt gwüſs ein gotsknecht *Roma. 13.*
Aber von der Geyſtlichen dienen
ſagt vns gſchrifft nun gar nienen
Deßglychen ouch du Purßman
der Oberkeyt thů Eer an
Sy treyt das ſchwärt nit vergeben
denn ſo du wirſt frommklich leben

2264 skuchen *B*, das fluchen *F*

That way, the blasphemers' curses would go away, which would make life pleasanter – just like getting rid of the pox. Would to God it might come to pass that anyone who swears by God's sufferings, young or old, would be dealt with – that they'd be taken straight to the pillory and left there until their spleen cooled down. Then you could teach them actually to praise God's sufferings. You'd use a neck-iron, and place the criminal's hat on that instead. Then for certain people would stop doing it, and God above would be pleased. That's the way to use the hangman's vice, which in good German we call the pillory. That's where you catch game without a dog.[188] Believe me, pious lords, such bird-catching pleases God much better than setting up a wine-bishop and opening up Caiaphas's court. And you authorities, don't doubt that you'll be serving God more by doing this than you would by sitting in a Charterhouse[189] and never coming out again – even if you did nothing while you were in there but fasted and prayed. For goodness' sake don't let your sword be idle. With it, you can truly serve God, and will be called a servant of God.[190] But as for serving the clergy, the Scriptures tell us nothing. In the same way, you farming man, honour the authorities. They do not bear the sword in vain. So if you live virtuously,

188 A pun on the fact that 'Brangen', or 'Pranger', can also be used of a stick for beating game.

189 i.e., a Carthusian monastery.

190 Romans 13:3–4 (see n. 87 above).

[Fv[r]] Wirſt du Eer vom gwalt empfahen
darumb ſolt nit gwalt verſchmahen
Du haſt bißhar pfaffen geert
das ſelb dich Gott an keim ort leert
Darumb hüt dich by diner ſeel
eer nit die pfaffen Ieſabel
Das ſelb ſind nun ſölich pfaffen
die nüt anders hand zeſchaffen
Denn das gotswort zewider fächten
ſchryend kätzer mit groſſem prächten
So ſy aber werdend fürgſtellt
vnd man inen dwarheyt fürhellt
gſtond ſy wie der Ritter Roßkamm
der was Edel von Klüpflis ſtamm
Der ſelb Ritter thett ein thaat
vff ein zyt er in ſim huß vmbgadt
Vnd ſicht zů ſinem laden vß
einen ſitzen in eim wirtzhuß
Der hatt jm thon ein widerdryeß
vnd ee er jnn on angriffen ließ
Zuckt er / vnd houwt vß zur ballen
das jm ſin ſchwärt můßt enpfallen
Vnn hüw alſo gegen ſim fyend mit ſtreichen
biß er*s* ſchwärt můßt im ſchißwinckel reichen
Glych alſo thůnd die touben pfaffen
jnen iſt yetz wie dem Affen
So der Aff kein lüß mee findt
dhut er nach den lüſen ſchindt
Pfaffen hand üch Puren gluſet
vnd in iren ſeckel ghuſet
[Fv[v]] So nun dlüß gar ſind verkrochen
fahend ſy an mit klauwen bochen
Vor denen ſolt du hüten dich
für ander aber bitten ich
Das iſt für all die yetz bißhar

2322 er *B*

you'll be honoured by those in power. So you shouldn't slander the authorities. Until now you have honoured priests – which God doesn't teach you to do anywhere. So be watchful of your soul. Don't honour the priestly Jezebel. For this is what those priests are who have nothing better to do than to fight against the Word of God, making a great show of decrying people as heretics. But if you could sit them down and expose the truth to them, they'd be like the knight Rosskamm,[191] who was a nobleman of the lineage of Klüppfi.[192] This is what that knight did: one day, as he was walking up and down in his house, he happened to look out of his window. There he saw a man, sitting in the inn, who had once angered him. And rather than just leaving him be, he drew his sword and hewed off the man's balls, so that his sword fell from his hand. And then Rosskamm hewed away at his enemy with many strokes, until his sword reached the man's shithole. This is just what the mad priests do. They've become just like monkeys. If a monkey runs out of lice, he scratches his skin for more. The priests have deloused you farmers, and have kept the lice in their own sacks. And now that the lice have been killed, priests have started to beat about themselves with clubs. Be on your guard against ones like this. But I pray for the other priests, for all of those who, until now,

191 Or 'horse brush'.

192 See n. 160 on the *Concilium*, p. 125 above.

nit beſſers gwüßt hand gantz vnd gar
Vnd ſind nun yetz in gůtem alter
die ſelben ſolt du by dir bhalten
Haſt du bißhar die böſen gneert
ſy mit hůr vnd kinden verzeert
So neer yetz all die gern wettind
daß ſy beſſers glernet hettind
Man findt noch vil frummer pfaffen
die nit beſſers mögend ſchaffen
Vnd woltend gern von Mäſshan lon
ſy wüſſend daß nit recht iſt gthon
Dennocht wil es ſich nit ſchicken
daß ſy ſich mögind daruß flicken
Den ſelben Pfaffen thů das beſt
es ſind fürwar gfangen geſt
Vnd ſtadt nit in irem gwalt
daß ſy thügind was inen gfallt
Biß ſy erlöſt ſelbs Gott der Herr
der ſelb all jrrend zů jm keer
Murriger Thomma loß yetz ouch
din kutten zum erſten wol erflouch
Erwäſch vor wol din eigen hut
ee du verachtiſt Gots ſtattut
Du ſchrybſt ein ſchantlich reſponſion
wär wäger du hettiſts in tütſch thon
[Fvi^{r}] So hette der gmein man verſtanden
du giengiſt taapen an der wande
All din ding iſt nüt denn gſchrey
du gaggeſt vil / vnd leyſt kein Ey
Denn allein die ſchal loß ſind
deren ich vil in diner gſchrifft find
Din reſponß iſt nun ſchyſſen vnd dräck
jch gloub das ein Apotecker in dir ſtäck
Du gaaſt mit wüſter vngwent vmb
zäch ſelbs in dim Myropoliumm
Du ſchilteſt der Eſel wie er dich
vnd ſechß ander Doctor Chriſtenlich

haven't known any better, and have now reached a ripe old age. These you should keep. But if you've been feeding bad priests – along with their whores and children – you should now feed those instead who wish they had learned a better way. Many pious priests are still to be found, who can't do any better, but would willingly be rid of the Mass. They knew something wasn't right, but didn't know how to get out of it. Do what's best for such priests. Truly they are exiles who've been taken captive; they don't have the power to act as they would like until they are set free by the Lord God himself, the one who brings all who are lost back to his side. You listen to me too now, moaning Thomas.[193] First, curse your monk's habit, then wash your own skin thoroughly before you go on despising God's statutes. The *Responsio* you wrote was shameful. It would have been better if you'd written it in German, because then the common people could have seen that you're groping about for the walls. All you do is shout. You honk a lot, but don't lay any eggs. All I find in your writings are empty shells. Your *Responsio* is just shit and dirt. I think there's an apothecary in you, since you go about with dreadful ointments. Drink from your own perfume shop.[194] You berate the donkey, how he put you and six other doctors (in a Christian way)

193 See n. 211 on the *Concilium*, p. 151 above.

194 A 'myropolium' would also sell ointments and essences of many kinds.

Habe in ein büchle geſetzt
darinnen hab er üch verletzt
So ich des Eſels bůch durch ſich
vnd din antwurt ouch nimm für mich
Thůſt du durch vß nüt denn ſchelten
ein gůt wort empfalt dir ſelten
Du thůſt wie vorzyten ein wyb
die was ſchebig an allem lyb
Von houpt ab biß vff die füß
eins mals ſy ſich vſs irem huß ließ
Vnd lüff mit bloſſem houpt härfür
jr Gfatter ſtůnd vnder einr andren tür
Vnn ſprach: Hey gfatter deckend den grind
die ſchebig erwuſt daz vnderhemd gſchwind
Dackt mit rock vnd hemmd das houpt
das arm wyb do ſich ſelbs beroubt
Ließ jr hinders vnd vorders ſehen
alſo Murnar iſt dir ouch gſchehen
[Fviv] Deß Eſel ſchelten iſt nit der grind
gegen dem das ich in diner reſponß find /
Doch du biſt kein Obſeruantz
du ſchrybſt ein rechten Thomma dantz
Du biſt ein gůter Conuentual
haſt dkutten von dir gworffen drümal
Der Bapſt gern mit dir diſpenſiert
damit der Thomman dantz werde gfürt
Ich denck du dantziſt nun als lang
biß dir pfyff ouch in ſelben ghang
Du werdiſt zletſt zů Babilon
nit ſingen ein gſang von Zion
Vnd ob man ſchon darnach wirt fragen
wirſt du glych wie dIuden ſagen
Wie kann ich ſingen Gott dem Herren
darzů jnn eim frömmden land Eeren?
Denn du můſt noch in ein land
daß dir yetz zmal iſt vnbkannt
Gott der Herr wöl dich ziehen

in a book. By doing this, it seems, he has done you wrong. But when I flick through the donkey's book, and then read the answers you give in it for myself, I find that you do nothing but scold him, the donkey. A good word seldom falls from your lips. You're like the woman, once upon a time, whose whole body was a mass of scabs, from head to foot. Then one day she came out of her house and ran about with her head uncovered. Her neighbour was standing at another door and said: 'Hey, neighbour, cover up your face'. The scabby woman straightaway took off her vest, and covered her head with her skirt and blouse. So the poor woman shamed herself, exposing her front and backside to view. The same thing has happened to you, Murner. The donkey's scabs are nothing to those I find in your *Responsio.* Because you really aren't an observant monk. You write a real Thomas's dance. You're a good conventual, having thrown off the habit three times.[195] The Pope is happy to give you a dispensation, so that the Thomas dance can continue. I think you'll keep dancing until even the pipe hangs in its skin. You'd be the last to go to Babylon and sing a song of Zion. And if someone should ask you for one, you will answer like the Jews: 'How can I sing of God the Lord, honouring him in a foreign land?'. For you'd once again be in a land you don't know.[196] May the Lord God draw you to himself,

195 Murner was indeed a conventual, and as such not required to wear a habit or to live on a long-term basis in the same monastery. This was, however, a point that he had to argue strongly following criticism from Wingersheim and others.

196 Another reference to Murner's peripatetic, unsettled career.

daß du ſim zorn mögiſt entfliehen
Ich ſolt dir vnderwyſung geben
wie gots prieſter ſöltind leben
So weiß ich wol es iſt vmb ſuſt
du haſt zum gotswort keinen luſt
Sagt ich dir ſchon das aller beſt
ſo hilffts als der fhür mit ſchyter löſt
Wirſt du mit ſchmächen nit nachlon
ſo wirt man gar gen Straßburg gon
Man iſt yetz nun gſin vff der bruck
da iſt ein gůter Mehokuck
[Fvii^{r}] Der hat vil anders von dir gſeyt
dann dir der Eſel fürleyt
Weyſt nit was da ſye Mehokuck
ſo ſetz dich zů dem Ofen vnd ſchluck
So empfindeſt du obs hebreiſch ſy
jch ſchleck es ab dem Ofen fry
Schleckt man hebreiſch ab dem Ofen? *ja als der Murnar ſchrybt.*
ſo ſchleckeſts du ab einem ſchrofen
(Heyßt hebreiſch Mechaſchephim)
diewyl du hörſt des Bapſts ſtimm
ſo biſt du ouch ſin Koſſamim.

Burgermeyſter Salomon.
Was wilt jm vil hebreiſch ſagen?
er kündte baß Parnößlin jagen
Der jm wölt bſchryben ſine thaten gmein
dem wurd die wyt Gouchmatt zeklein
Am Murnar iſt nüt mee zgwünnen
Man můß ander lüt fercken von hinnen
Es hat ſich ſunſt verzogen lang
darumb yetz yederman heim gang
Pur Eygennutz vnd kumpſt du hein
leg alle handlung für der gmein
Vnd ſprich daß ſy ſich fridſam halt

2436 fercken] fertigen *F*

so that you might escape his anger. I should instruct you about how God's priests ought to live, but I know it's pointless trying. You have no desire for God's Word. If I were to give you the very best advice, it'd be as much use as trying to use logs to put out a fire. You wouldn't stop slandering me, and so we'd go to Strasbourg. We have even been to the bridge, where there is a good Mehokuck. He's said many more things about you than the donkey does.[197] Don't you know what Mehokuck is?[198] So sit down by the oven and swallow it. Then you'll see whether it's Hebrew or not. I like to eat straight from the oven. Do you eat Hebrew straight from the oven? In the same way as you eat from a cliff (in Hebrew this is called 'Mechashephim'.) For as soon as you hear the Pope's voice, you are his Kossamim.

Burgermeyster Salomon

What do you mean by all this Hebrew? He could just as well go off and hunt for the donkey.[199] Anyone wanting to describe his deeds would find the broad *Geuchmat* too small. There's nothing more to be gained from Murner. And it's also time to get other people to leave. We've already wasted enough time. So everyone should now go home. Farmer Eygennutz, when you get home, please explain to your community all that has happened here. And tell them to live peace-ably,

197 A 'meho'kek' (*sic*) is a 'lawgiver', or 'scribe'. This seems likely to be an obscure reference to a Strasbourg-based opponent of Murner. At this time, the likeliest candidate would be Martin Bucer, whose *Grund und Ursach* appeared early in 1525, and was instrumental in driving Murner and others out of the city.

198 By this stage most readers will have doubtless concluded that these smatterings of Hebrew are not intended to mean very much. Rather, the Herald's lack of any command of the language creates a comic effect. 'Mechashephim' tends to be translated 'sorcerers' (see Daniel 2:2), and is used as an example of Hebrew also by Erasmus in the *Moriae encomium* (p. 186). 'Kossamim' are astrologers or wizards (see Leviticus 20:27).

199 Or possibly 'steward', even 'community leader' (Hebrew 'parnas', see for example Isaiah 22:15).

vnd nit mee überziech den gwalt.
denn es Gott gar nüt gfallt.

Pur Eygennutz.

Herr Burgermeyſter es ſol ſin
denn ich yetz der meinung bin
Ich wöll es alles der gmeind ſagen
[Fvii[v]] wir wend fürhin nüt mee tagen
Sunder vns halten wie von alter
Gott der Herr vnſer behalter
Wöll vns geben gůten friden
das wir mögind vfrůr myden
jch far dahin / wir wend vns lyden

Als Pur Eygennutz heym kam / verſamlet er die .XIII. Richter der gantzen Gemeynd / deren namen nach volgend / vnd redt der weybel Lätzkopff alſo:

Wolan Vogt Broſe Tubenkropff
Thoman Sackband / vnn Bentz Wydhopf
Küny Darmhaſpel / vnn Küre Zwilchback
Flure Fladenmul / vnd Lülle Senffſack /
Bläſe Hafenkäs / ouch Gall Pflegelskap
Wolf Schwynnetz / vnn Lentz muckenſchnap
Henſe Strownäpper / Fritſche Zettmiſt
hörend Eygennutzen der hie zů gegen iſt /
Drumb min Eygennutz vns hie ſag
was bringiſt von Fridberg ab dem Rychſtag.

no longer troubling their authorities; for this does not please God.

Pur Eygennutz

My lord Mayor, it shall be so. For I am now of a mind to tell the community everything. And from now on we'll never meet in a rebellious spirit, but behave just as we used to do. May God the Lord, our preserver, give us peace, that we may avoid unrest. I'm going. We'll live in peace from now on.

When Pur Eygennutz came home, he gathered the thirteen judges of the whole community whose names are listed below, and the Weybel spoke as follows:

So, Vogt Brose Tubenkropff,[200] Thomam Sackband,[201] and Bentz Wydhopf,[202] Rüny Darmhaspel,[203] and Rüre Zwilchback,[204] Flure Fladenmul,[205] and Lülle Senffsack,[206] Bläse Hafenkäs, also Gall Pflegelskap,[207] Wolf Schwynnetz, and Lentz Muckenschnap,[208] Hense Strownäpper, Fritsche Zettmist[209] – Eygennutz is present with us. Hear what he has to say. Therefore my dear Eygennutz, tell us what you have brought back from the Diet at Fridberg.

200 The surname means 'pigeon's neck' (or 'crop').

201 A 'Sackband' is a piece of string used to tie a sack; but since 'Sack' alone ranges in meaning from 'stomach' and 'swelling' to 'scrotum' and 'whore', the number of possible overtones are legion.

202 The crested bird known as the hoopoe (modern German 'Wiedehopf').

203 'Darm' means 'bowels'; a 'haspel' is a bobbin, but can also mean a poor worker, a madcap, or indeed the devil (see *SI* II, 1760–2).

204 The surname means 'Twill-cheek'.

205 'Flure Cakehole'.

206 A 'Senffsack' is a sack of mustard. One feels that Eckstein's invention is beginning to run thin.

207 Both of these names have to do with cheese ('Käs'): a 'Hafen' and a 'Skap' (see *SI* X, 10) are pots for storing it. A 'Pflegel', meanwhile, is a flail or whip (or an unruly young man).

208 The names of these two involve catching animals: 'pig net' and 'midge snatcher'.

209 The final two surnames are 'Hay-cutter' and 'Dung-spreader'.

Als nun die gantz gmeind by einanderen was / vnnd hören woltend die handlung / redt Pur Eygennutz mit etlichen vermanungen alſo.

Alſo frummen biderben lüt
jch weyß das mich min läbtag rüwt
Das ich bin eygennützig gſin
einr andren meinung ich gantz bin
Denn ich han nun ſo vil gehört
[Fviii^{r}] z Fridberg da man mich hat glert
Das ich fürhin rüwig blib
nimmer mee widern gwallt kyb
Wölt Gott jr wärind ſelb da gſin
jr wärind der meynung wie ich bin
Alſo hat man mir doch gſeyt
wie man ſöll halten Oberkeyt
Darumb ſind bätten lieben Meyer
zinſend fürhin hüner vnd Eyer
Wyn / korn / vnd was man höuſch
wagend recht kappen vnd fleyſch
Biß Gott der Herr ſelb kumpt
vogel vnd näſt hinwäg rumpt
Der ſelb mag vns wol erlöſen
man mag vns dennocht dſeel nit kröſen *Matth. 10.*
Darumb ſorgend der ſeel heyl
wir ſind nun deſt minder geyl
So man vns im zoum bhalt
drumb eerend nun fürhin den gwallt
Allein drumb das Paulus ſpricht
der wider ſtand empfacht das gricht
Drumb laſſend vns gwallt nit widerſton
es wirt vns vil deſter baß gon
Gott wöll die ſinen nit verlon.

Alſo ſprachend ſy all / was du vns heiſt / wöllend wir thůn. Gott wölle vns vnnd der Herrſchafft gnad vnd frid geben das wir einhelligklich miteinanderen läbind / hie vnnd dört in ewiger ſäligkeyt A M E N.

Now when the whole community had assembled, and all wanted to hear what had happened, Pur Eygennutz spoke, with several admonitions, thus:

My good fellow villagers, I know that I will regret all the days of my life that I have been selfish. Now I've changed my view completely because of what I've heard at Fridberg: they taught me that I should live peaceably from now on, and not struggle any more against the authorities. Would to God that you had all been there yourselves – you too would now be thinking as I do. They told me how we need to have people in authority over us. Therefore I ask you all, dear farmers, from now on to tithe your chickens and eggs, wine, corn, and whatever else you eat; to weigh poultry and meat correctly, until the Lord God himself shall come to remove all birds and nests. This can save us, so that no one can crush our souls.[210] Therefore look to your soul's health. We are much less wilful when we are held in a bridle. So we should honour the authorities from now on. This is what St Paul says, that he who rebels will be judged. Therefore let us not resist authorities, and things will go better for us. God will not desert his own. And they all said: 'What you have told us, we will do. May God give us and the lords grace and peace, that we may live in unity with each other, both here and above, in eternal blessedness. Amen'.

210 Cf. Matthew 10:28: 'Do not fear those who kill the body but cannot kill the soul; rather fear him who can destroy both soul and body in hell'.

Appendix
(additional material from
the 1526 text of the *Concilium*)

From text C of the *Concilium* (1526)

We here offer most of the common material found in prints C, D, and F, but not in A or E. Excluded are only a few very short additional passages, the wording of which we have been able to accommodate in the critical apparatus to our main *Concilium* edition. To facilitate comparison between the two versions, each additional passage printed here begins and ends with the lines from A which frame it. These are presented in italics, alongside the relevant line number from our main edition. The base German text used in this appendix is C; in all other respects the approach to editing and translating is the same as that described above (pp. 61–2).

Uorred

382 *gloub ims nit du frummer Pur*
Gott din Herr gibt dir gſatzen gnůg
ob du ſchon ſtaaſt hinder dem pflůg
Vnd werckest vmb das täglich brot
ſo du dennzmal trachtest nach Gott
Vergiſ nit ſůch ouch ſpyß der ſeel
růff an den starcken Gott Jsrael *Iosue. 14.*
Sunſt wil er kein opffer haben
Jm gfallt vnder allen gaben
Allein das man jnn loben söll *Pſal. 90.*
Jn trübſal zů jm keeren wöll
Das iſt ein opffer das jm gfalt
das man jnn allein für Gott halt
Er ſpricht klar man růff mich an
vnd so ich dir geholffen han
Denn wirſt du mich darumb loben
das gfallt Gott im himmel oben *Prouer. 23.*
Allein din hertz das wil er han
vnd nimpt on das kein Opffer an

Prologue

God himself gives you enough laws, even though you may spend your days behind the plough. And though you have to work for your daily bread, when you turn to God, don't forget to look for food for your soul also. Call upon the mighty God of Israel. He doesn't want any other kind of sacrifice; amongst all other gifts, the only one that pleases him is that we should praise him and turn to him in trouble. It is a sacrifice pleasing to him that we should worship him as the only God. He says clearly: 'Call to me and, as I have helped you, so you will praise me'. This pleases God in the heavens above. He wishes only to have your heart, and without it he will accept no sacrifice.

Er freyt nit nach ſilber vnd gold
dir iſt er on gelt hold
Allein tracht er nach diner ſeel heyl *Esaiæ. 55.*
ſin gnad findſt du vergebens feyl
Jst das nit gnůg ſo er ſelb ſpricht
der durſtig ſye / ſich zů mir richt? *Ioann. 7.*
So du nach Gott denn durſt haſt gwunnen
bgär zů jm wie ein hirtz zum brunnen *Pſalm. 41.*
Din hertz allweg nach jm fächt *Matth. 5.*
vnd hab Gott lieb / ſo läbſt du recht.
384 *Herold.*[1]

Paule Kachelmůs
869 *vff irem houpt wachßend nit lüß*
Mich wundret nun von hertzen ſeer
wohar den pfaffen kumm die Eer
Das man ſy gnad Heren ſchilt
ſo nun das S. Lux ſchrybt / gilt
Vnd ſol es ſin wie Chriſtus seyt
vnbillich der Bapſt das ſchwärt treyt
Denn es ſtadt heyter alſo gſchriben *Lucæ. 22.*
dIünger fiengend an all kyben
Welcher der höchſt vnder inen wär
do hatt ye gſprochen Gott jr Herr *Math. 20.*
Vnd der jügeren hochmůt dempt
gſeyt / Weltlich lüt man gnad heren nempt
Ir aber ſöllend nit alſo ſin *Marci. 10.*
pfaffen gwalt viel hie billich hin
Den ſchwärdt ghört zů weltlichem gwalt
geystlicher huf ſich Gotzworts halt *Roma. 11.*
Damit ſöllend pfaffen fechten *Epheſ. 6.*
kein Christ mit dem anderen rechten *Matth. 5.*
So es nit zimpt eim Christen man
mit Christen fahen hader an
Vil minder zimpt pfaffen ſchwärt
alſo Chriſtus ſant Peter lert
Welcher mit dem ſchwärdt fecht *Math. 26.*

1 A and E's line 383 is omitted.

He does not ask for silver or gold, for he loves you quite apart from your money. He seeks only the salvation of your soul, and you will never find his grace for sale. Isn't it enough that he says to you: 'Come to me, all who thirst'? If you are thirsty for God, desire him as a hart pants for cooling streams. Turn your heart towards God always, and love him; that way you will live rightly.

Paule Kachelmůs

I really do wonder in my heart where priests get the honour from that makes them expect to be called 'my lord'. If what St Luke says is still valid, and if what Christ says is to be heeded, then it's quite wrong for the Pope to carry a sword. For it states here clearly that the disciples all began to quarrel among themselves about which of them was the greatest, and the Lord said, condemning the disciples' pride: 'Worldly men are called "Lord", but you should not be as they are'. In our day the power of priests has rightly been overthrown, for swords belong to secular powers. The clergy should stick to God's Word; priests should fight with that. No Christian should quarrel with another. Just as it is not right for a Christian man to cause discord, still less is it fitting for priests to bear swords. As Christ taught St Peter: 'He who fights with the sword

werd er mit gricht / ſo gſchech jm recht
Drumb ſchwärdt das ſyg von pfaffen ver
alſo redt ſelber Gott der Herr *Math. 20.*
Daß mir dienet werd / bin ich nit hie
vnd herſchet über kein ſtatt nye
Sunder das ich dienen well
hör wie er ſin gwalt vff ein ort ſtell
Wie wol er ein herr über all ding was *Philip. 2.*
dennocht leert er dIünger das
Sy nit ſoltend herren ſin
wie wol der Bapst och fart harin
Schrybt ſich ſelbs ein knecht der knechten *Seruum*
ja deren die jm ſpyeß fechten *ſeruorum.*
Mit ſchryben nideret er sich gnůg
nempt ſich ein knecht / lebt herrlich vnd klůg
Wie ein herr ob allen herren
man dörfft volgen ſinen leren
Wär dero nit wil ghorſam ſin
den verflůocht er ins vierdt glid hin
Wär vff ſiner ſyten ſtadt
pen vnd ſchuld er nach ladt
Stirbt einer denn in ſinem ſtryt
das eewig läben er ouch gibt
Einer fart von mund vf zhimmel
ſchnäll wie S. Iörgen ſchimmel
Wär nit iſt vff ſiner ſyten
der můß biß in dHell ryten
Also regiert er lyb vnd ſeel
an Gots ſtatt / wiez zBabylon der Beel *Dani.14.*
Solt der Bapst an Gots ſtatt ſitzen
es wirt jnn frylich nüt nützen
Das er ſo vil zkaſten ſchlacht
ſo Gott von jm rechnung empfacht
Der Bapst denn ſpricht / Sichſt du Herr
wie ich dir land vnd lüt meer
Vil Küngrych hab ich an mich zogen
Gott ſpricht / Gytz hett din hertz btrogen
Do ich noch vff erdtrich was
zů Pilato ſeyt ich das
Myn Rych wär nit von diſer welt *Ioan. 18.*

deserves to be judged by it'. So swords should be kept far away from priests. This is what the Lord God himself says: 'I have not come to be served' (and he had no authority anywhere at all), 'but to serve'. Hear how he wielded his authority: although he was Lord of all things, he nevertheless taught the disciples that they should not be lords. Although the Pope too goes about and signs himself 'servant of servants' (at least of those who fight with lances) and humbles himself greatly in writing by calling himself a servant, he still lives in lordly style like a lord of lords. You have to follow his teachings, and anyone who isn't willing to obey them is cursed by him even to the fourth generation. Anyone who places himself on the Pope's side heaps upon himself trouble and guilt. He also gives eternal life to anyone who dies fighting his battles: a man can rise to heaven as fast as if he were riding on St George's steed; but anyone who isn't on the Pope's side has to ride to hell. In this way he rules over body and soul in God's stead, just as Baal did in Babylon. If the Pope does indeed rule in God's stead, it certainly won't benefit him when God demands a reckoning from him that he's filled his coffers in the way he has. Then the Pope will say: 'See, Lord, how I have increased your land and your people, and have drawn many kingdoms to myself'. God will say: 'Greed has led your heart astray. When I was on earth I told Pilate that my kingdom was not of this world.

do mir der Sathan nach ſtelt *Matth. 4.*
Bot er mir ouch land und ſtatt
wolt mir geben das ich vorhin hatt
Drumb Bapst du haſt das letz erwüſchet
hettist du nach menschen gfischet *Math. 4.*
Darzů hatt ich dich geſendt
jch ſprach nit / für das regiment
Denn ſpricht der Bapſt: Ich hab gfiſchet
mengen glerten mann erwüschet
Erfült in türnen / ouch verbrennt
darzů halff mir min Regiment
Spricht Gott / Das hieß ich dich nit
dem Tüfel haſt du dienet damit
Man ſol nyeman zum Glouben zwingen
allein mit güte zůhar bringen
Alſo haſt du die glöubigen gfangen
die bösen dir laſſen anhangen
Haſt allein tödt die frummen
die min wort habend angenommen
Du ſoltest ſelber prediget hat
das haſt du vnderwegen glan
Haſt ertödt die predigen wolten
ſy darzů Kätzer gſcholten
Daß du ſolteſt thůn / haſt du gweert
din wort / vnd nit das min gleert
Niemant dorfft vom Gots wort ſagen
er ward verbrent / oder veriagen
Du biſt nit min ſtatthalter gſin
vnd haſt mir gſchoren die ſchäflin
Inen abgſchunden woll vnd hut
hör wie ein ſpruch in Petro lut *2. Petri. 2*
Chriſtus der herr hett glitten
volgend nach ſinen füßtritten
Er hett vns ein exempel glon
das wir thügind wie er hett gthon
Do man jnn ſchmächt / er hatt nit tröuwt
vnd nit wie du dſchaaff zerſtröuwt
Diewyl denn Chriſtus dultig litt
warumb volgteſt du jm nit?
Alſo denn Gott zum Bapſt ſeyt

And when Satan pursued me and offered me lands and cities, he was only seeking to give me what I already owned. So, Pope, you've reached the end. If only you had been a fisher of men! That is what I sent you to be. I didn't say: "Be a ruler"'. Then the Pope will say: 'But I *have* been fishing; I've caught many learned men, made them rot in towers, or burnt them. Being a ruler helped me to do this'. God says: 'I did not command you to do that. You've been serving the devil by doing it. You shouldn't force anyone to believe, but rather bring them to faith only by doing good. But you have caught the faithful in your net and surrounded yourself with evildoers. You have only killed pious people who accepted my Word. You should have been preaching it yourself, but you've stopped doing that along the way. Rather, you've killed those who wanted to preach, and accused them of being heretics. You've prevented others from doing what you should have been doing yourself, and you have taught your words rather than my Word. No one can claim that he was burnt or banned by God's Word. You haven't been my representative: you have shorn my sheep, sheared them, and skinned them. Hear some words that St Peter speaks: "Christ the Lord has suffered: follow in his footsteps". He has left us an example, that we might do what he has done. When he was reviled, he did not make threats, and did not scatter his sheep, as you have. Since, then, Christ suffered patiently, why don't you follow in his footsteps?' That's what God will say to the Pope,

dennzmal er nit ein kron treyt
Das weyß ich wol / vnd bin ouch gwüſs
ſo ichs nun hin vnd wider miſs
Mag kein menſch an Gots ſtatt ſin
wiewol ich nun ein pur bin
870 *Darab bringt mich kein Cardinal*

Doctor Gryff

2759 *vnd bſorg wenn ich ſchon lang mach*
Das min ſagen lützel beſchieß
vnd gloub das man Gots lychnam nieß
Die wort redet Chriſtus heyter gnůg
ee er ſinen lyb ans crütz trůg
Sprach nun klar Das iſt min lyb
ſo waß es zwar / dwort ich nit ſchyb
Er ſpricht ye / Das iſt
nun wär ich doch ein frächer Christ
So ich (jſt) für bedüten näm
wenn nun Christus yetzund käm
Butte mir brot / ſpräch och darzů
Das iſt min lyb / den ich darthů
Ans Crütz desglychen mit ſim blůt
Es käme mir nit in min můt
Das mir das Gott nit halten ſött
welches er klarlich zů mir redt
Der Luther und Hans Pomerantz
ſind yetz der meynung gar vnd gancz
Habend vor beyd anderſt gſchriben
ſind aber nit darby bliben
2782 *Der Luther ſchrybt in einem bůch*

Doctor Gryff

2822 *bringſt mich drab / du můſt baß kychen*
Das wörtlin (iſt) truckt mich hart
denn es was nit Chriſti art
Das ers hette gſagt / vnd nit wär
ſin mund was alles lügen lär
Das düt myn lyb / hett er wol gſeyt

for he does not wear a crown. I know, and am certain of it (even if I forget it from time to time) that no man can take the place of God. Even though I'm only a farmer, no cardinal will be able to persuade me otherwise.

Doctor Gryff

I am worried that, if I speak at length, my words will have little effect. I believe that we do eat God's body. Christ spoke the words clearly enough before he bore his body to the cross. He said clearly: 'This is my body'. That indeed was it; I am not twisting his words. He said: 'This is'. Now if Christ were to come here now, offer me bread and say, 'this is my body which I am giving for you on the cross', I would be an arrogant Christian indeed if I understood 'is' as 'means'. And the same with his blood: it wouldn't occur to me that I oughtn't to hold to what God had clearly said to me. Luther and Pomerantz now share this view entirely: previously they said something different, but didn't keep to it. *Luther writes in one of his books...*

Doctor Gryff

If you're going to move me from my position, you'll have to argue better. The little word 'is' presses hard on me, because it wasn't Christ's way to say something that wasn't true. His mouth was free from all lying. If he'd meant 'this means my body', he'd surely have said it?

das wär ein groſſer vnderscheyd
Denn wölt ich mich gern wiſen lon
vnd gantz von miner meynung ſton
Er hat es gredt / drumb můß es ſin
wo findt man durch alle gſchrifft hin
Das er ſage (das ist) vnd nit ſy
by ſynem wort bſtand ich fry
Gott geb was die gantz welt ſchry

Claus Räbſtock.
So bring ich nun ein ſpruch baryn
ſag an / ſind xij.botten ſalcz gſin? *Matth.5.*
Ir ſind ſaltz. Ouch Chriſtus ſpricht
wie wol er kein ſaltzin xij.boten ſicht
Der glychen ſprüchen ſind nun vil
die ich dir yetz erzellen wil
Da Chriſtus ein ſöliche leer gab
ergert dich din fůß / how jnn ab
Vnd meynt da nit den fleyſchlichen fůß
anders man hie verſton můß
Chriſtus hat gredt vß ſinem mund
ein jrdiſch ding wirt offt kund
Man můß ein geyſtlichs daby verſton
das wil ich an all gleert lüt lon
Wie offt er mit den Juden redt
jre laſter darzů an tag thett *Matth. 23.*
Wee üch gleerten / er ouch ſprach
do er jren gyt ſach
Der witwen hüſer ir eſſend
ſo wir dwort ermeſſend
Ist es vnmüglich gſin
das ſy eſſind ein zyegel zum mul yn
Dennocht ſagt er / jr eſſend hüſer
loß ich wil es baß bwyſen
Moyſes vnd Paulus zween leerer thür *Deute. 4.*
ſprechend / Gott iſt ein verzeerend fhür *Hebre. 12.*
Hörſt: Gott wird hie fhür gnennt
wie wol die Gottheyt ſelb nit brent
Ist nit fhür / hats aber gmacht
das fhür den brendt / der jnn veracht

And that would have made a great difference, for then I'd let myself be persuaded otherwise, and completely change my opinion. But he did say it, so it must be true. Where can you find any passage in Scripture where he says 'this is', and it isn't?

Claus Rebstock

I'll bring to bear just such a passage. Tell me, were the disciples salt? 'You are salt', Christ says, even though he can't see any disciples made of salt standing in front of him. There are many sayings like this (I'll tell you about them now). Christ gives teachings like this: 'If your foot annoys you, cut it off'. There he doesn't mean your actual physical foot; you have to understand it differently here. Christ himself said that often an earthly thing is mentioned which you have to understand to mean a spiritual thing. I accept what all learned people say about this. Whenever he speaks to the Jews, he brings their sins to light. 'Woe to you scholars', he also said, when he saw their greed: 'You devour widows' houses'. As far as we can understand the words, it was impossible for them to eat bricks with their mouths; yet he said: 'You devour houses'. Listen: I will prove the point still better. Moses and Paul, two esteemed teachers, say: 'God is a consuming fire'. Listen: God is here called a fire, even though the Deity itself doesn't burn and isn't fire. But he has made a fire that burns those who despise him.

Vnd wie das fhür alle ding verzert
alſo vor Gott ſich keiner erweert
Wie wol das (Jst) nun klar ſtadt
vns der text zůladt
Drumb ein figurlich red iſt das
wie ouch der ſpruch Joannis was *Lucæ. 3.*
Ir werdend toufft im geyst vnd fhür
von dem der da ſamlet in ſin ſchür
Deſſe wurff ſchufel in ſiner hand
nit wie puren bruchend vff dem land
Chriſtus (wie puren) nit tröſchen het
ſin ſomen nit ins erdtrich gſäyt
Das man hie buwt mit dem pflůg
ſag an / ſind das nit ſprüch gnůg?
Kein ſchufel hat er in der hand
die wort habend ein andren verſtand
Die ſprüwer wirfft er in das fhür
weytzen ſamlet er in die ſchür
Die ſchür hie / den himmel düt
by dem weytzen verſtond frumm lüt
Sprüwer gottloß menſchen ſind
jch gloub du ſygiſt ſtarblind
So du fürhin nit verſtaaſt
das du ſo wyt jrr gaaſt
Noch eins frag ich / das ſelb mich wyß
iſts Sacrament des lybs ſpyß
Oder ſpyßt es dſeel allein?
laß hören was min Doctor mein

Doctor Gryff.
Es iſt nun gwüß ein ſpyß der ſeel
darfür ichs fürwar zel

Claus Räbstock.
Spyßt es denn die ſeel allein
ſo iſt der buch gnůg vnreyn
Das ſich Gott daryn laß
ein habermůß zimpt dem buch baß
Alles das in madenſack gadt
das ſelb dſeel nit für ein ſpyß hat
Vnd wie das Gotzwort nit vertrybt

And just as fire consumes everything, so no one can defend himself against God. Even though the 'is' stands clearly in the text, we're invited to see it as figurative speech. Just as the words of John were, when he said: 'You will be baptized in the Holy Spirit and with fire by the one who gathers the wheat into his garner and whose winnowing fork is in his hand'. This isn't the kind of fork that farmers use for working the land: Christ hasn't been threshing or sowing seeds in the ground or ploughing, as farmers do. Tell me: aren't those enough examples? He didn't have an actual fork in his hand; the words 'he casts the chaff into the fire' and 'he gathers the wheat into his garner' are to be understood differently. The garner here means heaven, the wheat faithful people, and the chaff godless people. I think you must be as blind as a bat if you don't now understand that you're badly mistaken. And there's one other thing I want to ask you: tell me, is the Sacrament food for the body, or does it only nourish the soul? Let's hear what the good doctor thinks.

Doctor Gryff
For certain it is a food for the soul – that indeed is what I reckon it to be.

Claus Rebstock
If it only feeds the soul, then the belly must be a very unclean vessel for God to enter; a dormouse would do the belly more good. The soul doesn't regard anything that goes into our maw as food for the soul. And just as God's Word doesn't prevent someone

das ein menſch zlang vneſſen blybt
Sacrament des brots dſeel nit füllt
also Gotzwort nit des lybs hunger ſtillt
Darumb die ſeel gar nit kennt
(für jr ſpyß) das brottig Sacrament
Man můß lang von Gott ſagen
ee Gotzwort ſpyß ein hungrigen magen *Deut. 8.*
Der Mag můß lang eſſen brot
ee es thüge der ſeel not
Alſo můſtu ewig eſſen
bröttin hergott in den Meſſen
Das din ſeel dauon ſelig werd
der ſeel ſpyß wachßt nit hie vff erd
Christus der iſt zhimmel gfaren
das ſach die Galileiſch ſcharen *Act. 1.*
Das ſchrybt ſant Lux der nit lügt
es wirt mit zweyen Englen zügt
Wie er zhimmel gfaren iſt
deſſelben du gnůg bezügt biſt
Er iſt vfgfaren hörſtu wol
eben alſo er wider kon ſol
Er für nit zhimmel in dem brot
Chriſtus warer menſch vnd Gott
Du magſt nit mit warheyt jehen
das du Gott ye habiſt alſo gſehen
Widerkom / wie er iſt vfgfaren
du vnd all Abgöttiſch ſcharen
Nemmend zhilff all welt ſchon
die kundtſchafft wirt ewig bſton
Denn es alſo gſchriben ſtadt
nit anders es ſich verſton ladt
Wyl du Gott noch nit haſt gſehen
als die Engel habend gjehen
Do er zhimmel gfaren iſt
gloub mir das du vnrecht dran biſt
Hörſt? er kumpt wider eben alſo
wie er vffůr / deß bin ich fro
Jſt noch nye kon von himmel nider
mit lyb / vff erdtrich zů vns wider
Am Jüngſten tag wirt er erſchynen

from fasting for too long, the sacrament of the bread doesn't fill the stomach – any more than God's Word appeases bodily hunger. So the soul doesn't in any way recognize the bready sacrament as its food. God has to say many things before his Word feeds a hungry stomach, just as the stomach has to eat a lot of bread before it ministers to the needs of the soul. So you have to eat bready hosts in your Masses for a very long time before they save your soul. The soul's food doesn't grow here on earth: Christ has ascended into heaven, as the Galilean crowds saw. That's what St Luke wrote, and he doesn't lie. His ascension into heaven was witnessed by two angels – so there's enough to confirm this all to you. Hear this well: he went up just as he will come down again. He, Christ, true man and true God, didn't go up to heaven in bread. You can't truthfully claim that to have seen God return to earth in the same way that he went up to heaven. You and all the idolatrous hordes can get the entire world to support you if you like, but the message will always remain true. It is written just as it is to be understood. You haven't yet seen God as the angels said they did when he ascended into heaven: believe me that you're wrong. Can you hear? He will return just as he went up. I am glad of this. He hasn't yet come down from heaven to us on earth in bodily form, but he will appear at the Last Day

wie er zhimmel fůr von jnen
Alſo haſtu Gott nye gſehen
es ſye denn an der Vffart bſchehen
ſo man jnn vfzücht an eim ſeyl
man findt all tag ſömlich hergott feyl
Vnd zücht man all jar vil hundert vf
es wurd frylich ein groſſer huf
So man ſy all zämen brächt
es wurd ein vnzalbar gſchlächt
Hett einer denn ein arm voll ſchyter
vnd fhür darzů ſy fürind wyter
Vf gen himmel alſo jm rouch
ſunſt zucht man ſy nymmermee alsh ouch
Vnd der dran zücht iſt ouch ein götz
den Dauid ich zů eim zügen ſetz *Pſalm. 113.*
Des glychen das brötti Sacrament
habend vil pfaffen nye erkent
Vnd wenn man ſchon ein pfaff fragt
was es ſye / ich weyß das er ſagt
Es iſt eins heylgen dings zeychen
das wirt vaſt vff min ſinn reychen
Denn iſts ein ſichtbar form oder gſtalt
die etwas verborgens innhalt
Die Difinitz iſt für mich eben
daran ſetz ich min leben
So nun ein herr nit drinn ſtadt
Es mag nit eins ſin / zeychen vnd herr
als wenig ich trinck vß eim gmalten meer
Vnd wie ein gmalet fhür nit brent
als wenig iſt Chriſtus im Sacrament
Eins heylgen dings zeychen laß ichs ſin
das aber Chriſtus kumme dryn
Gſchicht als wenig als ſo ich ſag
das ein floch das gantz erdtrich trag
So ich zů dir yetzund ſpräch
ob ein menſch Gott ſäch
Wo er by einer Meſſz ſtand
ſo ſprichſtu / Gott ſicht nyemant
Dann nye kein menſch hat Gott gſehen *Ioan. 1.*
hie zwingt dich gſchrifft du můſts jehen *1. Joan. 4.*

just as he was when he left the angels and the Galileans. So you haven't seen God unless you were there at the Ascension and saw them pulling him up on a rope. Every day you find many hosts for sale. If you picked up many hundreds of them every year, there would certainly be a great heap of them. If you brought them all together, they'd be a numberless race. If someone then had an armful of firewood, and a fire as well, then they could go on up to heaven in smoke. Otherwise you'd never get them to go that high. In the same way many priests have never recognized the bready sacrament, and if you ask a priest what it is, I know that he will say it is the sign of a holy thing. That is pretty much in line with my view – because if he says it is an outward form or figure which contains something hidden, the priest's definition supports my case. I will stake my life on this. If there is no divinity in it, then it can't be both a sign and God. Christ is not in the sacrament any more than I could drink from a picture of the sea, or than the picture of a fire burns. I'll accept that it's the sign of a holy thing; but Christ no more enters into it than a flake holds aloft the whole earth. If I asked you now whether anyone saw God when he was celebrating Mass and you said 'no one sees God, for no man has ever seen God', the Scripture forces you to concede, you must admit.

So ein menſch denn Gott nit ſicht
ſo ſind wir eins wägs gſchlicht
Wo man die oblatten vf hat
das ſich Gott nit ſehen ladt
Was ſicht man denn im vfhan?
brot můſt ſagen von ſtundan
Sich ich denn nun brot allein
vnd Chriſtum nit mit hut vnd beyn
Warumb ſagſtu denn daby
das Chriſtus mit blůt und fleyſch da ſy?
Wo Chriſti fleyſch vnd blůt iſt
da wont Gottheyt zů aller friſt
Vnd mag keins on das ander ſin
als wenig ich Gott vnd menſch bin
Vnd wie min lyb kein läben hat
ſo mir die ſeel vßgadt
Als wenig teylt ſich die Gottheyt
von dem fleyſch. Chriſtus hats ſelb gſeyt
Philippus fragt dem vatter nach *Ioann. 14.*
Chriſtus zum Philippen ſprach
Der mich ſicht / den vatter ouch ſicht
hör wie er jnn hat vnderricht
Wie man můß den vatter ſehen
es můß allein im glouben gſchehen
So man gloubt des ſuns wort
der iſt zum vatter der wäg vnd port
Hett der Philipp da dem ſun gloubt
er hett nit nach dem vatter toubt
Er meynt der vatter wär allein
vnd hette nit mit dem ſun gmeyn
Drumb zeig vns den vatter / Philip ſprach
vor vnglouben er jnn gwüß nit ſach
Alſo der vatter / ſun vnd heylig geyſt
teylend ſich nit / als du ſelb weyßt *Ioſue. 14.*
Man ſicht nit den ſtarcken Gott Jſrael
als wenig du ſichſt min ſeel
Lieber ſinn jm nun recht nach
ob es nit wäre Gott ein ſchmach
Das er ſich ließ in min buch
als in ein ſtinckenden kadtſchluch

For if a man cannot see God, then we're in agreement. Because if you elevate the host and God does not let himself be seen, what then do you see? If I can see nothing but bread, and not Christ in skin and bones, why do you claim that Christ is actually present in flesh and blood? Where Christ's flesh and blood are, divinity dwells at all times: there can't be one without the other. Just as I am not both God and man, and just as my body has no life when my soul leaves it, so the deity cannot be separated from flesh. Christ said this himself. Philip asked to see the Father, and Christ said to Philip: 'Anyone who sees me also sees the Father'. Hear how he has taught him, about how one must see the Father; and that this must happen through faith, when one believes the words of the Son, who is the way and the gate to the Father. If Philip had believed the Son, he would not have been so keen to see the Father: he thought the Father was on his own, and had nothing to do with the Son. That is why he said: 'Show us the Father'. Because of his lack of faith he certainly couldn't see the Father. So the Father, Son, and Holy Spirit are not divided, as you yourself know. You can't see the mighty God of Israel, any more than you can see my soul. Rather think of him in the right way, and think whether it wouldn't be a shameful thing for God to let himself come into my stomach as into a stinking, shitty hole.

Du magſt nit darwider ſin
alles das da gadt zum mund yn
Das ſelb der mag nit in jm ladt *Matt. 25.*
natürlich es wider daruß gadt
Alles / ſpricht der Text klar
nüt vßgnommen / ſo gadt zwar
Der brötin gott ouch in Magen
deßglychen der wyn gadt in din kragen
Gadt es denn dryn ſo gadts ouch druß
das wär ein vnsuber Gothuß
Wie wol wir ſind gotts tempel
ja alſo merck ein exempel *Exempel.*
So ich zů Gott ein liebe hett
vnd allweg gůtz von jm redt
Ouch bgirig wär by jm zů ſin
dennzmal ich gwüß in Gott bin
Ja mit dem gmüt on den lyb
loß was Joannes ſchryb *I. Ioan. 4.*
Gott ſelb die liebe ist
haſt jnn lieb / du in jm ouch biſt
Vnd er in dir / wie ich hab gſeyt
alſo wirt Gott ein tempel zůpreyt
Das aber Gott in der lyblich ſy
wie ein krutball / das iſt fantiſy
Es iſt ouch by vns ein gwonheyt
das ein mensch zů dem andren ſeyt
Du kumpſt mir vſſz mim hertzen nit
by welchem wir verſtond damit
Das eins dem andren ligt im ſinn
wie wol ich ſag / du ligſt mir im hertz dinn *Lucæ. 2.*
Alſo Maria trůg im hertzen
deß ſchwertz durchgang mit vil ſchmertzen
Kein ſchwärdt jr durch das hertz gieng
allein kummer ſy drinn enpfieng
Vnd ſtadt im text ouch ein ſchwert
ſchwärdt wirt hie für trübſal kert
Es iſt by den Hebreern gwon
ſo ſy ſagend etwar von
Nemmend ſy ein ander ding
hör zů wie vil ich ſprüch bring

You can't disagree with the statement that everything that goes into the mouth doesn't stay in the stomach but goes out again. This is true for everything without exception, as the text clearly states. So, yes, the bready god goes into your stomach, just as the wine goes into your throat; but if it goes in, it also goes out. That would make a very impure house for God to dwell in, even though we are God's temple. So listen to an example. If I loved God, spoke well of him at all times, and greatly desired to be with him, then indeed I would certainly be in God, in my spirit, not in my body. Hear what John writes: 'God himself is love, and if you love him you will abide in him and he in you' – just as I have said. In this way we prepare a temple for God. But that God should abide in you in bodily form, like some ball of cabbage, that's sheer fantasy. With us also it's usual for someone to say to someone else: 'You will never leave my heart'. By this we actually understand that the person remains in the other person's mind – even though we might say 'you are in my heart'. In this way Mary very painfully bore the sword's piercing in her heart, even though no sword actually went through it. Rather, what she felt was sorrow – even though it mentions a sword in the text. 'Sword' stands here for 'grief'. It's common amongst the Hebrews to say one thing and mean another. Listen while I give you lots of other examples:

Die berg ſpringend wie die Wider *Pſal. 135.*
berg ſtigend vf vnd nider *Pſal. 103.*
Wie mögends vf vnd nider ſtygen
du müſtiſt jnen lang gygen
Ee die berg anfiengend ſpringen
vnd das erdtrich ſingen *Pſal. 95*
Die Berg wie das wachs zerflieſſend *Pſalm. 96.*
lůg ob wir nit menſchen verſton müſſend? *Pſal. 67.*
Judicum ich ouch einen ſind *Iudic. 16.*
Die velſen werdend wie wachß lind
Mer vnd Jordan ſach vnd floch *Pſalm. 113.*
do Jſrael dardurch zoch *Exodi. 14.*
Des Meers flucht iſt on fůß gſchehen
vnd hat nit ougen / wie hats denn gſehen?
Dennocht ſpricht Dauid Es ſach vnd floch
noch ein ſpruch iſt / den merck ouch
Stadt in dem nümen Teſtament
den vns ouch der Paulus fürwendt *I. Cor. 10.*
Vnſre vätter habind vom velſen gnoſſen
ee Chriſtus hab ſin blůt vergoſſen
Wie mochtend ſy Chriſtum nieſſen
ſo lang vor ſim blůt vergieſſen?
Alſo trunckend ſy daruon
ſy gloubten Chriſtus ſölte kon
So gloubend wir ee ſye kommen
nit anders wirt die ſpyß gnummen
Denn ſo man ſich zů Gott verſicht
wir ſygind mit jm zfriden gericht *Roma. 5.*
On vnſeren verdienſt / durch ſin blůt *Epheſ. 2.*
der jnn alſo ißt / ſtadt in Gots hůt
der velß was Chriſtus / ouch hie ſtadt
der ſprüchen man nun vil hat *Lucæ. 6.*
Sant Lux beſchrybt ein wyſen man
der nun buwen hat gfangen an
Vnd ſin huß vff ein velſen geſetzt
für vngwitter / daß nit vmb viel geletzt
Ein puren huß meint er hie nit
das vff eim velſen ſtand / da man vff tritt
Chriſtus der velß was vnd der grund
das huß der glöubig / mit Gott im pundt

‘the mountains skipped like rams’. Mountains going up and down – how can they do this? You’d have to play your fiddle for a long time before mountains started leaping about, or the earth started singing. And when we read that ‘the mountains melted like wax’, see whether we shouldn’t understand this as referring to people. I also find something in Judges about the rocks growing as soft as wax; moreover the sea and the River Jordan ‘saw it and fled’, when the Israelites went through them. But the sea didn’t flee on foot, and it doesn’t have eyes – so how could it see? Nevertheless David says that it did see and flee. And here’s another saying to note, this time from the New Testament, where Paul sets it before us: ‘Our fathers ate of the Rock’. But before Christ had shed his blood, how could they eat of him – so long before the blood was shed? They drank of him in the sense that they believed Christ would come. We believe that he was not eaten in any other way prior to his coming. For if we trust in God we are satisfied indeed, without any merit of our own, but by his blood. Anyone who eats God in this way is in his care. The rock was Christ; that is mentioned here too. We have now had a lot of sayings. Also, St Luke describes a wise man who started to build and put his house on a rock, so that it would not be damaged by storms. By this he doesn’t mean an actual farmhouse standing on a rock that you might step on; no, Christ was the rock and the foundation, and the house was the faithful man, in partnership with God.

Ein menſch der in Gott allein truwt
vmb Gots willen laßt haar vnd hut
2823 *Der glychen ſprüch findt man noch mee*

Eygennutz's final speech (after 4198)
Ich keer mich nüt an das Concily
gelt wo ich nit das gwüſſer ſpily
Ich wil nun an ein ander ort
mir iſt zeſchwär diß gotzwort
Es brächt mich vmb min huß vnd hab
ich wurd zů letſt nun gar ſchabab
Müßt von huß zhuß bättlen gon
vnd nimmermee vſſz armůt kon
Sölt ich Edel vnd pfaffen neeren
ich mag mich kum der lüß erweeren
Vnd ſich nun wol wie es gadt
vns puren man nüt nachladt
Sunſt was bißhar ſitt iſt gſin
daruon fiele nun nit ein mydtlin
Hůrey / wůcher / ſchlemmen / braſſen
voll bübery ſteckend all gaſſen
Denen ſolt man ouch weeren
nit nun vns puren vmbkeeren
Wo iſt nur einer der yetz leb
nach dem wie Gott ſin leer geb?
Man kan vns puren gnůg ſagen
wir ſöllind Zinß zůhin tragen
Ouch Zähend vnd andrer bſchwärden
deren wir nit mögend abwerden
Allein darumb / daß die zween ſtend
vff vns puren vil deren hend
Nämind die pfaffen Zins allein
ſo hulff vns puren all welt gmein
das wir nüts mee Zinßen ſöttind
ja wenn ſy nit ſelb Zinß hettind
Diewyl aber der weltlich Stadt
vff vns (wie pfaffen) Zinß bat
So hilfft den pfaffen weltlicher gwallt
das man vns puren darzů hallt

A man who trusts in God alone leaves behind everything for his sake.

Pur Eygennutz

I'm not going back to the Council, I'm quite sure about that. I'm going to a different place now. This Word of God is too hard for me. It would do me out of my house and possessions, and in the end I'd be completely done for, I'd have to go begging from house to house and would never get out of poverty. If I've got to feed noblemen and priests I'll hardly be able to protect myself from lice. And now I see how it is: they're not letting us farmers off anything. Not even a tiny bit of all the stuff that's been going on until now will disappear: whoring, usury, gluttony, boozing. All the streets are full of mischief. They should see to that as well, and not just turn us farmers back. Can you find anyone today who lives according to God's command? They can tell us farmers as much as they want that we've got to pay our taxes, and also our tithes and other burdens. We can't get rid of these because the two other estates have a real hold on us. If it was only priests who took interest payments, that would help us farmers and everybody else – we wouldn't impose any payments if we weren't liable to them ourselves. But because the secular powers impose taxes on both us and the priests, they end up helping the priests –

Das wir müſſend Zinß geben
es hilfft nun kein widerſträben
Darzů helffend keinerley waaffen
es wärd ſy denn Gott ouch ſtraaffen
Vnd vns byſton mit ſinem arm
das er zletſt ſich vnſer erbarm
Sölt man den pfaffen nit Zinß gelten
ſy wurdind Zinſen ſelb ſchelten
Die wil man inen aber ſol
es dienet in dkuchin vaſt wol
Sy laſſends recht alſo har gon
denn ſy ſind vmbs opffer kon
Vnd vmb alle ir herligkeyt
dann man nit wie vormals zůtreyt
Nun hab ich ouch lange zyt gloubt
Gott hab inen ſölchen gwalt erloubt
Den ſy hand brucht gen yederman
darff man nun nüts mee druf han
Was darff man denn weltlichs gewalts
jch gloub ouch nit daß gſchrifft innhalt
Das ein Oberkeyt habind Chriſten
jch wil mich yetz heim rüſten
Vergangne Gſchicht mit mir füren
vnd gen Fridhuſen Appellieren
Daſelbſt wirt yetzund ein Rychßtag
da wird ich ouch thůn min klag
Wil wüſſen ob ein Chriſten man
ye ein Oberkeyt müſſe han
Denn zFridhuſen ſind vnparthygig lüt
ſy ſchonend weder pfaffen noch gwalt nüt
Gwünn ich das wir möchtind fry ſyn
wär aller puren nutz vnd min
Jch versůchs / aldee ich far dahin.

Vtz Eckſtein.

by forcing us to pay our obligations. Resistance is now useless. No weapons are of any help, unless God also punishes them, supports us with his arm, and has mercy on us at last. If the priests didn't themselves impose taxes, they themselves would complain about them. But while they do, their cooks are able to look after them very well. They let the law go to the dogs because they've lost their offerings and with them all their splendour – people aren't giving as they did. I've also believed for a long time that God let them have their authority, which they've been using against everyone. But you don't need to bother about that any more. And what do we need secular authorities for? I don't believe the Scripture says that Christians should have any authorities above them. So now I'll get ready for home, take all these stories with me, and go and make an appeal at Friedhausen, where a Diet is now taking place. I'll make my complaint there. I'll want to know whether a Christian man ever has to have anyone in authority over him. Because they're impartial people at Friedhausen, and they spare neither priests nor princes. If I persuaded them that we should be free, that'd be a great gain for all farmers and for me. I'll give it a go. Farewell – I'm off.

Utz Eckstein

Bibliography

1. Sixteenth-century sources

Eckstein, Utz: *Concilium. / HIe in dem bůch wirt diſputiert / Das puren lang zyt hett verfürt / Heilgen fürbit / ouch des baſsts gwalt / vom Fägfhür / ouch was dMäſs innhalt* ([Zurich]: [Froschauer], [1525])

Idem: *Concilium. / HIe in dem bůch wirt disputiert / Das puren lang zyt hat verfürt / Heylgen Fürbit / Ouch des Bapsts Gwallt / vom Fägfhür / ouch was dMäſs innhalt* ([Zurich]: [Froschauer], [1526])

Idem: *Concilium. / HIe in dem bůch wirt diſputiert / Das Puren lang zyt hett verfürt / Heilgenfürbit / ouch des bapſsts gwalt / vom Fägfhür / ouch was dMäſſs innhalt* ([Berne]: [Apiarius], [c. 1550])

Idem: *Der Bawren Reichßtag vnd Concilium. Weß ſicher die ſieben Bauren auß ſieben Landtſchafften vereynigt / vnd zů antwurt geben dem Cardinal Campeio vnd ſeinen mitgeſandten auff das verkündt Bäptiſch concilium,* ([Strasbourg]: [Cammerlander], 1539)

Idem: *Dialogus. Ejn hüpſche diſputation / Die Chriſtus hat mit Adam thon* ([Zurich]: [Froschauer], [1525?])

Idem: *Klag des Gloubens der Hoffnung vnd ouch Liebe, über Geyſtlichen vnd Weltlichen Stand der Chriſtenheit* (Zurich: Froschauer, [1525/6?])

Idem: *Reichstag: / oder / Verſammlung der Bawren / gehalten zu Fridberg im Rychthal [...] Concilium: / Darinnen die Bawren mit den Doctoribus der heiligen Geſchrifft von geiſtlichen Sachen diſputieren vnd entſcheiden. / Klag / des Glaubens / der Hoffnung / vnd auch der Liebe / vber alle Stend der Chriſtenheit* ([Basle]: [Henricpetri], 1592)

Erasmus of Rotterdam: *Desiderii Erasmi Roterodami opera omnia* (20 vols, Amsterdam: North Holland, 1969–2003)

Faber, Johannes: *Ain warlich vnderrichtung wie es zů Zürch auff den Neünundtzweintzigiſten tag des monats Ianuarij nechſtuerſchynen ergangen ſey* ([Freiburg]: [Wörlin], 1523)

Das gyren rupffen. halt inn wie Johans Schmid Vicarge ze Coſtentz / mit dem büchle darinn er verheißt ein waren bericht wie es vff den. 29. tag Jenners. M.D.xxiij. ze Zürich gangen ſye ([Zurich]: [Froschauer], [1523])

Hegenwald, Erhard: *Handlung der verſamlung in der löblichen ſtatt Zürich, vff den xxix tag Ienners / vonn wegen des heyligen Euangelij* ([Zurich]: [Froschauer], [1523])

'Karsthans'. Thomas Murners 'Hans Karst' und seine Wirkung in sechs Texten der Reformationszeit, ed. and trans. by Thomas Neukirchen, Beihefte zum *Euphorion*, 68 (Heidelberg: Winter, 2011)

Luther, Martin: *D. Martin Luthers Werke* (Weimarer Ausgabe), 120 vols (Weimer: Böhlau, 1883–2009)

Manuel, Niklaus: *Werke und Briefe. Vollständige Neuedition*, ed. by Paul Zinsli and Thomas Hengartner (Berne: Stämpfli, 1999)

Murner, Thomas: *Schelmenzunfft. Antzaigung alles Weltleüffigen můtwillens / ſchalckaiten vnn bübereyen diſer zeit Durch den hochgelerten herren Doctor Thoman Murner von Straßburg* (Augsburg, 1514)

Idem: *Murneri responsio libello ciuda[m] insigniter & egregie stulto Vlrici Zvuyngel apostate / heresiarche, ostendens Lutheranam doctrinam infamiam irrogare / & verbum dei humanum iudicem pati posse* (Lucerne: the author, 1525)

Scheible, Johann: *Das Kloster: weltlich und geistlich; meist aus den älteren deutschen Volks-, Kinder-, Curiositäten- und vorzugsweise komischen Literatur*, 12 vols (Stuttgart: the author, 1845–9)

Zwingli, Huldrych: *Sämtliche Werke*, ed. by Emil Egli and others, 14 vols, Corpus Reformatorum, 88–101 (Leipzig: Heinsius, and others, 1905–present)

2. Critical literature

Backus, Irena: *The Disputations of Baden, 1526 and Berne, 1528: Neutralizing the Early Church*, Studies in Theology and History, 1/1 (Princeton: Princeton Theological Seminary, 1993)

Bächtold, Hans Ulrich: 'Eckstein (Acrogoniaeus), Utz (Ulrich)', in *Biographisch-Bibliographisches Kirchenlexikon*, vol. 17 (Herzberg: Bautz, 2000), pp. 296–9

Baechtold, Jakob: *Geschichte der deutschen Literatur in der Schweiz* (Frauenfeld: Huber, 1892)

Barge, Hermann: *Andreas Bodenstein von Karlstadt*, 2 vols (Leipzig: Brandstetter, 1905)

Biographisch-Bibliographisches Kirchenlexikon, 28 vols (Herzberg: Bautz, 1990–2007)

Brady, Thomas A.: '"You Hate us Priests". Anticlericalism, Communities, and the Control of Women at Strasbourg in the Age of the Reformation', in Peter A. Dykema and Heiko A. Oberman (eds), *Anticlericalism in Late Medieval and Early Modern Europe* (Berlin: de Gruyter, 1993), pp. 167–207

Campbell, Fiona M. K.: 'The Dialogue as a Genre of German Reformation Literature' (unpublished PhD thesis, St Andrews University, 2000)

Corrodi-Sulzer, Adrian: 'Zu Ůtz Eckstein', *Zwingliana*, 4 (1926), 337–40

Davidson, Elspeth Ann: 'An Examination of German Reformation Dialogues, 1520–1525' (unpublished PhD thesis, University of Stirling, 1982)

Demandt, Dieter: 'Die Wirtschaftsethik Huldrych Zwinglis', in *Beiträge zur Wirtschafts- und Sozialgeschichte des Mittelalters. Festschrift für Herbert Helbig zum 65. Geburtstag*, ed. by Knut Schulz (Cologne: Böhlau, 1976), pp. 306–21

Dickens, A. G.: *Reformation and Society in Sixteenth-Century Europe* (London: Thames and Hudson, 1966)

Edwards, Mark Urban, Jr: *Luther's Last Battles: Politics and Polemics 1531–46* (Ithaca, NY: Cornell University Press, 1983)

Egli, Emil: 'Wer war Laurentius Fabula?', *Zwingliana*, 2/5 (1907), 147–51

Frühneuhochdeutsches Wörterbuch, 13 vols (Berlin: de Gruyter, 1977– [2015])

Füssel, Stephan (ed.): *Deutsche Dichter der frühen Neuzeit* (Berlin: Schmidt, 1993)

Gordon, Bruce: *The Swiss Reformation* (Manchester: Manchester University Press, 2002)

Gummelt, Volker: 'Die Auseinandersetzung über das Abendmahl zwischen Johannes Bugenhagen und Huldrych Zwingli im Jahre 1525', in *Die Zürcher Reformation: Ausstrahlungen und Rückwirkungen*, ed. by Alfred Schindler and Hans Stickelberger, Zürcher Beiträge zur Reformationsgeschichte, 18 (Berne: Lang, 2001), pp. 189–201

Hegg, Peter: 'Ein unbekannter Apiarius-Druck', *Schweizerisches Gutenbergmuseum*, 39 (1953), 51–65

Helbling, Leo: *Dr. Johannes Fabri, Generalvikar von Konstanz und Bischof von Wien, 1478–1541. Beiträge zu seiner Lebensgeschichte*, Reformationsgeschichtliche Studien und Texte, 67–8 (Münster: Aschendorff, 1941)

Iserloh, Erwin: *Johannes Eck (1486–1543). Scholastiker, Humanist, Kontroverstheologe*, Katholisches Leben und Kirchenreform im Zeitalter der Glaubensspaltung, 41 (Münster: Aschendorff, 1981)

Idem (ed.): *Katholische Theologen der Reformationszeit*, 4 vols, Katholisches Leben und Kirchenreform im Zeitalter der Glaubensspaltung, 44–7 (Münster: Aschendorff, 1984–7)

Jørgensen, Ninna: *Bauer, Narr und Pfaffe: Prototypische Figuren und ihre Funktion in der Reformationsliteratur,* Acta Theologica Danica, 23 (Leiden: Brill, 1988)

Köhler, Walther: *Zwingli und Luther: Ihr Streit über das Abendmahl nach seinen politischen und religiösen Beziehungen*, 2 vols (Leipzig: Eger & Sievers, 1924)

Laziadèr, Anton: 'Zur Geschichte des zweiten Kappelerkrieges', *Zwingliana* 6 (1937), 460–2

Lewis, Keith Dennis: 'Johann Faber and the First Zürich Disputation: 1523. A Pre-Tridentine Catholic Response to Huldrych Zwingli and his Sixty-Seven Articles' (unpublished PhD thesis, Catholic University of America, 1985)

Locher, Gottfried W.: 'Zwingli und Erasmus', *Zwingliana*, 13 (1969–73), 37–61

Love, Joel: 'Peasants in Dialogue with Authority: Three Literary Dialogues of the German Reformation' (unpublished MPhil thesis, University of Birmingham, 2004)

Idem: 'Dialogue and Disputation in the Sixteenth Century: An Examination of the Case of Utz Eckstein' (unpublished PhD thesis, University of Birmingham, 2008)

MacCulloch, Diarmaid: *Reformation: Europe's House Divided* (London: Allen Lane, 2003)

Michael, Wolfgang F.: *Das deutsche Drama der Reformationszeit* (Berne: Lang, 1984)

Moeller, Bernd: 'Zwinglis Disputationen: Studien zu den Anfängen der Kirchenbildung und des Synodalwesens im Protestantismus', *Zeitschrift der Savigny-Stiftung für Rechtsgeschichte, Kanonistische Abteilung*, 56 (1970), 275–334; 60 (1974), 213–364

Mortimer, Ian: *The Time Traveller's Guide to Elizabethan England* (London: Bodley Head, 2012)

Mosen, Paul: *Hieronymus Emser, der Vorkämpfer Roms gegen die Reformation* (Halle: Kaemmerer, 1890)

Moser, Dietz-Rüdiger: *Die Tannhäuser-Legende* (Berlin: de Gruyter, 1977)

Müller, Willy: 'Der Reformationsdichter Utz Eckstein' (unpublished *Lizenziatsarbeit*, University of Zurich, 1970)

Muralt, Leonhard von: *Die Badener Disputation 1526,* Quellen und Abhandlungen zur schweizerischen Reformationsgeschichte, 6 (Leipzig: Heinsius, 1926)

Neue deutsche Biographie (24 vols, Berlin: Duncker & Humblot, 1953–present)

Ozment, Steven E.: *The Reformation in the Cities. The Appeal of Protestantism in Sixteenth-Century Germany and Switzerland* (New Haven, CT: Yale University Press, 1975)

Pée, Herbert: *Jörg Syrlin d. Ä. Das Ulmer Chorgestühl 1468–1474* (Stuttgart: Reclam, 1963)

Potter, G. R.: *Zwingli* (Cambridge: Cambridge University Press, 1976)

Schweizerisches Idiotikon, 17 vols (Frauenfeld: Huber, 1881– [2022])

Schwitalla, Johannes: *Deutsche Flugschriften 1460–1525: Textsortengeschichtliche Studien*, Reihe Germanistische Linguistik, 45 (Tübingen: Niemeyer, 1983)

Stricker, Hans: *Die Selbstdarstellung des Schweizers im Drama des 16. Jahrhunderts*, Sprache und Dichtung, n. s., 7 (Berne: Haupt, 1961).

Vasella, Oskar: 'Neues über Utz Eckstein, den Zürcher Pamphletisten', *Zeitschrift für schweizerische Kirchengeschichte,* 30 (1936), 37–48

Vögelin, Salomon: 'Utz Eckstein', *Jahrbuch für schweizerische Geschichte*, 7 (1882), 91–264

Wandel, Lee Palmer: *The Eucharist in the Reformation: Incarnation and Liturgy* (Cambridge: Cambridge University Press, 2006)

Weber, Walter: 'Die Datierung von Zwinglis Schrift *Was Zürich und Bern not ze betrachten sye in dem fünförtischen Handel*. Versuch einer Lösung', *Zwingliana*, 12 (1965), 228–31

Zinsli, Paul: 'Notvolles Prädikantendasein', *Reformatio*, 9 (1960), 327–33

Index

Note: the references to the parallel texts of the 'Concilium' and 'Rychsztag' are made to the English translations

Frontispiece: Dance in Tokelau. From left the performers are Pua, Makalika (seated) Hiokave, Towhitea, and Hipiliano. Behind the dancers are drummers seated on the ground playing the wooden *papa* to accompany the dance.

Photo Father MacDonald, Nukunonu, c. 1964

NEW SONG AND DANCE FROM THE CENTRAL PACIFIC

Creating and Performing the *Fātele* of Tokelau in the Islands and in New Zealand